SWE
Gulf of Both
S.
R.
Kokkola
Vaasa
Lapua
Iisalmi
Nurmes
Lake Pielinen
Koli
Kuopio
Kristiinankaupunki
Haapamäki
Jyväskylä
Kuusjärvi
Joensuu
Ilomantsi
Tuupavaara
Tolvajärvi
Äglajärvi
Suojärvi
CEDED TO U.S.S.R. 1940
Pori
Tampere
Savonlinna
Mikkeli
Punkaharju
Sortavala
Kitelä
Rauma
Lake Vanajavesi
Heinola
Lake Saimaa
Elisenvaara
Valamo
Hämeenlinna
Lahti
Imatra
Enso
Käkisalmi
Åland Islands
(Ahvenanmaa)
Turku
Viipuri
Laatokka
(Ladoga)
Lovisa
Hamina
Järvenpää
Porvoo
Kotka
Summa
Lake Muolaa
Koivisto
Stockholm 23 miles
Helsinki
Joutselkä
Hanko
(LEASED TO U.S.S.R., 1940)
Gulf of Finland
Terijoki
Rajajoki
Leningrad
Tallinn
ESTONIA
20° E.
24°
28°
32°
64°
W
E
N
S

FINLAND FOREVER

Hudson Strode

Other books by Hudson Strode

SOUTH BY THUNDERBIRD

THE PAGEANT OF CUBA

THE STORY OF BERMUDA

IMMORTAL LYRICS: AN ANTHOLOGY OF ENGLISH LYRICS

THE ECONOMY OF FINLAND: THE WOODS, THE FIELDS, THE RIVER, AND THE PULP MILL

Finland Forever

by

HUDSON STRODE

hb

NEW YORK

HARCOURT, BRACE AND COMPANY

first edition

PRINTED IN THE UNITED STATES OF AMERICA
BY QUINN & BODEN COMPANY, INC., RAHWAY, N. J.

TO

MARY and ALBERT SPALDING

"The Finns are the most gifted of all people."

SIGRID UNDSET IN CONVERSATION.

Contents

PREFACE

"I saw a people who were able to do everything except betray their honor." JOHAN LUDVIG RUNEBERG

Preface

The very word *Finland* has power to stir the hearts of men. It arouses the hero-worshiper that abides in most of us. We still think of the Finns and their superhuman defense with admiration and with wonder.

What was the motive force of the unparalleled resistance, which made the international press in various quarters of the globe spontaneously recall the story of David and Goliath, of St. George and the Dragon, and declare that Finland's heroism surpassed Thermopylae? What are the special inner qualities which give the Finns such power?

In *Omoo,* published in 1847, Herman Melville pointed out a curious feeling current about the Finns almost a century ago. He wrote: "It is a circumstance not generally known, perhaps, that among seamen, Finns are regarded with peculiar superstition. For some reason or other which I could not get at, they are supposed to possess the gift of second sight, and the power to wreak supernatural vengeance upon those who offend them. On this account they have great influence among sailors."

Everybody knows that if Finns are in a brawl in any of the world's seaports they are supposed to come out victorious. For an ally in a fight, sailors of all nationalities would prefer to have the help of a Finn to that of any other breed of man. It is not because of the Finn's physical endowment. The average Finn is no bigger and looks no stronger than another man. But whatever a Finn does that is worth doing, he puts his heart and soul into it with every ounce of energy he possesses. And as men under certain hallucinations and compulsions often possess super-strength and super-cunning, the Finn seems endowed with preternatural powers when forced into a fight. But to have this strength—this help from beyond—a Finn must know in his heart the cause is just. When aroused to righteous indignation, a Finn's fury can be that of a diabolically cool avenging angel.

From the astounding Finnish victories against overwhelming odds, it would almost seem that the Finns do possess the gift of second sight. They met Russian strategy with such shrewd and swift counter-strategy that to the Reds it must have seemed beyond human insight. The phantom squads of white-cloaked Finns on skis led the Reds on hopefully into the whitened forests, confused and harried them, and left those they did not kill to perish in the blinding snow.

The Finnish vengeance Melville spoke of was felt painfully in Soviet Russia despite the final costly victory. It was not Russia's loss in comrades, twisted and frozen in death on Finnish soil, that hurt her, but the stinging humiliation of being held at bay for over three months by an opponent one-fiftieth of her size. Red Russia's prestige went down in the mire. And she lost not only prestige, but almost all the foreign well-wishers she ever had. By a criminal attack on the integrity of a little nation of only 3,750,000 people, the Russian Communists became discredited and ridiculous and evil in the sight of just and civilized men. Finland wreaked vengeance not only by making Soviet Russia a most hated nation, but by showing up many of her militaristic weaknesses.

In accounting for the Russian defeats it may be significant to note that the Reds have put their faith in the power of machines. The Finns were fortified by the power of mind. Finns have individual thinking minds, which have been cultivated by democratic independence.

Because of their faith and inner grace, they fought with superhuman courage and endurance. Finns did not mind dying for an honorable cause. They had no fear of death, and they did not whine, because there is nothing in a Finnish throat capable of making a whining sound.

But in the end, their government made a peace. And though it was a bitter peace, it preserved what they were fighting for—their independence.

Until this present generation Finland was hardly more than the name of a far-flung land in arctic and subarctic regions along the eastern shore of the Baltic, a protectorate of imperial Russia. On the very maps it looked remote and cold, lying wholly north of the city formerly called St. Petersburg and falling within the forbidding latitudes of Greenland. It lay on the way to nothing but the icy abode of the god Boreas. Throughout the march of time it was among the least visited of nations.

At the beginning of this century the one personal name familiar to the foreign public was that of a man of music, Jean Sibelius. Through his immortal compositions only did distant Finland communicate anything of herself to the outside world. Music lovers wondered vaguely about the land where the woods sang as they did in tone poems of Sibelius and where the burdens in the hearts of alien men could be so stirring. Yet few knew anything that was directly significant about the land and the people.

Then, at Antwerp in 1920, Paavo Nurmi ran into the world's arena, bringing tidings of the birth of the brave new nation. In that year Finland, having just gained her complete freedom from Russia, entered the Olympic contest as an independent country for the first time and won sensational victories.

In the years that followed, sporadic spotlights turned on this corner and that activity of the nation invariably revealed facts that redounded to the glory of that distant land of Nurmi and Sibelius. Tourists who desired the untried began to poke about the sixty thousand lakes and to push up to the Arctic Ocean. Social and economic investigators came to look at progress in Finland and write admiring monographs. Then Helsinki was chosen as the seat of the 1940 Olympic Games. Finland was preparing for a universal house-warming when the second World War broke.

Everyone knows how marvelous the Finns proved as soldiers—their record in war is unsurpassed. But few know much more of Finland than pertains to feats of battle. Few realize how admirable were the Finns in peace. So in this book I have endeavored to reveal the proved power of Finland in peace—to show the simple pattern of daily living and daily thinking that made the heroic Finland possible. Their achievements in the brief twenty-two years of peaceful independence were as unparalleled as their deeds in war. In attacking their domestic problems they used the same courage and faith and indomitable will that they employed in conducting a war.

My wife and I were in Finland when the European war began, and though our visit was cut short we had already been in all parts of the country—from Helsinki to the Arctic Ocean, from Turku on the Bothnian Bay to Karelia and the Russian frontier. And because the whole picture of the land and the people has sunk forever into the depths of my heart, and because I wish more men to know the inspiring truth about the Finns, I have written this book, revealing Finland as it appeared to me just before the tragic events of the war. I have tried to interpret the human heart of the nation by recounting what I knew intimately of the Finns in 1939. Conversations appear virtually verbatim, since my wife and I separately wrote them down before we retired each night of the day on which they occurred. The purpose of the selected talk that is recorded herein is to throw a little light here, a little light there—until the Finnish character as a composite whole becomes illuminated.

In her design for living Finland created a pure democracy that is worthy of the world's remembrance. How long she can hold it no one can foretell. But Finland's spirit will never be enchained. Whatever happens, the little nation has earned a glorious immortality. I give you Finland as a model on which to start the world anew.

"Shadow Lake"
Near Mount Pinson
Alabama
November 30, 1940

PRELUDE

"The remembrance of beauty, the beauty of a thing, or of personal relationships, or of a country, has always seemed to me the chief end of life. . . . Remembrance is the one sure immortality we know." STRUTHERS BURT

Finlandia

When the Creator made Finland, he was not in that mighty mood of genius that fashioned Norway. Nor at his most charming as he was when he conceived Denmark. Nor yet in the orderly state of mind that designed Sweden. In Norway, Denmark, and Sweden, he followed a plan, chose details with care, worked for effects. When it came to Finland, he relaxed. He took water and earth and trees and spread them about casually, as a sower broadcasts seed. He let everything lie as it dropped—in wooded hills and rocky fells, rivers, marshes, archipelagoes, and sixty thousand still blue lakes dotted with verdant islands. Finland is a simple land.

Everywhere there is feeling of infinite space beneath the sky. Space for a grown man's breathing. It is not the same sort of open space one finds in the monotonous pampas of Argentina, where one may suffer acute agoraphobia. It is a companionable space, where man can speak to the earth and where nature knows the code that reaches mankind's heart through the pulse. Unless a Finn looks up to the heavens, he never sees "as far as the eye carries." He is always met by the evergreen trees, by the familiar but magical forest. Here in the free, wild woods his deep individualism has been nurtured.

There is nothing in the Finnish landscape to live up to in a worldly sense. Each man may call his soul his own in his own peculiar way. He answers to nothing but nature and the elements, arbitrates only with atmospheric conditions and bodily hunger. The pure quality of Finland's landscape has bred an integrity in its people that is rare in the contemporary world. The Finns know things other races have forgotten. They know what is wrong and what is right. They know how to endure hardship and how to draw spiritual sustenance from natural forces about them. Because they have faced all the dark menace the forests hold, they do not fear what civilized man can do. Fortune's fingers cannot play whatever tune she likes on Finnish pipes. No matter how dismally the winds of fate howl or how sweetly blow propitious zephyrs, the Finns can temper the music. They know their way too well about their bogs and marshes to lose themselves following will-o'-the-wisps of prosperity or gloom.

Finns do not look on nature as the garden-loving Danes do in their perfectly groomed Eden. In Finland nature is impregnated with harshness. The stubborn soil does not render fruits in exchange for loving words or some hits with a hoe. It likes a tough struggle. Nature and man in Finland have many of the same traits of temperament. They are both like wrestlers who will never admit that they have been vanquished. But nature in the last decade has met her master in the Finn. Today the harvests of Finland are bigger per cultivated acre than those of the United States.

With all its masculine simplicity, Finland is a land of moods and contrasts. One continually meets with the unexpected. The very newest is to be found close to old and timeless things. In the dead of winter, while the Gulf of Bothnia is held in the grip of ice and the most powerful ice-breaker ever constructed must plow a lane in the Gulf of Finland for ships to reach the southernmost coast towns, the Arctic Ocean harbor of Liinahamari, warmed by the Gulf Stream, remains open, ice-free. Far above the Arctic Circle the summer sun becomes so hot that children go barefoot, clad only in cotton trunks, and field hands and carpenters work stripped to the waist like stokers in a ship's boiler room. At Rovaniemi on the Circle, where stands the most spectacular modern hotel in the Northern Countries, reindeer graze at the town edges and the champion bear-killer of the district raises specimen fuchsias.

For generations the Finn has cultivated his love of solitude. The solitude accounts for Finnish silence. The Finns average only a dozen persons to the square kilometer. When a man's nearest neighbor often lives three miles away, he finds little need for the faculty of chatting agreeably. Because Finns do not like to talk much, they dream the more. When the hard day's work is done and the Finn rests, he sees strange, appealing things in his mind's eye. Perhaps this habit accounts for that distant gaze in the eyes of Finns who have never sailed. That look which one is accustomed to see only in sailors' eyes one often meets on country lanes and on concrete pavements in inland towns.

"In our Finnish world where everything must be paid for, we have our solitude in exchange for our endless space," a young poet named Lorenz von Numers said to me. "And the darkness of our winters, rich with snow, against our marvelous summers, brimful of light. The melancholy you find in our music and in our poetry is the black flower of the silent wilderness. You cannot find it among orange blossoms."

"To understand what makes us tick," said Ralph Enckell of the Foreign Office, "you must remember winter and what it does to us. It is one of the keys that give access to a comprehension of the Finnish soul. The other three key-words are space, solitude, struggle."

Later I learned another keyword—more significant, perhaps,

than the others. It is the Finn's favorite word. It is *sisu,* pronounced "see-su," with the accent on the first syllable. It cannot be translated, and even the Finns have difficulty in defining it. For like so much of Finland which eludes definition, it is a thing felt, like religion or love.

Sisu, a Finn will tell you, thinking very hard, means something still more. It surpasses fearlessness and extraordinary endurance. It is a kind of inner fire or superhuman nerve force. It makes an athlete forget fatigue and pain and risk his life to win. *Sisu* made Paavo Nurmi and Taisto Mäki break world records again and again.

Sibelius defined *sisu* as a metaphysical shot in the arm, which makes a man do the impossible. At the Helsinki station on the September afternoon I left Finland, Nurmi gave me his favorite definition. *"Sisu,"* he said, with quiet understatement, "is patience without passion." And then added, "It comes to men miraculously in times of stress."

I first heard the word at Ilomantsi, the last town in eastern Karelia before one reaches the Russian border. I was having coffee with the sheriff of the district, and we were listening to the radio report of Hitler's army, poised, ready to descend on Danzig. The sheriff drew a knife from his pocket and handed it to me. It was sturdy, executive-looking, not long, not short. Its black bone handle was trimmed with narrow silver bands and red enamel. The handle fitted snugly, companionably in the grasp of the fist. The six-inch blade ended in a curving point like the tip of a new moon. The sheriff had carried it for fifteen years for sentimental reasons as well as for protection.

"The young fellow who owned this knife," my host said, "had more *sisu* than anyone I've ever known. Six older men attacked him and tried to kill him. He was in the right, but he had only this one blade between him and death. They fought for an hour.

He cut the six to pieces. I saw the finish of the fight—it was a glorious display of *sisu*." The sheriff took the knife and held it lovingly in the embrace of his fist for a moment and then slipped it into its embroidered leather holster. "We shall have need of *sisu*," he said gravely, "to face what may come shortly." He turned off the radio and glanced out the east window that looked toward Russia. "But in the world we live in today," he said, as if the idea were being born that moment, "*sisu* is the Finn's minus as well as plus. For it makes it impossible for him to compromise with his ideals."

The Finn is not well understood, even by his nearest western neighbor, the Swede. Despite a similarity in landscape, the northern winds, the white nights of summer, the red farmhouses, the shared boundary, the Finn is something quite different from the Swede in temperament and character. When I was leaving Sweden for Finland, the editor of Stockholm's largest newspaper said to me, "You will find the Finns unique—different from all other people on earth. There are spiritual forces stirring among them that we know little about. If you notice carefully you will see it in their eyes. You must remark them closely, though, for on the surface they are a very simple, natural people."

The Finn has a fresh, unspoiled, primitive side that exists in close harmony with nature. He feels stirring in his blood a special kinship with the wilder variety of nature—with virgin forests, unproductive fells, and the animal life that haunts them. There is something about him rugged like the boulders, something untamed like the elk and free like the wild swan. Wherever his foot wanders in the city, however far fortune lets him ascend the wheel, his roots remain deep in the soil.

The rural Finn—and three-fourths of the population is still rural—has been self-educated in a heroic school. He has been brought up on generations of scanty rations. He is the modern

Spartan. When famine years came in the past, he nibbled at the roots of trees and unflinchingly ate bread made of pine bark.

"A typical Finn," a countryman said to me, "is an obstinate sort of fellow who believes in getting the better of bad fortune by proving that he can stand worse." Yet he is no grim fatalist sitting doggedly immobile, waiting to receive fortune's blows. He is resourceful to the end, and cheers himself and his brother by declaring, "There's always one trick left, and even that isn't the last." In whatever part of the land a Finn has made his home he has never lacked a grindstone on which to sharpen his worldly wits.

But his Spartanlike qualities carry with them no hardness of heart, no selfishness. There is nothing mean about a Finn—nothing petty. He has always been one to help his neighbor, and he can be sympathetic in time of trouble. "Pity never harmed a a man," he says, "except when he pitied himself." And though a Finn is hospitable and quick to recognize a duty to a fellow man, he does not open both doors of his heart to everyone he meets. Once his friendship has been won, however, it lasts for life.

A Finn is as honest as the days of mid-summer are long. The stranger senses security and fair-dealing straight off. Even in the cities one feels no necessity for bolting doors, and above the Arctic Circle it is an unwritten law that doors be left unlocked, for on winter nights the difference between a locked door and one that opens quickly may mean death or life to a freezing traveler. The oft-told tales of found purses being nailed to trees and retrieved by their owners months later are not exaggerations.

A Finn can't see why people praise a man for anything as natural as honesty. In regard to the famous debts to the United States, the Finns say it is pointless to make such a fuss. "Is it such a marvel," they ask, "that I repay the money you have lent me? We did not intend to keep it, of course."

The Finns detest boasting and pretentiousness as much as dishonesty. They do not encourage "personalities" among their compatriots. They are apt to discredit all "chiefs," and particularly those who rise too fast. Paradefulness and artificiality are foolish vices in Finnish eyes. The Finns have a modesty that goes with a woodman's shyness and awkwardness.

Though they are not big talkers, Finns can make excellent conversationalists. But when they have nothing to say they keep silent. "One can take back a good silence, but not a bad hurry," is a favorite proverb. When something that matters is at stake—something that touches his patriotism—a Finn can be eloquent with passionate appeal. The love he has for his country, which he calls *Suomi,* is a beautiful thing. Patriotism is his real religion. It is something ingrained in the fiber of him, like that spiritual force that stirs within the breast of the nation.

Because the Finns are at base a hardy race of dreamers and demand fewer of life's superficialities, they are less materialistic than other peoples. Through centuries they plodded half-asleep in involuntary communion with the nature about them. Yet strangely their awakening had to come in a large measure through practical things—through that stirring business activity that flamed with the new century. Then the outside world made them aware of the value of their material resources. And their ideas and requirements and hopes began to expand into a passion for self-improvement. But while gratefully accepting the material aspects of better living, the new conveniences of modern culture, the Finns have never been bemused into imagining false values. Finns above all races seem to understand that spirit is fundamentally life's only substance and reality.

PART ONE

"Man's bounden duty is everywhere and in all things to forward the progress of humanity." GIUSEPPE MAZZINI

White City of the North

BY WAY OF TURKU

We went to Helsinki by way of Turku. The overnight trip from Stockholm across the Baltic in the immaculate little steamer was comfortable and pleasant. It was quiet, too, with the same Scandinavian quiet we had become accustomed to in five months among the Northern Countries. But it was a strange, many-voweled tongue that we heard spoken for the first time. And the people were more foreign-looking than the Swedes, who are not foreign-looking at all. The faces were broader, the features less mobile. There was less color in the cheeks, but more yellow in the hair. Some indescribable quality in their composed façades challenged one to get at the heart of their mystery.

The evenness of the crossing was broken by a brief two-in-the-morning halt at Mariehamn in the Åland Islands. Local vacationists returning from Sweden disembarked, and Finnish vacationists returning to the mainland boarded the ship. The Swedish and Finnish tongues mingling together in the early morning merged dreamlike with the ship's muted noises. I did not get up to peer at the controversial islands that Napoleon called the Key to Stockholm and that Finland and Sweden almost went to war over in 1919. I recalled that these islands were so maritime that every little boy went to sea at eleven or twelve, and with his first savings bought himself a share in a ship. I remembered, too, vaguely how Sally Salminen had poignantly described the sorrows and joys of the islanders in a book called *Katrina.* Then I dozed off again and slept until we reached Turku, or Åbo, as it is called in Swedish.

We did not stay in the oldest of Finland's cities, but took the Helsinki express at the dock. The train, however, ran the length of the city slowly, and the glimpses were pleasing in neatness and cleanness. Along the tracks working people lived in the ivory-colored one-story wooden houses, built in the 1820's, and set around grassy courts. In the middle distance were shops of pressed glass and chromium, and concrete apartment houses, and farther off, the famous cathedral that had its ceremonious dedication in 1290. The word *Sauna,* signifying the famed Finnish steam bath, caught the eye every few blocks. In the open spaces between factories, florists cultivated flowers for the market. Small parks with benches under silver birches were set here and there for people's enjoyment, like a loose chain linking the city with the countryside.

Beyond the town the fields were rich with ripening wheat, and in the pastures fat red cows chewed their morning cuds. Shallow drainage ditches, bordered with feathery elk's grass, divided the whole land into regular rectangular patches. The open landscape in the distance looked like acres of pale green corduroy spread out on the low-lying hills. But the nearer rectangles were varied with the greens of rye and oats and sugar beets and potatoes. No matter what else was growing on a man's land, there were always the hardy green potato plants. Sometimes there were beehives between the house lot and the flowery meadows; always there was the bathhouse, and close beside it the piled cords of birchwood. Farmsteads with apple orchards flashed upon the view, framed by coniferous forests. Clusters of red houses and lone white churches broke the stubbly bronze of reaped hayfields. Black crows sunned themselves on the tips of poles around which drying hay was neatly stacked. A forest of spruce trees brushed by the train, and the clean odor of woods surged in the window. Then came a field where twenty farmers were experimenting co-operatively with a new, bright yellow farm implement. Finland was a simple land. It made the pulse steadier to look at it.

BRONZE MESSENGER

It was almost noon when we reached Helsinki. The sun lay in warm abundance upon the world's most northern capital. My admiration for the Finns rose the instant a little porter smilingly began to strap all our seven bags about him—before, behind, on both sides. All but his head and feet completely disappeared. The bags were heavy. When I insisted he call an extra porter, he scorned my implication. Smiling reassuringly, he said what I imagined to be "This is nothing"—not boastfully, just run-of-the-day courtesy—and walked off stout as a load-bearing ant.

We started following him into Eliel Saarinen's famous station, reputed to be the finest architecturally in all Europe. I stopped short. I had run into myself in the crowd at the gate. There I was held in the hands of a smiling young girl I had never seen before. A Swedish friend had sent the girl's Finnish employer one of the lecture circulars my agent got out with my picture on it. He had sent his secretary to meet us and to see us to our hotel. She was using the photograph on the folder for identification. It was pleasant to be unexpectedly welcomed.

The entrances to Helsinki by land and by sea are planned to give the stranger a spacious impression. In front of the railway station and on the sides is space to match the great cathedral square in Mexico and San Marco's in Venice. But in Helsinki there are flower beds and trees besides flagstones. And the neighboring buildings are not the usual bobtail conglomeration to be found about most American and European stations. The National Theater, the Athenaeum Museum, the yellow Post Office, the headquarters of the Finnish Co-operative Wholesale Society, S.O.K., and two of the best hotels open directly upon the square. And across the elevated street to the west stands the most imposing parliament house in the North.

We stood and marveled at the urban space under the noon-blue sky. But where was the famous silence? We knew Helsinki was noted for noiseless streets—that by law no motor horns honk, no bicycle bells tinkle, no street vender cries his wares, no factory whistle sounds the time. And those unlawful noises were absent. But there was a hubbub of excavating and drilling, of blasting and building. A vast new hotel was going up over there on the edges of the open space—foundations were being laid for a mammoth bus station on the opposite edge.

"All over the city it's like this," said the Finnish girl, as we got into a taxi. "Building everywhere. Four other hotels are being built. Dozens of new apartment houses are going up, and hundreds of villas in the suburbs. We have so little time. All must be ready a year from today—the Olympic Games, you know." It was July twentieth, and the Olympic Games were scheduled to begin in exactly one year.

Through the streets, in the shop windows, like a Mercury bearing good news, the green-bronze nude of Paavo Nurmi was running on posters announcing the Twelfth Olympiad to be held at Helsinki.

"The posters are done from Väinö Aaltonen's famous statue in the Athenaeum," our friend said. "They are printed in twenty languages. They are running like that all over the globe." There was buoyant enthusiasm in her voice, and bright assurance. "We must work fast to be ready." As if no rumors of impending war had reached her, Finland was building furiously to entertain the world in the summer of 1940. The intensity of preparation to get her house in order for her guests was almost like a mobilization for war.

FIRST WALK

We did not tarry in the Hotel Torni, but went out at once to look for a place for luncheon. Poking about unfamiliar streets and sniffing out agreeable restaurants has always seemed to me the quickest way to get the feel and flavor of a new country. So we strolled off, looking at façades and shop windows, at statues, at passing men and women. The people in the streets were a mixture, like those in all city streets. Inexpensively but tastefully dressed girls in neat suits and smart hats were returning to their offices and shops. Occasional distinguished-looking gentlemen with gloves in their hands raised their hats to other gentlemen dressed like themselves. Purposeful errand boys dashed in and out of the crowd. A few old women in white head-kerchiefs tied under their chins sat on street corners selling flowers.

Aleksanterinkatu, the principal business street, was substantial with gray granite—blocks of solid, dignified structures broken two or three times by one-story wooden buildings from the early nineteenth century, like bits of an outdoor museum the commissioners had forgotten to have carted to their proper place. Blocks of modern buildings, sporting-goods shops, hat shops, drugstores, furniture stores, and bookstores branched off from the solidity of banks, office buildings, and department stores.

The distinctive feature of the business streets was the artistry of the window displays. Creative energy had gone into the designs of fruits and vegetables from Holland, France, Italy,

Smyrna, far-off California, and farther-off Chile. The grocery stores and butcher shops glistened with cleanliness.

Helsinki's shopping district was up-to-date, adequate, and attractive, but there was no nonsense about it, nothing faddy. And only in wood carvings and hand-woven rugs and fabrics did it seem regional. Antique shops displayed some relics of Czarist Russia, but American tourists had already bought up the cream.

The sea laps eternally at Helsinki's front gate and all her side gates because the city is situated on a slight promontory indented with bays. An invigorating, faintly salted breeze blows refreshingly in every byway of the town, and sooner or later if you follow the path of the wind you will find yourself at some water's edge. When we reached the South Harbor, a brigade of vigorous cleaners with hose and scrubbing brushes were making the cobbles shine like a Dutch hearth. An open-air market with its booths and stalls and produce boats from the island farms hold session there from early morning to noon. But by noon tradesmen, shoppers, weighing scales, stalls, everything, must be gone, or the men with the hoses will wash them into the sea. Some stallkeepers gamble with time and flee with their unsold goods just in the nick of time before the flood. And the pigeons audaciously pick crumbs to the very last moment. Like an auxiliary corps of cleaners, the flocks of blue and white pigeons that live on the Esplanade descend to help with the tidying. They devour the bits of fish, grain, vegetables that fall between the tables. By a quarter to one the pavement and the concrete quay were restored to their clean nakedness, and we could have eaten our dinner from the street as safely as from a scrubbed deal table.

From the whiteness of the market place and the immaculate cathedral of the great Suurtori Square high on the hill two blocks behind it, Helsinki is known as "the White City of the North." Today the market place was blue and white like Finland's flag, which flew above the Presidential Palace. The canopy of sky stretched above the market was a cloudless azure, and the water of the harbor a deeper blue, like that of the sapphire-colored awnings of the Swedish Embassy. Out on the surface of the bay the sails of yachts reflected their graceful white triangles on the rippling mirror.

At the west end of the market place began the Esplanade, where a slim Finnish girl in bronze rose in the great basin of the fountain like Aphrodite naked from the waves. Two parallel streets with rows of shops, banks, hotels, office buildings faced each other across seven blocks of rectangular islands of green growth. At the harbor end of the parked center an expansive open-air restaurant consumed one whole green rectangle. At the restaurant Sibelius' youngest son-in-law led the orchestra that drew crowds to the al-fresco tables. At the farther end were the Royal Café and the white modern Swedish Theater, round like a cheesebox.

On the seven blocks of benches that stretched in two rows down the gravelly center of the Esplanade, citizens were sunning themselves and watching each other go by. In the old days under Russia the upper classes took possession of the place. Russian officers in high patent-leather boots and dazzling uniforms would parade like peacocks before the girls sitting under bright parasols. Children of the well-to-do played about the lilac bushes under the surveillance of uniformed nurses. Dowagers in mauve silk and old men with gold-headed canes and silk hats conversed in Russian, Swedish, French, and German. Common people would have been frozen with dismayed glances had they presumed to sit among the privileged.

Today half the sitters were what is called the proletariat. Some looked like farmers unused to city sights; some were bricklayers and carpenters from near-by building projects. Some were soldiers in rude gray cotton blouses and crushed boots, and some were jaunty sailors. Several girls were dressed in the peasant costumes of blue and henna hand-woven stuff with gold-figured embroidery and sheer white blouses. An occasional old woman in white head-kerchief sat with a market basket on her knee, placid as a Rembrandt figure. Several youths wore the white velvet student caps with the golden lyre badges which proved they had passed their entrance examinations to the university. The people all sat quietly, as if in church. Many of the heads were tilted back, faces uplifted to the sky, for they were worshiping the sun while they rested.

In natural niches among the shrubs, bronze statues perched on pedestals—charming young girls with freshly budded breasts—were half-hidden by the lilac bushes, as if playing hide and seek. Runeberg, the national poet and Finland's Robert Burns to young lovers, had the place of honor. His statue, done by his son Walter, rose high above all the rest in a circular space planted with some unfamiliar gold flowers, which were all feathery bloom with no foliage. In blocked letters the base bore the first verse of Finland's national anthem, *Our Land*.

At the street crossings horse-drawn droshkies with top-hatted coachmen waited for fares in the checkered shade. Blue pigeons returned from marketing fluttered about white news kiosks that were as innocent of advertising posters as mosques in Mecca. A red-headed youngster knelt on a strip of purple cloth and shined a man's shoes with prideful energy. A pigeon, a soldier, and a toddling girl came in turn to drink from a shallow dipper that lay chained to a fountain.

At the end of the Esplanade the flambeaux of the chestnut trees caught the flame of the sun, and the Royal Café spread its many-leveled terraces under rust-colored awnings and behind railed rows of blue hydrangeas. The shade of a giant chestnut in full bloom fell in sprawling pattern on the white linen of our luncheon table. The Russian émigré waiter knew how grapefruit should be served, and we did not have to tackle it with the tablespoon and the tiny fork they always gave us for implements in Sweden.

Though the waiter had lived for nine years in America, he preferred Helsinki. "There are not many rich here," he said, "but neither are there many poor. There is a decent living for all. In America I made so much, much money, but what is the use of money if you have to rush your life away? Life is made for living, not rushing."

When the bill came we knew why Finland could boast of the most reasonable prices in Europe. The food was excellent, yet the luncheons, with fillet of beef, cost only twenty-eight cents each. The pigeons fluttered about the grass, making cooing noises of delight. The people on the terraces and those passing on the gravel walk looked happy and alert and full of hope for the future. Democratic Helsinki was charming that sunny July day in 1939.

PORTRAIT OF A BUSINESS MAN

"From any part of Helsinki you can be in the deep woods or on the water in a quarter of an hour," said the gentleman named Paloheimo, as we drove along the next day.

His brother in New York had written him, and he had come to show us about and to take us to lunch. He was one of the many sons-in-law of Sibelius: not the banker, nor the actor, nor the orchestra leader, but the manufacturer of glassware and the country gentleman. He was sorry his wife couldn't have us at their country place that day, but it was the preserving season. The canning of the summer's fruits was a sacred time in Finnish households. The World's Fair Committee had invited her to come as her father's representative to the Sibelius Celebration in New York, but she couldn't make up her mind to leave the preserving.

"Besides, Finns are limelight-shy," Paloheimo said. He began or ended almost every sentence with a smile of some sort. If he spoke of a real-estate development, or of a remembrance of childhood, he smiled. His attitude toward any subject could be judged by the quality of his smile. He seemed to regard all human beings, including himself, as children who made forgivable mistakes and had fun and suffered little disappointments. Whatever was bad would pass. And hardships could always be endured. Nothing was worth ponderous worry.

He was a tall, handsome, vague fellow, a youngish fifty, with an Anthony Eden Homburg pushed back from his tanned forehead. His shoulders were uncommonly broad, like his brother's in New York. His hair was not Finnish blond, but chestnut; his eyes were dark hazel, with a perpetual twinkle. There was a flavor of Rhett Butler about him without Rhett's trickery or ruthlessness.

He drove his car himself. Therese sat in front beside him, and I learned about Finland from the back seat.

He waved casually toward a tennis court where some youths were leaping in the sun. "No tennis courts are allowed at our country place," he said with a grin. "My boys can play tennis at school if they like. At home in summer they are in the fields with the laborers at seven every morning. They work until the laborers quit in the evening. It hardens their muscles, stores up strength for a lifetime. They get the peasant's point of view. When you sweat side by side with a man and call him by his first name, you learn what's in his heart.

"At home my boys are given plain food, and eat only hard peasant bread in the summer—horse bread—it's good for teeth. See—" he turned and bared his own strong, even white teeth at me "—I was brought up like that—on horse's bread—thick, tough, black bread. I haven't got a plug in my teeth today." He laughed and righted the car, which was heading for the ditch. He sighed. "My boys have stopped eating that kind of bread now, though. They didn't have so good an appetite, and their mother, hearing all this new talk of vitamins, got afraid they wouldn't get enough to eat if they ate no bread at all. So I had to give in. But I—I still eat good old horse bread." He laughed at his own eccentricity and clamped his strong teeth together. "My father never permitted my four brothers and me to comment on food at the table. We were to eat what was set before us. If hard times came, as they did in 1917-18, we were ready for them. My father made only one mistake—he didn't pay us wages. I pay my boys wages."

"The same wages as your laborers?"

He nodded. "Less room and board," he added, laughing. "Last year the sixteen-year-old one saved his summer's money and bought an accordion. It meant something to him."

"Don't they ever get a vacation?" Therese asked, feeling sorry for the poor little rich boys.

"Oh, yes, the nineteen-year-old one is on vacation now. He's helping to build anti-tank fortifications near the Russian frontier, fitting the granite boulders in the holes."

"That's a vacation?"

"The best sort. He's doing something for his country. He's a Civic Guard volunteer. That's the way most of the young Finns, married and single, are taking their vacation this year. They have a big time—all sorts and kinds of men together, from all parts of the country, working and singing and eating at the kitchens where the girl volunteers, the Lotta Svärd, cook the food and serve them."

We crossed a bridge and then another. Helsinski broke away from urban restrictions into spatterings of islands separated by little inlets. Thirty thousand islands stretch out to make the Finnish archipelago that protects the coast. Summer cottages crouched beneath the trees that grew to the rocky shore line, and here and there people were swimming in their own front yards or sunning themselves on grass and rocks. The fast-growing capital had reached hungrily into the surrounding forests and meadows and islands, and had incorporated more acres within its limits.

We came to a new residential section that was being opened up for the well-to-do—expensive houses being erected on expensive lots that had been without value a decade ago. A golf course was being laid out, a clubhouse being built. *En tous cas* tennis courts shone richly red in the open spaces. "Like America," Paloheimo said, smiling. "One of my brothers is going to build over there." He pointed vaguely and laughed. It amused him to think of the money many of his friends had already sunk in the enterprise. It seemed kind of silly—all this sort of thing—dressing up the woods. "I'd rather be out in the fields or forests with a gun and a dog."

"Are you a good farmer?" I asked.

He smiled and didn't answer directly. "Well, I wouldn't try to make my living that way. Farming is no good for business, but it's wonderful for the heart."

We turned off from the real-estate development and were going down a dusty, old-fashioned dirt road. The car suddenly stopped in the midst of nothing. Paloheimo just sat there, vague and puzzled. He pushed his gray Homburg to the very back of his head as if to give his brain more air. He jiggled the mechanism, shifted gears, and laughed. We got out, lifted the hood, poked about. "It's a new car too," he said, perplexed. "American. I've only had it three months." A truck passed with two young Finnish laborers and a load of lumber. They stopped cheerfully and came and tinkered with the mechanism. The gas line was plugged, and there was no water in the battery. The car had to be abandoned.

We laughed and considered. Paloheimo's Homburg and Therese's blue-fox scarf and city clothes seemed to go just as well with the dusty country road as atop the pile of lumber in the truck. We decided to walk back to a filling station we had passed on the main road. The truckmen said they would send help if they saw any.

We trooped down the road gaily, Paloheimo with a perplexed apologetic grin, his hat clean on the back of his neck.

On the roadside a young woman and a little girl were picking raspberries—the couple had seemed to appear from nowhere. I said something pleasant in English and, to my surprise, the woman answered me in English. She was studying the language in a neighborhood study circle. She offered us some berries. They grow wild all over Finland along paths through the woods and on roadsides. They are delicious, but these were coated with dust and needed washing.

We went on and met no one else until a bus came behind us. We hailed it and climbed in the back. At the filling station we got out. The driver wouldn't accept any money—the ride had been too short, he said. A boy from the filling station was sent on a bicycle to the nearest telephone to call a taxi from Helsinki. We sat on a white bench and talked of farming and shooting and country life in general as compared to Finnish town life.

"Society life, diplomatic life," Paloheimo smiled wryly with a headshake as we taxied into town. "I was briefly in consular service in Turkey, but I had to give up that sort of thing. That's no life—it's not living—lunches half the day, dinners into the night!" He laughed at his own distaste. "Not living at all."

We asked him what time the Finns usually dined at home.

"At six."

"Then you don't have the tea custom?"

"No—never." He looked as if that were no life either. "Women," he said vaguely, "at parties—maybe." He laughed at the prospect.

"Your wife—does she ever go to them?"

"No—not she—never." That sort of thing was all a joke in his family. "In Russia we did sometimes, when we lived in St. Petersburg—I had business there before the war. I suppose it's all right for Russians or English."

As we went into the dining room of the Societet Huset, a familiar-looking thin-faced Englishman came out. Paloheimo recognized him vaguely and then spoke pleasantly. "That was Noel Coward," he said. "We took him out to see Sibelius yesterday. They had a big chat together."

The waiter showed us to a corner table. "We are more polite than the English," Paloheimo said. "We men shake hats when we pass each other." He made a motion of raising his hat. "An Englishman never thinks of shaking his hat at another man." We didn't correct his verb—it was too expressive the way he used it.

"I'll take you to see my father-in-law soon—some afternoon when Mme. Sibelius is able to see you, too. She isn't well just now. There's a rare woman! I've never seen any to compare with her in intelligence, charm—quality. It's not glamour. She's too natural for that. It's a kind of magic."

He rose and said, "Shall we fill our plates?"

The Finns in their hotels and restaurants follow the Swedish custom of elaborate *smörgåsbord.* In the center of the dining room stood the long table laden with hors d'œuvres. Their variety was as remarkable as their flavor and quality. The platters and plates and bowls and covered dishes crowded the white tablecloth more thickly than the thirty thousand islands of the Finnish archipelago crowded the water. There were half a hundred different dishes to tempt the gourmet and ravish the average appetite. Our choice lay among the long slabs of smoked salmon, the salted salmon, the *pâté de foie gras,* smoked reindeer meat, herrings smoked and herrings raw in sauce, Norwegian sardines, fresh radishes, tidbits with truffles in aspic, chicken mayonnaise, small whole tomatoes, cold chicken, reindeer tongue, calves' tongues, liver sausage, Swedish red caviar, lettuce salad, baked ham, cold roast beef, cucumbers in sweet sauce, scrambled eggs, boiled shrimp, lobster salad, beet salad, vegetable salad, pickled pigs' feet, kippers, shredded horse-radish, prawns, a fruit salad of oranges, grapes, and prunes, veal brawn, kippered herring, potato salad, smoked goose, and anchovies. In the center were stacked six kinds of breads and four varieties of Finnish cheese, including the sweetish peasant goat's cheese, the color of brown sugar. At each end of the table in burnished copper dishes set over spirit lamps were chanterel mushrooms, hot boiled new potatoes, spaghetti au gratin, and lambs' kidneys sauté with sherry sauce.

Our delay on the road had given us an appetite to do justice to the feast—or rather to the first course.

"Hard, black, horse bread!" I said derisively to our host, looking at his loaded plate of delicacies.

He grinned like an irresistible youngster caught at the jam pot. "Makes one properly appreciate the good things of life," he retorted.

When we returned to our table, the waiter set small glasses of white aqua vite before us, and tumblers of amber beer. Paloheimo raised his schnapps glass and said with casual grace, "Skål—welcome to Finland."

"You skål here as in Sweden?" Therese asked.

"Oh, yes, we always skål." Then he added, with mock solemnity, "But we don't make a drama of it as the Swedes do."

"How much Swedish and how much Finnish are you?" I asked.

He shrugged expressively. "Who knows? Our family has been Finnish for at least three hundred years. But in any Finn there may be Swedish blood—and in some even a drop of Russian—though one hardly dares to admit it. We have some Scotch blood in us. Our family name is really Brander, from a Scotch great-great-grandfather. In one day about thirty-five years ago a hundred thousand Finns changed their names from Swedish to Finnish. The name-changing was a nationalistic means of resisting Russification under Nicholas II. It was a patriotic thing to do to show national unity. It was as exciting as Adam's naming the animals in *Genesis*. We took the name Paloheimo because in ancient times it belonged to the family. It means 'Fire Tribe.' People with Latin names, like Sibelius, kept them. They were considered Finnish. But some of the Swedo-Finns, rather than change the names to lowly Finnish, would have preferred to die, then and there, so as to have Swedish names on their tombstones. Hundreds of the upper-class families did change, however, and thousands of peasants who had Swedish names that Swedish-speaking priests had given them."

The waiter held the menu before him to order the main course. All menus in first-class restaurants are printed both in Swedish and Finnish. Paloheimo put a monocle to his right eye, read over the dishes, and ordered squab chicken en casserole with fresh green peas.

"You can see the language change, right in our family. In

MARKET SQUARE, SOUTH HARBOR, HELSINKI

HELSINKI: THE MONUMENTAL STATION BUILDING IS A WORK OF ELIEL SAARINEN AND WAS COMPLETED IN 1919. THE NEW GENERAL POST OFFICE IS SEEN IN THE BACKGROUND

earlier times the cultivated families all spoke Swedish. My father is the eldest child—now in his seventies. He had seven sisters; to the first four he always spoke Swedish—to the last three he always spoke Finnish."

We went on with our food. "The linguistic point of view is not so acute now," Paloheimo said optimistically. "The bitterness between the Swedo-Finns and the Finns over the language is dying out. The Finns have learned they can live without the Swedo-Finns, but the Swedo-Finns couldn't live without the Finns."

Paloheimo looked up and bowed to a white-haired old gentleman who was leaving the dining room. The old man lowered his glasses and looked over them at our host with a cabalistic glance. "He has a perpetual joke on me," Paloheimo said. "He's a friend of my father's. He was there when I was born—on an island on a fishing trip—one August third. I came before I was expected. My mother thought she oughtn't to go. 'But,' they said, 'you come on—just a nice sail.' The weather turned out to be very rough. And in the middle of the night I was born. The man who went out says he has never forgotten the sight of my father running about in the moonlight with his trousers hanging about his ankles because he couldn't find his braces in the excitement—trying to decide whether to try to sail back. But I made the decision for him. And my father had to use his fishing knife."

Paloheimo told it with gestures to help out his rarely practiced English. "I've always had to wear a leather belt—so—about my middle." He laughed like a boy confessing something he wasn't quite sure was proper. "Because of that fish trip."

"And your mother?" Therese asked.

"Oh, she got on fine. Finnish women are wonderful."

When the waiter brought bowls of fresh chilled raspberries with frozen cream for dessert, our host said, "This was George's favorite dessert. A funny fellow, that brother of mine in New

York—I suppose you'd call him an idealist. He left Finland because he said he couldn't stand the friction in the air between capital and labor. We sent him to study cellulose in the States for a while so he could come back and manage one of our plants. He stayed six weeks at the factory, then threw it up. He wrote that he couldn't stand 'all that materiality.' " Paloheimo was delighted at such absurdity.

"He inherited an estate right next to Sibelius—with three large houses on it. He's letting relatives live there now. He and Sibelius were great friends. He's been gone six years. Did he say when he was coming back?"

"When he closes up the Finnish Exhibit at the World's Fair," I said. "He's coming home to stay."

"What's he going to do?"

"Turn his three houses and his grounds into a psychiatric hospital for the poor."

"My God!" The elder brother's eyes widened, and in his surprise he stuck his monocle into his eye. Then he smiled. "And what's *he* going to do?"

"Live in a one-room log hut with a dirt floor."

"Idealist!" He chuckled derisively at the lengths to which idealism could lead you. "It's just like him." He smiled expansively. "I'll bet he enjoys it too. Let's drink to him with a typical Finnish liqueur." And he ordered *Mesimarja.*

The liqueur was red and sweet and had a special taste of almonds, strawberries, and apricots. It was made from dark red bramble berries that grow only in burnt-over land in Lapland. The berries require wood ash, and birch ash gives them the richest flavor.

When the host kissed Therese's hand in farewell, he did it with the ease and grace of a Dane.

"These Finns are something different," I said, when we were alone. "Full of surprises."

"And so charming and natural," Therese said. "I wonder how he ever runs a glass factory."

COLOR AND LIGHT

One does not take in all Helsinki in a day—it is not all of a piece. It must be explained and returned to if one is to get the flavor and the variety—to see the wise planning, from the areas of public building to the sports fields and the industrial sections.

If there is a dominating color in the capital it is certainly white, ranging from bone white to lustrous white, ivory white, oyster white, and thence into shades of pearl gray and granite pink. The new public schools, hospitals, and various sports stadia, the arresting new Agricultural College, and hundreds of modern apartment houses in white stucco and concrete have strengthened the impression of whiteness. Certainly there are more white structures in Helsinki than in any other European city. Buildings remain white for years, for although the capital is also the republic's largest industrial town, it is virtually smokeless. Instead of coal, birchwood is used for fuel, and birchwood gives off almost no smoke. Rains in summer and snow in winter keep the houses well washed, and the fresh sea breezes help the sun to dry them.

As in Stockholm, the visitor to Helsinki is always impressed by the harmony of color of the better apartment houses. They are not monotonously white, but are relieved by bright awnings of deep sea blue or rust or orange, or aquamarine or pale lemon yellow. Often the buildings are painted a wheat-color or a whitish-green like Malaga grapes. Invariably when color is used on the new buildings it is pastel and chalky in effect, never violent, never murky. Some of the architects have selected colors that seem intended to reflect the luminosity of the aurora borealis—the cool glowworm green or a diluted heliotrope much like that of light bulbs filled with helium.

Although Helsinki's charter dates back to 1550 and the city has occupied its present protected site since 1640, it is hard to find here a structure built before the nineteenth century. Before Finland came under Russian suzerainty in 1810 it had suffered a devastating fire and three Russian occupations. After the capital was moved from Turku to Helsinki in 1812, the building program instituted in the new capital in the 1820's under Ludvig Engel proceeded uninterrupted for three decades. Helsinki was metamorphosed into a city of dignity and beauty in a serene modified Empire style. Engel's work did not stop with a few churches, governmental buildings, and the university. He built barracks, stables, and country villas and whole rows of one-story dwellings strung together.

The buildings of 1820 to 1850 are so persuasive that Engel is to Finland what the Adam brothers were to later eighteenth-century England. Few structures erected between 1850 and Finland's independence year of 1918 are worth recalling. But ever since gaining her freedom Helsinki has been diligent in improving her appearance. Along with the development of freed genius in many national endeavors after the winning of independence, there emerged a new crop of architects led by Eliel Saarinen. To Saarinen and Sirén and Lars Sonck must be accredited the most impressive buildings of Helsinki since the completion of Engel's great church in Suurtori Square. But in the last decade a younger generation, led by Alvar Aalto, in employing the modern style which dominates the contemporary architecture, has made spectacular architectural history.

In the last two decades Finland has surpassed all other countries of Europe in architecture, with the possible exception of Sweden. And even Sweden has no library to compare with the one Aalto built at Viipuri, no railway station half so handsome as Helsinki's, no modernly equipped hotel so attractive as the one in the little town of Aulanko. And beside Sirén's magnificent Parliament House, Stockholm's meeting place for legislators is a poor thing indeed. Yet it is in the provincial schools, the co-operative shops, the rural sanatoria, that one finds the most striking advance in the new architecture.

Finland has been as blessed in her architects as in her city administrators. Like the Swedes, Finns possess an uncommon knowledge of what is good taste and what is bad. And Finns have had no false allegiance to the past when the period was wrong. The city fathers have torn down individual buildings and whole blocks that impaired the general appearance. Private owners have followed the good example and razed and rebuilt. No nation's architects have had such steady employment as have Finland's. The colleges and institutes have hardly been able to turn out enough draftsmen for the demand.

Finland has not hesitated to experiment. But though her architects have been audacious, they have avoided freakishness, the pitfall of many another nation's use of functionalism. And to the new bright styles designed for economy, Finnish architects have added a sense of beauty and sometimes a relieving sense of humor. Everywhere they have sought to catch the light, making abundant use of glass. The lines are severe but graceful, with sudden surprises, like the round tower of sun balconies on a corner of the Military Convalescent Hospital.

One special distinction of Finnish architecture, which Eliel Saarinen pointed out to me, is the harmony between the outside and inside of a building. "The architect in Finland," Saarinen said, "is his own interior decorator. He chooses the fabrics, the fixtures, the furniture, as well as the material for the ceilings and the colors for the walls."

We were sitting in his study at his country place twenty miles from Helsinki. That afternoon he had just received a marked copy of *Time* with the account of his winning in collaboration with his son the $7,500 prize for the plan for Washington's new art gallery. Though the Saarinens—like Sweden's foremost sculptor, Carl Milles—have lived for many years at the Cranbrook School in Michigan, they return to Finland every summer to the rambling house on the hill by the lake. It was built in Saarinen's romantic period before the first World War, and he looks at it oddly now as if he wonders how he ever came to conceive such a setting for a Gothic tale.

"The Finns have never been slavish imitators," Saarinen said. "In the Polytechnic Institute I mainly studied how not to do architecture. People speak of my style. I have never had a style or a favorite building. I like best always the next building I am going to do. Style should proceed from architecture, and not architecture from style. When the Parthenon was built, Greece was in a mood for that sort of style. But we had to forget old classical design and keep out tentacles for new impressions, forms, functions. Of course, I believe in functional architecture, but not functionalistic. Every brick in a building has a function . . . just as every note of music must have a function in an orchestral composition."

He reached over and took up a spray of yellow mimosa from the coffee table and broke open one of the feathery balls.

"Every part of this flower has a function. The so-called functional in architecture should be looked on so. Architecture should be a steady progression—the development, gradual. It's easy to play with architectural forms, but it's dangerous. An architect should always remember that a building will last. A bad picture a painter can destroy. But once you build a building, it stays there, good or bad."

We went out into the garden to join our wives. Under a huge orange and white umbrella Mrs. Saarinen was pouring tea. Her dress of yellow organdy with her floppy garden hat of woven straw and ribbon made her look very summery. The sun beat down with such intensity on the northern setting that we all hovered on the shady side of the table.

"Well, the Finns in general are certainly not concerned about any possible European war," Mrs. Saarinen said as we looked up at a passing military plane. "Today one of my maids overheard Nina Strandberg saying there wouldn't be many tourists from America this summer because of the war scare, and the girl said in surprise, 'Oh, do they have war in America now?' "

"FOR THE PEOPLE"

If ever a city was framed for the enjoyment of its citizens it is Helsinki, and many of those citizens in gratitude have left her enduring public legacies in the form of parks and buildings. Lallukka House for artists, for example, was the gift of a rich merchant of Viipuri who believed that a nation's greatness was best reflected in its art. It is a building of forty-six studio apartments, endowed in perpetuity. Here painters, sculptors, musicians, actors, or writers, and their families could live in three times the space and charm they could ordinarily afford. There was a home for old bachelors, a bequest of a rich gentleman whose own bachelordom had been lonely. A series of Flower Foundation Houses for old ladies had grown from an idea spread from Stockholm, by which instead of sending flowers to a funeral friends of the deceased sent checks to the Flower Fund to make the last years of the living more comfortable. In the exclusive district of Observatory Hill, with a view of the South Harbor and Suurtori Square, the Social Museum had been placed. Here women of all classes learned the art of housekeeping and the science of child-welfare work and practical nursing.

The flats for the working people in the factory districts have been so arranged that there is a plenitude of playgrounds and green open spaces. Because there are no slums in Helsinki, there are consequently no slum smells or slum noises or slum attitudes of mind. Poor people there are, but they live in modern apartment houses, plain, serviceable, workmanlike, but light and airy and conveniently equipped, with nothing unpleasant to see from the windows.

On one of the most valuable pieces of real estate in the city, across the street from Stockman's (Finland's greatest department store), stands the Students' Corporations House, where university students have their clubrooms and libraries. Following the Swedish practice of "nations" or provinces, the Finnish students have divided themselves according to the districts from which they come, and each group has its floor or at least its series of apartments. Some of the groups have grown quite rich from the accumulated legacies of well-to-do alumni, who have left their compatriots not only cash and bonds and preferential stocks, but tracts of timberland, dairy herds, and even pleasure yachts.

From the bottom of the sea the city administrators have dredged sand to provide seven municipal bathing beaches for the health and pleasure of their people. One of the public bathing places, on a sloping hillside of spilled rocks and boulders, is reserved for men only, and here bathers may bask in the sun naked like seals and practice diving from granite ledges. Wherever you may abide in Helsinki, a two-cent bus or trolley ride will get you within twenty minutes to the water, with sand beach or rock shore, for mixed bathing or restricted nudity, as you choose. The moving-picture houses are all municipally owned, and the profits go back in benefits to the people themselves. The Opera and the National Theater are subsidized by the government so that the poor man may see the best performances for a pittance.

For flat-dwellers who hanker after gardens, the city has provided tracts in the suburbs called "colony gardens," and there a man may build himself a little summer house to take his family to for week-ends and raise vegetables and flowers on a few hundred square feet of good soil.

Scattered here and there, like healthful oases in the blocks of brick and concrete, sports fields and running tracks have been laid out for youngsters and oldsters, champions and novices, to indulge in athletics, build up their bodies, and have democratic fun.

Impressive orphanages and homes for the aged and charity hospitals are attractive in settings of apple orchards and rose gardens; for in Helsinki today, as far as possible, the curse is taken off misfortune. And the lowly are not made to feel like outsiders, but are welcome at least to some morsels of the national pleasure.

SHARPENED VIRTUES

During the following fortnight I went here and there in the capital observing, meeting, questioning. I wanted to know how Finland, a little nation of not quite 3,800,000 population, had accomplished within a score of years such an exemplary state that commissions from foreign countries came continually to study details of the model.

With a smile, the youngish foreign minister, Eljas Erkko, gave me the best and simplest answer: "Because they are a gifted and intelligent people." He used the pronoun "they" as if he and the other leaders of recent years had merely carried out the general will. "And—" he paused significantly—"because the domination of Russia under the last Czar sharpened every virtue they possessed."

"And they have not overdone," he added after a moment, "because they have continued to practice their inherent sense of restraint and discipline. But, mark you"—his friendly eyes shone frank and keen behind his nose glasses—"neither have they been timid about experiments, innovations. As you know, they were the first European country to give the vote to women, and you have seen the modern influence in the new architecture. Yet—and this is important—they have not been remiss about curbing any dangerous manifestations of what you in America quaintly call 'rugged individualism.' " He leaned his Wagnerian bulk back in his chair and smiled knowingly. When he was a boy his family had lived in Brooklyn and he had gone to school in America. Like so many cabinet ministers in the Northern Countries, he had been raised to his high position from an editorial desk. He was still editor of Finland's leading liberal daily, *Helsingin Sanomat*.

"The Finns *planned* their future in accord with their natural resources and their native mentality." He emphasized the word "planned." "You can notice what town planning has been to Helsinki—it will give you an inkling of what has taken place throughout the nation. Finns have too much respect for their hard-earned freedom to allow a few unconscionable individuals to upset the general harmony. I want you to meet Erik von Frankel, Helsinki's first vice-mayor. He's responsible for much you have been complimenting in the city."

The Foreign Minister arranged an appointment for the next day with one of the busiest men in the republic.

Like many Finns, Mr. von Frankel was a controlled dynamo with magnetic charm and a sense of humor. He was as energetic and hard-punching an individualist as I had met in the Northern Countries. His mind seemed as poised and alert as his will was relentless. He looked like an American business man with a difference—his expression was that of a man who had turned his major talents and energies to his country's upbuilding. He was framed to achieve success and cultivate enemies in the process—the sort of person one likes instinctively for his ability and high spirits, or dislikes intensely because of a latent ruthlessness. At the end of the first minute I knew I liked him. At the end of a quarter of an hour I wished we had his double in every city in the United States.

We talked in his new office in the building hired to house the Olympic Committee. He had been lent by the city to head one of the Olympic commissions. I asked him to explain some of the operation of the Town Planning Law, which had been in effect since 1930.

The mayor and four vice-mayors are chosen by the Town Board, consisting of fifty-nine members who are themselves elected every three years by the vote of the citizens. The mayor and vice-mayors are called "immortals," because they serve until death or resignation.

The job of looking after Helsinki's welfare and improvements is divided among the vice-mayors. The first vice-mayor has under his supervision the estates, grounds, houses, markets, sports, and traffic. The second vice-mayor supervises the fine arts. Number Three has charge of technical matters: water, electricity, gas, harbors. Number Four looks after social matters: schools, hospitals, all charities and charitable institutions.

Von Frankel took me to a map of Helsinki on the wall of an inner office. "See, we have drawn upon our map in different colors. These quarters are for industry, these for living, these for official buildings. Parks and public gardens are placed here—new ones to be in those marked spots." He offered me a cigarette, and we sat down on a divan before the map.

"We are not concerned about real-estate values as they affect individuals, and we do not encourage speculation in real estate," von Frankel went on, his eyes on the map and then on me. "No one can build a house in Helsinki before he submits his plans to the city board. We have a special façade committee that can forbid monstrosities. When I first began to stop people who wanted to build high, ugly houses for rent in sections where there were mostly low houses in garden plots, I was called 'Communist,' though I had been Parliamentary leader of the Conservative Party for twelve years." He smiled sardonically. "It's funny, isn't it, when a man tries anything for the good of the town, he is howled against if it affects any individual's pocketbook adversely. But here, we try to protect the mass of citizens from the few. No man can cut down a tree in his own front yard unless he gets permission. In America I hear you actually allow men to cut down beautiful trees on an avenue to erect a filling station."

I admitted that the principal avenue of my own home town had been despoiled by the chopping down of century-old oaks for the erection of filling stations. Von Frankel shook his head—it was hard to conceive that America was so backward.

"In Helsinki a man must paint his house every seven years, if it needs it," the vice-mayor continued. "If he refuses, the city has it painted and sends him the bill—which he must pay. A property owner in Helsinki is not permitted the indulgence of holding an eyesore for speculative purposes. Nor is he allowed to paint a house or an office building 'a color that cries.' No one is permitted to express himself at the expense of the city's good taste. Before a man paints a house he must submit his proposed colors to a city official. He is never told what color he must use, but he is often told what colors he cannot use. If the chosen color is glaring or out of harmony with the surroundings, he must choose another. The committee offers the assistance of first-class artists and architects to help him. Of course, the right sort of citizen is grateful for the service."

"In Helsinki, then," I said, "it is *all* restricted area."

"Why not?" von Frankel answered, sparks of energy glowing in his eyes. "If a restricted area is good for one part of a town, why isn't it good for the whole town?"

The first vice-mayor got up to show me his plans for making a park, with willow walks along the lake, between the railway yards and the sports stadium. He was trying to get the unsightly freight depot that faced the Parliament Building moved to the suburbs. But he was having a terrific fight with the state railway chief, who not only opposed his admirable park scheme but was endeavoring to get the government's permission to fill in half the lake and build more tracks. Von Frankel's strong jaws clamped together as he talked of it. The fire of battle flashed in his eyes for a moment, as his hand unconsciously formed a rocklike fist.

A secretary interrupted to remind him that he must be off to make a speech. I had heard that von Frankel could make speeches in six different languages—and with continental suavity cloaking the Finnish drive. Besides doing a strenuous job as first vice-mayor, heading one of the Olympic committees, and holding a seat in Parliament, von Frankel sat on countless boards, received scores of foreign visitors, was in charge of entertainment of foreign athletic teams, carried on a voluminous correspondence, and attended all important sports events and innumerable social functions. Yet he did everything without any appearance of strain.

"What's your secret for keeping your manifold jobs hitting on all cylinders?" I asked, as we walked down the hall.

"I belong to a club," he replied with a grin. "It's called the Five-Minutes-Before-Twelve-Club." He punched the button for the elevator. "No matter what the function, members are pledged to be gone home—like Cinderella—before midnight."

PERENNIAL RECORD-BREAKERS

After leaving von Frankel, I stopped by to see Olaf Gummerus, a secretary of one of the Olympic committees. He had been brought up mostly in Rome, where his father had been Finnish minister from 1919 to 1935. This father was that noted professor of archeology, Herman Gummerus, who had headed the Activist Movement against Russia and encouraged the student patriots to slip off to Germany to train secretly at Lockstedterlager for the day of revolt. Because he had spent only five of his twenty-six years in Finland, young Gummerus had the manners of a cosmopolite. He looked as much like an English pre-Raphaelite as a Finn, wore three rings on one finger, and rose at six in summer to keep fit by rowing a shell in the bay. No one knew more about the history of Finnish athletics than this cultivated former expatriate.

We drove out to Olympic Village, where three hundred men and two hundred women were working to prepare for three thousand foreign athletes. The thirty modernistic apartment houses with shops and rock gardens were set on a hilly slope among tonic spruce trees some four miles from the center of the city. Pretty girls with long-billed carpenters' caps worked side by side with the brown-bodied men. Husbands and wives came to work together and ate out of family-sized lunch pails. Women perched on scaffolding, wielded hammer and saw with dexterity. Some carried hods of mortar with easy skill. They looked proud and happy and not in the least imposed on, for they were working not merely for the wage they received, but for the glory of *Suomi.*

With the usual Finnish astuteness, Olympic Village had been planned for permanent use. The up-to-the minute apartments were already being bought on the co-operative plan. And when the games were over, the furniture and the two hundred miles of linen were to be auctioned off, and citizens of Helsinki would move in. In another quarter of the town a half-constructed building of concrete and glass was to house seven hundred and fifty female athletes, and later it was to become a permanent nurses' training college and recreation home.

"Sport in Finland," Gummerus said, as we drove from place to place, "is not only an intensely patriotic expression, but it serves to foster the democratic spirit. We have no professional athletes. Our sportsmen run, wrestle, leap, and ski for fun and national glory. In Finland, varsity athletics do not exist in the American sense. The Finnish student engaged in some phase of sport usually belongs to an ordinary athletic club, outside the university. In earlier days of Finnish sports history, students were generally the best athletes. But now in later years the laboring classes have sprung into the best positions and still hold them."

Virtually all the Finnish champions and potential champions, I learned, were from humble backgrounds and had simple jobs. Among the fifty athletes who had hitherto succeeded in capturing the sixty-nine gold medals for Finland in preceding Olympics, only about five had attended the university.

Finland's rural population takes a keen interest in various sports activities, and farm workers walk away with many of the most prized ribbons. Of the thirty-four most promising athletes in 1939, four were still farmers, five policemen, six laborers, seven office clerks, three technicians. Only four were university students. The rest were variously employed: one was a store manager, one an army officer, another a railroad man, still another a shop salesman, and the last an engine fireman. The best wrestlers of Finland are policemen or laborers, though there are among them several promising farmers from South Ostrobothnia. The majority of the Finnish long-distance runners are from the country, though they have come to take city jobs to be nearer training fields.

Within pleasant walking distance from the center of the city, Helsinki's Stadium Tower shoots straight as a javelin from the rocks of Eläintarha toward the mid-heavens. Lustrous-white against the blue sky, it is stirring as a clarion call.

"The Stadium belongs to the people," Gummerus said. "The people built it. By means of flag days they have been collecting the money since 1927. The poorest citizen contributed as much proportionately as the wealthy—and often more. A state subsidy laid the financial foundation stone. A site was chosen among these birch groves and pine forests of Eläintarha. Architectural plans were submitted and selected, and the work began in the winter of 1934. At first, because the possibility of an Olympic contest was not even dreamed of, the seating space was no more than 30,000. That large gap there on the east side, called jokingly 'Olympic Gap,' was left open against possible additions. In April of this year they began closing the gap. That new higher addition to the south has been added, too, so now the spectator accommodation will reach 63,000.—And the tickets are almost all sold, a year in advance."

Altogether on an organized basis there are 975 different clubs belonging to the Finnish Sporting and Gymnastic Federation. But the place of honor in sport must go to ski-running, Gummerus insisted. It is a universal diversion that many practice as a prime necessity of routine living. Little beyond the coastal edges of Finland would have been settled if men had not been able to go on skis in winter. It was through ski races that the Finnish countryfolk got their first initiation into competitive sport. And today almost a million pairs of skis are in annual use among a population which numbers less than four million, young and old. Country children are set on skis almost as soon as they can toddle. For one week at the end of February all the nation's schools declare a skiing holiday.

"In international skiing meets held in Finland," Gummerus said, "Finns are invariably victors. And Jussi Kurikkala last winter won more major international ski races than any champion from any other country. He amazed the experts, who insisted one man couldn't be succesful both in skiing and running, by a surprising success in the marathon at Helsinki. Now he's running twenty miles a day training for the Olympics."

We sat talking in the empty stadium watching Tuominen, third-ranking distance runner, at his job of keeping the emerald turf and the brick-dust track at perfection. The twenty-three-year-old Tuominen had been a policeman, but because the pavements hurt his feet he had been given a softer job at the Stadium. Here he had his sleeping quarters and could make practice runs at dawn or any hour of the white nights he chose.

"Despite the universality of skiing," continued Gummerus, "long-distance running still holds first place in the ambitions of athletes seeking fame—and it is the champion runner who receives the most fervent plaudits."

"It is strange," Gummerus answered, when I asked about boxing, "that in a country where men are so handy with their fists prize-fighting is looked down on. A promoter could never draw a vast crowd to watch two human beings give each other bloody noses *pour le sport*. Most Finns regard such a spectacle as either childish or barbarous. Pugs have no followers in Finland. And a

Finn, who will gaily join a free-for-all and fight with gusto, scorns American football as too rough and messy for good sport."

Gummerus opened a fresh box of Finnish cigarettes, "Club No. 7." They were long and slender, with an inch of hard paper holder attached in the Russian manner. "In attitude toward sport," he said, "the Finns are more Greek than any nation since the glory of Greece. And the discus and javelin have recaptured the place they once held in Hellenic sports. Our javelin throwers are perennial champions. But in these last few years Finland has developed a new sport that has gone like a forest fire throughout the nation. It is called 'orientation.'"

That was a new one on me. "What's it like?" I asked.

"It's a game of pathfinding through unchartered wilderness. A man goes off with only a compass and a map to guide him and some food. The object is to reach a certain known objective miles away in the shortest time. It's a sport for winter and summer, with the divers hazards of the season. As gentle as 'orientation' may sound, there is nothing tender about it. It calls upon all a man's resources of stamina and speed, and it sharpens his wits. It makes him at home with unknown regions of his country, and it will stand him in good stead in a defensive war.

"Another popular sport," he went on, "that the Finns can turn to advantage in case of war is target practice. Finns are unsurpassed in marksmanship. Today there are 605 separate clubs scattered through the land that affiliate with the Finnish Marksmen's Association. Finland encourages sport, as she does education and art. Sporting associations receive regular state grants."

"I see," I said. "Sports here have certain aspects of military preparedness. Orientation, skiing, shooting, and throwing things like discuses for hand grenades."

"But it is entirely voluntary," Gummerus added quickly. "Not something required in military service. However, it does seem to add up. And it's all to the good for national health and pluck."

As we got up to leave we paused and looked back on the great oval of emerald surrounded by the terra-cotta ring, and the rising tiers of gleaming white concrete. "On June sixteenth, for the first time a world record was made in the new Stadium," Gummerus said. "Taisto Mäki ran the 5,000 meters in 14 minutes 8⅘ seconds. That's beyond anything anyone had believed humanly possible. The 5,000-meter record has been Finnish property for twenty-seven years. In 1924, when Paavo Nurmi brought it down to 14 minutes 28⅕ seconds, the press asked him how fast he thought he could run the distance if he trained for it alone. Nurmi said he might be able to make it in 14 minutes and 12 seconds, but he didn't think any human being could ever crack 14 minutes 10 seconds. Last month Mäki did the incredible and cracked 14 minutes 9 seconds."

We drove back into the heart of the city to see this phenomenal Mäki, who also held the world's record for the 10,000-meter, the two-mile, the three-mile, and the six-mile. "Remember," Gummerus reminded me with emphasis, "Finland does not pamper her champions. Mäki works for his living as a baler and wrapper at the Alcohol Monopoly. He lives in the village of Rekola and commutes. He must get up before six in the morning to run up and down the road by his little half-acre place. Then he takes a train to Helsinki. He works from nine to four, handling bundles and receipts. Then he runs in the Stadium and afterward takes a train for Rekola. His salary is about forty dollars a month—hardly a widow's mite to an American world-record breaker."

Although I had heard Mäki was the most popular athlete that the North had ever known, I was still unprepared for the Mäki personality. We found the contemporary idol of the Finns in a below-the-pavement office behind the Alcohol Monopoly's retail shop on the Esplanade. As he came forward he smiled—the most engaging smile I ever saw. It was quick, frank, and warm, and lifted the heart. He looked more like a handsome Irish-American than a Finn. He was middle-sized and rather slight of build, with wavy brown hair and dancing eyes. In the midst of the city he carried an atmosphere of new-mown hay about him, and his twenty-nine years had not robbed him of his eager-little-boy charm. Superlatively likable, he was a bit shy, and he flushed rather easily but pleasurably. About him there was no hint of heroics or pose or championship.

I regarded him almost incredulously and looked down at the famous feet in their cheap, rusty shoes. Here was a fellow the gods liked, for they had blessed him from toe to crown. They had given him legs to outrun the world and a smile to outface victory as well as defeat.

Mäki was the son of a small farmer, he told me, and in his youth he had been a shepherd boy. He did his first running after lost sheep. While hired out as a farm laborer, he ran in local rural competitions. And then in 1934, at Tampere, he entered the 5,000-meter race as a dark horse and won. Nurmi coached him a few times, and in 1937 he broke the world's record for the 10,000-meter. Then he broke it on the two-mile and the three-mile, and then he started in beating his own world records. "Nurmi was Mäki's idol," Gummerus said in English so that Mäki would not understand, "and he is not quite happy over taking so many honors from him."

The Finnish athletes live normal lives, with no great palaver about training, according to Mäki. He said he eats just as he pleases, whatever he likes—ice cream whenever he wants it, though not just before a race. He smiled and showed his white, even teeth. He does not smoke, however, and he drinks no alcoholic beverages. "Sometimes at a party to be sociable I'll sip some beer," he said, "but I don't really like the stuff."

The visit was brief because the champion was called back to his bread-winning job. I promised to drive out to Mäki's little place in the country to meet his wife and his little daughter Maire Anita, and to see his vegetable patch some Sunday. "It's only a half acre," he smiled as he shook hands.

CRAYFISH AND DOUBLE F'S

Because Lapland is at its best in early or middle August, between the end of the mosquito season and the first frosts, we were advised to go to the Arctic now while the immediate weather as well as the season was salubrious. At five o'clock the day before we left for Lapland we were invited to a private showing of Finnish films at the Suomi Filmi offices at No. 12 Bulevardi. Some friends wanted to show us what to expect in Lapland and to give us an idea of the aims of Finland's motion-picture industry, which is not excelled in any other of the Northern Countries. Many experts consider the Finnish pictures superior even to the Swedish. "Technically the Finns are as good as the Swedes," a movie critic said to me, "and the Finns have more courage—they are not afraid to experiment."

Mr. Otto Schreck, the manager of the company, had arranged a program that would give us some insight into Finnish character and the factors that influenced it. He explained that he was entirely "self-taught" in the business. A lawyer by profession and a bank director, he had had to take over a moving-picture concern in the 1933 depression.

In the small air-conditioned show room, hung with gray-green linen, Aino Schreck, his wife, the golden-haired young concert singer, received us. We sat in armchairs and watched Finland unroll before us. First, because we were going to Lapland, we were shown what to expect in summer, and then what to expect in winter. Borje Sandberg translated the Finnish captions as they appeared on the screen. We saw the endless forests, the log cottages, the grazing herds of reindeer, the swarms of mosquitoes, the salmon fishers with pitch-smeared faces and mosquito veils, the logging, the breaking of new ground for farms. And then the scene changed to winter, when the land stretched in immaculate solemnity under its awesome burden of snow. In the midst of a desertlike whiteness appeared a large modern sports hotel, reached only by reindeer sleds. Because there were not sufficient snowplows to keep the roads open in remote districts, reindeer were still used for transportation, as the Lapps had employed them for centuries. We saw the terror of blinding blizzards—lonely farms buried in a sea of snow. We saw endless white forests of firs, their branches sparkling under the moon as if a powder of diamond dust had been sifted over them. And where the snow fell softly, the trees stood knee-deep in swansdown. From the comfort of armchairs in an air-conditioned room we saw the same uncompromising landscape which was to blind and bewilder Russian soldiers four months later. As they sank down on the silken quilts of snow under the death-still trees, their last astonished gaze was to be on this same quintessence of whiteness.

Parts of a picture called "The Log Floater's Bride" followed the snowbound scenes of Lapland. Its story depicted the intimate life of people near the Arctic Circle, the earning of their daily bread by floating the logs down the rivers and rapids, their loves, sins, and retributions. In the summer, when the ice is melted, logs are made into rafts and men steer them over the rapids. It is a dangerous game at best, and in the movie the villain played an ugly part in cutting a rope so that the hero's raft would split. But the villain was caught in his own trap and the hero went to his rescue, and in turn they were both saved by the heroine. It was not like a film, but like a life drama enacted before our eyes, revealing the courage and endurance and fortitude of Finns in their daily existence. The star was a girl of compellingly quiet beauty who played with an emotional intensity and restraint that was admirable and moving.

The next picture, a dramatic story of Finland in the last years of the Czarist regime, showed the Russian tyranny, the plotting of the Finns, their grace under pressure, the assassination of the hated Governor Bobrikoff, the escape of the Jägers to Germany to train for fighting, the Red uprising and the fight for independence. It was an exciting picture, skillfully directed, with details worked out in the subtly natural manner of the Moscow Art Theater. We saw that Finland owes much more to Russian theater art than it does to the American.

When we thanked Mr. Schreck for the lessons in history, he said, "For several hundred years we made history for Sweden rather than for ourselves—I hope the future will give us a chance." *

At the Hotel Kämp on the Esplanade, the Paloheimos and another gentleman guest were waiting for us in a private dining room. We had not yet met Mrs. Paloheimo, the daughter of Sibelius, who could not leave her preserving to go to represent her father at the World's Fair music festival. She was particularly happy tonight because her sixteen-year-old son had just returned from his volunteer work on the tank traps at the frontier.

Great platters of cold scarlet crayfish, decorated with dill, were already spread on the table—four huge platters for eight persons. Because this was a crayfish party, none of us were in evening clothes—you can't do justice to crayfish in evening clothes, we had been told.

* In February 1940 he made his own contribution to history by a soldier's wound that almost cost him his life.

We knew that a crayfish dinner was something very special, but we were not prepared for the ritual. Mrs. Paloheimo took off her rings and bracelets and laid them beside her plate. The hostess took off her rings and a string of aquamarines. Paloheimo took off his wrist watch and hid it in his pocket. We wondered if we were being kidded, but Therese took off her one ring and laid her pearls beside it by her plate. Mrs. Paloheimo tucked the napkin in the bosom of her flowered chiffon dress, and the party began.

A glass of schnapps was tossed off to "skåls," and then we set to work. The technique of eating crayfish must be learned. It requires an informality of table manners to the point of abandon, and there is a special knack to getting the last morsel of meat. The first step is to break the crustacean in two and then to suck the cool, dill-flavored juice from the top end of him. We tossed back our heads and partly poured the juice, partly sucked it, into our mouths.

I had had crayfish twice before as an hors d'œuvre at men's luncheons, but Therese had to be instructed. The host at her left picked out an especially fine one for her, and showed her the delicate points of getting the most delicious morsels tucked away in crevices and how to suck to the best advantage.

Soon we all sounded like happy pigs at a trough, for it is good form to eat crayfish noisily. The fashionable Swedes had so decreed. The Swedes in Sweden are formal fifty weeks out of the year; but for one fortnight in August they relax for crayfish season, gorge themselves on the delicacy, abandon proprieties, drink a glass of schnapps with each crayfish, sometimes with each claw, they say—and make an hilarious, rip-roaring, un-Swedish holiday. One was invited to Sweden for the crayfish eating in August just as one was invited to Scotland for the grouse shooting.

Hands reached out freely for another crayfish and another and another. The broken scarlet shells piled up in the dinner plates. When they were dangerously near toppling over, the waiters removed them and brought fresh plates, followed by replenished platters of crayfish. The men "skåled" and drank the white fiery liquid at a swallow. The three ladies sipped thimblefuls in response.

Mrs. Paloheimo was absorbed in arranging a canapé of delicate slivers on a square of buttered toast and decorating it with feathery threads of dill. "The choicest bits," she said, instructing Therese in etiquette, "are to be saved and sent to your favorite gentleman at the end of the course." Therese, having already had more than enough of crayfish, spent the rest of the time arranging a masterpiece. Of course, she presented it to the host.

The hostess made an open-faced sandwich for me. We wondered what Sibelius' daughter was going to do with her tidbit, for there were three men besides her husband and the host. When the waiters finally removed the plates and began setting large fingerbowls with floating lemon slices before us, we asked Mrs. Paloheimo what she had done with her carefully prepared canapé. She confessed she had eaten it herself, blushing like a child caught eating all the jam.

We had a real bathing of hands and mouths and chins. Then rings were put back on, necklaces and wrist watches replaced; lipsticks repaired damages, fresh napery was laid, wineglasses were set, and the dinner was ready to proceed with the second course—stuffed squab and fresh peas and green asparagus.

In the interim, green velvet curtains were drawn back; a stringed orchestra appeared and played compositions of Sibelius. Then our host made a speech of welcome and told us what he was trying to do in Finnish films—to show the actual life of the Finns, their struggle, their modest achievements, the poetry of their lives as well as the stark reality, the hope as well as the melancholy. We "skåled," and I made a speech of appreciation, and we "skåled" again.

Our hostess then sang Finnish folksongs for us. Her voice was one of those lovely, clear, resonant voices that come forth as naturally as bird song. Standing there so simply, her hair gold against the emerald curtains, singing her native songs with such feeling and understanding, like the very embodiment of the spirit of Finland, she created a charm not to be forgotten.

One song she sang in Swedish, with music by Sibelius, particularly delighted us. It had such a haunting appeal that we asked her to repeat it twice during the evening. Mrs. Paloheimo explained the words to which her father had composed the music. It was the sort of story that is written in many languages. A peasant girl comes home with her hands all red; her mother asks her why; she says she has gathered roses and they pricked her fingers. Another evening her mother asks why her lips are so red: she has gathered strawberries and they have stained her mouth. A later evening she is pale as death, and when the mother asks why, the girl says she wishes only to die, and asks her mother to put an inscription on her tombstone, saying, "Here lies a girl who came from her lover with hands red from pulling against the crushing pressure of his entreaties, who came again with lips red from his kisses, and who now comes deathly pale from his deceit."

It was hard to tell which was more charming—Aino Schreck's singing in her appealing voice or Mrs. Paloheimo telling the story in her naïve manner. When she came to the line "her lips were red from her lover's—kisses," she flushed and touched her own lips as if to help her somewhat halting English.

When the dinner was over at the end of three hours and the women were sipping Finnish liqueur made from Arctic bramble berries and the men were enjoying brandy, Therese and I both tried to get the conversation on the Russians during their domination of Finland.

Why was it, Therese asked, that though the Russians had obviously played a significant part in Finland's history, and the movie this afternoon showed their extravagant activities in Helsinki, no one would ever point out anything Russian, not even where they had lived? She had not met a single Finn who had ever been to a Russian's house or a Russian's party, or even had a speaking acquaintance with a Russian. Ever since we had come to Finland we had felt this strange conspiracy of silence, as if they wanted to deny that Russians were ever there.

"Certainly not," they all shouted as one voice. "We had nothing to do with them."

"I've never seen people so united in detestation as you Finns are for Russians," Therese said, "except an old-time Southern Confederate for a Yankee." They had all read *Gone With the Wind* and understood and agreed.

"Didn't any Finnish girls ever go to Russian balls? Didn't any Finnish girl ever marry a Russian officer stationed here?" I persisted.

"Of course not," they cried. "Certainly, no nice Finnish girl would have gone to their parties. Perhaps some Swedo-Finns did."

"But you," I said to Paloheimo, "you and your wife lived for a while in St. Petersburg before the war. You said you went about there and had delightful Russian friends and liked it."

"Oh, yes," he admitted. "But that was different—that was in Russia."

"I knew a Russian scientist in Peru once—Baron Korff," I said. "His father was governor-general of Finland when the Revolution came, I think. He seemed a very good chap. Did you know the Korffs?"

There was no recognition in any of the faces about the table.

"Korff wasn't as bad as the other governor-generals, was he? He didn't leave such a bad name, did he?"

Paloheimo slanted an eye at me and grinned almost sardonically. "No name that ends in two *f*'s is any good in Finland."

We gave up.

"Bobrikoff," said Mrs. Paloheimo, "was the name ending in double *f* that children of my generation were brought up to hate, like Southerners the name of Sherman. I remember one day when I was ten my mother took me to the dentist. I was afraid, and after I got in the chair I refused to open my mouth. No coaxing could make me. Finally my mother said patriotically, 'Eva, remember Bobrikoff!' I immediately opened my mouth wide, determined, brave, ready to bear any pain in my hatred of Bobrikoff. When the dentist yanked out my tooth I refused to cry out, I was so busy hating Bobrikoff."

She laughed and then added, "Oh, we were all brought up to be very patriotic because of Russia. I remember once, shortly after my father had composed *Finlandia,* I had some ailment and was ordered to lie with the back of my neck on a cold wet compress. I refused. The family gathered at the bedside. They coaxed and commanded. Finally my father said sternly, 'Eva, do you love Finland?' 'Oh, yes,' I cried ardently, and threw myself on the cold compress, giving myself up to my country."

At midnight we rose to go. We men had emptied several glasses of brandy, and now the whiskies and sodas had come. We thought our rising would break up the party, but after we said good night they watched us go—and then settled themselves down for a good talk in Finnish. In the hall we met the musicians coming back to play again; they had merely been taking an intermission. They looked at us in amazement, as if we were committing a *faux pas.* But the party had begun for us at five o'clock—and I apologized to myself by recalling von Frankel's Five-Minutes-Before-Twelve-Club.

PART TWO

"Hard work conquers even the worst of luck. Ay, if we once start on the job, we'll stick to it with clenched teeth. But the matter needs thinking over—wisely from the roots upward."

ALEKSIS KIVI

To the Arctic Circle

THE PRIME MINISTER IN THE SLEEPER

Despite all we had read and what we had been told, Lapland proved to be a region of surprises. We began our journey to the Arctic Ocean on the crowded two-o'clock train from Helsinki. The sleeping car to Rovaniemi was to be attached to the train at Haapamäki before bedtime.

I had just got pleasantly settled in reserved seat Number 32 facing Therese, when two gentlemen arrived, one of them holding an identical ticket for Number 32. I had met one of the men at a sports contest. He was a government official who received foreign diplomats at stations and docks. He introduced me to the gentleman he was seeing off, a tallish man with a mild expression and a sandy mustache that cascaded completely over the lower lip. He was the Prime Minister, Dr. Aimo Cajander. We bowed and scrutinized each other's reserved seat coupon. Both were plainly marked Number 32.

On this day the Prime Minister was even more, the official said: he was the acting President of Finland because of the current illness of President Kallio. I was no more eager to stand for the President than for the Prime Minister. However, I moved my things out of 32 over to the seat beside Therese. The Prime Minister remained patiently in the aisle. The official sought the conductor on the platform. I foresaw the Prime Minister and myself taking turns at standing in the aisle during the seven hours' journey to Haapamäki, unless some of the patriotic Finns arose to give their chief a seat. But no one stirred with offers. The Finns were quite indifferent to the situation.

The conductor finally settled it by allotting me the seat next to Therese. The Prime Minister was to have the space opposite us. The engine gave its characteristic shrill little toot, and we were off.

I began a conversation with Doctor Cajander and discovered he spoke no English. Since I didn't speak Finnish, our conversation was confined to gestures and a few Swedish words and phrases. Doctor Cajander was on the way to Oulu to a board meeting of the pulp mill there. In Finland, cabinet members are on the boards of the greater industries so that the government can know how the businesses are run and assist them in export trade. Doctor Cajander was Finland's foremost forestry expert and had been a professor of forestry before he became Prime Minister. Shy like most Finns, the Premier had the apologetic air of gravely trying to deny that he was anything so important. His glasses were a screen for his pale, thoughtful eyes, and the waterfall mustache was a hideout for his in-drawn, careful mouth. He was still the professor, with a cautious, modest demeanor. His severe black clothes were as somber as a Presbyterian minister's. This mild gentleman the Russians were to denounce within four months as "squirming grass-snake, clown, and warmonger."

As we approached Haapamäki, where we were to change to the sleeping car, an anxious look crept into His Excellency's pale eyes. He glanced at his tickets and looked at me surreptitiously. I glanced at mine and looked at him. I knew he had faced for a moment the possibility of our sleeping together or in turns.

"You may have to sleep with the President of Finland," I said to Therese.

When the train stopped at Haapamäki, Doctor Cajander grabbed his bag and umbrella and with moderate haste made for the door. He was the first one out onto the platform.

We were quite as anxious about our reservations as His Excellency. But we smiled pleasantly at each other on the platform while waiting for the sleeping car to be joined to our train. The moment it was coupled, the Premier did not wait for the female porter to get his bag, but with dignified alacrity he hoisted it into the vestibule and mounted the steps.

Five minutes later the conductor assured us of a whole compartment next to Doctor Cajander's. As we passed his open door, he was hanging his umbrella on a hook. We said good night in Finnish, and he stopped to shake hands. Neither dared smile as broadly as he might have liked.

"You'll never have such a chance again," I said to Therese, as the Prime Minister slowly drew his door shut.

The sleeping coach was an old-fashioned one with gas for illumination. In our compartment the light was in the ceiling—a large, shallow, inverted bowl-like globe. It had a divided brown cloth hood to be drawn down about it to make a night light. We decided we did not want the gas lit for fear it would smell. But the gaunt, amiable female porter made desperate signs of command. "It will smell," I kept saying in English. She talked Finnish back at me. We smiled and frowned at each other like friendly enemies, I barring her way to the light. Finally a Finnish lady at the other end of the corridor heard the commotion and came to the rescue with a fair knowledge of English. "It *must* be lit," she said.

"But it will smell," I protested.

"Yes," she agreed heartily, "the smell will be awful. But it *must* be lit."

Lit it was. And it did smell to heaven. I wanted to turn it

off. Therese was afraid it would asphyxiate us or blow up the train. I called for the porter.

"It smells," I said, sniffing the air violently. "Turn it out."

The porter nodded vigorously, holding her nose and making a face in enthusiastic agreement, but tossing off signs of helplessness. The lady from down the corridor called out, "It must *not* be turned off. The whole train would be in darkness and we might all be gassed."

I acknowledged defeat, and with a bitter-sweet smile climbed up to my berth and lay between pure linen sheets in the softest bed I had found in Finland.

The gas must have acted as a soporific. Neither of us woke until the cheery porter called us next morning.

We had a station breakfast at the lumber town of Kemi, on the Gulf of Bothnia, where the trains switch to the northwest to go to Sweden. Breakfast was spread out on a counter. You could order a beefsteak if you liked, but there were no eggs or bacon. We took open-faced cold veal sandwiches and coffee.

We had invited the lady who saved the train from darkness to breakfast with us. She turned out to be a medical doctor of Rovaniemi returning from a vacation in Iceland. Her name was Tyyne Jyrhämä. She was a bright, attractive woman, lavender-scented and rather smart in a gray tailored suit. We asked the rawboned porter to join us too. The porter was a widow with six children—the doctor told us—her husband, a railroad employee, having been killed in an accident. All sleeping-car attendants in Finland are women. The railroads take care of the widows of employees by giving them jobs as porters.

A huge lumberman with most of his front teeth gone came and ate his porridge at the same table. He spoke some English, for he had once worked in Canada. "Eggs are scarce here," he explained. "Chickens don't do so well in the cold. Hens won't lay during the dark months, and people can't afford to feed them just for the bright months."

After we had had mid-morning coffee at Koivu, a pretty little station where Lapland begins and where coffee and cakes were spread on long tables under bright awnings between grass plots and red-berried mountain ash trees, the train passed through a monotonous uninhabited region with sparse woods and forbidding bogs. To look at it gave one a sense of approaching desolation. But in less than an hour we had reached Rovaniemi, the capital of Lapland, with its gay, gypsy-sounding name.

THE BUSIEST MAN IN LAPLAND DRINKS LEMONADE

The Pohjanhovi Hotel stood boldly white and modernistic against the sparkling blue Ounaskaski Rapids to the east and a yellow hayfield to the north. The lobby was three stories high, with enormous round columns of lustrous white enamel supporting an electric-blue ceiling, like pillars of ice holding up the heavens. The east wall, built of glass blocks, opened on terraces where people sat under sky-blue umbrellas and looked across the wide, rushing rapids to the bathing beach and houses on the other side. The furniture was of chromium, glass, and gray-blue leather. The dining room with its mirrored walls was elevated at the back of the lobby above wide-spreading stairs, and some of it turned into balconies like boxes at the opera.

No one expects to find such a hostelry at the edge of what was an almost trackless wilderness not many years ago. But it was most fitting for the entrance to the domain of the icy god Boreas. It was like a palace in a frosty fairy tale. But when the clerk asked for our passports to send to the police for overnight examination, it became immediately contemporary. Therese mildly protested that we had already been in Finland a fortnight. The clerk trembled at the gentle reproof, and said, "But you do not understand! We are near Russia, Madame!"

A glass elevator took us to the lounge of the third floor, where mirrors reflected daisies, cornflowers, and baby's-breath in vases on tables of glass and chromium. Our room and bath were all one might expect in smartness, comfort, and mechanical equipment. In colors of silver, beige, and midnight blue it looked cool and clean as an iceberg. A great corner window gave on the swirling water where men fished from boats, and on hayfields where girls in red blouses and men naked to the waist raked fresh-scythed hay and stacked it in cocks. The Arctic Circle lay less than five miles to the north.

A lithe, blond young man who spoke some English and carried a red pocket dictionary in his hand came to fetch us for lunch with the governor. He said a friend of mine from Helsinki had telephoned the governor to look after us. By profession a lawyer, he was on the governor's staff and adjudged cases of social relief. He bore the easily remembered name of Eero Eho and the title of judge.

Although Rovaniemi had received its city charter only in 1938, it had been the capital of Lapland in reality since its founding in 1929. It was a junction for traffic. Dirt roads leading in six directions and important channels for log floating converged here. Fairs were held in February and at mid-summer for trade and merrymaking. The winter fur market was attended even by foreigners. It was the center of summer tourist traffic north of Tampere, and in the past three years it had become noted as a winter sports resort. Just now it was in the throes of acute growing pains.

Rovaniemi was a market town of wood that was fast turning into a town of concrete and stucco. One block gave the impression of a mining town in gold-rush days of Forty-nine, and the next belonged to an architectural dream of the future. Sidewalks of plank merged into concrete pavements. At one end of the main street a canvas shooting gallery played gramophone records at top volume to attract the visiting traders. In the middle of the town co-operative shops displayed cameras from Germany, fancy fruits from California, topcoats from London. At the other end of the town, reindeer grazed in primeval peace. And through the main street ran the great blue fish truck carrying electrically cooled fresh fish from the Arctic down to Helsinki—the entire length of Finland. Rovaniemi had the positive, vital air of a town that meant to be of note.

The governor of Lapland and his lady lived in a recently completed modernistic mansion as substantial-looking as a Renaissance palace. The ultra-modern architecture seemed the right expression of a vigorous new country. In its modern furnishings the main rooms had no tie-up with the past, except in the sturdy artistry of old Finland displayed in fine handicraft work and carved birchwood bowls two centuries old. The walls were mostly chalky blue and beige, the favorite colors of modern Finland. Silk and wool draperies were silver green in herring-bone pattern, rugs pale water-green and champagne-colored. The Finns have an inherent sense of good taste. Even when they are audacious their colors never clash. White vases held a profusion of blue cornflowers, and in the window ledges miniature tropical gardens of cacti caught the August sun—for Finns have a penchant for bringing a hint of the tropics into their arctic climate. The governor's mansion at Rovaniemi was the brightest, least cluttered, most cheerful, most thought-cleansing official residence I had ever seen in any land.

The governor himself gave the same impression as his house. He was clear-eyed, youngish, unbound by tradition, and stout as an oak stump. He had a powerful chest, a determined jaw, an iron grip. He radiated good nature, purpose, limitless energy. His lady was a tiny thing, pretty, blonde, and bubbling, with enormous quick blue eyes in a pert head. She was like a child making a lark of playing house in a palace. Neither the governor nor his wife spoke English, and so "the Judge" turned his tongue to English and Finnish as rapidly as possible, while his fingers flipped pages in his red pocket dictionary.

It was a delightful meal. We all smiled a great deal and laughed to make up for not being able to speak. The governor's lady had an infectious giggle. She acted as if as punishment her mother had forbidden her to speak, and she discovered it was grand fun to giggle instead of talk.

With our luncheon we drank iced lemonade. There were no cocktails, no Finnish schnapps with beer, no wine, not even native liqueurs. The governor was a teetotaler; the young judge was also a teetotaler. They had always been teetotalers. They thought a man must be pretty sorry if he couldn't create his own energy with what nature had given him.

It was refreshing to see how happy they were about it. The food was perfectly cooked, with one course of whitefish caught that morning in the river. We had little new potatoes decorated with dill—the most delicious we had ever tasted—the first of the season and from the governor's garden. For dessert were great bowls of golden berries called "cloudberries," a Lapland specialty. In shape they are something like loganberries with swollen seeds, and in texture like the insides of pomegranates. The last three Russian czars, the governor said, were especially fond of cloudberries, and the Russian court got them from the very district these came from. I thought the berries overrated; they tasted faintly fermented. The crisp seed required a lot of crunching.

The Finns swallowed the seed; Therese probably horrified them by spitting hers out.

Maaherra Kaarlo Hillilä, the governor, was the busiest man in Lapland. By car, by boat, by ski, and afoot he traveled 20,000 kilometers a year. He commanded one-third of the territory of Finland; he ruled over more land than the King of Denmark; his province was as large as Hungary. He had his fingers on the pulse of every section of his commonwealth. As he talked I could feel that those fingers were like electric wires that set things humming—whether in mining, electric-power development, industry, agriculture, or the fisheries. When he went about inspecting, advising, encouraging, he always took his rods or his gun with him. A sportsman governor, he lived daily life fully while he built for the future.

After luncheon the governor and Eho and I went into the governor's private study. It was furnished in white enameled peasant furniture from the eighteenth century. The simple lines of the furniture blended well with modernistic walls and fixtures. We looked at maps and planned special things for the northern trip. The governor would arrange for us to visit the nickel mines at Kolosjoki in Petsamo. We had to have a special permit, for they were not in operation yet.

"We are beginning to develop our water power in Lapland now," the governor said. "At Jäniskoski we have four thousand people working on the dam. It will supply all the power for the nickel mines. At Rovaniemi soon we shall begin construction of a dam on the rapids so that we can supply the rural districts with cheap electricity. Now it is too expensive, because all the electric power comes from burning birchwood. Of course that's an economic waste that must soon be remedied."

He listed schools and hospitals we might be interested in visiting. "Tuberculosis," he said, "is our big problem now. We have done pretty well with our fight in the rest of Finland and now we are beginning to go at it here. You know, of course, we've done remarkably well in routing tuberculosis in cattle. We adopted from Denmark the Bangs system of segregating all the cows reacting to the tuberculin test. In the past forty years Finland has spent millions of marks compensating farmers for the condemned tuberculous cattle they killed. But in two generations we have virtually eradicated the disease from our herds. At the government abattoirs less than one-fifteenth of one per cent of the cows slaughtered are found to be affected with tuberculosis. No other country in the world has such a record. In the various districts of Finland all people feeding or milking cows are examined thoroughly by district medical officers—*to keep the cows from being infected by humans.* All those cowhands or dairymaids found to be infected are straightway removed for treatment, or if that is impossible at the time, they are forbidden by law to come into a cowshed or handle the utensils. We have to keep our milk pure"—he smiled—"because we are a race of milk drinkers. You know, there is one cow for every three persons in Finland."

"Yes, I've heard that. What do you pay for milk in these northern regions?"

"In your money, here at the Circle, we pay about four cents a quart."

"Four cents a quart!" I reiterated. "Why, we pay fourteen at home—in the South, where the cows can be out of doors all winter."

He looked at me as if there must be some mighty poor management somewhere.

"The price goes up farther north," he said, "where the cows have to be stable-fed nine months of the year. At Liinahamari on the Arctic Ocean milk is six cents a quart."

"Six cents a quart," I repeated, to make sure of the figure. "Why, in Florida where the cows stay out of doors all year, the price is sixteen to eighteen cents."

"Our farmers can manage a profit at four and six cents, because they get 85 per cent of the retail price themselves. That's the value of co-operative selling. Our farmers got rid of middlemen a long time ago."

He smiled broadly, as if to say the United States had a long way to come.

The governor wanted us to see a fish-breeding establishment about forty miles from Rovaniemi. A renowned angler himself, he knew the importance of keeping his rivers and lakes well stocked with fish for his people's recreation and sustenance. "The poor in Finland," he said proudly, "have all the blessings of hunting and fishing that only the privileged enjoy in England."

I learned there are twenty-nine fish-breeding establishments in various parts of Finland. Five are maintained by the great wood-products companies. The industries are forced by law to replenish the waterways they use for log floating. The rotting bark from logs that sinks to the river bottoms is detrimental to fish, so the companies must provide a fresh stock of young fish each season. No Finnish industries, however powerful, are permitted to dump into the waters chemicals and waste that may destroy the fish as they wantonly do in so many countries where wealth controls.

"Remember," the governor said, "we have only commenced our work. Lapland is a very poor country, and it is for the poor and underprivileged that we must work hardest. But they are good stock, and they will be a better people. Finns have an indomitable spirit that has been tempered by hard times. We have all slept on hard beds and eaten coarse food. We were long under the rule of foreign powers, but all the time we have been growing slowly—like these northern trees that take two to three hundred years to mature."

A servant interrupted to say the governor was wanted by long-distance telephone.

"You'll enjoy Lapland, if you don't look for things that aren't there," the governor said as he rose. "And don't expect to see Lapps everywhere just because the province is called Lapland. There are not more than two thousand Lapps in all Finland. Sweden has three times as many and Norway has twenty thousand."

In a minute he was back from the telephone.

"You may even get a case of Lapland fever, if you aren't careful," he said, taking up the conversation, his eyes twinkling. Eho laughed as he translated. "But as a rule it doesn't get one until he's spent a winter here. We've never enjoyed an illness so much. I'm afraid we're incurables—like one of our police officers. He had spent five years in Lapland when he was ordered to return to Helsinki to hold a life job. They thought they were doing him a kindness. He made such an awful row they had to let him stay here. 'What crime have I committed,' he wrote, 'that I must be condemned to spend the rest of my life in exile in the tropics?' "

As we were leaving, the governor's lady brought her three pretty stair-step daughters in to meet us and stood pertly at the head of them, looking like a fourth step and not a day older than fourteen herself.

From the third-story window at the head of the great stairs, the governor paused to point out the buildings going up all over the town—a new officers' barracks, a new school, new shops, new homes: everything modern in style, and everything in good taste. Progress was in full swing, no more to be stopped in its natural, man-benefiting growth than a blade of wheat in July—unless a blight from Russia came out of the east like a destroying frost.

A BEAR-KILLER RAISES FUCHSIAS

Later that afternoon we spent an hour inspecting the complicated arrangements of troughs in the basement of the fish hatchery. The infinitesimal orange-colored balls turn to tiny salmon, and when they are three and a half months old and about three inches long, they are put outside in great rectangular ponds of fresh water. The water is controlled by a motor pump and kept at the right temperature. But the director prepares them for active life by an ingenious invention. As a practice ground for the young he has had constructed a zigzagging rocky waterway down a miniature hill. As a fresh stream of water poured down it like a mild cascade, the baby salmon got proper exercise by struggling up the winding stream and dodging among the rocks. Salmon delight in swift, down-plunging water, and even the youngest instinctively seek to go up against the current. By October they are prepared to face the rushing, rocky river like grown-ups.

After two years in the rivers they are ready to brave the sea. Salmon grow slowly the first three years. When they return to the river from their first year in the sea, they are mature. But they may keep on growing to any size after that.

The director breeds a million salmon a year, and 80 per cent of them live to go into the Kemi River. He has brought salmon spawn from Alaska, Canada, and the United States, and has bred them in Finnish waters. Here was another example of Finland's interest in nurturing her natural resources. And Finland's care of its inland fisheries has brought fishermen from all over Europe for the sport.

It had rained off and on during the afternoon, but now as we left the fish hatchery the late sun came out full and bright. The landscape was very appealing, with the freshened green fields and the platinum river winding through the wet woods and meadows. Stray reindeer loped off into the fir forests as our car approached. Manly little boys on the roadside took off their caps and gravely bowed their towheads as we passed. I thought it was because of the blue and white flag of *Suomi* and the governor's Number 1 license plate. But Eho said it was merely a polite country custom.

I wanted to see the inside of a Lapland farmer's house, and Eho said he knew a man down the road at whose house he had stopped for coffee on a skiing trip. Besides winning prizes at the agricultural fair, this farmer was the champion bear-killer of the district.

Lapland farms are not beautiful as Danish farms are beautiful. The arctic climate forces too much attention on survival to leave energy for decoration. Everything must be done practically and with stringent economy. The days for plowing, planting, reaping come bunched close together. Farmers and their families often work in the light months sixteen hours a day merely to be sure of living through the winter.

Even old farms on this Lapland landscape had the air of having been put together to await more prosperity and better seasons before being built in finer style. Houses of squared logs were scattered haphazardly about a *piha* or courtyard. Beside the dwelling house there were always the cowstable and the hay barn, the *sauna,* and an earth-covered house for winter potatoes and root vegetables. And always the well-sweep with the tree-tall shaft making a right angle between earth and sky, and the bucket dangling from the rope. The richer the farm, the greater the number of outhouses. As a Chinaman's prosperity was often judged by the number of his concubines, so a Finnish farmer's success could be guessed at by counting his outhouses.

The farm we stopped at was beyond my expectations. The tan-colored houses were built around a court, but the stables had a back entrance and were not too close to the dwelling. Flowers grew, if somewhat carelessly, and grass covered the ground of the court. The wife came from the "summer sleeping quarters" to greet us in her bare feet. She was slight and fair. She asked us to the main house and went back to put on her shoes, just as the farmer, who had been helping a telephone linesman detect some disruption caused by the rainstorm, appeared to receive us. He welcomed us with that unmistakable smile of a man who is making a success of life.

Like most of the better Finnish farmhouses, this one had a jutting vestibule painted white, with green plants and vines in the glass windows. Before the outer and inner door lay doormats of fresh spruce twigs. Inside there were one huge room and two small rooms at one side. Three walls of the living-dining-cooking room were largely double windows, with box couches spread with handicraft fabrics. In the window ledges fuchsias bloomed in pots. (Fuchsias seem to grow better in Lapland than anywhere else in the world.) The curtains and rugs were hand-woven in bright, attractive colors—all the work of the mistress done in the long winter evenings. There were white rocking chairs and a big table for eating and for study. The room was so spotlessly clean that I felt we should have left our shoes at the door as in Japanese houses, instead of only wiping them twice on the fresh spruce mats.

The heart of the room was the enormous stove, which was open fireplace, oven, dryer, storage place for wood—everything a stove for cooking and heating could possibly be. It took up at least a sixth of the floor space. It was built of iron and brick and glazed tiles. Flowered curtains hung in front of various compartments in the structure. I pictured the snug winter scene with arctic winds howling outside, the mother at one side of the open fireplace busy with sewing, the father at the other cleaning his gun for a bear hunt, the three children grouped about the long table doing their lessons. The open corner at the side of the stove farthest from the vestibule was the pantry and scullery. Here were the mixing bowls, the built-in cupboards, the sink. On open shelves in stair-steps stood crockery jars ornamented with field flowers marked in gilt Finnish letters for flour, sugar, salt, and a whole string of spices.

The bear-killer and his wife took us into a room beyond the scullery. It was a white-curtained bedroom with a single bed. "Chaste as a virgin's bower," Therese said. But at night the bed for one was pulled from underneath and made into a bed for two. The master and mistress slept here.

I looked at the huntsman-farmer, standing there smiling proudly in his rough boots and sweaty work clothes. He and the room didn't seem to go together. But apparently he was quite delighted with it. The Finns are inherently orderly and cleanly. Doubtless he left his clothes in the big room by the warm stove.

The small room at the other side of the stove turned out to be a sitting room without a couch, and not the children's bedroom as we had supposed. It had a telephone and a radio, and a shelf crowded with silver trophies: vases, cups, statuettes with engravings.

"For bear-killing?" I asked.

The farmer grinned. "For motorcycle racing," he said, proud and sort of sheepish. "Before marriage," he added significantly. He had given up such youthful and dangerous sport since he

SIRÉN CHOSE NATIVE PINK GRAY GRANITE AS MATERIAL FOR THE PARLIAMENT BUILDING

ST. NICHOLAS CHURCH WITH THE STATUE OF CZAR ALEXANDER II IN RIGHT FOREGROUND

had taken on the responsibility of wife and family, for he had to be sure to keep his neck attached to his shoulders. For sport now he hunted bears. On the table beside him four bear skulls lay white and still as monuments.

"Lord Byron would have loved this room," I said to Therese.

"Shall I show you the bear I got last month?" the farmer said.

But I was still concerned about the sleeping quarters. "Where do the children sleep?" I asked, looking about.

"Here," the farmer said, and went into the big room and lifted up the box seat. There were blankets and a mattress underneath. He turned up one, two, three, grinning more broadly at each turn.

"And the maidservants and—the guests?"

The mother lifted up two more seats. "Here and here," and revealed bedcovering and bearskins and reindeer robes. They went on lifting up seats all about the walls and banging them shut delightedly.

At night children and servants and guests slept around the edges of the room on the box couches they sat on in the daytime. It was as modern as efficiency apartments in New York and as primitive as the days of Beowulf when the warriors slept on the mead-hall benches.

But these were the winter sleeping arrangements. Now the family slept in the next house, because it caught the coolest breezes. In the summer this room was used only for entertaining and eating.

The happy farmer brought forth from an outhouse a gigantic bearskin and spread it over the well base in the center of the yard for inspection. It had covered a grand old bear. The pelt was thick and shaggy. But it smelled raw, for the curing was not complete. For each bear he killed the government gave him five hundred marks—and the neighboring reindeer owners' association gave him another five hundred marks. Twenty dollars in American money.

"A thousand marks and bear meat and a rug, for a load of fun," the farmer said, slapping the bearskin affectionately. "This old honey-paw had killed two reindeer in the neighborhood before I got him. You have to be cautious with a bear. Off the highway he can run as fast as a horse and leap twenty feet."

"Unless you make a bear mad, he isn't vicious, is he?"

"When he comes out of his winter sleep the old-man-of-the-forest is hungry. If he can't break through the frozen snow to get the roots and vegetation he needs, he will attack cows and men as well as reindeer."

"Will he attack a woman?"

The farmer grinned. "Well, I wouldn't trust him. But the Lapps say that a bear will not attack a woman—if she *shows* him she's a woman."

Two cream-colored bear dogs who had smelled the hide were barking frantically and trying to tear themselves loose from their chains by the pighouse. The farmer went to quiet them.

"Want to see my bachelor owl?" he called to us.

Behind the chicken run, a huge eagle owl with great yellow eyes kept a bachelor establishment. He had taken up with the place on his own volition. The farmer had built him a ten-foot-high wire house about a tree and a little wooden doghouse for bad weather. He had lived there for years.

"But doesn't he ever try to fly away at mating time?"

"Not he," the farmer's wife said contemptuously. "He doesn't like desert life, and he gets full board here."

"Last year a passing lady owl slipped through a hole in the wire roof and tried to tempt him," the farmer said. "He would have none of her. He sulked in his corner the whole time. She fluttered about him for a week, flying up to the hole in the roof and back, urging him to flee with her. He had no intention of giving up security for the hazards of love and adventure. Finally in disgust and fury the lady owl flew away. But he didn't feel safe and wasn't really happy until I patched the hole."

It had begun to rain again. So we did not get to go over the farm or accept the refreshment of milk in great pitchers which the barefoot serving maid was bringing from the cooling house. But we glimpsed the wood stacks, high and long as the summer sleeping quarters. We saw the fat hogs grunting in their pens and the white cows in the pasture. We saw the rain-drenched wheat fields rambling down the hill to the lake, and the woodlands with sufficiency in perpetuity for the farmer's sons and sons of sons. Here were happy Finns, loving life and proud of what they possessed; not desiring more, but desiring only to continue to improve themselves and what they had.

We wished the farmer good hunting and good crops forever.

WHAT A CITIZEN SHOULD EXPECT

The next morning Eho took me to see other evidences of Finland's forward-looking interest in its people. We visited the modern hospital and the almost completed modernistic school that would have done credit in its architecture and equipment to a city of two hundred thousand.

The Finns have such a respect for education, Eho said, that the Lutheran church forbids illiterate people to marry. The law is no longer significant, however, since illiteracy is only a small fraction of one per cent. In northern Lapland when the winter days are dark as night unless the moon shines, children gather in groups and go to school by the light of pocket torches. Sometimes in the worst weather fathers go on skis, carrying the smallest children on their backs. In remoter parts of Lapland, where transportation is impossible in frozen months of winter, children board at the school. The state pays 90 per cent of the pupil's living expenses. The district, which is poor, pays only 10 per cent.

Such is the wise planning of the Finns. They look upon the children of the poor districts as citizens of the nation tomorrow and not just as the underprivileged of the less fortunate region they inhabit.

At the new school in Rovaniemi, which was designed by one of Finland's best architects, 50 per cent of the children were to be given breakfasts and lunches free. The others who could afford it were to pay less than four cents for their lunches. They were to have porridge or thick soup, with all the milk they wanted, bread, and stewed or fresh fruit. A trained nurse had her apartment in the school, and doctors were to come to give examinations and treatments twice a week. The school commissioners were very proud of a loud-speaker system which had been installed so that the daily chapel service could be conducted in the individual rooms. "It is better," one commissioner who was a timber foreman said, "not to have the children dirtying up the gymnasium floor by gathering there to listen to prayers. They can get the service sitting at their desks and not have to waste time. And the gymnasium is busy every hour in the day with body-building. We've got to keep our young strong and healthy as well as make 'em smart."

The domestic-science departments and the manual-training departments were fully equipped with the latest devices. "Every girl in this district must know how to cook and keep house and take care of children," Eho said. "Every boy must know how to build things and make a living with his hands, no matter if he becomes a doctor or poet. A Finn can't be sending for a carpenter every time he needs a little patching done."

The new hospital had been running smoothly for a year. It was constructed in functionalist style on a point jutting out in the river, all the windows had a view, and along the south side sun verandas on the roof terrace looked down upon a garden and to distant Pöyliövaara Hill with the three-hundred-foot ski-jump. The wards were divided into rooms with beds for four or six patients for easier sociability. The children's rooms were equipped with nursery toys for all ages. Everything possible was planned for human comfort.

In one of the operating rooms two young gauze-swathed doctors were removing gravel from the throat of a nickel-mine worker. He had been injured in an explosion and brought three hundred miles from Kolosjoki by private motor. A Lapp with a ruptured appendix had just been brought down by airplane ambulance from Ivalo. The Lapp was a charity case. Most of the patients were charity patients.

"A citizen of a good country," said the doctor in charge of the hospital, "should have among other benefits the right to good health and free medical treatment, no matter in what remote district he lives or how poor his worldly circumstances. That is a doctrine on which we are building for the future of Finland."

THE LADY DOCTOR'S RETREAT

We were invited for coffee after luncheon to the home of the lady doctor we had met on the train. She turned out to be the maiden sister of the governor's childlike wife. Doctor Jyrhämä lived on the top floor of the new four-story bank building above her medical office. It was a cheerful, spotless apartment with Biedemeyer chairs and sofas against the walls and four white rocking chairs around a white center table. In the library were rows of books in five languages—but her special treasures were her shelves of books in English, especially those of O'Neill and Maugham, her favorites among the contemporaries.

Eho came, and we sat in the white rockers. The maid who brought in the coffee was a pretty, shy girl fresh from the country. She flushed crimson when I said good day to her in Finnish. Finns blush quickly at unexpected pleasantries.

As we drank coffee and rocked, the doctor explained that she was both a private practitioner and an employee of the state. She had an exciting practice that extended over a radius of sixty miles. In winter she had to make some calls by a combination of motor car and wagon, afoot and on skis. Her eyes danced as she described difficulties with mud, ice, wind, and snow. "And what it means to the poor people," she said, "to know that I will come—if I am sent for. That no blizzard, nothing can stop me, if they need me. If I am sent for, *I will come.*"

The maid brought in a bowl of golden cloudberries, and we drew closer to the table.

"Besides my own practice and my hospital duties here," the doctor went on, ladling the berries into dessert plates, "I have twenty idiots." They were in an asylum in the country twenty miles away because the distractions of Rovaniemi might be bad for their nerves.

"What do you do to treat them?" I asked.

"I give them medicine," she said.

"But medicine doesn't help the mind," I said.

"Oh, yes! My idiots, they cannot sleep, they are so unhappy. I give them medicine—and they sleep. Here in Lapland we have much idiocy—in the fall, when the dark is coming—in the spring, when they have had so much dark. It makes them quite idiot to think about it."

"But besides medicine, how do you treat them?"

"I keep them busy," she said wisely. "They must do something. Always something. They weave. They cut wood. When the snow is away, they tend the fields."

"Are they ever cured?"

"Sometimes. Quite often. But my idiots, sometimes they cry—oh, it is very bad. The dark is terrible for them. We have to be very gentle with them."

The doorbell rang. The maid said the doctor's car was ready.

"I do wish I could take you to see my idiots, but your time is so short and tomorrow my vacation ends. Now I must show you my retreat, my little farm, where I 'get away from it all,' as you say in American books."

At the curb a young tow-headed Finn, eager-faced as a sailor on shore leave, shook hands with Doctor Jyrhämä enthusiastically and opened the Chevrolet's doors. He was the chauffeur who drove her on her calls into the backwoods, she explained. She did not maintain a car of her own but used a taxi and this special driver. It was easy to see he adored her, that he would get her where she was going if he had to carry her pickaback.

We started off with a roar. The chauffeur handled the car with gusto, as if it were a wild buck reindeer. Finns excel in reckless driving. Cars have come into general usage only during the last ten years, and many Finns are not quite used to them. But they have no fear of fast going. They laugh and say, "Nothing fiercer than death can come of it."

This bright-eyed driver was the most original we had encountered. He had a style all his own. Of all the spectators in the car he was the most interested in the view. Every time Doctor Jyrhämä, in the back with us, or Eho, in the front, called our attention to anything in the landscape, the chauffeur would stare at it delightedly. Splitting the wind at some terrific number of kilometers an hour, he'd turn around in his seat and have a good long look and smile his approval and glance at us to see how we reacted. After we had faced death a few times, I urged him to keep his eyes on the road and waved my hand to indicate the front. He thought I was playing a game with him. He sort of waved his eyebrow at me over his shoulder, as much as to say, "Yes, we're having a jolly time, but I really think I'm going as fast as I should."

We turned into a country road with bumps and holes that any ordinary chauffeur would have paused and shifted gears for. But not our debonair towhead. He did not even slacken his speed, but going full-speed ahead, he twisted his head from side to side in his animated inspection of rural scenes. He would suddenly wheel around and pop his eyes at us brightly to see what we thought about it. Everything pointed out to us appeared to him a spectacle of wonder. Had he been transported to the Yosemite Valley, he could not have suggested more fresh interest than in this same route he had been over a hundred times.

A spotted sow with a litter in a ditch made him thrust his neck to the right to get a look at the extraordinary phenomenon. We hit such a bump this time that the three of us in the back rose clean to the top together and came down in a scramble. The doctor, instead of saying, "Slow up!" began searching for the strap on the back of the front seat. That was all she asked—to find the strap to cling to. When the chauffeur realized what she was doing, he completely gave up driving to come to her assistance, turning all his energies to help her locate the strap that was lost under a lap rug. The car flew ahead in leaps and bounds. If we had been going to the deliverance of quintuplets we couldn't have made better speed.

Under the Pöyliövaara ski-jump we stopped abruptly. The chauffeur hopped from the car, grinning, as if to say, "My, but that was a swell ride we had, wasn't it?"

We got out under the bony skyscraper structure that shot into the void above our heads. Therese and I felt as if we had just landed after our first ski jump. Even the judge had lost some of his color.

I began to laugh. "You say this fellow drives you on your night calls in winter?" I said to the doctor. "Congratulations on being alive."

"The Finns of the district always win the skiing contests here," said Doctor Jyrhämä, not seeing anything funny.

"But the champion Norwegians—do they never jump here?"

"They jump here, but they never win. Always Finns."

"Do the Finns ever win in Norway?"

"Never. Only here, where they know their jump."

"Everyone is accustomed to his own hill," Eho said. "That is when he wins best. Is it not so in most things of life?"

I thought of the roads we had just been over. Of course, with anyone but a local Finn driving so audaciously, we should have been dead many times over. But here we were alive, happy, even invigorated.

The judge tactfully suggested that the chauffeur proceed more slowly, so the foreign visitors could better take in details of the Finnish landscape. The chauffeur agreed amiably, but looked as if he thought those flashing panoramas were much more to his taste.

Where some old women were gathering raspberries on the ditch bank, we turned off on a side road. It led to a group of red houses on the river bank, flanked by fields of hay and groves of birch and aspen. It was the doctor's farm. Around a *piha* the little houses clustered under mountain ash trees, their branches thick with red berries. Above each doorway was a weathered pair of antlers; before each doorstep was a doormat of fresh spruce twigs. A hammock was slung between two slender silver birches. Chairs were grouped casually about it. Foxgloves and poppies bloomed in the flower garden. Potatoes, beets, carrots, spinach, and sugar-peas grew in the vegetable plot which the hired girl tended.

Therese stretched out in the hammock and lay looking at the sky. It was pale blue, without a wisp of cloud. Only a single summer swallow, barely visible, glittered brightly, darting hither and thither in some strange delight. The river flowed behind the house, deep blue and silent. A soft wind brought the refreshing scent of cut hay that hung yellowing on lines of wire in the bronze, stubbled fields. The crook-horned cow returned, tinkling her bell faintly along a heather-decked path. The afternoon was full of peace and Lapland simplicity.

Along the bluff above the river an aspen walk led to the old-fashioned smoke *sauna*. It was the doctor's pride and joy. Any parvenu could have a fine modern *sauna,* but a mellowed old one like this was rare.

"It is a poor *sauna* in Finland that hasn't been built by a lake or a river," Eho said. "The right location solves the water problem for the washing and for the cooling plunge after the hot bath."

This *sauna* was an unpainted weathered log hut. Outside by the door grew the birch trees from which one pulled the twigs to make a bundle for beating the body into a tingle. It was low-ceilinged and divided into a dressing room and steamroom. It smelled clean and mellow, of old wood fires. The walls were so smoke-blackened that I pictured a bather entering white and coming out in burnt cork. The judge must have read my thoughts. He smeared his palm over the dark walls and exhibited it white and pink. "The black will no more rub off," he said, "than the pink off a salmon."

Lying in one corner of the smoke-cured room was the *sauna's* heart, a nest of rounded stones. Underneath the stones was the iron fireplace for burning the birchwood to heat them. Beside a wooden pail of water lay a wooden dipper, used for throwing water on the hot stones to make the steam. Five steps led up to a platform where the bather lay to sweat. In more elaborate *saunas* platforms rose in tiers higher and higher. The higher one went, the more intense the temperature.

"While the fire under the nest of stones is heating—so—the smoke goes out—so—through this smokehole and the door," the doctor said, pointing. "After the stones are thoroughly hot and the fire has died down, we throw water on the stones to clear the air. The hot vapor drives out the last smoke. The air stays smoke-flavored, but is fresh, and pleasing to taste."

"The advantage of the smokehole instead of a chimney," Eho said, "is that on each heating the *sauna* is thoroughly fumigated and kept dry as an old bone between baths."

"Smoke routs bacilli," the doctor added. "That is why Finnish women in olden times used to go to the *sauna* to have their babies—there was no danger from infection."

"Most of the country folk in times back first opened their eyes on the world in a *sauna,*" Eho said. "Maybe that's why we're so attached to them."

"No one knows where *sauna* originated," the doctor said. "But it was a custom with Finnish tribes more than a thousand years ago. Every farm in Finland has its *sauna*—every farm. They often build the *sauna,* then the house. Every Saturday in winter the *sauna* is heated. In summer during the haymaking, on Wednesday and Saturday. At threshing time, every day. All the family bathes—all the hired men and serving girls. In the backwoods they all bathe together. Now in the more cultivated families the menfolk and the womenfolk bathe separately."

"We may not bathe as often as the Americans," Eho said,

laughing. "But when we bathe, we bathe. One Finnish bath is worth a dozen of your American hoppings under a shower."

Although this day was Saturday, the *sauna* was not heated. The doctor was sorry—she would like to have given Therese a bath, followed by a quick run down to the river and a naked plunge in the water. But she was just back from her vacation and nothing was in order yet.

As we drove home, Eho pointed out smoke curling from the smokeholes or chimneys of little bathhouses at every farm. Saturday was the Finn's night of pleasure. The smoke plumes were like banners announcing a festival.

HEROIC BATHING

The Finnish *sauna* is a place not only for family bathing, we learned, but for entertaining one's friends. It has a special social value like the Japanese tea ceremony. The offer of a *sauna* bath is the height of Finnish hospitality. Sometimes as a special treat for guests Finns will heat the *sauna* stones on days other than Wednesday or Saturday. If you are visiting a country home on Saturday, it is taken for granted you will join the family bathing.

The superintendent of the hospital had invited Eho and me to have a steam bath at the *sauna* for resident doctors and nurses. The staff bathed in relays. I had seen the schedule typewritten and pasted up on a bulletin board. Doctors, 4:00 to 6:30; nurses, 6:30 to 8:00; doctors, 8:00 to 9:30; nurses, 9:30 to 11:00. We accepted the invitation for the eight-o'clock bathing.

Eho and I arrived at the hospital just before eight. The evening air was so cool we were glad we had worn our topcoats. We joined the two young doctors we had seen operating on the miner's throat. They were not long out of medical college. The shorter dark one had grown a crisp little black mustache to make him look more professional. The other was taller, clean-shaven, and auburn-haired.

The hospital *sauna* was an impressive affair, built in modernistic style of brick, with a small veranda with benches, a vestibule, a dressing room, a steamroom. It could accommodate comfortably five or six persons at a bathing. In the dressing room were a couch and chairs spread with bathrobes and towels. On the table were bottles of mineral water and *Valencia,* a Finnish orange drink.

We stripped to our skins and went into the breath-taking hot air of the steamroom. The inside walls were paneled with small split logs to soften the atmosphere and consume moisture. On scrubbed wooden benches lay bars of soap and gourd sponges. On the floor were wooden buckets and basins for washing and throwing water over the body. Utensils of metal would be too hot to the touch, just as stone benches would be impossible to sit on. In the corner was the nest of rocks above the breast-high, round fireplace, incased in sheet iron. The rocks were fist-sized, from boy's fist to lumberjack's fist. They were black, rounded cobbles that had lain in the wash of a shore. These were the favored stones in *saunas* because they were accustomed to variations of temperature and moisture. Now they were grayish-white with heat. In old-fashioned *saunas* like Doctor Jyrhämä's, one had to throw dippers of water on the stones, but here one could merely turn a spigot that sent water from a pipe flowing onto the hot nest. Coils of pipe among the stones furnished the hot water for the afterbath. Another spigot let in cold water for the douche.

Reached by eight broad steps—like the bleachers at a ball park —was the slightly sloping platform where the bathers lay with heads toward the back wall and where they could just sit up straight and miss bumping their heads on the ceiling by a few inches.

I waited to follow the moves of the initiated. The short doctor with the black mustache turned the spigot, and a hot vapor rose from the sizzling stones and swirled about the room. He paused and turned it again. The stones sputtered as if they had been scalded. The vapor became hotter and thicker. Eho wondered how I liked it. I liked it fine.

They had forgotten the birch twigs for the whipping. So the auburn-haired doctor went out, naked as Adam, into the garden, and tore off two fistfuls of leafy twigs about a foot and a half long. He brought them back and seared them by switching them briefly against the hot stones. Then he dipped them in a bucket of warm water. A pungent, tonic scent, faintly medicinal, filled the air. Eho told me to cap some water on my hair and face. The black-haired doctor took his place on the platform by the wall where he could manipulate the spigot and the intensity of heat. There was another gadget on a chain by which he could open or close the shutter in the fireplace, through which the hot air poured into the room. By opening the shutter the temperature could be raised thirty degrees Centigrade in a few minutes.

The black-haired doctor made himself comfortable, flat on his back. Then in one athletic movement he hoisted his legs high in the air and hooked his heels over a rounded beam. The beam extended like a chicken roost above the platform and about a foot beneath the ceiling.

"It draws the heat to the feet and leaves the head cool," Eho said. Then he ordered, "Climb aloft."

He stretched by the farthest wall and hooked his heels over the beam. I went up the steps into the hotter air and lay back on the warm planks. I raised my feet to the ceiling and flinched when my heels hit the hot wooden beam. The red-headed doctor climbed up, bringing his wet whisks with him, and slung his heels over the beam.

More water was turned onto the rocks. The hot vapor bulged out, enveloped us. My skin began to tingle. I opened my mouth to breathe. Perspiration drenched me from head to foot. The sensation was pleasant as when a kind of pain makes pleasure. We all lay quiet, with occasional gasps for air and a wiping of the sweat away with our hands. To a person entering the door we must have looked like eight fresh-slaughtered hams hanging from ceiling hooks.

"The use of the bathhouse was a cult among the ancient Finns," Eho said, taking down one foot and swiping the sweat off the other leg with it. "It was a sacred place where the bathers sat quietly and refrained from singing and spoke only in subdued tones. In the deep country the people still use the *sauna* as a sort of rite. They are quite solemn in the bath."

"In Finland," the black-mustached doctor said, "the *sauna* is not merely a matter of hygiene. It is one of the great pleasures of the nation."

Again we lay in silence, the black head, the red head, the brown, and the yellow all pillowed in puddles of sweat. I could feel the wooden boards beneath me getting hotter. The heat crept into every pore and routed out every impurity. My toes were becoming parboiled. I withdrew my feet from the beam and sat up. It was as if I had plunged my head in a bucket of hot water.

"Are you ready for the whipping now?" the red-headed doctor said, climbing down and dipping the birch whisk in the water bucket. He handed Eho a bunch of twigs to beat himself with. Since I was a foreign guest, he paid me the honor of beating me.

In public *saunas* in the cities all the beating is done by female bath attendants; and on farms the hired girls whip the family and the male laborers. When men take *saunas* without female attendants, they either beat each other or beat themselves.

With the crash of aromatic birch leaves against my skin, I began to sting and tingle. "This will induce a more complete perspiration," the doctor said, dripping with sweat. I turned from side to side, on my belly and on my back. When he had finished, I was glowing like a peeled birch sapling in the sun. I politely returned the compliment and beat him. Eho passed his bunch of twigs on to the other doctor.

After the several beatings, we lay back down again and sweated in quiet gusto for another ten minutes. The black-headed one opened the draft of the oven, and the heat became too intense even for the seasoned Finns. We climbed down to the less hot regions of the floor benches.

Then came the washing with soap and warm water, the scrubbing with gourd sponges, followed by relentless pouring of buckets of cold water over each other's glowing bodies. The black-headed doctor finished his bathing first and went out to sit on the veranda to cool. It was the kind of bravado uninitiated Americans might think the shortest route to pneumonia. But if doctors did it, I thought there must be little harm in it.

"And now for a quick plunge in the river," said the red-head, leading the way. I paused on the veranda steps. The hospital clock chimed nine. The river at night on the Arctic Circle? I had arrived an hour ago in a topcoat, and now, completely naked, I was supposed to run along the grass path down into the river. I shivered at the thought, and then boldly tossing to the winds any cowardly belief in catching cold, I ran leaping down the path after the leader. As I struck the river I let out an unrestrained yelp of horror and delight. The water was shockingly icy and quite wonderful.

"In the winter," Eho called out, "we roll in snowdrifts."

THE MICHAEL AGRICOLA CHURCH BY LARS SONCK IN HELSINKI

TOWER OF OLYMPIC STADIUM RISES THEATRICALLY TWENTY-TWO STORIES TALL

We tore back up the path and began drying off with towels on the veranda. In the northwest a fiery sunset glowed like a furnace and streaked the river with little tongues of flame like burning surface oil. The rearing ski-jump in the distance caught the reflection and glittered with dancing colors as if it had been illuminated for a night contest.

Back in the dressing room we sat about in bathrobes to complete the cooling process. We drank mineral water and bottled orange juice and settled back for quiet talk and a smoke and a surrender to a preternatural sense of well-being. A delicious feeling stole through nerves and sinews like some pure sort of intoxication that lifted the head and cleared the brain, adding power to the body and fleetness to the feet. I began to have an inkling of why Finns are champion runners, why they never get flustered, and why sometimes their strength is as the strength of ten.

By Post Bus Beyond the Circle

EXPERIMENT STATION

There was no railroad between Rovaniemi and Petsamo, and no airplane service, though the airports and landing fields were under construction and scheduled for completion by June 1940. But the world's only motor road to the Arctic Ocean lay before us. It had been opened in 1929. By *Posti Bussi* it was a two-day trip, with an overnight stop at Ivalo—531 kilometers in all, or, in English miles, 184 the first day, 144 the second. We had had both warnings and misgivings about the trip, for people back in Helsinki had shaken their heads doubtfully and one man had told me the bus ride had jolted his front teeth loose and damaged his bridgework. So it was almost a wrench to leave the excellent beds and cuisine of the smart Pohjanhovi to jolt two days into the wilderness. But we were spared the first fifteen miles of discomfort, as the governor sent us in his car with Mr. Eho a couple of hours ahead of the bus to visit Lapland's brand-new agricultural experiment station.

From Rovaniemi to Liinahamari each of the 531 kilometers is marked by red poles, with two white boards meeting at the ends to form an arrowhead, the distance covered being painted in black figures on one and the distance to go on the other. Eight kilometers north of the capital and 523 south of Liinahamari, another signpost announces the Arctic Circle in four languages, thus: Napapiiri, Polcirkel, Polarkreis, Arctic Circle. As we approached the pole we saw its rocky base was animated with reclining humanity. A male figure detached itself from the group and rushed to the car with his hands up. I thought there had been a Finnish motor accident. The chauffeur threw on his brakes.

It was a thin young man with an open shirt, a battered hat, and a most engaging smile. "Could you possibly take us with you?" he asked in charming Oxford, but not ultra-Oxford, English. "We want to get to the Arctic Ocean." The two loungers behind him grasped the straps of their rucksacks.

The chauffeur made a disgusted "Tcha!" sound and waved the back of his hand emphatically toward the eager face. Never before had the governor's car with its Number 1 Lapland license plate and official blue and white flag been halted by hitch-hikers.

We explained from the back seat that this was not our car, that we were going only a few miles ahead, and that the regular post bus would be along in an hour or so. The young man thanked us ingratiatingly. The chauffeur muttered under his breath, then laughed as we began to laugh.

The most northern agricultural station in the world lay on both sides of the Arctic Highway. It had been a large private farm before the government bought it, and now it looked quite neat with all the houses freshly painted the rich country red and the fences white as milk. "Red is very cheering on a snow-covered landscape—like Christmas cards," Eho said. "And red paint is by far the most economical," he added.

Flat fields exposed to sweeping winds stretched between two lakes ringed about with somber firs. There were acres of rectangular patches of flourishing wheat, rye, oats, barley, and potatoes. More than a dozen species of wheat were undergoing cross-breedings and experiments for cold and frost resistance and quick maturity. A special strain called "speed wheat" had been produced to accord with the brief summers of Lapland. Various fertilizers were being experimented with to see which would most benefit the pale, thin soil.

The farmers thereabouts had not believed in store-bought fertilizer, the director's assistant told Eho in Finnish. They felt it against nature to use anything but cow manure. Lapland farmers were hard to convince; they didn't like to change their customs. "The land sticks to its ways," they would say, "no matter where the new master comes from." Demonstration took time. But they would learn and be grateful later. Already they were coming to the station to watch the experiments.

I went up and down the potato rows and learned that Vesijarvi potatoes had the best flavor of all, but that Green Mountains gave the biggest crop. A rich man might grow Vesijarvi, but a poor man should grow Green Mountain. The potato plants looked luxuriant and green, but this was August seventh and they were still in bloom. It had been a cold, late summer. The station had not been able to plant before the twelfth of June. The life cycle of these potatoes lay between the twelfth of June and the end of August. Every fourth or fifth season a killing summer frost might be expected. But in a few years they hoped to have developed varieties that would survive the hazards of frost. Even as it was, the assistant said, nature had its ways of compensation. For there were no bugs to fight, and up here where there was sunshine for twenty-two hours a day in summer they raised the biggest potato crops per acre in Finland.

The director's wife joined us. Her husband was away, and she was eager to be helpful and explain the little she understood of his work. She spoke a bit of English. She had been a school teacher in the south of Finland and had been here only since December. It was all very strange to her in the north, but now it was her life and her husband's work, and happiness would come in the success of their experiments.

Eho said we must accept hospitality by going into the director's house. The wife had made meringue cakes with shredded cocoanut for us, and she set a tray of bottled fruit juices on her living-room table.

"This is only our temporary house," the hostess said hesitantly, spreading blue prints before us on the grand piano. "Next year the government will build this large house there—on the edge of the lake—and I can help the neighborhood children with their lessons in this big room."

She pointed on the drawing. Her eyes shone with the eager anticipation of a child as she looked at the blueprints, yet with a child's shyness lest it dare not come true.

"At the new place I shall make a real garden," she said.

On the side of her house grew rows of vegetables which she had planted and cultivated herself: carrots, beets, parsley, spinach, beans, sugar-peas. We plucked off pods of the sugar-peas and chewed them. They were sweet and very tender. Green peas are cooked whole in Lapland, for they never grow large enough to shell. The season is too short. But the vines were full of pods and flowers and they would go on bearing until heavy frost. Vegetables in the arctic regions of Norway, Sweden, and Finland grow in profuse bounty, and because they mature with such rapidity, owing to the long hours of sunlight, they are richer in flavor than vegetables in the south.

In a special sheltered plot Brussels sprouts, celery, and cauliflower were growing. "Celery and cauliflower in the Arctic!—Would they produce?" we asked.

The ex-teacher laughed wonderingly. "Would they?" She did not know. She was only here this season. The seed had come in packages. She had planted them. They had come up. They were growing. Later she would learn. This was an experiment station.

DELIVERING MAIL

The indispensable Mr. Eho had reserved seats for us on the yellow *Posti Bussi,* which stopped to pick us up at the agricultural station. It was well that he had, for the three English boys had taken up the last free seats. We crowded into our places while the passengers scrooged together to make room for us. There were no individual seats with arms. But brass place numbers said that five were to sit on a row, regardless of individual bulks. A fat man in Number 8 might spread half again into Number 7 and take up half of Number 9 also. And the other four would have to manage as they could. The knees of tall men shoved deep against the back of the seats in front. But being packed tight as tinned herrings kept us from jouncing about.

Besides the Oxford students, a librarian from Dartmouth College, and ourselves, the other twenty-odd passengers were Finns. A mother with two obedient little tow-headed children and a baby at her breast sat in a row behind us with two shaggy ax-bearing woodsmen and a grave, toothless old woman with a head rag tied under her chin. Several farmers in Sunday clothes were just going down the road a piece. A group of townspeople on vacation were going north for the fishing. A huge fiery-bearded Finn with a salty look and old sea captain's clothes was squeezed so tightly in his place that he had to keep his arm folded above his great chest. Even though this was the day after *sauna* night, there was a musty kippered-herring smell in the bus. It was a characteristic smoky smell that we came to expect among the rural people of Lapland.

In the right-hand forward corner of the bus the sharp-eyed postboy sat wearing his yellow-billed cap. He never relaxed for a moment, his eyes alert to warn the driver when to stop. The post bus delivered mail to the farms and villages all along the road. That was its chief function. The passengers' accommodation was a by-product of the mail service.

The events of the journey were the mail deliveries and collections. On the edge of the road, by a gate or an open yard, or sometimes at the end of a path leading into the dark shadowed wood, stood yellow wooden boxes set on posts. When there was a letter to be collected, a little flag was affixed to the box. When the postboy left a letter, if no one was there to receive it, he would take the flag from inside the box and raise it. At most farms someone stood expectantly on the roadside waiting for the mail—a man or a woman or a child, sometimes an entire family. If it was only a newspaper to be delivered and no people were in sight, the driver would honk and the postboy would aim the paper at the box or toss it into the front yard as we sped by. Now and then someone would come rushing from a house at the last minute, waving a letter at the bus. Letters to be mailed were invariably wrapped in newspaper. The postboy would carefully unwrap it, and examine it to see who was writing to whom. Then he would shake from the newspaper wrapping a smaller package wrapped in more newspaper. It contained the exact change for the stamp.

We collected and delivered not only mail but cans of milk and empty milk cans, flowering plants, sacks of grain, squawking hens. During the first stretch of the journey there were frequent farms and paths leading through the woods that told of clearings out of sight. Berrypickers were gathering berries along the dusty ditches. And then came miles of nothing but dry pine woods carpeted with blueberry bushes and streaked with purple heather. In the low places black ditches were lined with Lapp cotton—silky, feathery plants that looked like dandelions in fluff, useless as a commodity, but delicately decorative. The clamor of the empty milk cans in the vibrating bus and the constantly changing passengers added to the confusion and the informal sociability. When there were no vacant seats and the driver would decline to take in the passenger standing on the roadside, the passengers within would sometimes raise a racket and scrooge together still more and invite the fellow mortal to share a few inches of seat.

The road was unpaved, and the white dust flew when we passed another car. The bus vibrated so that if we didn't hold our teeth together on the bad stretches, they began to chatter violently.

At intervals we stopped for coffee at farmhouses which carried on a refreshment business in the front rooms. The interiors were always painted white and immaculately clean, with muslin curtains at the windows and pots of flowers on the ledges.

About five o'clock we stopped for supper at Södankylä, a church village that resembled a Bret Harte crossroads town. The meal began with conventional smörgåsbord of herring and reindeer meat and radishes, followed by a hot dish of meat and potatoes, and ending with soup. Why the soup came last, we never learned.

To none of the stops in the 294 kilometers between Rovaniemi and Ivalo had modern plumbing penetrated. The W.C.'s of both post-office settlements and the farms were out-of-door affairs. It was illuminating to compare the W.C.'s of Finland with those of Latin countries or Russia or the Balkans. In the wilds of Finland they are austerely clean; not a scrap of litter on the floor, not even a cigarette butt. At Södankylä a discreet arrow pointed to an outhouse painted red like the neighboring buildings. It was a commodious affair, well lit from a long window above the door. At the back, like a three-chaired throne on a dais reached by three ascending stairs, the smooth flat boards were scrubbed clean as a

Dutch table. The pit was deep as a cellar and empty as a coal bin in late spring. And so it was in the hamlets clear up to the ocean, and at any farmhouse where the bus stopped for coffee.

Farms became scarcer after Södankylä. Few of the houses were painted red now. The buildings were cruder, clearings more raw, hayfields smaller, hardly any wheat at all. Some of the log cabins were single-roomed—the rude dwellings of woodsmen, not regular farmers. Stumps still stood fast-rooted in the clearings about the houses. These woodsmen had come out of the deep forest to build habitations by the road. Before long they would clear land and raise crops and become farmers—cultivating the land in summer and felling trees for timber companies in winter. Few Lapland farmers made their full living from their farms. Most of them worked in lumber camps in January, February, March, and April, and with cash in their pockets returned home in May in time for plowing.

I thought of Aleksis Kivi's shrewd knowledge of Finnish peasants and how he made them talk like themselves.

"The savage in the forest had to keep far from the bridal bed, the man who can hardly fill his own rumbling belly, let alone those of a wife and children. But if we clear these backwoods into meadows, hoe this sloping sunlit clearing into fields, and around this house, round its echoing yard, gradually build stables, a cow house, a barn, a store room and other buildings as they are needed, that will be a different matter."

Now savage Lapland was becoming a very different matter indeed. Farms had been wrenched from the wilderness by ceaseless toil and teeth-clenching hardship. Around stout-walled cabins here and there were grouped other buildings—as more swamplands were drained and former woodlands became acquainted with the plow. There was poverty in Lapland, but Finns could hold their necks well above it. There was no degradation in it, no cowering, no sloth, no apathy. The poorest could look his fellow steadfastly in the eye. Men, women, children all had self-reliant expressions. A Finn asks no favors. And howsoever humble a home he makes, it is clean and neat and always in repair. And it is his own, for there are no tenants or sharecroppers in Finland.

We came to long, unbroken stretches of woods without sign of habitation. But great stacks of cordwood were piled by the roadside to be trucked to market. And sometimes the postboy would fling a paper where there seemed to be only a vague track through the forest. Occasionally a reindeer feeding by the roadside would be startled into the woods, his top-heavy antlers flashing like sabers in the sun.

THE ELF LAPP

At a place called Vuotso, where rude buildings gathered about a yard served as restaurant and post office for the community, we stopped for evening coffee. Because it was Sunday, several Lapps from a Lapp village not far away had come dressed in their costumes for a holiday change. They were sitting about the stoop in thick blue woolen suits embroidered in colored wools of red, yellow, and purple. The long, skirtlike jackets which flared at the bottom were belted in low on the hips and made them look incredibly long-waisted. Lapps have short legs at best because, it is said, for generations they have squatted on the floors of tents around the central fire, and accommodating nature has shortened their legs to make squatting more convenient.

The men all wore "Four Winds" caps, with the points sticking out alertly in four directions like the pricked-up ears of a dog listening to the wind. The women wore billowy skirts and blouses of bright cotton prints and headkerchiefs tied under their chins.

A few of the Lapps bore a faint resemblance to Mongols, but if a Lapp were to stand beside a Chinaman, a Tibetan, or an Eskimo, one would see how slight the resemblance is. Their cheekbones are high, but no higher than those of the Finns, and their eyes do not slant.

One of the older men, who stood with arms folded, had a sweeping sandy mustache that drooped at the ends like those in the pictures of old Viking chieftains. The carved bone handle of his knife hanging in a leather holster looked apt to spring into action. I had not yet learned that the Lapp people are exceedingly peaceable and gentle, and that where much strong drink may make a Finn run amok and clean out a tavern, alcohol makes a Lapp increasingly affectionate and gall-less as a dove.

In the tremendous oven-stove of the restaurant a big fire was roaring. The room was stiflingly hot for the Lapps' benefit. Living in Arctic climate, they seem never to get warm enough even in hot Augusts. While we drank weak, bitter coffee and ate delicious fresh-baked bread from rough planks like picnic boards, the Lapps on the stoop came in to inspect us. They sat on board benches against the wall and stared at us frankly.

One fair, slightly built youth with an elfish expression on his face leaned forward with elbows on knees, cocked his head to one side, and regarded us with the eager curiosity of a daft wood creature. His childish-soft lips smiled and his blue eyes were wistful as if he were eager to learn about the outside world whose breath we brought into the hot, smoky room. With a little encouragement he might leave the nomadic life of Lapps and seek with us this strange great world.

The youth turned to a black-haired, dull-looking Lapp beside him and began to whisper little confidences. With his "Four Winds" cap and sidelong whimsical glance, he was like a court jester just come to life after several centuries' sleep. The older Lapp with the sandy mustaches, at his other side, sat regal and proud with folded arms, as if he would never stand for any desertion—the youth must stay Lapp, be proud always he was a Lapp.

It was a strange meeting of two worlds at this crossroads where the yard was littered with reindeer antlers and the pine forests stretched limitless beyond. Strange to us, for it was the first time we had seen these people in whose language the word Lapp means "banished" and who in Norway, Sweden, and Russia as well as Finland had been pushed out of the fertile south farther and farther into the cold and unproductive north, with only the reindeer to save them from extinction.

Out on the stoop again, we loitered while the other passengers finished their coffee.

"Ah," said a Swedo-Finnish girl, a university student who was cashier in the hotel at Ivalo, "everywhere you look now is beauty." We gazed at the rigid buildings around the bare, shaly yard, at the dusty road, the dry pine woods, the stubbly blueberry bushes. Yet as I looked deep into the forest I became conscious of shafts of pale gold light between the red trunks of the pines, and saw the wildness stretching endlessly as though earth had no time, no end. The light from the sun was that subtle green gold that turns this simple northern region into something mysterious. "I should like to walk on and on through the forest forever," the girl said quietly, staring a hundred miles before her. I saw what she meant. In the feeling of infinitude lay the beauty.

From Vuotso we could see to the northeast the light on the outer fells of Nattastunturi. At the 252-kilometer sign we came to the southern boundary of the commune of Inari. A pole painted the sky-blue and white of *Suomi* stretched across the road. A custom's officer came to examine our passports.

"Again the imminence of Russia!" Therese said.

The pole was lifted, and we proceeded into the largest rural commune in Finland. In area it is about one-half the size of Belgium, while its population is less than twenty-five hundred. Almost half of the inhabitants are Lapps.

Farther on we stopped on the edge of a river to wait for the ferry. A concrete bridge was being built—to be ready for the Olympic Games in 1940. We wandered off into the near woods to gather blueberries. There were millions of great juicy berries on the low green bushes. But battalions of mosquitoes rose from ambush, swarmed about, clustered on our faces, hands, ankles. Stamping, brushing, slapping had no effect. They clung stubbornly, having no fear of death. "Like the Finns," the girl cashier said, smiling. "Like the Finns who will cling to their land, no matter what is done to them."

It was our first encounter with arctic mosquitoes, but this brief fierce struggle made us grateful our visit was in August, not July. By August the pests retire to the woods. But in June and July they swarm over the highroads, the gardens, and into the houses if they can. In July people smear their faces with pitch oil or go about in nets and gloves like bee men. The natives carry bottles of pitch hanging from their belts like medieval purses. Tourists often wrap their ankles in newspapers.

The ferry was a pontoon with railings. It was operated by a man pulling a stout, squared stick with a transverse groove over a stationary wire cable that stretched across the river. There was a knack to manipulating the stick with just the right twist. Passengers took turns helping the ferryman pull. Of course, they were awkward and we lost time, but no one cared. You lose sense of time in the vastness of Lapland.

LUMINOUS FELLS AND LAPP FEVER

Beyond the river the road began to climb. The trees grew sparse and dwarfish. Even the pines faltered and finally drew the last drop of nourishment from the stony earth, and ceased altogether. We had come into the region of the fells, those rounded mountainous piles of naked rock.

Soon the bus turned off the main road and climbed until it came to the top of a fell that seemed to be the center of the group. We got out and looked in every direction of the twelve-winded sky. Ringing us about were undulating ranges of rounded fells within other ranges, like amphitheaters within amphitheaters. Not a tree in sight, only patches of mauve arctic lichens and a few low bushes crouching protectively close to the ground. The light of the descending sun lay in subtle splendor upon the rocks. The whole panorama of the idle earth was tinted lavender. In the distance the rims of the mountainous fells were violet-colored. The universe seemed a vast immensity of luminous sky, shimmering and white gold, stretching like a benediction over the silent wasteland. Remote and ten times lonelier than any spot in Wuthering Heights, the scene made me think of sea-loving Conrad's belief that only a thousand miles from land can man communicate with his own soul. In these stark fells a hundred shrines for contemplation lay uncontaminated by anything human or mundane. And here now at evening the stony wilderness seemed to be making up to man for its harsh uselessness by this offering of evanescent beauty, this enchantment of sterility.

Over a lap of fell that folded in upon itself, seven reindeer quietly appeared as if called up by conjuration. Two were grown and five were hornless young. One of the Oxford boys dropped to his knees and got his camera ready to snap as they approached. But the reindeer lifted their heads to sniff the scent in the wind, the young and old together. Then, as if answering a cue, they turned in profile to make a Grecian frieze, and descended into the lavender nothingness.

The air grew cold, and we needed our topcoats. But it was time to go.

The Oxford youths' eyes were wide. "I live near the Scottish border," one said, "and I know downs and fells, but, by Jove, I've never seen anything so extraordinarily lovely at home. What makes it?"

"It's the light," I said. It is this special Lapland light that gives the key to the fascination of Lapland, that gives the region its character, flavor, variety. The superabundance of light in summer, the mysterious light of winter when the snow glows blood-red at noon and in an hour turns pale silver as if lit by a wax candle.

The bus crossed the watershed, which now sent all the rivers flowing north to the Arctic Ocean instead of to the lakes or the Bothnian Gulf. At the top of the watershed amid treeless wastes it seemed there must be nothing ahead but desolation. But when we started down and crossed the timberline again, the pine and spruce and birch came to meet us—little fellows at first, then whole virgin forests, with tall straight trees standing among their fallen ancestors. The dead trees on the ground had stood for centuries without ever having been seen by man, and then had dropped onto their shadows from old age. Now they lay there, bleached pale as skeletons by snows and summer suns, their whitened roots and branches spreading out like mammoth antlers from prehistoric reindeer.

Swamps and forbidding bogs broke the monotony of the woods with their own special monotony. Goldenrod and magenta mid-summer flowers grew by the ditches. And soon clearings with new houses and white cows grazing in the meadows appeared. We sat up alert, sensing civilization.

The postboy flung his papers merrily again. Peasants and woodsmen began to get on and off the bus more frequently. Though it was nine o'clock and cold in the night air, farmers with their wives were still raking hay and hanging it over the hurdles. Soil became more fertile and hay abundant. Wheat in the patches grew straight and tall. Potatoes were thick and luxuriantly green. The road wound down into the valley of the Ivalojoki.

The bus turned into the drive of the New Ivalo Inn. It was a pleasant, stout-walled building of squared logs stained red. The university-student waitresses stood on the steps to receive us in native costume. One of the girls with a watering pot was sprinkling a row of sweet peas trained on cotton strings against the wall. The plants were yet only a foot high, and there already was a feeling of frost in the night air.

Inside, a cheerful fire blazed on the hearth and brought out the bright colors of the hand-woven rugs and curtains. In our room upstairs I touched the radiator. The steam heat was on. Our windows faced the west and a silver river with a sand beach on the opposite shore. The sun was still above the horizon, although it was after half-past nine. The sunlight turned the sand across the river to grains of gold. A canoe glided swiftly beneath the window, leaving a chain of glinting ripples. When it was gone around the bend, a young stag came across the green fields down to the yellow beach to drink.

"Don't look," I said to Therese, who was taking off some travel dust, "unless you want to catch Lapland fever. I've got it already."

But she looked—and tired though she was, she got it too.

After a light supper we threw on topcoats and took a brisk

stroll down to the village of Ivalo, about two-thirds of a mile away, to see if the young Britishers had found a place to stay. They allowed themselves about a shilling a night for lodging. From behind the red and white cabins of the older inn we heard splashings in the river. There, by the fading light of half-past ten, the Oxford men were plunging about in the arctic river. They came out dripping, clutching their bed blankets about them, grinning broadly. They had all got bad cases of Lapp fever, too, they confessed, shivering delightedly.

It was almost eleven when we walked back to our hotel. The sun was gone. Mists rose from the swampy places that divided hayfields from small groves of slender birch. The pools in the swamps were still lavender-pink from the afterglow of evening. A curved young moon lay cool as a silver shaving against the faded flush of sky.

When we got to our rooms I turned to switch on the electric light. There was none. I lighted a candle and turned off the steam heat. "Central heating, modern plumbing, but no electric light!" I said. It was characteristic of Finland to take what was needed from modernity and retain what was adequate from the past.

The next morning after breakfast, waiting for the post bus that was to leave at seven, Therese and I sat on stumps on the river bank and looked across to the sand beach and the hayfield between two patches of fir forests. The morning was warm with the sun, which had risen at two. A sun-browned peasant family arrived in a motor-propelled rowboat with their rakes to gather the hay and hang it up on wires to dry.

"It's strange," Therese said, "how this land where there's really so little to see reminds you of so much else." The people across the river might have been forgotten Indians in the depths of Wisconsin. The crossroads settlements we had stopped at were like Western frontier villages. The log cabins in raw clearings and the berrypickers on the dusty roadsides were familiar scenes in the backwoods South. The sparse pine forests and cut-over woods were like the dry, palmless sections of sandy Florida. The heather-clad moors and the rocky fells recalled bleak and rugged parts of Scotland. Yet here the reindeer and the Lapps, the reindeer moss, the Lapp cotton, the endless light of summer days, the never-ending stretches of dark woods, the immensity of sky, the looks on men's faces, the uniform blondness of broad-cheeked children, the woven stuffs and the costumes, the alien language, made one aware of strangeness in the midst of familiar memories.

SLOT MACHINES ARE FOR CHARITY

The road to Petsamo proceeded northeast from Ivalo, keeping close to the eastern shore of Lake Inari. Beyond Ivalo the forests had had a housecleaning. For miles and miles they were owned by the government, and the underbrush had been cut out and all the dead branches piled in neat stacks like pyres for Hindu suttees.

At Virtaniemi, a fishing resort in a lush green setting with gigantic ferns, axes were crashing, hammers pounding, saws flashing in the sunlight—all the thunder and lightning of building that had spread like a contagion through Finland. Here they were doubling the size of the inn to take care of the next year's tourists. Three smart British-made cars belonging to British sportsmen and overrunning with rods, reels, nets, gaffs, and suitcases were parked at the edge of the wild ferns. It was little wonder that rich Englishmen let out their estates with the fishing and shooting rights to wealthier Americans and flocked to Finland for sportier sport at the proverbial song. Near the Virtaniemi inn there were well-stocked rapids. The state controlled the fishing rights. Permits could be obtained by foreigners for half a dollar a day, or a few dollars for the season. A double room in the inn cost only seventy-five cents, and meals were twenty to forty cents each.

After Virtaniemi, miles of uninhabited lands stretched between huts. There was no more purple heather in the woods—only the close clusters of arctic moss, the sole food of the reindeer in winter. The gray-white moss covering the Lapland ground looked like soft snow melting after rain. Here and there, scattered nearer the roadway, were wooden racks and pens heaped with the moss. Lapps had gathered it to help the reindeer in the winter feeding when the snow was frozen hard.

At the 368-kilometer line the bus crossed the parish of Petsamo. This most northern district of over 10,000 square kilometers belonged to Russia until 1920, when she ceded it to Finland. With Petsamo, Finland acquired the valuable ice-free harbor on the Arctic. In 1938 there was only about one person to every three square kilometers. Of the 3,400 inhabitants the guidebook said 400 were Karelians, 200 Russians, 400 Greek-Orthodox Lapps, and 60 Lutheran Lapps. The rest were Finns. The opening up of the nickel mines and the construction of a large hydro-electric plant at Paatsjoki had recently brought several thousand more Finns into the district.

From ancient times Russians, Finns, Swedes, and Norwegians have contended for Petsamo. Near the middle of the sixteenth century a Russian monk named Trifon founded a monastery at Yläluostari. Trifon was aided and abetted by Ivan the Terrible, who, under the guise of religious zeal, sought to increase Russian colonization. But in 1590 a Finnish peasant led a marauding expedition against the intruding Russians, sacked the monastery, and routed the monks.

When by international agreement between Russia and Norway in 1826 the boundaries were settled, Finland was deprived of a right of access to the Arctic Ocean which had been hers under Sweden. She pressed her claims so hard, however, that finally in 1864 Russia promised her the district of Petsamo for a strip of land north of St. Petersburg which the Czar had appropriated illegally. But Russia never carried out her promise. In 1918 Finland made a gallant effort to seize what was rightfully hers by sending a force of a hundred Finns to take over the region. But the Finns were stopped by an English expeditionary force which had occupied Petsamo in the last year of the war because of its strategic position. Finland did not get Petsamo with the outlet to the Arctic until 1920, by the Treaty of Tartu.

Starting from Nautsi, at 379 kilometers, the river called Paatsjoki forms the frontier between Finland and Norway. At 425 kilometers, in pleasant, open lake country, we passed the village of Pitkajärvi. The Finns were to fall back to this place in their retreat from the ocean in December of 1939.

Some Norwegian hikers, who had joined the bus, began pointing ahead, not to shores of their country across the river, but to the northeast to the great white smokestack of the Petsamo Nickel Company—the highest smokestack in all Europe. Thirty kilometers on a branch road to the right was the newly created, almost completed, model mining village of Kolosjoki, where by concession the Canadian International Nickel Corporation was boring for nickel and copper. The smokestack, white as a wax candle and ten times taller than any topless tower in Ilium, stood like a symbol of tomorrow.

The village of Salmijärvi lay by the lakeside open to sky and wind. It was an important postal center, as it was also the district's center of traffic, agriculture, and mining. There were a new school, new co-operative shop, new post office, new restaurant, new houses. The parking spaces were filled with cars. Across from the restaurant a pavilion where sweets, coffee, postcards, and knickknacks were sold was kept by the girls of the Lotta Svärd, the Finnish women's organization for helping in the defense of the country. A landing field was being constructed for the Helsinki-Petsamo Air Service, to be instituted in 1940. Salmijärvi had the vital look of an adolescent town that might think nothing of quadrupling its population within a year. No one dreamed that the lively spot would be a mass of blackening debris before four months had passed.

In the crowded restaurant where we had lunch, the radio was playing marching tunes, and men were lined up to get to the slot machines. When our little bus driver stood ready to put a mark in the slot machine, I indicated I would try to give him good luck, and flipped his coin. He pulled the lever. It dropped in a winning groove, but the machine jammed. He shook the cabinet and a fistful of marks clattered into the metal cup. I helped him gather up his money. His eyes were wide with astonished delight; he got ready to play again. I put my hand over the opening and took him by the arm, suggesting he had had all the luck possible and should leave while he still had the money.

But he looked at me in surprise, said something in explanation. One of the men in the crowd said in English, "It's for charity. All slot machines in Finland are run for charity to provide increasingly better hospitalization for the poor. Finland permits no private gambling devices. And when a fellow wins he is supposed to keep playing his marks until he loses them all again in the good cause."

Even in Salmijärvi I learned a lesson in Finnish concern for general welfare.

Green Pastures on the Arctic Ocean

THROUGH THE BACK GATE TO NORWAY

Of all the places in Finland, there was none that amazed the eyes and won the heart like Kolttaköngäs. The village lay romantically in a sylvan valley along foaming blue rapids, sheltered from arctic winds by a protecting wall of gray granite cliffs that rose with jagged grandeur like fjord mountains in Norway.

The bus stopped under an overhanging cliff a few hundred yards from a bridge in process of construction across the highest fall of rapids. The village was a mile and a half away. Ahead of us a string of cars were parked in front of the toolhouses and offices of the bridge builders. The workmen had gone home for the day.

Everybody got out of the bus.

"But we aren't there yet," I protested.

All luggage was unloaded and deposited on the roadside. The Norwegians shouldered their rucksacks to start for the bridge. I didn't see how I was going to carry three heavy suitcases a mile and a half. The strapping bus driver looked husky enough to carry two of them. "What do we do now?" I asked him in English.

He shrugged. I made signs of asking if he could lend me a hand. He made signs he must stay by his bus.

"Maybe they will send a horse from the hotel," one of the Norwegian girls said.

"But a horse couldn't cross the half-built bridge any more than the bus can," I said.

"We'll stop by the hotel and tell them you are here," said the girl. It was about a half hour's walk.

We sat on rocks, wondering. The bus driver was unconcerned. I gave him a cigarette. He smoked it standing. After a minute or two he looked at his watch and drove off cheerily.

"Why in hell didn't the tourist agents tell us what to expect?" I grumbled. It was not untypical of travel in Finland. Virtually no one in Lapland, except a few at the tourist hotels, spoke English. And no one ever told us anything. The Finns did not even tell each other. No one ever seemed to know exactly what to do; the Finns were as uncertain as the foreigners. But somehow it had been planned, and when the time came we did as we were supposed to and we arrived on schedule. Finns seemed to have little necessity for knowing ahead.

I was in a hurry to get to the hotel, because I had an appointment with one of the engineers of the Kirkenes iron mines in Norway to show me over his plant that afternoon. Mr. Carl Hambro, the Conservative speaker of the Norwegian Parliament and President of the League of Nations, had arranged for the visit. He wanted me to inspect an industry where the contented workers all voted the Conservative ticket.

We saw some people picking their way across the bridge, coming toward us, carrying their own luggage. It looked more hopeless than ever. I went to question them. Among them was a Finn I had met at Rovaniemi. He had come for week-end fishing. He proudly exhibited two fine salmon.

"But what do we do now?" I asked him.

"The hotel sends a rowboat from the other side to get the luggage across the river, and then a horse to take it to the hotel."

"But they aren't here. Shall we leave our bags?"

"Ah, yes, they will send."

"But they should have been here. They knew we were coming. I telegraphed."

"Yes," he smiled. "They are a little late."

We all laughed together. Finnish placidity is disarming.

The Finn and his friends drove off with their salmon. We sat on.

Suddenly a Lapp boy appeared above the bank and seized a suitcase and disappeared down a path. I went to the edge and looked. He put the case in an old rowboat that looked as if its hours were numbered. He scrambled up the bank and got the other bags. Therese and I started with coats and briefcases for the bridge. We picked our way along planks over the swirling water.

The sunlit road to Kolttaköngäs lay along an open grove of slender birches by the rapids. Eighteen cream-colored horses grazed on lush grass among the silver trunks. To the left of the road behind a field rose a thick wooded hillside studded with gray boulders. Ahead, on either side of the road, lay a helter-skelter Lapp village. Twenty-odd weathered gray cabins stood askew and on stilts, with haphazard fences dividing some of the patches of hay. In the fields little old men with curly beards and little old women in faded pink skirts were busy as ants, raking hay. By a one-room lemonade bottling works near the river a flock of sheep lay basking in the sun. Before an open front door of a hut on "chicken-leg" foundations a girl was milking a nanny goat. On a green point of land that jutted arrow-shaped into the river arose a theatric salmon-pink church with five aquamarine-colored domes.

On the river two men with mosquito veils over their faces were lolling in boats with two-handed rods affixed to a device in the bows, while two Lapp boys rowed furiously to hold the boats against the swift current.

We stopped in our tracks. We had been told of a new hotel and the fishing but not of the church or the Lapps. Amazement must have been on our faces as the Norwegian girls appeared from the small co-operative shop with hunks of cheese in their hands.

"Your hotel is just behind the shop and the church," they said, laughing, "through the graveyard."

And there it was, a three-story modern hotel in white concrete. It had just been completed in April. Its front garden was an ancient graveyard with Greek crosses, among boulders under the birch trees. Near the center stood a wooden chapel—not much bigger than a *sauna*. It had been erected by a Russian monk in 1569 in memory of two young Russian princes, Boris and Gleb, who had been murdered by heathen about the year 1000. Before Finland took formal possession of Petsamo on St. Valentine's Day in 1921, the village had always been known as Boris Gleb. But the Finns named it Kolttaköngäs after the tribe of Koltta Lapps and the rapids, which are *köngäs* in Finnish.

Kolttaköngäs was like one of those places that get incredibly mixed in a dream. Memories and realities of ancient orthodox Russia and forward-looking Finland converged about the ageless Lapps. And Norway proper began virtually in the back garden of the tourist hotel. Finland's possession was evident in the new bridge, the roads, the post service, and the modernistic hotel.

"Norway's by nature, Russia's by inheritance, Finland's by treaty and improvement," Therese said as the horsecart arrived with our luggage. We were shown to a room done in attractive modern style, where the beds were perfection and the bathroom equipped with all the gadgets of a metropolitan hotel.

A quarter of an hour after I had taken a shower, I was walking into Norway. The engineer from Kirkenes had come by the larger motorboat, which could not return for a couple of hours, because of the low tide. We decided to walk the few miles to the river village in Norway where the engineer had left his car. Passing through the ancient emerald cemetery and by the brown chapel that merged into the hotel garden, we swung into the new road that ran high behind the Lapp village. At the top of a rise in the road by a refreshment shop for road builders, we passed another graveyard, a newer one, in use today. The graves were boarded up with weathered planks that looked like coffins left on top of the ground. Rusty ax heads, spades, or spade handles lay on top of the boards—bits of tools men had worked with in this life that would help to make the next one feel less unfamiliar. At each grave head was a crude, slanting Greek cross. Thin-necked cows belonging to the hotel and the Lapps walked among the graves, the sunlight sifting through the birch boughs making patterns on their white hides.

"A mighty lot of graves for such a small village," I said to the engineer.

"It's tuberculosis," he said. "The Lapps are easy victims. They stay shut up in their houses all winter with their windows sealed with woolen. But the Finnish government is putting on a campaign to save them. They send the bad cases down to sanatoria further south and send nurses here to teach the Lapps sanitation and hygiene. Koltta Lapps are not very strong. When they hire out to work they don't last at it. They're not lazy; they just haven't the strength. It's generations of undernourishment and privations. These frail, impecunious Lapps acknowledged allegiance to Russia from earliest times. The stronger, wealthier Inari Lapps, who despise the Koltta Lapps, have always been men of Finland. These Lapps here are eating better now, though. Finland has been excellent to them. They have education and cash, as well as insurance against starvation. All the fishing fees here go to support the Lapps, and the Lapp boys have exclusive rights to row the boats for the fishermen. It's big money to them."

On one side of the road rose mountainous piles of pink granite. Purple and gray arctic lichens spread over the boulders scattered about the base. Ferns grew rank in the rich earth of the crevices. In the damp black ditches silky-white Lapp cotton plants blew about on their slender stems. Grass grew luxuriously in the yards of Finnish farmhouses right up to the fenced chicken runs where white leghorns made contented noises in the sun. Four big black rabbits sat impudently in the grass watching us, as we stepped aside for a flock of sheep that came down the road kicking up dust.

The road gave out and narrowed into a mere path. "Precaution," the engineer said. "We're not building a Norwegian road to connect with the Finnish road yet. If the Russians ever decided to try to capture Kirkenes, we wouldn't want to make it too easy for them."

Through a wooden gate in a hedgerow we stepped from Finland into Norway. We were on a farmer's land. The farmer and his little daughter were hanging hay on hurdles. They acknowledged our greeting cheerfully. When we passed the house, we heard a woman's racking cough from within.

"Tuberculosis," said the engineer. "Even some of the sheep have it. It's our biggest problem in the north."

At a cabin in the spruce woods my passport was stamped by the Norwegian control. Then we began climbing up over boulder-strewn hills that looked like a Wagnerian opera setting. From the top we could see Kirkenes and the sun on the ships in the blue water of the Bøk Fjord. A mile farther on we reached the lumber town of Elvenes, where the engineer's car was parked, and drove to Kirkenes to see the mines and the workers' houses.

Before the war Kirkenes had been quite Red, the engineer said. The workers had struck repeatedly. Finally the strain of constant strikes broke the company. The workers had killed the goose that laid the golden egg and there was no more money for them to live on. After the war new capital had started operations again. The workers had learned their lesson and they foreswore labor unions. Now they felt a part of the company, building their own houses with the company's aid, and seeming content even in the dark months of winter.

After several hours of visiting the mines and the bright-painted homes of the workmen, and having enjoyed a real Norwegian supper, I was brought by the engineer to the landing stage at Elvenes. He had telephoned for the motorboat from Kolttaköngäs just as one telephones for a taxi. It was waiting at the landing when we arrived.

THE LYRICAL BOATMAN

Behind the hills the northwest sky was still flushed crimson, and the pinkish reflection was mirrored in the river. The boatman started his motor and we shoved off. To my surprise he addressed me in English. I looked at him closely through the twilight. As he smiled, his white teeth shone like an Arab's in his lean bronzed face. He had extraordinarily good teeth, a rarity in Lapland. His name was Reino, he said, and he came from Helsinki. He had studied English in the schools. He was eager to talk, not because he particularly liked talking, but because he wanted to practice his English. He spoke his words carefully and rather slowly.

He had hoped to enter the university, but his father, who was a small tailor, had died, and he had been earning his living since sixteen. He had come as a carpenter's assistant last fall to help to build the hotel and had stayed in Petsamo through last winter. He never wanted to go back to the capital to live.

"There is nothing like it here—the stillness of winter," he said. "It is so beautiful—the stillness on the white snow. You go on skis far off alone. You can't imagine how still it is on the snow-covered meadows. The only sound you hear is the call of grouse. But you cannot see them, because in winter they are white as the snow." His deep voice rose and fell softly above the chug of the boat. "In winter in Lapland we cannot work much because of the darkness, but we have time to think and read and study. When the moon is full, the reflection from the snow gives so much light that you can read all day by moonlight. The moon shines all day, just as it does at night, for there's no sun to make it pale. I must have read fifty books last winter after my work hours were done."

He adjusted the rudder wire and sat nearer me.

"I should think this place would be fine for writers in winter," he said, "because they could keep their minds on what they were doing. I don't see how they think straight in cities." His teeth showed white in the twilight as he smiled again. "I don't like cities, with all the noise and hurrying about on business that pretends to be important. There is no peace, no freedom in cities—no beauty in them like this, now."

He made a slight gesture to take in all the river and its banks. A mysterious midnight twilight had silvered everything—the water, the rocks, the trees, the sky, the village behind us, the face and figure of the boatman.

Reino turned off his motor. We glided up to a pier. A lamp shone through window shutters up a path.

"What's this?" I asked.

"Norwegian passport inspection."

We tied the boat and went up the path to the house. The Norwegian questioned me, and then stamped permission to leave his country.

"Do you think there will be war?" he called as we started down the path.

"Not in this territory, surely," I called back, making a sorry guess.

"Listen, how still it is," Reino said, as we got back into the boat and sat there a moment before he started the motors. "Is it not as full of peace as it could possibly be?"

He skirted the rocks in the rapids with the ease of experience. It was growing colder. He pulled a leather jacket over his woodsman's plaid blouse.

"Are you staying long?" he asked, after a bit.

"No. I must go tomorrow. I have an appointment Tuesday at Liinahamari. I'd like to stay through a winter, but I'm afraid."

"Afraid?" He looked at me in surprise. It's a word that always astounds a Finn.

"Because I might get Lapp fever so bad I could never go home."

He laughed softly. "Oh, you have heard about that—Lapland fever? Yes, you might get it. People are funny. Some get it, some don't. Some go out of their senses here in winter. You never can tell. A lawyer from Helsinki was sent to Petsamo for two years to take a public office. After he returned south he got a fine promotion—became a supreme-court judge or something like that. One night at a banquet in his honor he looked very sad, and when he rose to speak he said, 'Gentlemen, tomorrow the first sunlight of the year will be seen on a certain Lapland hill. I can't stay here. I must beg to resign and go back.' And he came. I think I should feel that way."

He was silent for a few moments. As we drew into sight of the hotel he said, "You cannot imagine what it's like here in the valley at the end of January when it's time for the sun to come again. The people are quite mad. They speak only of the sun.

'Will it come?' 'Do you think it will come before time?' 'I think I saw signs yesterday.' 'We have only five days more now.' Talk, talk, talk. A nervousness in the air. And when it does come, it shines first only on the hills. 'Now, it is coming!' they cry, and run to tell everybody who is not watching. Everybody is quite mad with joy."

It was midnight when we reached Kolttaköngäs. The landing stage lay between the white hotel and the painted Russian church. The salmon-rose walls and the aquamarine-onion towers of the church were fantastic in the silvery dusk. A determined Englishman was still on the river hoping for a fish. A hatless Lapp boy was pulling hard at the oars.

"No luck yet?" I called through the stillness.

"No luck," he answered. "Think I'll give it up."

"When do you sleep?" I asked Reino, as I got out, apologetic for keeping him up so late.

"From now till four," he answered, smiling amiably. "Ah, it's quite enough. I catch up in the winter."

FAIRY-TALE TOWN

I had no salmon-fishing equipment, and the hotel had none to rent as I had expected. It was quite expensive to buy, and they could not afford to stock it, they said. So after breakfast the young woman who managed the hotel and whom the Lapps had received as a friend took us about. The morning was as gold as the midnight had been silver. The air was brisk and tonic. The rapids were indigo blue, the sky only two shades lighter. While a Lapp woman who kept the church keys was sent for, we waited in the graveyard where the humble wooden monuments were fenced off in rectangles among great natural boulders fit for an emperor's tomb. The custodian came picking her away among the graves, clanking her great iron keys and looking like something from a picture book. She was a dried-up little woman with a wasp waist and bright figured skirt of yellow and tomato red. A faded cotton rag was tied about her head and under her chin. So fragile she was that she looked as if a wind could blow her away like dandelion fluff. She bore the fine Russian name of Natalia Fedotoff. A sturdy, taffy-colored reindeer dog accompanied her like a shepherd protecting a lamb. He had the Finnish name of Hupi. He waited respectfully at the doors when we entered the church and the chapel.

The ornate church had been built in 1874 close by the simple brown log chapel that the monk Trifon had erected more than three and a half centuries ago. It was because of this miniature chapel that Kolttaköngäs was now part of Finland instead of Norway. When the international boundary was settled between Norway and Russia in 1826, the little valley about the chapel was included in Russian territory, although it lies on the west, or Norwegian, side of the river.

Both churches were seatless in the Greek Orthodox fashion, and their altars were a mass of gilt filigree, rosy madonnas, and tawdry saints in mediocre style. When I gave Natalia Fedotoff money to burn some candles, she took it shyly, smiling with such childish delight she almost showed her toothless gums.

The gentle Natalia was quite willing to pose for a picture, but she preferred to put on her proper tribal headdress to show she was married. We accompanied her to her house by the road. It was a one-room structure with a kind of entrance hall at the side. In the hallway two small, bloody fish lay on the floor waiting to be cooked for dinner, and a bowl of dirty water stood on a shelf that served as a washstand. We had to stoop to get through the doorway. Lapps build their doorways low because they are a short race, and for generations were used to stooping to get through a tent flap.

An unmade cot bed with ragged quilts and furs stood in the corner, and over it, hanging from nails in the wall, was a violin that belonged to one of Mrs. Fedotoff's five sons.

Natalia Fedotoff sat on a low chair with a six-inch square of cracked mirror on her knee. She took off her cotton kerchief and put on a high, stiff-wired yellow headdress. It was like the contraption the Czarina often wore when she wasn't adorned with the court jewels. Natalia regarded her lined parchment face in the glass, turned her head critically from side to side. Then she spit on her two fingers to wipe the loose hairs carefully from the nape of her neck. We smiled, and she laughed shyly at her own vanity.

When we thought she was all through with her primping, she carefully took up the faded cotton rag and placed it over the headdress and knotted it under her chin. There was little to see more than at first, except a bit of gold braid peeping from the head rag that was now reared high up in the air.

With her wool-lined moccasins turned up at the toes and looking three sizes too big, she posed before a reindeer sled by the side of the house.

"Where are the reindeer?" I asked, adjusting my camera.

The reindeer were in the mountains, the hotel director explained. They went to the high mountains in summer to avoid the mosquitoes. But the Koltta Lapps had very few—just enough to pull the sleds and furnish them with meat for themselves. There were only two cows among the sixty Lapp villagers. They mostly used canned milk. Most of the hay they raised they sold to the hotel.

The Finnish girl said they were grateful for the hotel, because the sportsmen who came meant money to them. Some of the Lapp girls were employed as kitchen maids. The Koltta Lapps had had a precarious existence before they came under Finland. Russia did not bother them, but she did not bother with them. If they died of starvation or disease like wild animals, Russia paid no attention. Now the children were sent to boarding school in Salmijärvi. They spoke Finnish besides Russian and Lappish and some Norwegian. The young men also had a bit of English they had picked up from rowing for the English fishermen.

But the hotel director sighed to think what it would be like when the bridge and road were finished. Cars would be coming —so many cars, she said, right through the Lapp village—noise and confusion. Before it was so quiet. "Before the tourists came," she added naïvely. The blessings of civilization were a bit mixed. The Lapps owned their tiny village all together. There were no deeds to the property. Each one just took whatever he seemed to need. The dividing fences served only to keep the animals out of the hay and potatoes. She was afraid the government would come and say, "Now you have that," and "This boundary is yours," and they might learn to quarrel over possessions. Now they never quarreled over what they owned. It was not in their nature to quarrel. They had ever turned the other cheek.

"And see what it got them," I said, as we wandered off. "They have been pushed almost out of existence into the Arctic Ocean."

We stood on the hill overlooking the whole Lapp settlement. An old woman was working with her husband in the nearest field. Her full skirts were tucked up to her knees. She raked with vigor, swishing her skirt violently like a ballet dancer. She regarded us hostilely, for I had my camera in hand; but her husband, who was piling the hay on a rack, smiled up at us friendly-wise. A young man was nailing boards on one of his outhouses, which stood on a chicken-leg foundation. A fisherman was squatting on the ground mending his net. Everything was makeshift, pieced together, irregular, and memorably picturesque.

"But it's the kind of patchwork poverty," I said to Therese, "that lends a certain charm to the Negro cabins of the South."

"It's like a fairy tale, too," she said. "Such little huts, such small patches of hay, such tiny people. Like a miniature of something created and set up for the delectation of a fanciful child. There's something so unreal about it—as though Hans Andersen might have imagined the whole thing and it wasn't really here."

We did not dream then that within four months the fires of war would have reduced the village to embers, and the Lapps would be fleeing over the hill through the little wooden gate into Norway, driving their flock of sheep and two cows before them, carrying their ikons and whatever household goods they had time to snatch.

A young Lapp woman in a tailored skirt of gray wool and a yellow cotton shirtwaist came out to tether a calf to the hodgepodge fence about her potato patch. The hotel director knew her well. We went down to meet her. The woman was friendly and smiled. She was rather good-looking, with strange, great gray eyes, but most of her front teeth were already gone. She asked us into her house. In contrast to the gentle church custodian's, this one-room house was clean as a pin. Newspapers lined the wall, where bright copper utensils hung. A samovar shone on a shelf. We sat on a wooden bench that would be a fur-covered bed in winter. The young woman sat in the only chair. Sunlight streamed in the one window over a struggling yellow calendula in a pot and a brindled kitten that sat by it catching at flies. Wool-lined baby boots hung from a rafter.

"Your baby's?" Therese asked.

The young woman looked slightly embarrassed. She wore no married woman's headdress.

"She has a little girl, but no husband," the hotel director said in English, which the Lapp woman did not understand. "But moral irregularities are most unusual among the Lapps," she added.

We changed the subject. Therese got up to show interest in a hand-sewing machine, which explained the tailored skirt and waist. I admired the brass samovar and picked up a small ikon from among several others on the shelf beside it. I held it in my hand, looking at it. It was a triptych in deep blue enamel on bronze, and beautifully wrought. In bas-relief Christ was healing the sick.

"Ask her," I said to the Finnish girl, "since she has so many ikons, if she could possibly sell me this one. I've taken a great fancy to it. I'd like to keep it as a remembrance of Kolttaköngäs—if she has no special attachment to it."

The Finnish girl interpreted. The Lapp woman was quite still.

"I will pay her well," I said.

The Lapp woman looked at me with her strange gray eyes steadily for a moment. Her face was thoughtful and sad in the window-filtered sunlight. Then she said quietly, "No one has enough money to buy that. You see, it is a picture of God."

We had an early supper that evening and began to walk leisurely to the bridge to take the bus for Liinahamari. (Our bags had gone on by horsecart.) The little Lapps were busy at their evening tasks—moving about like marionettes—raking hay, tending sheep, washing bottles before the one-room lemonade factory. The young woman who prized the ikon was leaning on a rake laughing with a young Finn.

There was a great naturalness about it all and a timelessness like that in Hardy's poem beginning "Only a man harrowing clods." I quoted aloud the last stanza:

Yonder a maid and her wight
  Come whispering by;
War's annals will fade into night
  Ere their story die.

Bells tinkled about necks of the horses grazing among the birches by the water. Mewing seagulls wheeled above the rapids. The evening air was cool and sweet. At the bridge we took a long, last, affectionate look at the fantastic but strangely simple place. We did not need to take away the Lapp girl's picture of God to remember the village. For the picture of Kolttaköngäs would remain in a special niche of our memories forever.

MONK GOLDILOCKS

To get to Liinahamari we had to return to Salmijärvi and change to the direct Post Bus that left there at nine. From Salmijärvi to the harbor of Liinahamari, the distance was 79 kilometers. On the maps Finland's narrow corridor to the Arctic Ocean extends between Norway and Russia like an arm upraised to protect the slender Norway from the gross Eastern empire. The road wound through open spaces and marshlands. The birch trees, crouching close to the ground from their lifelong battle with winds, were gnarled and twisted like old apple trees in abandoned orchards. Snow shields, tall as billboards, built of slanting planks, stood on either side of the roadway at strategic places to defend the road against winter snows. Evening mists rising here and there from the lowland pools suggested an army bivouacking in the swamps.

For miles there was no habitation. And just when we might have expected a more complete arctic desolation we came into a region of well-tended meadows. At a group of houses that looked like both school and farm, the bus stopped and a young woman with three little boys ranging in age from six to three prepared to get off. The little boys' eyes were big with inner excitement as the woman straightened the caps on their yellow heads and adjusted their collars. She glanced at the buildings questioningly and then turned a caressing smile of reassurance on the big-eyed youngsters. The postboy helped them out.

"It's an orphan asylum," a Finn explained. "She's not their mother. She's just taking them there."

The woman walked ahead with a suitcase. The three manly little shavers walked behind, each carrying his bundle of clothes. The door opened and a woman appeared to receive them. Well, we knew they would meet kindness there and get good schooling and doubtless grow into husky men, and do their mighty bit in the upbuilding of Lapland.

In half an hour or so we saw to the right down a branch road the onion domes of the church belonging to the most northern monastery in the world. Then we drove into the yard of the red inn and post station of Yläluostari.

Before the inn steps towering above the crowd about him stood a black-gowned man with a golden beard and golden curls rippling over his shoulders. His hands were folded statuelike into the breast of his robes. Therese gasped. Was there no limit to the unexpected in Lapland?

As the last passenger collected his parcels and left the bus, the monk detached himself swiftly from the group. He jumped into the bus and slid into a vacated seat in front of Therese, as if he were afraid he might not get a place. After he got settled he became fearful lest he might have taken the seat of someone who had just stopped off for coffee. He quivered nervously and turned to us appealing for help. He twisted his tongue to Finnish, Russian, Polish, and Swedish. We indicated in English and a few Swedish phrases that he might stay where he was. He was grateful, and his expression full of apology for not speaking English.

"He's downright pretty," Therese said, staring at the gold hair streaming down his broad shoulders from under the black velvet cap, high and narrow like a Mohammedan fez. "I'm sure he gives his hair a hundred strokes a day." His beard was a full Van Dyck, as golden and silky as the hair, and his features were chiseled like a matinée idol's. The women in the bus became patently or surreptitiously excited. The back seat, full of noisy camp girls, became suddenly silent as they gazed at the handsome monk with awed admiration and then began to whisper. The monk couldn't keep his eyes off them. He twisted about with eager, almost girlish, movements to get better looks at them.

"Poor thing," Therese said. "A monk and so beautiful."

I supposed of course he was a Russian, but a Finn who spoke English said he was a Finnish convert, that he had come a year ago from the great monastery at Valamo in Lake Laatokka. It didn't make sense—a tall, strong-bodied Finn with girlish ways and prettiness. "The monks got him young, when he was an orphan at their school," the man added. Apparently he was known in the district and was a sensation wherever he appeared.

He did not remain in the bus long. Seventeen kilometers ahead at Parkkina, the most densely populated town in Petsamo, he got out at a pink church with green bulbous towers. He stood like a statue again, straight and tall with arms folded impressively, as a parishioner came forward to meet him.

The Finn who spoke English said the gold monk was a legend wherever he appeared. There was a rumor that he had been sent from the rich Valamo monastery to the poor arctic monastery of Yläluostari as punishment for an escapade. To a masked ball at

Viipuri he had gone as a guest disguised as a monk, and he had danced and been a sensation. The unmasking had come before he expected it, and it was discovered he really was a monk.

"Those Russians!" the Finn said contemptuously. "Dirty people. You should see how those monks keep that monastery. The smell is awful. They never bathe. They raise cows and try to have a dairy, but they are so filthy no one would dare buy their milk. Of course they're old now—all except that one young Finn—and they can't work much. But if they can get up at two o'clock in the morning and go to prayers in an unheated church, they could take a few *saunas* and wash out their cowsheds and milkpails."

Between Yläluostari and our journey's end was a string of new villages with functionalist co-operative shops and schools. At Alaluostari, the administrative center of Petsamo, were the frontier guards' barracks, the district attorney's residence, the hospital, a row of up-to-date shops, and a substantial jail with a maximum capacity for seven malefactors in a district of ten thousand square kilometers. But at the town's edges and along the way between the villages were some miserable-looking turf and board huts. By some of the huts fish nets were spread and fishheads were drying, to be used for sheep food in the winter.

It was eleven o'clock when we got into the modernistic hotel in Liinahamari. The lobby sitting room and dining room were crowded and full of the chatter of a seaport and a tourist center. Before I got into bed I took a long look out the north window to the granite-walled fjord that opened out into the Arctic Ocean. By the faint light it looked as impressively grand and still as it must have in the nights when the first Vikings anchored their high-prowed ships in the bay.

DAISIES ON THE ROOFS

Liinahamari, like Rovaniemi and Salmijärvi, was obviously teeming with future. Seventy trucks were lined up on the harbor front road, one behind the other, close as the segments of a backbone. Supplies for constructing the new hydro-electric plant and for building the model mining village at Kolosjoki, fifty miles behind us, came through Liinahamari. The products of the Petsamo Nickel Company would go out to the world through Liinahamari. Dredgers were further deepening the deep-water harbor, so that quantities of the ships of great tonnage could find anchorage at the same time. Trawlers from Italy, Spain, and Africa, having discharged their cargoes of olive oil, fruits, and vegetables, were loading up with salted cod. The fish-meal factory was temporarily closed—business had been so good the stock was entirely sold out. Though already prepared to handle seventy tons of herring daily, the fish-packing plant was extending its warehouses. The whole semicircular water front was in a state of building, or of blasting earth in preparation for building.

Captain Haikola, the harbormaster, spread blueprints and architectural drawings over his office table to indicate the future Liinahamari that the new prosperity would bring about. It was a beautiful layout, with the residential streets winding charmingly as in an English village instead of being a hopscotch pattern of right angles as in an American mid-western town. There were to be parks about the schools and hospital and library. And before all the public and administrative buildings was to be space for planting. In this protected spot, warmed by the Gulf Stream, shrubs and flowers and birch trees grew well. A garden city on the Arctic Ocean—this the landscape gardener had planned.

In Liinahamari as everywhere in the New Finland there was plan, a striving for order and harmony. Each citizen had to submit his plans and his color scheme to a committee before proceeding to build or paint. These independent Finns at the edge of the Arctic had no patience with an individualism that might spoil the beauty of their town.

Captain Haikola took us out on his boat to visit coves of industry on the ocean. With us came the manager of a cod-liver-oil factory and the three Oxford students, who turned up cheerily at the psychological moment. The sun was strong and golden and the water blue like the Gulf of Mexico, but a cold wind was blowing. We sat all together on the bow deck on robes made from reindeer faces. The cheek of the reindeer is the softest, silkiest part of the hide, and by far the most costly.

"The wind is always cold here," said Captain Haikola, who wore no topcoat, "and it blows constantly winter and summer." He sounded slightly bitter, and he had an air of resignation as though tied to something against his will. He was tall and thin, with strange hazel eyes. An attractive fellow, as distinctive as a character in a Conrad novel.

"The winters must be hard," Therese said sympathetically.

"They are hard," he said, "because of the wind and damp—though we rarely have snow before December. Often there is snow in Helsinki seven hundred miles south before we get it here."

"But the long dark days—" Therese suggested.

"No," he said quickly, "the dark isn't bad." He looked off—his strange seaman's eyes peering into the distance. Then, coming back to reality, he turned to her and said gently, as if explaining to a child something he did not expect it to understand, "The dark isn't bad. We work as on ordinary days and we read much. But once you know its spell, you can't be happy anywhere else.

Two years ago I thought I couldn't stand it any more. I asked to be sent South. They sent me. I had a good post and life was easier, much easier, and better for the health of my wife and child. But I couldn't stand it. I wasn't happy. I asked to be sent back here." He paused—he had read Therese's thoughts. "My wife, she felt the same. Though it was better for our little son there, we had to come back."

He stopped suddenly and went to give an order to the pilot.

So that was the harbormaster's resignation—tied to the fascination of darkness and light, of cold and wind and sea, just as Reino the boatman was enthralled by the peace of it. When Captain Haikola came back, he said—again as if reading our thoughts—"Besides, there's so much to be done. We've only just started in making a new country up here."

Seven miles from Liinahamari we turned from the ocean into a little harbor sheltered by gray rocks with racks for drying cod and stockfish. Here the blue sea washed gently against a white sand beach. Turf-walled huts and log cabins belonging to fishermen were scattered in the deep green grass like occasional mushrooms. White daisies grew in tall clumps on the sod roofs of the houses. We climbed a makeshift ladder up to the deserted pier. There was no one in the factory or in the huts now—the season's work was over. Again that feeling of unreality came over us as if we were looking at something that existed only in fancy.

But the grass was real grass, thick and deep. Belled horses had come the seven miles over the spine of bare rock cliffs to graze at the edge of the Arctic Ocean. Buttercups and bluebells bloomed as naturally as on a Devon meadow. Anemones were scattered like stars through the grass. Wild shredded carnations, fragrant as spice pinks, grew bounteously. The Oxford boys jumped from boulder to boulder over the lush grass like happy young goats. One of them—the one who was president of the

Young Socialists of Oxford—dug up wild-flower plants and wrapped them in moss to send to his mother for her Yorkshire garden.

We climbed the hill to a chapel built by fishermen. It stood on high rocks, a poor thing of brown-stained boards, its metal cross silhouetted against the northern sky like an everlasting petition to the winds. Before us lay the whole expanse of the ocean. Directly north of where we stood there was no more land between us and the North Pole.

Back on the boat we followed close to the shore for some distance, and passed another half moon of white beach backed by jade-green hills. The water before the beach was intense aquamarine. I had seen precisely that setting before—in Bermuda.

We came out into the open Arctic and started for the western shore of the Rybachi Peninsula, which projected from the mainland—half Finnish, half Russian. The waves dashed spray in our faces, and we licked Arctic salt off our lips. We chugged among the bare rocky islands where vast communities of seabirds made their home: gulls, guillemots, and puffins. Of their own free will—like the men who got Lapp fever—they chose to live exposed to the everlasting punishment of the elements.

After an hour in the open sea we wound into a fjord and thence to a protected bottle-necked cove. It was called Paitahamina, which means Shirt Harbor, because this was the only place on the Arctic coast where sailors could undress down to their shirts and be assured no sudden storm might wreck their vessel before they could get dressed.

Beyond the pier a large warehouse was stacked to the roof beams with bales of dried codfish to be shipped to ports in the seven seas. One great room was filled with little cod, not considered good enough for sophisticated trade, but much in demand with the Negroes of western Africa. "The savages make very profitable customers," the fish-oil manufacturer said. "But of course our chief customers are the Roman Catholic Latin nations, who must have their Friday fish."

Along the slope that rose from the beach, wooden racks extended to the sheer mountainous wall at the east. The racks were strung with drying fish like those we had seen in Hammerfest, Norway. In the strong sunlight they looked like long bronzed gloves drying after being dyed. In the patterned shade of a thousand stockfish three magnificent reindeer were resting under the racks enjoying shelter from too much sun, like Turkish *effendi* under their own grape arbors.

As I approached to take their picture, the great-antlered creatures started up and ran along the beach, silhouetted against the blue bay. We watched them until they began to climb the rocky hill, beyond which lay Russia. These three reindeer had been coming for four summers now to rest in the shade of the fish racks. They were quite as much at home in one country as in the other.

"Too bad men can't be as international as animals," said the Oxford student who was studying medicine.

"Does England think there will be war?" the fish-oil director asked, after we had got back in the boat and started for Liinahamari.

"Of course we hope not," the medical student answered. "If we could get a decent treaty with Russia, it might stop Hitler. But something's *got* to stop him."

"I thought you were Socialists and didn't believe in fighting to maintain your Empire," I said.

"We don't give a fig for the Empire. But we've got to have our freedom. We couldn't live under a Hitler, bottled up and suppressed like German boys we saw in Germany this summer."

"Yes, it's *freedom* we'd be fighting for," interposed the president of the Oxford Socialists. "What's an empire? We've got the greatest empire in the world, yet after seeing these Northern Countries and comparing them with our city slums and a lot of rotten conditions in general, I'm almost ashamed of being an Englishman. Look at this little country. Finland's been an independent nation only twenty years, yet look what it's doing for its people."

"It's blessed in not having had much culture or money in the past," said the red-headed student, whose father was a millionaire wool importer. "The population didn't have to break through all that class distinction and a sentimental clinging to old things. I was talking to a Finnish girl who'd been to Cambridge on a scholarship. She was amazed at the dampness and coldness of some of the rooms and the evil-smelling drains. 'It's not healthy nor sanitary for people to be in such places,' she said. 'Why don't you tear the buildings down and build new ones?' Just like that. She had no patience with such sentimental nonsense as living in discomfort to preserve some old relic."

We all laughed.

"Tearing down a building at Oxford or Cambridge would be a bit radical even for a socialistic England," the medical student said.

Cold spray began dashing over the bows again, and we had to move down and sit in a close-huddled group against the pilot box.

"But," said the president of the Socialists, pulling his battered old raincoat high up about his neck, "England has got to break away from her feudal ideas of keeping the lower orders in their places. The world has grown beyond that sort of foolishness. At Oxford the idle rich sons with their special valets and exaggerated accents are very much discredited now. Most of the good professors are Socialists, and the students are leaving the university with a clearer understanding of the necessity for England's future."

"On the other hand, present-day Finland already is the future," the son of the wool importer said. "When dear old England can get herself and her people in the healthful state of this little Finnish republic, she'll deserve an Empire."

Captain Haikola stood listening with mild surprise to English youth talk. "I suppose we've done pretty well with what we have," he said at length. "And undoubtedly our government is ruled by men of integrity and judgment. One thing I can certainly say: a Finn is not a profiteer in political life, and our men don't sit down to make a parasitical living on the stock exchange. But we are not a rich country—we can never be. And we have the misfortune to have a one-commodity economy—wood. Our export is dependent on world conditions. Right now we are at the height of our prosperity, which must seem a small thing indeed to rich British and American eyes. We try to distribute what we have so that all can share to some extent. But we are poor. I am a civil servant, the harbormaster for a port of growing importance—my salary is seventy-five dollars a month."

The English boys whistled with surprise.

"I don't want to dampen your enthusiasm," Haikola went on, "but I want you to think over what it would mean to live within the confines of your own country, before you throw away your Empire. Besides, beyond those rocks over there lies Russia. Russia has been watching this development in this ice-free harbor. Liinahamari has a special strategic military value—perfect for a submarine base. We don't want to fight—but like you, we may have to, to preserve our freedom. Like you, geographically we have some natural protection, in our network of lakes and marshes in summer and in the snows and terrible cold of winter; but we have no great fleet as you have, no formidable air force, no gold reserves—no allies. I'm not trying to discredit your admiration, but I want you to see us for what we are—a simple land, an almost defenseless people."

We all sat silent. We had been pleasurably excited by the plans for the future, the blueprints for a model town, the teeming port of Liinahamari, the fishing industries in the white sandy coves on the Arctic where flowers bloomed in the grass and daisies flourished on the sod roofs of huts. The Oxford boys looked grave. What could be made of a future without security? Without some international protection could this civilization go on?

"Tell them that in England," Captain Haikola said. "Tell them our danger in America."

HOSPITAL WITH SUN BALCONIES

THESE PRETTY GIRLS WERE HELPING TO BUILD OLYMPIC VILLAGE INTENDED TO HOUSE VISITING ATHLETES IN 1940

Heat Wave in the Arctic

THE NICKEL MINES

On our return journey when we stopped at Salmijärvi, where the director's car came to fetch us to the nickel mines at Kolosjoki, it was so warm men were going about in shirtsleeves and boys were swimming naked in the lake. At the door of the modernistic clubhouse at Kolosjoki the thermometer stood at 93 degrees in the sun. It was to touch fifty-four below zero in January 1940. In the private dining room where we lunched with Ivor Simcox, the Montana-born director, the temperature was seventy-seven. The sun lamps which the company had provided in the municipal bathhouses to give the workers beneficial ultraviolet rays in the sunless winter seemed a quixotic thoughtfulness.

Kolosjoki was still in the process of building to make a perfection of workers' living conditions. What was not already completed in the way of school and apartment buildings and landscape gardening, I saw on blueprints just as I had at Liinahamari. But here the work was three-fourths done. Kolosjoki in the Petsamo fells, less than fifty miles by crow flight from the Arctic Ocean, was to be a model mining town. Human considerations in comfort and attractiveness were the first dividends to be paid from the mineral rights.

Besides the gymnasium, the athletic fields, amusement hall for movies and amateur plays, and *saunas* with sun lamps, the management had provided public washhouses with electric driers and washing machines so that the workers' wives would not suffer the distress Finnish women often experience when doing the family wash in winter.

The apartments of the workers we visited were neatly and pleasantly furnished, and invariably potted flowers grew on the ledges of muslin-curtained windows. The cooking, dishwashing, and garbage riddance arrangements had all been designed to save housewives inconvenience and give them leisure for that self-improvement which Finns and Scandinavians make so much of.

We look back now on all these evidences of consideration for the Finnish proletariat and think of Red Russia's rallying battle cry to deliver the Finnish slave workers from the dog-hearted capitalistic oppression. We think of the sad and lowly condition of Russia's subnormal masses, of vermin and torn towels and muddleheaded inefficiency in Leningrad's better hotels. Because of the Reds' pious mission, the comfort of Kolosjoki was shortly turned to fire-blackened, windowless walls, slashed by arctic winds. Its happy, well-housed workers became homeless refugees, or frostbitten soldiers, or mere idle corpses, frozen and useless to the world's good.

Except for fishermens' huts, occasional Lapp villages, a Greek Orthodox monastery, and a few onion-domed churches, Petsamo had been a roadless wasteland. Now with roads and bridges, the developed nickel mines, the electric power station, schools, hospitals, modern hotels, and towns planned by first-rate architects and landscape gardeners, Petsamo was a living testimony to what could be done to bring prosperity to a forbidding region.

THE MINISTER'S WORK AT INARI

When we got back to Ivalo the next night, the arctic heat wave had not abated. It was so warm in our bedroom I thought the steam heat was on. We went to sleep with only a sheet for covering. The next morning when I slipped out, leaving Therese sleeping, and took the seven o'clock mail bus for Inari, it was already quite warm.

All the tourist hotels in Lapland seemed to be run with love, but at the Inn at Inari there was a special atmosphere that made it the favorite with tourists who knew all Lapland. In the center of reindeer country, it was the most typically Finnish of them all, a wooded retreat twenty-five miles from the highway, deep in the forest beside a wild and rocky stream.

In the attractively furnished red log house the fourteen rooms were provided with hot and cold running water, and two pet reindeer fawns wandered about the drawing room like the most honored guests. Even into the dining room the fawns, against orders, sometimes stole. Tourists fed them delicacies and wiped their fingers on the soft furred muzzles.

In the yard a special help-yourself hostelry had been constructed for the Lapps. Bunk beds were built about the walls and provided with bearskins. Stoves and utensils for cooking their home-packed food were furnished, and silverware, china, and even racks for drying their mittens. Doors were never locked. Lapp guests were free to come and go and cook and sleep as they pleased. Here they stayed when they came for their semiannual marriages and christenings at the Lutheran church. Here they stopped for a night or a hot meal on their way to round up their reindeer herds or to take a seasonal job somewhere or to shop at the Ivalo co-operative. Because they were such good friends and helpful neighbors, the Inn charged nothing for the use of its house, but merely asked that the Lapps leave everything spick and span, to gather wood and draw water for the next comers.

The lady manager of the Inn took me to see the minister at the village a mile away. One of the fawns came with us, trotting along as naturally as the black Scotty, but a bit uncertain of his first antlers, which were still tender to the touch. The Scotty got chased by four of the minister's white cows all at once. The fawn did not like excitement and returned to the more civilized atmosphere of the tourist inn in the forest. As he trotted away, the upstanding white splotch of undertail was as distinctive as the black tip on the white tail of an ermine. "It's a light to guide them in the dark winter days," the lady said, "when they are following the leader."

Like the bear-killer farmer of Rovaniemi, the minister of Inari specialized in fuchsias. His veranda vestibule was a conservatory, and in the drawing room two sixteen-year-old plants were more than five feet tall. They were heavily blossomed with a tropical luxuriance. Six-year-old ivy made draperies over the inner windows, and in the center of the room, hanging from a basket like a chandelier, was a cactus with one spectacular, rich red blossom. "The first time a cactus has been known to bloom above the Arctic Circle," the minister said with gratification.

Like a European in Tahiti, the minister wore only a pair of trousers with braces and an undershirt and slippers. His comely wife and the two Lapp maids were barefooted, and his two little boys wore nothing but green shorts. The drawing room was furnished in white-painted wicker, as if it had been in Barbados, and for summer carpets six long strips of white dish toweling were stretched tight across the red shining floor.

Besides being a successful farmer, the minister was a specialist in Lappish language and dialects. When we called he was in his study translating a volume of Lapp poems into Finnish. The poems were written by a Finnish Lapp named Pedar Jalvi. The first four titles in their English equivalent were *Snowflakes, Wave on the Lake in Autumn, The Funeral Bell, To My Little Son*. The minister read some of the verses in Finnish, and the inn manager translated them to me in English. The verses were all about simple, universal things, and charming and full of feeling. One the poet himself especially liked was called *I Ran Toward a Sound*. It was about a man so in love that everything in nature reminded him of his beloved. He heard the cuckoo call, and he ran toward it because he thought it was the voice of his sweetheart.

Like Michael Agricola, who made the first Finnish ABC book in the sixteenth century, the minister had published an ABC book in Lappish. Foreigners who wanted to learn Lappish, as well as Lapp children, used the book. It had gone into several printings. Sometimes the minister preached his sermons in Lappish, for there were eight hundred Lapps in his district. There were only three ministers north of Rovaniemi and the Arctic Circle—in a territory the size of Hungary—and all three of them had to know Lapp.

The Lutheran Inari Lapps were far better off than the Greek Orthodox Koltta Lapps. Some of them owned reindeer herds worth 200,000 marks. The minister estimated there were altogether 200,000 reindeer in Finnish Lapland. Reindeer meat, the staple food of the Lapps, was considered a *délicatesse* in Helsinki, Stockholm, London. In Helsinki, where other meat was cheap, reindeer meat cost as much as eighty cents a pound. A fairly young and tender reindeer would bring twenty dollars or more.

In reindeer culture and economy the Lapps were co-operative.

The smaller reindeer owners found it convenient to add their few to larger herds and to let experienced watchers and dogs look after them. All reindeer owners were registered in reindeer associations and paid so much per head for grazing rights in the state lands and for any damage to farmers' crops.

The minister said I should be there for calving time to see Lapland in the height of activity. The excitement begins about the middle of May. The hinds are tethered to trees before the calving, so that the owners will be able to identify their offspring. Watchers are busy everywhere. The moment the young is cast, men must be ready to tag the ear, else it might stray off and be claimed by some other owner. The special mark of the owner is cut on the margin of the ear, and the markings are registered, copyrighted like a trade-mark, with the association.

St. Erik's Day, May eighteenth, is the favorite day for the birthings. In the forests it is the busiest day of the year. Men, dogs, reindeer—all busy. The dogs run about like excited midwives as the men rush from hind to hind. There is no more privacy for a reindeer at birthing time than there was for French queens before Marie Antoinette's almost fatal accouchement.

"A stolen reindeer," the minister said, "can be recognized by the mark on the ears, as a criminal can be by his thumbprint. The penalty for stealing a reindeer is two or three years' imprisonment. But though very few are ever stolen, it is the one crime in Finland that doesn't carry a serious stigma with it."

The Lapp utilizes every part of the reindeer. The skins make coats and bed coverings; the horns they carve into knife handles. Since time immemorial the Lapps' existence has depended on the reindeer. These furnish not only their food but are their beasts of burden and constant companions. The reindeer are to Lapps what the llamas are to Indians of the high plateaus of Peru.

Reindeer, like the llamas, are most economical beasts to own—they get their own living. They feed on grass in summer and in winter on arctic moss. They can scent the moss and root it out even when it is buried in three feet of snow.

"Of course, the Lapps may disappear," the minister said in answer to a question. "There are less than twenty-five hundred of them left in Finland. And they are becoming more like Finns in many ways. When they make money and build themselves good houses, they often begin to call themselves Finns."

We went out to see the minister's garden—or rather his wife's garden. "Women do the gardening," he said. "The man looks after the fields." His wife took care of the flowers; the Lapp girls worked the vegetables.

The flower garden was in full bloom. Except that the roses grew in tubs, it might have been a June garden in Virginia, with spring flowers and summer flowers blooming at the same time. There were sweet peas, nasturtiums, cornflowers, red double poppies, California poppies, daisies, pansies, zinnias, and clarkia.

In the vegetable garden they raised all that the family needed for summer and winter. They got in three plantings of lettuce and radishes. From a few short rows they pulled 140 pounds of carrots. A cultivated acre produced 30,000 pounds of Irish potatoes. "Potatoes make the best sort of winter cowfeed," the minister said.

For his six white cows he raised all the hay and sold what they did not need. Here was a self-contained farm, which lay in sub-zero weather seven months of the year. Here was a useful minister of the gospel, who served his fellow man, made his happy family a comfortable living, kept the common touch by working his own fields, and yet saved plenty of hours for his scholarly and linguistic inclinations.

"And the peace of it all!" said the minister's wife, who had been brought up in Helsinki and educated at the university. "Pity not those who live in the wilds of Lapland."

RETURN TO ROVANIEMI

The Arctic heat wave had not abated when we took the eight-hour bus ride from Ivalo back to Rovaniemi. It was really hot, and the heat added to the discomfort of springless seats and dusty road. But the Finns of Lapland were happy in their abundance of warmth. In almost every stream children were bathing. Tots ran naked about the stacks of hay in the fields, where bronzed-skinned men worked stripped to the waist. In almost every settlement boys were practicing pole-vaulting or hurling homemade javelins.

But despite the heat and the monotony of returning by the same road, we were content with the day and our remembrances, except for an encounter that was disturbing.

A group of German boys in shorts, with heavy rucksacks, traveled on an extra bus close behind us. I had seen them at Liinahamari and felt rather sorry for them, for they seemed more or less set apart in a hostile world. The Oxford students had tried to be friendly there, but had been repelled with a formal politeness. The boys were not allowed to speak with strangers unless their tutor permitted. At one of the stops I spoke to the tutor, and soon the whole crowd gathered around us.

They were nice-looking boys ranging in age from fourteen to seventeen—Prussians from well-to-do families, students in an upper-class preparatory school. Every one of them was studying to be an aviation officer. They all lived in East Prussia—not far from Danzig, they said, with a kind of challenge, seasoned with contempt. Two of the youths already flew planes solo; they pointed to badges on their shirts to prove it. And although all of them somehow gave the impression of itching to get into the air to drop a load of bombs, I smilingly took a picture of the group.

There was a polite air of friendliness all around now, until I suggested that there might be happier outlets for their talents than handling bombers. "If all your best young men take to the air," I said amiably, "what future can there be for your good countrymen on the ground?"

They became silent, looked at me suspiciously, and began to draw away even though the bus driver had not honked his "all-aboard." I had cast aspersions at what they had been trained to believe was the noblest of professions.

Later at another stop, when we halted for coffee and the passengers began to gather blueberries by the lake, we ran into a group of them. We spoke to them pleasantly, but got a cool response. They had quite done their duty in being polite to aliens. We were rather shocked at their hostile manner. It was alarming to see youths trained in arrogant self-sufficiency.

We began to wonder if their trip to inspect the Arctic coast and its ice-free harbor had been purely for vacation purposes. We remembered them pointing out this and that, making sweeping gestures, exchanging glances as if they were appraising everything they saw with an eye to future possession.

Back at the sparkling hotel at Rovaniemi, where we spent another night and day before returning south, we sat on the terrace having after-dinner coffee and savoring the experiences of the crowded days that had passed.

It is difficult to explain the spell of Finnish Lapland—and photographs do it a sorry injustice, except in winter months when snow covers its naked reality like a cloak of ermine. It is not what is seen that is memorable, but what is felt—the fascination of a mood. Out of simple things like illimitable forests, wild and barren fells, and lonely smoke-gray cabins squatting by secluded lakes, is distilled a lingering essence. And here in summer the strange light of evening may cast a spell of unreality over a scene that in the white glare of noon reveals nothing but stark infertility. Under a twilight illumination the monotonous rounds of fells are transformed into a solemn and matchless beauty.

On those clear summer nights, when the light comes from somewhere underneath the horizon, wiping out all outlines and depriving everything of its shadow, the familiar forest becomes enchanted. One's sense of vision is upset, for he cannot tell whether that yellow line stretching across the north is sunset or sunrise. In fact, it is both. And he hears the mighty night cry of a water bird mingling with the lark's greeting to the day.

There is a constant activity in this region of infinite space and timelessness—where men and women wrest a livelihood for the day and for the savage winter that always comes so early and stays so late. Inconspicuous tracks leading off into the maze of forest tell of other people farther in the depths, clearing meadows amid century-old spruces. Pioneers are breaking more and more of the Lapland earth into clods and "digging eternal graves for the bilberry bushes."

New heroes and heroines of colonization are giving all they possess to push civilization deeper into the forests. Their hearts, impregnated with a love of land and yearning for independence and a home of their own, have accepted the grim challenge of the wilderness. They have schooled themselves for contention with virtually every obstacle that nature can put in man's way. And the supreme lesson to be learned from their way of meeting life is that poverty need not be sordid.

Again and again, strange as it may seem, parts of Lapland had reminded us of the pine-woods regions of the Deep South. After a doze in the bus, when we opened our eyes, we would seem to be looking at rural Mississippi or Alabama. The dry woods, the unpaved roads, the goldenrod by the ditches, the unpainted cabins with the little potato patches, looked like the backwoods at home. The difference lay in the faces of the people. Here was no apathy, no hopelessness, no sloth. In the poorest region there was nothing akin to the spiritual degradation of *Tobacco Road*. Everything, however meager, was tidy and in repair. The attitude of mind was right, it was independent and self-reliant.

A Swede who knew Finnish Lapland well said to me, "Where penury makes some people mean, it makes Finns more willing to help others in greater distress than themselves." And penury didn't seem penury where almost every small farm had at least one cow, where each family raised enough potatoes and root vegetables for its own use. The Lapland farmers managed to feed themselves and their beasts largely from their own place, and to supply the rest of their family needs they worked in the forests in winter.

One felt so strongly in Lapland the cheerful independence of individual man. Of course, all struggled alike to live. Whether a man had many reindeer or few, great fields of hay or only small patches, he had to work. There were no lazy loafers lolling in the shade or the sun. Nor was there any upper class to make one man feel inferior to another. All men under the Lapland sky had an even enough chance to prove themselves. And they knew they must make themselves content with modest living in a region where nature and climate will play stern roles throughout eternity. The vapory wastes of fells and swamps, the reluctant soil, the dark days of winter, and the burden of snow will ever put a curb on man's ambitions. But Lapland is a superlative school for turning the sons of Finns into Finns.

Stop-overs Among Industries

OULU

We wasted a night and a day going to Vaala to shoot the rapids in a tarboat. It was a heavily advertised tourist "must," but it wasn't half worth the bother. The industrial towns of Oulu and Tampere were far more rewarding.

A dapper young man with his English hat at an angle and a stick in his hand found us at the Oulu station and said the Governor of Lapland had asked him to show us about. He turned out to be an architectural engineer who had deisgned the cellulose mill the Prime Minister had been going to inspect when we met him on the first lap of our arctic journey.

Though its name reminded me of a Biskra hoochy-koochy dancer, Oulu was the capital of Ostrobothnia, that province noted for its sobriety, where black-clothed people of a religious sect called the Pietists went about bareheaded with fanatically zealous expressions. A trading post from medieval times, Oulu was completely rebuilt in 1822 by plans drawn up by the great Engel. It was once the center of the world's tar exporting, but it never recovered its tar trade after an English battleship destroyed its harbor warehouse and mercantile ships during the Crimean War. Although Oulu grew into an important industrial town in later decades, it preferred to speak of itself as a scholastic center. Three of Finland's most famous sons, Runeberg and Snellman and Topelius, the writer of fairy tales, all attended school in Oulu.

The engineer drove us up and down the town to let us see how Oulu had jumped a century in its architecture and retained an harmonious impression. The one- and two-story Doric wooden structures after Engel's plan in the 1820's fitted in happily with the new functionalist style.

Beyond flowering parks and promenades along the water, we came to the cellulose mill on Nuottasaari Island. It was an impressive pile of red brick with straight modern lines and a decorative square chimney shooting four hundred feet into the air. By elevator we shot up to the roof terrace and looked down the Oulu River to the Gulf of Bothnia. Before us the illuminated sky was flaming orange, the river burnished copper, the Gulf of Bothnia a distant streak of apple green.

Behind us from the ground rose mountainous piles of stacked wood. "A million dollars' worth," the engineer said. "Only enough to last for one year. The yards are full now—for we cannot get any more before next June, after the ice breaks."

The mill was losing money at this time, he added, because the world market price of brown paper was low, owing largely to recent expansion in pulp mills in the South of the United States.

I asked him how much the Finnish mills paid per cord. "About $10, counting cost of transportation." I compared the figure with the $3.50 to $5 the paper mills in the South paid for wood "delivered at the mill." I thought of our comparatively high cost of living and wondered why we Southerners were so simple.

"With the market prices of pulp the same, why are workers' wages here lower than those in Sweden?" I was asking as we watched the sunset.

"Because our cost of transportation is greater," the engineer replied promptly. With his cane he began lining diagrams on the roof's pavement, stained with the colors of the sunset. "In

Sweden, the rivers run down so—direct to the mills. In Finland, they run across—so—and are all intersected by lakes. We must pay men to guide the log floats, and often we have to transport the wood part of the way by train and truck."

Even in the way the rivers run Sweden had the natural advantage.

As we walked about the plant, the engineer commented on something Therese said in praise of living standards at the nickel mines in Petsamo. "Workers are often a pain in the neck," he declared. "They asked them up there what they wanted, because they are a foreign concern. We know our workers. We never ask. At the mill I built before this one, I put in fine showerbaths as I always do. The men had never seen showerbaths and they refused to use them. They preferred to go home dirty—the *sauna* on Saturday suited them. We finally made it a rule that no worker could leave the factory until he had taken a shower. We stationed a factory policeman at the exits to see that they did. Three months later, when something happened to the water supply, they refused to work, because they'd get dirty and couldn't take a shower. You have to know your own men."

We went to dine at his club. I had thought the young man was no more than thirty at most, despite his experience and his two years in America. But when he spoke of his school days—how he was forced to study Russian in 1908—I knew he was older. I heard more distinctly the faint clicking of his false teeth as he talked. He was forty and looked ten years younger. Holding to youth in Finland, I ruminated, comes from close contact with the outdoors and sports, but it doesn't seem to save the teeth.

"Germany is as great a danger as Russia to Finland," our host affirmed while we were drinking whisky and soda. "But the man in the street doesn't think so. He fears Russia, because he knows what it is to be under Russia. He doesn't know Germany and what it would be like to be under Germany." He paused to take a big swallow, and then went on: "The man in the street remembers that Germany helped us in our fight against the Reds in 1918. But he doesn't know we paid her a billion finnmarks in gold. Very few Finns do. And that we also had to agree to give her part control of our government. Of course, the Finnish people did not agree—they knew nothing of it—some of our diplomats made the bargain. Fortunately for us, Germany lost the war—else we would be under Germany's 'protection' right now. But the man in the street doesn't realize this." He took another swallow. "'It wasn't Finnish interests,' Ludendorff himself said, 'but purely German ones that took our troops to Finland.' We have paid our debt to Germany. We owe her nothing."

Returning to the subject of workers and their demands, the engineer revealed that it bored him. It was not up to the factory to build houses for its workers. The paper mill had no concern with where its employees lived. Oulu was a city and it was a city's business to house its people, not the factory's. If a factory were set up in the wilderness, that was a different matter—they had to build houses for the workers to get them to stay and work. Altogether he feared too much was being done for the workers. The white-collar-job men were the ones that needed assistance.

"But they won't organize," I said.

"No, thank God, not yet. But it's not for a noble reason. It's a class-consciousness—they feel to join a union would put them on a level with the laborers in the blue jumpers."

"How are living standards here—say, for an architectural engineer?" I asked with a grin.

"We have a ten-room apartment, keep two maids, maintain a car and a boat," he replied genially in clipped phrases.

"Not bad," I said.

"No, but this is Oulu, not Helsinki—and," he smiled broadly, "the boat is only a little fellow. We Finns are really rather easily satisfied, you know. I never could get used to my friends in America apologizing because a neighbor's boat was two feet longer than theirs. Honestly, we don't make a virtue of keeping up with the Joneses here—not even the most new rich."

At the station when we left for Tampere, he said, "You wouldn't live in Tampere, but I'll bet you'll praise it to everyone else and say you've never seen anything like it."

MODEL FOR AN INDUSTRIAL TOWN

The factory town of Tampere lies between two lakes on two sides of the Tammerkoski Rapids. Because it uses its water for power it is as clean as Garden City, Long Island, and it was built at a better period architecturally.

Founded by King Gustavus III of Sweden three years after the American Declaration of Independence, it received in 1819 a royal visitation from Czar Alexander I, who saw such possibilities in the place that he decreed factories here might import machinery and raw materials free. Though blessed with kingly godfathers, the real father of modern Tampere was a Glasgow-born machinist named James Finlayson. He moved from Moscow in 1820, the year after Alexander's visit, and set up a machine shop. In 1828, Finlayson's shop evolved into a cotton mill, and in the decades that followed, factory after factory was established in Tampere, until today the city has two hundred separate industries, which provide employment for three-fourths of its people. Tampere manufactures textiles, footwear, metalware, paper, and

THE ANCIENT CASTLE OF OLAF AT SAVONLINNA. IN THE RIGHT DISTANCE A SMOKESTACK OF MODERN INDUSTRY

THE SNOW-COVERED FELLS AT PALLASTUNTURI GLISTEN LIKE WHITE SAMITE

leather products. It has weaving mills and power stations, linen mills and locomotive shops.

The Scotch Finlayson who came from dirty Glasgow called Tampere "Finland's Manchester." But the English Manchester and Finnish Tampere are different as smoke and sunlight. The curses that lie on most industrial towns were taken off it in Tampere by promenades, tree-shaded boulevards, statues and gardens, waterside restaurants, municipal bathing beaches, and the blocks of white modern apartment buildings to house the workers. Some factories were surrounded by parks. Others spread their many-windowed buildings with the decorative chimney towers along the banks of the rapids. The bus station which looked like a vision of tomorrow was perhaps the most striking structure in Tampere. But one remembers the pavilion of the Nasijärvi Yacht Club and the old church by Engel and the State Airplane Factory and the murals of Hugo Sinberg in the cathedral.

Nothing was huddled or crowded or niggardly. There were spaciousness and light and open places. The harbor for lake steamers lay beside the market place. The water-divided city was spanned by graceful bridges, one adorned with sculptured figures by Väinö Aaltonen, a gift from an industrial magnate, Rafael Haarla. A goldsmith named Kustaa Kiekka gave an art collection with a building to house it. An industrialist named von Nottbeck left his villa on the rocks for a museum. A state theater and a workers' theater and an open-air theater, together with sports fields and swimming beaches and gifts of museums, were all there to relieve industrial fatigue.

If Tampere could have had these amenities for its proletariat in 1918, there would have been no war between Whites and Reds. Tampere was the site of the decisive battle in the so-called War of Independence, when the Red workers put up a stout and terrific resistance to General Mannerheim's White Guards. From the debris and blood of that battle rose the new Tampere—an industrial city unsurpassed for cleanliness and comeliness and convenience. Wisely, as soon as she was able, Finland saw to it that her laborers got a squarer deal. Yet there was no unpleasant feeling of paternalism in the place. Tampere seemed to belong to the worker, as if it all had been planned and developed by him.

"I can't help noticing," Therese said as the train pulled away from the station, "that the industrial centers with the best conditions seem to have been Reddest before the compromise between capital and labor."

PART THREE

"In my time I have seen many a cause that seemed hopeless carried through to triumph, and many a man, beaten to his knees, rise to prosper."

History

BRIEF TALE

When we got back to Helsinki I indulged, with the help of many Finnish friends of diverse political creeds, in a fortnight's intensive study of Finland's history, before we did any more traveling. I had read widely, if desultorily, in the subject during the previous year and had taken many notes, but there were gaps in my understanding. And now that I had observed daily life and landscape from the Gulf of Finland to the Arctic Ocean and had met a variety of people of varying views and sympathies, I was better prepared to make my own discounts. For Finnish historians are by no means of one mind, and the Swedish and British commentators each have their special bent.

To the ancient geographers Finland was the utmost northern limit of the world. They called it Ultima Thule. The early chapters of Finnish history are shrouded in unusual obscurity. Until the nineteenth century the chronicles of Finland recorded virtually nothing but the doings of Swedes living on Finnish soil. The Finns themselves had only a mythological or legendary account of their people which they preserved orally in poetry and song.

From the beginning of time, the Finns have been a mystery people. No one knows for sure just who they are or where they originated. The scholar and anthropologist cannot tell us anything with assurance. Some of the most reliable authorities believe them to have sprung from regions about the upper Volga and to have wandered westerly to the shores of the Gulfs of Finland and Riga. Others say they came from the northern slopes of the Himalayas. But the available facts reveal nothing of the earliest known Finns beyond the Baltic basin. If the Finnish language were not so radically different from the Scandinavian languages, the Finns might always have been accepted as true northern Europeans—as true as a world of mixed races permits. Today only the Estonians have the same language roots as the Finns and are their only existing relatives, with the probable exception of the Hungarians.

In the first century after Christ, Baltic Finns began going to the land now known as Finland to hunt and trap animals, for furs were a commodity always in demand. When these Finns arrived, they found the country sparsely settled by peace-loving nomadic Lapps. These gentle people they began to push up into the colder northern regions, as English settlers in the United States drove the red Indians westward. The Baltic Finns had a rudimentary knowledge of agriculture, and they cultivated land in the new country, as they needed it, by burning the surface growth and harrowing the earth with wooden-toothed harrows. They learned to do the needful things men must do in rigorous northern climates to survive. They built rude cabins and insulated them with moss and birch bark. They turned birch bark to a dozen other utilitarian uses—snowshoes, baskets, ropes. They used the plentiful wood for skis and sleds. They scooped out boats from tree trunks, fashioned juniper into household utensils. They also built bath huts, where they cleaned themselves in the intense steam that rose from water thrown on heated rocks—the custom of *sauna* that every Finn indulges in today. In the evenings they chanted folksongs to the accompaniment of a five-stringed zither, called a *kantele*.

The prelude to an association that was to bind Finland's destiny with Sweden for over six hundred years came between the years

1156 and 1160, when Erik Jedvarsson, King of Sweden, professed such a passionate devotion to Christianity that he felt impelled to undertake a crusade against Finland. On his holy mission he took with him a Scottish-born bishop named Henry to baptize the heathen, and to establish the Catholic Church for the benefit of the rude population. When the Scot was later murdered by a peasant, he was canonized, and the Finns were persuaded to accept this alien saint as their patron.

By 1216 the Pope himself had sanctioned the Swedish protectorate over Finland. And in this thirteenth century commenced the prolonged struggle between the Swedes and the Russians for dominance over the Finns. Finland as buffer state was to withstand the shock and horror of future war after war.

Except for the granting of large tracts of land to certain Swedish nobles, who established a kind of personal rule over parts of Finland, Sweden did not molest the Finns or make any serious effort at subjugating them. The Finns continued on in their wonted simple ways, yet became more and more under the influence of Sweden. In 1362 representatives of the Finnish people were granted the right of voting in the election of Swedish kings, and Finland was represented in the Parliament, just like the other provinces of Sweden. The bishops' court at Turku became a flourishing intellectual center, and many students from Finland were inspired to study at the foreign universities, particularly at Paris. During the period from 1350-1450 there were in Paris more students from Finland than from any other northern bishopric.

DISCIPLES OF LUTHER

Early in the sixteenth century the most promising intellectuals of both Sweden and Finland began going to Germany to study.

Some of these scholars came under the influence of Martin Luther at Wittenberg. They listened to the new doctrine of the Reformation and approved of it. Thus when Gustavus Vasa, the greatest of the Swedish kings, shrewdly embraced Protestantism as a political aid to his country, the Finns were prepared to accept it painlessly because of the preaching of those young Finnish clergymen who had studied under Luther. One of these, the famous Michael Agricola, became the first truly renowned figure in Finnish chronicles. While rector of the Latin school at Turku, he translated the New Testament into Finnish in 1548 and thus gave Finland its first literary language. But even more significant was his publication in Finnish of an ABC book by which the unlettered people might learn to read.

With the religious question settled without bloodshed or even animosity, Gustavus Vasa served the Finns well by holding in check the greedy proclivities of the nobility. In 1556 he did Finland the honor of a personal tour of inspection. On his departure his last royal gesture was to make Finland a duchy and to set up Prince Johan, his second son, at the head of the ducal court. Prince Johan proved his interest in his new responsibility by undertaking to learn the difficult Finnish language. And his court was more gorgeous than anything Finland had ever seen before.

During the brilliant twenty-one-year reign of Gustavus Vasa's grandson, Gustavus Adolphus (1611-1632), the Finnish people received the traditional protection of the crown from their nobility. But Finland paid heavily for her protection by the prodigious levies of cannon fodder exacted from the Finnish populace. To feed the insatiable ambition of the warrior Gustavus Adolphus, the Finns gave so plentifully of their lifeblood that, when the King himself at last expired on the battlefield, Finland was in a state of exhaustion. The Finns had fought fiercely for Sweden's triumphant victories, but the bravery and sacrifices earned them little more than the empty breath of local praise. The substantial rewards in Finland went to the Swedish generals, who received vast grants of Finnish territory to establish estates.

Twelve years after the death of Gustavus, by 1654, approximately three-fifths of Finland was in possession of the Swedo-Finnish nobles. But few of the nobles erected magnificent manor houses and castles on their Finnish property as they did in Sweden. Most of them remained absentee-landlords and used the new income, bled from the peasants, only to make their milieu in Sweden more luxurious. The farmer class, which had been depleted by sending its hardiest men to fight for Sweden, now was further weakened by an excessive taxation, which left them with barely enough to hold body and soul together. To avoid the hardships of taxation, many farmers gave up title to their land and became tenants and crofters.

As the soldier-nobles who remained in Finland grew in wealth and power, they became more and more class-conscious and ultra-Swedish in outlook. Finnish ceased to be spoken at all in cultured homes, and Swedish became the required language of the schools as well as the law courts. The fashion to be as Swedish as possible seeped down into the lesser ranks. Lower officials, the clergy, and small-town bourgeoisie aped those of higher prestige. Pure Finns who spoke only Finnish and clung to Finnish customs were scorned as belonging to the uneducated lower classes.

Disheartened at this new attitude and the dark turn of fortune, the depleted Finnish peasants began drifting to ruin. When the crops failed in 1696, famine stalked the landscape. Mass deaths from starvation were followed by deaths from contagious diseases. Within a few years more than a quarter of a population naturally endowed with super-vigor lay rotting under the ground.

Before the next generation of Finns had time to reach maturity, that strange boy genius, Charles XII of Sweden (1714-1721), had been crowned and had rushed off to battle. Again the loyal Finns were called to arms for Sweden's glory. While the young king was leading his fantastic, fruitless campaigns in far-flung lands, soldiers of Peter the Great were laying waste to Finland. For seven years the Russians wrought havoc among the Finns, massacred and tortured thousands of citizens, and carried off great masses of them to serfdom in Russia. The people today speak of the period as the Great Wrath.

When the peace of Nystad was made in 1721, Sweden had lost almost everything she had gained during an agitated century and a half of conquest. Finland was shorn of the district of Southern Karelia, including Viipuri on the Gulf of Finland, her most important market town and seaport. The Russian bear had sunk its teeth into a great chunk of Finnish territory, and for some time the Finns existed under the threat of being entirely absorbed. The Finns had fought too long against Russians, had tasted their cruelty too often, not to have ingrained in them an active and traditional hatred of anything Muscovite.

In spite of the fact that the Finnish people had been treated by the Swedo-Finnish ruling class with cavalier contempt, and robbed not only of their dignity but of the opportunity to make more than the barest living, their loyalties were bound stoutly to Sweden. They looked to Sweden to protect them from the greater evil of Russia. Yet Russia's rise to the dominant position in eastern European politics made the Finns begin to doubt Sweden's ability to save them.

However, the two small wars between Russia and Sweden that occurred during the last three-quarters of the eighteenth century did not do great harm to Finland. During the second war (1788-1790), which ended in a mild Swedish victory, a portentous revolt occurred among the officers, the leader being a Swedo-Finnish colonel named Sprengtporten, who devised a plan whereby Finland would become a republic governed by the aristocracy under the protection of Russia. Though this scheme did not come to fruition, Sprengtporten's dream and his flight to Russia, his residence there and friendship with Czar Alexander I, all stood Finland in happy stead when, in 1809, Finland passed from Swedish to Russian rule.

Despite the two little wars, the last half of the eighteenth century was a relatively prosperous period for Finland. A trade in tar began to supply the needs for the mercantile fleets and navies of western Europe, which were doubling and quadrupling their tonnage. Finland became the world's foremost country in the export of tar. Sawmills began to spring up near the coast towns to meet the demand of foreign markets for sawed timber. In seasons when the crops were better than normal, Finland could even export a little grain. But although more and more acres came under cultivation and Finnish pioneers underwent the cruelest sort of hardship to wrest a living from the grudging land, nothing was done to improve the low technical level of agricultural production. In one year out of three or five, farmers in the north and central regions still expected to add ground-pine bark to their bread dough. Yet in the six decades between the middle of the century and the year Finland passed from Swedish control to Russian, the population of the country doubled.

Napoleon was directly responsible for Sweden's loss of Finland. To punish Sweden for refusing to aid him in a continental blockade against Great Britain, Napoleon persuaded Czar Alexander I to make war on Sweden. The prize offered for victory was Finland. On February 21, 1808, the Russian army entered the country treacherously under white flags and marched straight to Helsinki without declaring war. The Swedish generals fought the war by moving north out of the way of Russian troops. The Swedo-Finnish upper classes of Turku ingratiated themselves with the Russian officers. But for a year and a half the Finnish peasants fought with all their might to defend their lands from the Russians.

They had little substantial help from Sweden, but by clever guerilla tactics and daring heroism they won victories against Russian forces that outnumbered them four to one. Though the result had been inevitable from the first, the Finns went on dying fruitlessly. They were in the mood to continue as long as there was any unspilled blood in their bodies, but Sweden gave up the struggle in September 1809. By the treaty of Hamina, Sweden relinquished to Russia that eastern third of her kingdom which had been in her possession for six centuries.

UNDER THE FIRST ALEXANDER

What Finland had feared most dreadfully had come upon her. She was a conquered state under Russian dominion. But doomsday did not dawn; for Alexander was an unaccountable man of oddly liberal views. The Finns had one of their greatest surprises in history: the autocratic Czar did not annex Finland. He proclaimed that Finland's constitutional laws would be preserved. Finland was to be an autonomous state. The Czar was to be Finland's Grand Duke. Although Alexander ruled an empire whose common people were still in a condition of serfdom, the Finnish peasants were left free.

In Finland the Czar was to be represented by a governor-general. An administrative council and a senate composed of Finnish subjects appointed by the Czar were to direct the state's internal affairs. The man selected for the governor-generalship was not a Russian but a Swedo-Finn, Colonel Sprengtporten, who had fled to Russia with the idea of a Finnish republic under Russian suzerainty. Fortunately Alexander had liked him and listened to his scheme, just as he liked and took advice from another Finnish refugee, Gustav Armfeldt, an able soldier who proved to be also a gifted statesman. Because Alexander admired Armfeldt's liberality and his soundness, he gave him his ear, and now he made him what amounted to Finland's first foreign secretary, the chairman of the committee that reported on Finnish affairs to the Czar. One of Armfeldt's first achievements was to persuade the Czar to restore the Finnish territory lost to Russia in 1721.

In 1812 the capital of Finland was moved from Turku on the Baltic coast to Helsinki on the Gulf of Finland. After a devastating fire in Turku which destroyed the university buildings, the university also was moved to Helsinki. A building program in the 1820's began to change the aspect of the straggling town into that of a real capital. A statesman named Ehrenström was made chairman of the building committee. His appointment of the German-born Ludvig Engel as city architect conferred a superlative blessing on the city. Engel's masterpieces in modified Empire style set such a high standard in urban architecture that Finland escaped most of the bad taste of later periods that infected other European capitals.

Finland had been uncommonly lucky in drawing a sovereign as generous as Alexander I. She was autonomous to a degree she had hardly dared to dream. She possessed her own law courts and schools. Her religious services and church administration were not a jot interfered with. Finland was more free to manage her domestic affairs than she had been under Sweden. Internal independence was such that she was allowed to maintain her own customs and, moreover, a customs frontier against Russia herself. Her taxes were reduced and allotted to her own upkeep—no more did they pour into Sweden's royal treasury. Finns were even exempted from military service and no longer had to think of protecting themselves, for they were assured protection by the Imperial Russian Army. This was a boon, indeed, for in almost every generation Finland had been called upon to help Sweden fight her battles—and not out of a single war had Finland received anything but death, misery, and a heavy tax burden. Her peasants were no longer called from their plowing to fight for ambitious kings who did not even speak their language.

When in 1812 Napoleon turned against Alexander and made war on Russia, the Czar did not call a single Finn to aid him. During her entire domination by Russia Finland was at peace, except for a brief bombardment of some of her forts by the British fleet during the Crimean War.

It might be supposed that Finland would have made herself content under the new regime. But on the whole she was not really happy. Much of the Swedo-Finnish aristocracy was exuberant at first because of the added power that fell to their class. There were high positions and sinecures to dish out among themselves with lavish gestures. And as they built more splendid mansions to house their greatness, they did not neglect to erect higher and more formidable walls of class distinction to keep the rude Finnish-speaking populace in its proper place. Yet even these Swedish-speaking bureaucratic gentry felt a vague discontent. For in their ambitions, thoughts, and deeds, they took sustenance from the Scandinavian mother, and now they found themselves under the guardianship of incomprehensible Slavs, whom they had been bred to hate and with whose temperament and civilization they could feel no sympathy. After some years of drinking their fill at the fountain of bureaucracy they had a sour, dry taste in their mouths.

By the change from Swedish protection to Russian, the Finnish peasant had gained nothing except the release from soldiering. Intercourse between the Swedish-speaking upper classes and the Finnish masses was virtually non-existent. The Swedo-Finns used every device at their command to hold tightly to the strings of privilege and to keep from becoming Finns. The landowning ruling class did nothing to make the peasants' lot easier or to encourage their self-development. They made exclusive use of Swedish in the law courts; judges who understood no Finnish tried cases through interpreters. The laws of the land were printed in Swedish for the benefit of uncomprehending Finns. It was illegal even to teach Finnish in secondary schools. The common man had small redress from upper-class oppression and contumely. His inferiority was constantly held up before him, until he came to feel no more important than a clod.

Hardly a decade had passed after the union with Russia before a nebulous dissatisfaction had brought to light the beginnings of a Finnish nationalist movement. Its first sponsor was a Swedo-Finnish historian and journalist named Adolf Ivor Arvidsson. He was one of those anti-Russians who strongly felt the superiority of Swedish culture. But he was acidly critical of the selfishness and indifference of his own class—their struggle for sinecures and pensions which left them "no time or inclination to consider and work for the welfare of the country as a whole." In 1821 he wrote passionately, "Anger fills my soul when I consider how little the words 'people' and 'fatherland' are understood by our flint-hearted contemporaries." To him is attributed, though without absolute authority, the well-known slogan: "Swedes we are no longer, Russians we can never be; we must therefore become Finns." But to accomplish this aim Arvidsson realized that the linguistic gulf between the Swedish-speaking classes and the Finnish-speaking masses had to be closed. So he advocated that the teaching of Finnish should become general and that universal education should be the privilege of common people as well as the Swedish-speaking gentry, that Finnish be accorded its proper place in government, school, and society. He urged the Swedish-speaking upper classes to make Finnish their mother tongue.

Arvidsson's views did not set well with either the Swedo-Finnish office holders or the Russians. They both tried to silence him by stopping the newspaper he had established for his cause. So he wrote for other journals. Finally, after he published a belittling observation on the military which was interpreted as revolutionary, life in Finland was made too uncomfortable for Arvidsson and he was forced to emigrate to Sweden in 1823.

But the lamp of national consciousness lit by Arvidsson was not allowed to be blown out by the indignant puffs of reaction. The idea that Finland's future would never come to much unless the peasants were given a fairer show was nourished among a small gathering of young men connected with the university at Helsinki. These advanced students and junior instructors, inspired by the Romantic Movement that was stirring in Europe in the 1820's, used to meet informally on Saturday evenings in one another's rooms to discuss literature and learning.

POWER OF WORDS

In 1831 the Saturday Circle founded the Finnish Literary Society and set about "to collect the spiritual treasures stored in the minds of the people." They believed that this was one of the best ways of promoting the cultivation of the Finnish language. Since pagan times the Finns had recited tales and legends of heroic life and conserved the fruits of their simple wisdom in proverbs.

Among the Circle members were three men who saw the necessity of developing a Finnish secular literature as a spur to make the educated learn Finnish and look at the common people with new eyes. These three contemporaries, destined to become immortal like Shadrach, Meshach, and Abednego, who came forth triumphant from the fiery furnace, were named Lönnrot, Runeberg, and Snellman.

Perhaps Elias Lönnrot was the greatest influence of them all, for he gave to Finland her first significant literature in the Finnish language. He compiled and presented the national epic, *Kalevala, Land of Heroes.* His discovery of the rich spiritual heritage among the Finnish-speaking people quickened the awakening of a national consciousness.

Elias Lönnrot, son of a backwoods tailor, began his career like the poet Keats as an apothecary's assistant, and he entered the university in 1822. By a casual newspaper article on Väinämöinen, prime hero of Finland's folktales, Lönnrot was inspired to select that hero's exploits as the subject of his university thesis. In October 1828, returning from a "poetry-collecting tour" in Häme and Savo, he entered the medical school, where he completed his studies in 1832. After he received a state appointment as a physician in a country town in Savo near the boundaries of primitive Karelia, he spent more time in listening to rune singing than in doctoring. For years he wandered from village to village, playing his flute and writing down the words of the unwritten Finnish poetry that had descended from mouth to ear for generations. The epic, amazingly rich and varied, Lönnrot gathered piecemeal from shack to shack along the lake shores or deep in the forests —the more remote from civilizing influences, the fresher the poetic imagery. Lönnrot's method was to recite the parts of the folk poem he had learned and beguile his listeners to chant what they knew. One old peasant, blessed with an astounding memory, once kept him writing steadily for "two whole days and part of a third."

In 1835 Lönnrot published his first edition of *Kalevala* and in 1849 a revised, larger edition. The Finns now possessed a folk epic to make the masses proud of their heritage. It was like a rediscovered mislaid banner about which they could rally for advancement. For in the *Kalevala* the heroes are not aristocrats; they are simple men whose daily life is fraught with primitive obstacles that make lesser achievements heroic.

The loosely constructed story follows the careers of many men, and its theme is the gradual triumph of Finnish heroes over neighboring enemies. It begins with Creation and ends with the coming of Christianity to Finland—when a virgin named Marjatta swallowed a cranberry and conceived. Her baby, born on the hay in a horses' manger, grew into "a youth most beauteous" and was crowned King of all Karelia. The hero Väinämöinen, recognizing the superior power, sang himself a copper boat and sailed away, bequeathing his songs and his *Kantele* for the "people's lasting pleasure."

The heroes of *Kalevala* are no blood-stained killers. The chief hero, Väinämöinen, does not fight by the sword; he sings his treacherous foe, Joukahainen, into the swamp. He sings away the plague. When a man refuses to go to distant Pohja, Väinämöinen sings up a whirlwind to blow him there. By the magic of song the hero wins his way for his people.

When Väinämöinen sang in wrath and indignation, lakes swelled up, the earth was shaken, and the coppery mountains trembled. As one reads the *Kalevala* and then remembers how in the winter of 1939-1940 blizzards arose to confuse and paralyze the Russians, how whole divisions were led into death traps on frozen lakes and in freezing forests, one may imagine the ghost of the singing hero returning to help his people.

The *Kalevala* furnished the proof of Finland's right to be regarded as a distinctive nation. And Finland's national poet, Johan Ludvig Runeberg, aroused the interest of the aristocracy in the peasants by his idealistic portrayal of rural life. In *The Elk Hunt-*

ers, published in 1832, he showed Swedish-speaking upper classes the first living pictures of Finnish peasants. He revealed profound virtues of endurance and comprehension of life's verities among the humble country folk. He awakened a new interest in the forgotten masses. And in his war poems, called *Tales of Ensign Stål,* he fired the slumbering nation with a new patriotism. The tales in verse relate to the Finnish struggle against Russia in 1808-1809. Many of them are like the heroic stories told today of the winter campaign of 1939-1940. A favorite one was of the mentally defective Sven Duva, who "got the command to retreat twisted in his head" and single-handed held up a whole Russian detachment at the bridge.

The heroine of one of Runeberg's poems is Lotta Svärd, the courageous, self-sacrificing woman who accompanied her husband through all the dangers of wars. The story of Lotta inspired Finnish women during the War of Independence in 1918 to form the Lotta Svärd Association, a voluntary women's association which became famous in the war of 1939-1940.

Though Runeberg performed a great service for the patriotic movement, his work was done in Swedish. A Swedish-speaking instructor in classics, he was never able to learn Finnish sufficiently to write it well. Yet a Finnish contemporary wrote, "We recognized ourselves and felt we were one people, that we had a fatherland and were Finns." Another wrote, "We are Finns, the voice of the poet said in Swedish, and we understood him."

The third member of the group to become a leader in the movement to raise the condition of the masses was the philosopher J. V. Snellman. He knew that the ruling class and even most university graduates would ignore the misery of the rural districts until they learned to converse with the peasants. From his post as schoolmaster in Kuopio, Snellman waged a victorious editorial fight in Swedish to bring about education in Finnish.

In 1844 Snellman established two newspapers. One, called *The Farmer's Friend,* was published in Finnish for the benefit of the masses—it was the only Finnish newspaper of the time. The other, *Saima,* was published in Swedish for the Swedish-speaking upper classes.

Snellman preached that the spirit of nationalism, "based upon a clear perception and systematic development of the individuality of the nation to which an individual belongs," serves in the last analysis as the only directive for the life and labor of the true patriot. The Swedish-speaking part of the population he called "a mere denationalized appendage." The Swedish language and nationality belonged to a foreign nation, he maintained. He urged the Swedo-Finns to amalgamate with the purely Finnish part of the people and the upper classes to become Finnish in speech. To bring about national unity he devised a complete reorganization of the educational system on a more democratic basis. He emphasized in strong printer's ink that the physical and spiritual well-being of the peasants could never be improved as long as Swedish remained "the language of administration and education."

His systematic defense of the idea of a Finnish national state was stopped after two years by the Russian governor-general. The Russians feared the uplifting of the masses as much as did the Swedo-Finnish upper classes. In 1850 the publication of literature in Finnish other than that on religious or economic subjects was forbidden. But the fertile seeds Snellman had sown through his vigorous prose, along with those encased in the poetry of Lönnrot and Runeberg, did not become sterile through the droughts and frosts of suppression. Their proper germination and growth were merely retarded.

In the meantime Lönnrot spent eighteen years working on a Finnish dictionary; and, in accordance with Snellman's program, many of the educated upper class began to study Finnish and formed a nucleus of a Finnish-speaking cultured class.

If Lönnrot, Snellman, and Runeberg had not sung the forgotten peasants onto the stage of Finnish affairs, it is entirely possible that Finland might not yet have achieved an identity of her own or have been spiritually prepared to meet the onslaught of the Russian army with such unprecedented courage as she showed in December 1939.

FINLAND FOR THE FINNS

With the accession of Alexander II in 1855, the Finnish nationalist movement was surprised to gain a royal ally. Like his grandfather, the first Alexander, this absolute monarch sometimes indulged in notions of advanced liberalism. Besides, just at this time Sweden was casting longing glances at Finland, now that a new prosperity had arisen there. Partly to offset the effect of Sweden's beguiling overtures, Alexander decided to please the Finnish masses by granting long-needed reforms.

The first secondary school ever to teach Finnish opened its doors at Jyväskylä in 1858. In 1863, for the first time in history, some university lectures were given in Finnish. That same year, through Snellman's influence, an imperial edict announced that Finnish was to be put on an equality with Swedish in all affairs relating to the Finnish-speaking population. Within twenty years officials would be forced to conduct the district courts in the language most prevalent in the district. In 1863 Finland was granted her own coinage—and in the same year local self-government was allowed to rural districts. The next year a decree provided for the founding of state-helped elementary schools.

But the senate would not yet tolerate the idea of allotting public funds for Finnish-language secondary schools. Such schools had to be established and run by private means. Nor would it permit the lowly language to be spoken in its own august chambers until the very last decade of the century, in 1894. Neither Runeberg nor Snellman nor Lönnrot lived to see that day.

Despite reactionary opposition to every advancing move, Snellman and his co-patriots had won substantial victories. The echo of a new political slogan, "Finland for the Finns," penetrated the farthermost depths of the wilderness. Re-echoes, faint and confused from some districts but as clear as a bell from others, came to cheer Snellman on his deathbed in 1881. That same year marked the end of the man who, by fortuitous circumstances, had been one of Snellman's most valuable collaborators: Alexander II, "the noblest of Finland's Grand Dukes," was blown to bits by an assassin's bomb in St. Petersburg on March first.

In 1894—the year Finnish was first permitted to be spoken in the senate—a splendid bronze statue of Alexander II was unveiled. The sculpture was the work of Walter Runeberg, son of the national poet. Erected by the grateful Finnish nation to honor the man who had honored Finland's law, it was given the best place of all memorials in Helsinki. In the center of the great and beautiful Suurtori Square, it stands before the five-domed church designed by Engel under the first Alexander. The statue of the statesman-philosopher Snellman is just around the corner in front of the Bank of Finland. But Snellman had to wait until 1923 for his monument. By that time a new generation had matured. Ninety per cent of the population now spoke Finnish in their daily intercourse, and the university professors who lectured in Finnish outnumbered those lecturing in Swedish.

The quarter of a century under Alexander II, terminating in 1881, was the brightest and most prosperous period Finland had known. In the sixties and seventies the Industrial Revolution began to make a change in Finland's economy. Water power was used for industrial purposes. A great canal for commerce between Lake Saimaa and the Gulf of Finland was built in 1856. The first railroad train made its initial run between Helsinki and Hämeenlinna in 1862.

In the *Kalevala* the bard sings of a magic mill, the Sampo, that ground out riches and happiness and which an enemy power stole. In the tale the Finns fought bitterly to get it back; but in the battle, which took place on the sea, the precious mill fell overboard and broke to pieces. Now, in the days of Alexander II, the Finns endeavored to reassemble the legendary pieces. They succeeded in turning out factories, modern minotaurs that demanded every day thousands of trees, which they spat out as planks and pulp and paper. These products were loaded on foreign ships for export. Here was the foundation of that plenty which was to permit the Finnish people to live more comfortably. The small land holders in the north who tilled a stingy soil and got such sparse reward for their everlasting painstaking were relieved by work in the forests. In winter they felled trees, transported them to the nearest point of the lake system, got cash for their labor. Money began to replace the old subsistence economy. Dairy farming forged ahead of the cultivation of traditional crops. Farmers produced butter for export in increasing quantities. The textile industry started humming, and the adjacent Russian market consumed its output. The labor movement began to grow.

Under Alexander III (1881-1894), the Russians came to regard Finland's new prosperity with greenish eyes. Certain Russian newspapers attacked Finland's autonomy. Just what was Russia getting out of the relationship? they inquired. Finland furnished no conscripts for their army and put a duty on Russian imports.

Finland paid no taxes into the imperial treasury. Adherents to the Pan-Slavic movement in Russia started hinting that the time for Russification of Finland had come.

Alexander tentatively proposed certain changes, which the Finns indignantly protested were infringements on their liberty. To keep Finland friendly, because of her strategic geography, Alexander did not push the matter.

He had more sense of political expediency than his weak and willful son, Nicholas, who became Czar in 1894. That Nicholas II was the last Czar to sit upon the imperial throne was due in considerable measure to his obstinate reactionary principles. Finland soon felt the dampening force of tightening reaction. In 1898 began the period of Finnish suppression that awoke the national consciousness with a stirring vengeance. It was this attempted Russification that made Finland steel herself and begin in deadly earnest the struggle for freedom. Systematic efforts to crush the independent spirit of the Finns commenced when the domineering General Bobrikoff, a man known to have no sympathy with Finland, was made governor-general.

The clouds lowered ominously at Bobrikoff's arrival. The credentials he brought gave him virtually the powers of a dictator, and the thunder of Russification was not long in coming. First came the new army bill, by which Finland's forces were to be abolished and Finnish youths to be drafted for the Russian army—for a period of five years' service. By the notorious "February Manifesto" in 1899 the Finnish Diet was shorn of its highest authority. Henceforth it would only be required "to express its views" on subjects relating to matters that concerned the empire as well as Finland. Political liberty in Finland was to be wiped out.

The protest against imminent abolishment of constitutional

rights was nation-wide. Over half a million citizens signed a petition to the Czar. Five hundred chosen men went to St. Petersburg to bear the appeal. But Nicholas refused to receive the "Great Delegation." He likewise refused to grant an audience with a committee of distinguished European scholars and statesmen, bearing a similar petition signed by many of the greatest names in contemporary Europe, among them Ibsen, Björnson, Georg Brandes, Anatole France, Zola, Florence Nightingale. Even the plea of European intellectuals for Finland's autonomy did not budge the Czar and his reactionary advisers from their determination to subjugate the little country.

Imperial Russia ignored the European gestures in Finland's behalf in 1899 and redoubled her efforts at domination. A Russian was appointed foreign minister for Finland. Finnish police were replaced by Russians. Finnish heads of provinces and municipalities were removed from office. Russians who spoke neither Finnish nor Swedish were substituted for Finns in hundreds of civil-service posts. It was decreed that by 1905 Russian should be exclusively employed by all civil servants responsible to the senate and even to the provincial governors. A Russian text of the collection of Finland's laws was made the official one instead of the Swedish or Finnish version.

In 1901 an unconstitutional conscription act was forced on the country. By its terms Finnish recruits were to serve with Russian troops under Russian orders. When the young Finns refused to answer the call to military conscription, Bobrikoff threw out the whole Finnish soldiery and stationed garrisons of Russian troops in the important towns. In 1904 Russia gave up the conscription idea perforce, and substituted an annual payment of ten million marks to the Russian treasury.

The press was muzzled. A secret police system, with spies and informers, was organized. Several leading defenders of the constitution were exiled. The crowning ignominy and rawest source of irritation to both Swedo-Finns and Finns was that the teaching of Russian in the secondary schools was made compulsory.

When Bobrikoff asked a Finn how long it would be before all of them were speaking Russian, the Finn replied that it was not an easy question to answer. "You see," he said impassively, "for over six and a half centuries we were closely connected with Sweden, but only ten per cent of us speak Swedish." The pupils refused to learn. For the required seven-year period they attended Russian classes, unprepared, glum, antagonistic, and came away almost ignorant of the despised tongue.

The hatred for Bobrikoff and all things Russian was instilled even in toddling children. There was virtually no intercourse between the races. When Russians tried to beguile the Finns by inviting the society set to their elaborate parties, no loyal Finn would accept the invitation. The resistance to Russification drew all classes and parties closer into a nationalistic solidarity.

In April 1903, the Czar conferred upon the governor-general extraordinary powers to last for a three-year period. By this decree Bobrikoff was empowered to prohibit any public and private writings, to dissolve all clubs and private associations, to close bookstores, hotels, and commercial or industrial establishments.

As the situation grew more tense, there were many who believed that peaceful opposition alone would prove inadequate to save Finland's national integrity. When they saw that protests were of no avail, they quietly began to plan for revolution. Led by K. Zilliacus, a highly respected and able patriot, the Finnish Activist Opposition Party came into being in 1903. This group got in contact with undercover revolutionaries in Russia, bought arms and ammunition abroad, and smuggled them into Finland.

Then, one July day in 1904, a young former government clerk, known to be shy and slightly deaf, shot Bobrikoff dead in the streets. Then he committed suicide. The patriot's name was Eugen Schauman. In his pocket was found a letter to the Czar, swearing by God that there had been no conspiracy, that he alone had decided on his course of action. "I sacrifice my own life by my own hand in order to convince your Majesty yet more fully what grave evils prevail in the Grand Duchy of Finland." Schauman was given a hero's funeral.

Just what part young Schauman's dramatic sacrifice played in the subsequent events of Russo-Finnish relations can never be determined. But the Finns were stirred with gratitude to have the despot removed from their midst. And perhaps the startling deed encouraged them to carry out a program of passive resistance led by the Social Democrats.

The defeat of the Czarist forces by Japan in 1905 was followed by revolutionary uprisings among the oppressed people all over Russia. A general strike among the workers in St. Petersburg spread to Finland. The Finnish industrial workers, who had begun at the end of the century to take an active interest in the new doctrine of socialism, now gave their strength a trial. They called a general strike. They dropped their tools in the factories, stopped all the machines. The rest of the country joined in the strike. No trains or service boats budged. No communication by telephone or telegraph was possible. Schools closed. Shops and restaurants locked their doors. The streets stood as empty and silent as if a plague had devastated the towns. The police laid by their uniforms and badges of authority.

The Czar and his advisers became increasingly disturbed at this strange passive resistance of a united people. Its potential effect on the muttering Russian citizenry was too dangerous. After five days the Czar promised that Bobrikoff's unpopular decrees would be annulled and constitutional rights restored. The Diet was to be convened at once and reforms instituted. A more representative electoral system was to be devised.

When the Diet did meet, it made sweeping changes. In one stroke Finland advanced from medieval representation to the most democratic in all Europe. The Diet abolished the system of the Four Estates that had existed since the Middle Ages and transformed itself into a single chamber of representatives. It decreed general and equal suffrage and gave the vote to women. No other country in the world except New Zealand had yet adopted woman suffrage.

In 1907 the Social Democrats gained eighty seats out of the two hundred. It was an astounding victory for the progressive new ideas. The Social Democrats loaded their program with reforms and admirable innovations for the uplift of the masses. At a convention at the wood-industries town of Oulu in 1906, the Social Democrats had drawn up significant demands, almost all of which became laws. In these reforms the Finnish workers anticipated much of the social legislation in the United States and England by a quarter of a century.

The future of Finland seemed to glow with the rosy dawn of a millennium. But the Russians had contrived to pacify the Finns by creating a mirage. The new parliament found that it possessed faint powers of execution. The Czar procrastinated in confirming the new reform laws passed by the representative legislature. By 1908 the parliaments were being dissolved almost as soon as they convened. In June of that year a new period of suppression was inaugurated, when the Czar was persuaded by his Pan-Slavic advisers to put the control of Finnish affairs under the Russian Council of Ministers. One of the first acts in this next attempt at Russification was to demand $2,000,000 a year to be paid in lieu of compulsory military service.

In June 1910 an edict was issued that far exceeded the notorious February Manifesto of 1899 in robbing Finland of independence. By its decree the Czar and the Duma were given the sole right to pass laws for the whole Russian Empire, including Finland. The nations of western Europe were shocked. Representatives of the British Parliament and the French House of Deputies protested against the injustice. But the Russians were not moved. The new governor-general, Seyn, proved more poisonous than Bobrikoff. When Finns resigned from the senate as illegal measures followed one after the other, Russians filled the empty seats. Finnish officials who refused to execute the unconstitutional laws were sent to Russian prisons. Senator Per Svinhufvud, the leader of the Young Finns Party, was transported to the horrors of Siberia for speaking strongly against injustices.

The Finns were now in despair. Russification was enveloping them like a cloud of noxious gas. Russian spies were everywhere. Anyone who spoke against Russia or the governor-general suffered severe punishment. Finland's society retired into mourning, but with stiffened backbone and a mighty determination to resist adoption of Russian ways. The violent hatred smoldered in an intense passivity. The Finns did not see how they could ever fight the Russian Empire single-handed, but there were a few Activists furious and desperate enough to plan for such a step.

Suddenly, in August 1914, at distant Serajevo rang out the shot that plunged Europe into war.

"WAR OF INDEPENDENCE"

Although Russia did not call a single Finn to arms, the First World War changed the Finnish policy of passivity to one of action. The world upheaval gave that group of patriots known as

Activists the cue to work swiftly for a complete separation. In 1915 many university students, abetted by their professors, started slipping over the Russian-guarded frontier into Sweden and thence made their way to Germany to receive military training. They were to be ready to strike against Russia when the psychological hour arrived.

When the first Russian Revolution burst forth in the spring of 1917, the thoroughly aroused Finns were ready for a daring move. In July the Finnish Diet passed a bill designating to itself those powers over Finnish affairs formerly held by the Russian Czar. The provisional Russian government under Kerensky, although favorably disposed toward Finland, declared the bill unlawful and dissolved the Diet. Kerensky decreed that the people should express themselves at a new election.

In the meantime Bolshevism reared its head in Finland. The Russian soldiers stationed there rose against their officers. Russian workers impregnated Finnish workers with Bolshevik doctrine. Strikes were instigated. Various social classes began to look at each other with a new mistrust and resentment. The bourgeoisie began to arm secretly, and imported a shipload of weapons and ammunition. Russian soldiers provided guns and bullets for the Finnish workers.

In October the Bolsheviks took over St. Petersburg, and the moderate Kerensky was forced to flee. Lenin assumed dictatorial powers. The Finns decided to make a clean break with Russia. On December sixth, Finland declared her independence.

Great was the amazement when Russia—on January 4, 1918—was the first foreign country officially to acknowledge the new nation's sovereignty. Soon after the New Year most of the European powers had followed suit. Finland had achieved freedom without bloodshed. There was uncommon reason for national exultation.

But the people were too agitated to rejoice. Too many conflicting elements were demanding to know what kind of new nation they were to have. The proletariat and the bourgeoisie faced each other with mounting suspicion and antagonism. Each wanted a lion's share of power. The troops proved more disturbing and unruly day by day. Although the Russian government had recognized Finland's independence, it did not recall its soldiers. It was soon patent that together the Bolsheviks and the extreme Leftists among the Finns were plotting against Finland's brand-new independence. The Red forces, including the Russian soldiers, numbered about 75,000. They were, on the whole, respectable workingmen, a large proportion of whom had been forced into the Red Guards on threat of reprisals against their welfare (through expulsion from the labor unions) or against their families if they refused to join. Some of the workers who had lost their jobs when the Russian war orders ceased became affiliated with the Bolsheviks. Many of them, too, were sincere in the belief that a new order for the workingman was forthcoming out of the chaos of the Russian revolution. The miserable landless part of the rural population and many ill-fed, ill-housed crofters and tenants hearkened to the promises of Communism. The Social Democratic leaders lost control to the more violent elements in the party. The Red Guard which they had created to counter moves of the Conservatives' White Guard at the time of the general strike now became actively Communist. The new leaders were chiefly irresponsible, mostly opportunists pursuing their own personal advantage, seeking the overthrow of the parliament in order to seize power for their own hands. Armed bands of Reds and Russian soldiers, taking no notice of the lawful government, began to roam the country, pillaging and threatening and sometimes murdering the peasantry. To swell their ranks, the Reds set free the inmates of several Finnish prisons, and perhaps many of the Red atrocities can therefore be credited to these former convicts.

Finland had possessed independence for a meager seven weeks when a coup was effected that led to civil war. The Bolsheviks and the Finnish Reds took over the public buildings in Helsinki on the night of January twenty-eighth, 1918. In all the districts where the Red Guard was sufficiently concentrated and organized they assumed authority by threat of sabotage or war.

The next day in the capital the three leading Social Democrats, the president of the parliament, the chairman of the senate, and the chairman of the trade unions, formed a committee and declared Finland a Socialist Worker's Republic. The majority of Finns felt that the workers had betrayed their own people and delivered them back into the hands of Russia. And this strange, unpredictable new Russia they felt to be more sinister than the hated empire.

The Social Democrats had not counted on a war. But they got it. Straightway the White Civic Guard in the west prepared to resist the new order. The White Guard in all numbered about 37,000 more or less trained volunteers. The commanding officer, who was in the process of training an army at Vaasa when the Red coup came, was General Gustaf Mannerheim. Baron Mannerheim was a Swedo-Finnish nobleman who had served with distinction as an officer in the Russian Imperial Army. When Finland had declared her independence, he handed in his formal resignation from the Russian army. Retiring to Finland, he arrived just at the time that the Finnish senate was casting about for a capable leader who could organize the untrained Civic Guards into an army capable of dealing with the critical situation.

Mannerheim accepted the command of the Finnish nationalist

THE AUGUST ROADS ABOUND IN COMPOSITIONS FOR THE ARTIST

PUNKAHARJU

forces—the White Guards—only after he had been assured by the senate chairman that no foreign help would be sought. He believed it would be better for the future of Finland if the Finns achieved their independence unaided. His Civic Guard lacked trained officers as well as men and ammunition for a pitched battle. But Mannerheim ordered the guards to surprise outlying Russian garrisons in the north and west. The guards scattered Russian detachments and appropriated their arms and equipment. After some sharp fights the Whites were in control of the north down as far as Kuopio. As Mannerheim's men came south, their ranks were augmented by small farmers who looked upon Russians as Russians and something poisonous, no matter what class they belonged to.

On the last day in February the first shipload of those young Activists who had gone to Germany for officer training with the Jägers arrived at Vaasa. They began rigorously to train the local volunteers. Svinhufvud, who had been released from exile by Kerensky, now escaped from Helsinki and went to Germany to solicit military aid. By March twentieth Mannerheim, having successfully won all the districts in his march south, was ready to attempt to take the strategic industrial center of Tampere, the stronghold of the Reds in the southwest, and an important railway junction.

In the meantime the workers' government at Helsinki was furiously trying to whip its army into better shape. Lenin poured Red troops across the border. All over the country local scraps and sporadic killings occurred. Incited by the Russians, the naturally calm and peaceable Finns committed deeds of violence.

Exaggerated tales of atrocities began to be circulated. The peoples' minds were confused. Hunger further clouded sane judgment. Food supplies had run short, for the Allies had blocked ships carrying foodstuffs to Scandinavia for fear they might get eventually to Germany. People living on the large estates went to bed fearfully. If they had expressed White political sentiments strongly, they were in danger of having their houses raided or burned and their own lives taken. In communities where Whites predominated, the Whites retaliated with needless cruelty on the muttering Reds among them. In the cities the Reds killed wantonly. Children sitting at their own windows in the towns could see pantomimes more thrilling than Punch and Judy shows, when private citizens walking quietly down a street would suddenly pitch forward on their faces, shot from some cellar window. The Reds rounded up noncombatant university students as well as men of position and wealth and shot them down in cold blood. The great Sibelius, Finland's national idol, was kept a prisoner in his own house. Again and again his place was searched, and as he learned of the murders of his friends, he expected his last hour would come any day.

The siege of Tampere, a peculiarly bloody affair, lasted from the twenty-third of March to the fifth of April. The Reds, who had characteristically killed off their officers and elected inexperienced workmen to the commanding posts, fought with ferocious bravery. Even the workers' women and children joined in the defense. The wounded, groaning in agony, were left neglected on the sidewalks for hours. As the dead piled up in the streets, men paid no more attention to them than if they had been shrubbery.

"I had to sleep in a house where on both sides of the steps were heaps of corpses," Jaakko Kahma, head of Finland's export bureau, told me. He was caught in Tampere during the siege while engaged in his mission as food supplier. "From childhood I had been unreasonably afraid of dead bodies. Now I had to sleep in a ground-story room where from my bed by the window I could reach out and touch the pile of corpses. I deliberately touched the top one. Then I read a book and went to sleep. In the ghastliness I lost my fear of death."

The undisciplined Reds finally fell before Mannerheim's well-ordered troops on April fifth. The prisoners numbered some 10,000. Though Mannerheim opposed asking German aid, the government had sent urgent calls for Germany's immediate assistance. But the Germans were slow, and he had managed to conquer the Red stronghold without foreign aid. However, just as the Whites completed the victory at Tampere, 12,000 Germans, under General Von der Goltz, disembarked at southern ports in Finland. A week later, on April twelfth, the steel-helmeted Germans took the capital, just as a section of the German fleet arrived in the harbor of Helsinki. The Reds at Turku began a cross-country retreat toward the Russian border. They were intercepted, and 20,000 of them surrendered and were made prisoners. When the fortified town of Viipuri was abandoned by the Reds, who fled across the Karelian Isthmus into Russia, the war was over.

On the sixteenth of May, General Mannerheim entered the capital with his troops. He rode on a prancing white charger and wore a white fur hat that glittered like a crown in the spring sunshine. All the florist shops of Finland had been denuded of flowers to strew in his path. In the Great Square a triumphant ceremony of celebration took place. The bronze replica of Czar Alexander II, with its inscrutable, benign expression, stood serene on its pedestal in the midst of the history-making, while the gravely smiling Mannerheim, handsome on horseback, received the plaudits of the liberated.

Finland had won her independence. And the westward-moving tide of Communism had been halted and pushed back across the

Russian border. Again there was great cause for rejoicing. But it has never seemed that Fate intends the Finns to receive blessings unmixed. The joyous scene was haunted by the thirteen thousand ghosts of the slain. Both sides admitted shameful cruelties. Even yet dark passions still surged in men's breasts. Bloodshot eyes had not lost all trace of their menace. The compulsion to revenge smoldered. Seventy thousand Red prisoners, their inwards gnawed by hunger, cramped and anxious, awaited trial.

ALMOST A KING

It was weeks before the unnatural frenzy abated and the tempered Finnish rhythms replaced the disharmony. When the Finns finally cooled down, they were ashamed of themselves and each other. They were shocked at what they had learned about themselves. Fear and hate had stirred up a virulence and savagery they had been unaware of.

Finnish historians insist on calling the four-month struggle the War of Independence. But despite the roles played by Russia and Germany it was also unquestionably a civil conflict. It had the elements of a class war with the Swedish-speaking gentry, the clergymen, the industrialists, and the Finnish farmers who owned their land fighting to retain their position against the more radical element of the proletariat and the unpossessing country folk.

Now that Bolshevism had been routed and Finland had complete freedom, the people waited eagerly to see what kind of government would emerge. Before the momentous month of May ended, the Diet convened, minus the ninety Social Democratic members, who were denied seats whether or not they had taken an active part in the revolution. The patriot Svinhufvud was elected Regent.

Then in August an astounding thing happened. The people learned there was to be no republic. Free Finland was to become a constitutional monarchy and a king was to be selected.

Considered rationally, nothing could seem more unnecessary or un-Finnish than a crowned king and a royal court in Helsinki. Historians have not yet satisfactorily answered the why of this question. Such an unexpected decision may have come about as a reaction against the Communistic uprising. Many believe the choice was due to a bargain Svinhufvud made with Germany for the aid of Von der Goltz's battalions and the detachment of the German navy. Finland was told she owed her freedom to Germany, and she was convinced that Germany would win the war. The administrators of the newborn nation may have thought it expedient to be under the protection of the dominant Baltic power, which would be certainly Germany.

On October ninth, less than five weeks before the Armistice was declared, the Finnish parliament in session with only half strength, chose Prince Frederick Karl of Hess, the Kaiser's brother-in-law, to be King of Finland. The vote was 75 to 25. If the 90-odd Social Democratic members had been reinstated, of course no king—and certainly no German king—would have been elected. The hero Mannerheim did not approve, for his sympathies lay with Great Britain and the Allies, and he felt that their friendship would mean far more good to Finland.

But Prince Frederick Karl was never crowned; he did not even get to Helsinki. For Germany's army shortly collapsed. Two days after the Armistice, Svinhufvud resigned the Regency. The pro-British Mannerheim was given the office.

When the momentous year of 1918 came to an end, Finland was completely free of all entanglements. She had escaped German domination through Germany's unexpected defeat. She was free, but depleted. And she was still full of distress. During the great influenza epidemic of 1918, because of the acute shortage of foodstuffs and medical supplies, some twenty-five thousand persons died in Finland, of whom about ten thousand were Red prisoners in the overcrowded prisons. Her future was yet a slapping big question mark.

THE REPUBLIC IS BORN

Though Finland was independent, the economic situation was such that the masses were in a worse material plight than they had known under Russian domination. Along with the phenomenal gain from exports which made many new fortunes among Finnish business men during the first half of the war, the cost of living had risen far beyond any increase in wages. The mark had lost 75 per cent of its value. Many peasants were forced back to the older necessity of mixing ground pine bark with their meager bread. The roads were full of ragged folk with the asking eyes of beggars.

The war over and the blockade lifted, the United States, through Herbert Hoover's Relief Administration, now began sending shiploads of food and lent the Finns $10,000,000 to purchase supplies. But Finland still had to decide on what kind of nation she was to be. There were varied opinions among the five important political parties. The two conservative parties, the Concentrationist and the Swedish People's Party, both favored a constitutional monarchy. The liberals, who called themselves Progressives, and the Agrarians wanted a liberal republic. The Agrarians also definitely wanted to break up the large estates and to divide tracts of uncultivated land among the landless and give them government aid. Although the Social Democrats were still the largest single party, most of their leaders were in prison and they did not care to be too much in the foreground just yet.

In April, when the Diet convened, a constitution was drawn up by a committee headed by Professor Stålberg, the leader of the Progressive Party and a lecturer in administrative Law at the University. Stålberg had studied the constitutions of all the democratic nations and had adopted the best features and those most suitable to Finland from each. The new constitution was ratified on July seventeenth. It was so skillfully drawn that in all important aspects it was to remain virtually unchanged.

Two days later the Diet elected a president. The Concentration (Conservative) Party and the Swedish People's Party cast their 50 votes for the aristocratic Regent Mannerheim. The other parties combined to give the more liberal Professor Stålberg 143 votes.

Against the will of the Conservatives and the Swedish People's Party, the first amnesty law was passed in December, and forty thousand prisoners were released from prisons and concentration camps. The prisoners came out considerably sobered and glad to go back to work. The Social Democratic Party cut its Communist wing adrift. Wounds on both sides began to heal after the men returned to freedom and their accustomed ways of life.

After they had a taste of raw Communism served to them in their own homes, the upper classes were in better mood to compromise with liberal ideas. And if their tenets of privilege did not fit naturally into schemes for a fairer distribution of the nation's soil and wealth, they were wise enough to grin and bear it.

By 1920 Finland's people were sufficiently united to begin the creation of a new nation. But her boundaries were still unsettled. Russia had recognized her independence, but precisely where Finland left off and Russia began was undefined. By the Treaty of Tartu, signed in Estonia, the boundaries were amicably fixed.

Finland relinquished two southeastern provinces which she had taken in 1918, and gave up her claim to that part of East Karelia which lay across the Russian frontier and was populated by Karelian Finns. But Finland had made an excellent bargain by the acquisition of the Petsamo district with its ice-free harbor on the Arctic Ocean.

With her international problems disposed of, Finland at the beginning of 1922 was at last ready to begin to prove what she could do with herself.

Modern Finland's Progress

WITH THE AID OF TWO LEADERS

The two men who were particularly helpful and illuminating on Finland's history from 1900 to the summer of 1939 were those two public figures most talked of for the next presidency of the republic—Väinö Tanner, the incumbent minister of finance and the leader of the Social Democrats, and Risto Ryti, governor of the Bank of Finland and a Progressive in politics. Mr. Tanner's special aid came in the history of Finland's famous co-operatives, and Mr. Ryti's in the unparalleled progress in the two decades following the War of Independence.

Väinö Tanner and Risto Ryti are often referred to as the Thomas Jefferson and the Alexander Hamilton of the New Finland. But they were more dissimilar even than the two politically opposed early Americans. They possessed little in common besides their clever brains, patriotism, blond complexions, medium heights, and proprietorships in country estates. The thickly built former Premier Tanner had rather bluntish features, keenly intelligent ice-blue eyes, and tow hair turning white. A self-made man, he had risen to the top because he had more sense and more well-directed energy than his fellows. He understood the common man, his virtues and weaknesses, and he had devoted his life to uplifting him.

Risto Ryti, the financial genius of the North and the famous debt-payer, was slight of build, delicate of feature, and quietly charming in manner. He was a soft-voiced, all-Finnish Finn with an international bearing—one who would have been equally at home at a ducal houseparty in Devonshire or a 'possum hunt in Mississippi. His fair hair was thinning into baldness at the top and his mustache was merely a straw-colored wisp. His high intellectual forehead was that of a scholar, and his speculative pale eyes belonged more to an idealistic philosopher than to a man soon to have the burden of the premiership thrust upon him in Finland's most tragic months.

Risto Ryti was the man responsible for Finland's being virtually without foreign debt in the summer of 1939. And because he had used his financial genius in the service of his countrymen and not for piling up personal fortune, he was admired by every political party and, as far as I could learn, by every thinking individual in Finland. He had placed his country, poor in resources, on a solid financial basis, and it was due in considerable measure to his astuteness that Finland was enjoying a period of well-disciplined prosperity.

"It is easy for people to get out of the ditch of poverty, when wealth lends them a hand," Governor Ryti said to me in his office at the Bank of Finland.

As I smoked the cigarette he offered from a silver case and as I regarded the calm-featured face with the faint line of a smile, I recalled the story of how Ryti saved his own life and his wife's during the War of Independence. While they were staying with some friends at a country house in the east, Red soldiers came and slaughtered the host in the night. Ryti and his wife were making their escape unarmed through the woods early the next morning when a Red guard intercepted them. As the man leveled his gun at them, Ryti noticed that a button was missing on his blouse. He so fixed his attention on the place of the missing button and was so solicitous about it, that the fellow began a lengthy explanation of how he came to lose it. Apologizing for the slackness and the loss, he let the Rytis walk away from death.

"There is no limit in respect to the amount of land a man can own," the bank governor was saying in answer to my question, "but when land hunger becomes too great, the state has a right to confiscate. If we had passed the Land Reform Bills ten years before we did, we should not have had that Communist uprising."

"The state," he explained, "is the greatest landowner in Finland. After the business crisis of 1933, many great farmers were afraid of debt, so there were many voluntary sales of estates. One special economic advantage to the commonweal of Finland is that a small holder can get his children to work on his own farm, whereas a proprietor cannot use his tenants' children. Of course, hired child labor under fourteen is unknown in Finland."

"The co-operatives," said Mr. Ryti, when I shifted the subject by another question, "are good as long as they have competition. The private shopkeepers have now organized themselves on competitive lines."

I wanted to know how much of the inherent good taste of the Finns was due to Swedish influence.

"Swedes have never had anything to do with the color of the peasant rugs," he answered significantly. "It is difficult, as you know, to combine blue and red, but the Finns do it extraordinarily well. As for all the criticism of the Swedo-Finns and their top-lofty attitude, it was a big piece of luck for us that we came into contact with Western civilization as early as the twelfth century. Mark you, those of Swedish descent here in Finland have no allegiance to Sweden. They are 100 per cent for Finland."

After a pause, he answered my next question.

"Finland has achieved what you call a spectacular success by calm, prudent, long-sighted methods. She had no illusions about creating a Utopia. She merely experimented with a common-sense means of self-help in the solution of her economic problems. She bore in mind always that it was the lowest economic group that must be raised to higher levels of daily living if the new nation was to prove worthy. Her achievements for the general welfare have been patent enough to encourage the underprivileged of other lands to lift themselves by following Finland's example.

"The quintessence of democracy, of course, is the common good for the common whole. Proper housing, adequate hospitalization, decent restaurants for all the people have given the individual self-respect. In having self-respect he has an individual pride in co-operating with his fellow men to keep his state in good condition. Rather than emotional adherence to a cause or leader, the Finn has a cool, intellectual loyalty. Ruled by common sense, he cannot be swept this way and that by demagogues with a gift of oratory."

Mr. Ryti's fine line of a smile grew deeper.

"One thing remember—no matter what a Finn may be in business," he said, leaning forward to offer me another cigarette, "he is never a profiteer in political life."

Then the Bank of Finland's governor touched on the chapter of Finland's two decades of independence.

PRESCRIPTION FOR LAND HUNGER

The republic's first significant problem was to supply land for the have-nots. Although Finland's population is even today three-fourths rural, in 1910 not quite one-fourth of the families who lived in the country owned the land they worked on. The nation had tragically found out that landless people offered fertile ground for the cultivation of Communistic propaganda. The Agrarian Party in 1918 had stated that its principal policy was to break up the largest of the great estates, to arrange for tenants to purchase the farms they rented, and to open up new lands for cultivation. In September 1922 the leader of the Agrarians, Kyösti Kallio, was made prime minister in a coalition government that included the Progressives and the Social Democrats. Kallio's first effort was to find land for the rest of Finland's unpossessing country folk who were worthy. During his ministry the famous land act known as "Lex Kallio" was drawn up and made a law. It provided for the acquisition of unworked land for colonization purposes. It aimed to provide responsible peasants with twenty-five to fifty acres of arable land and the same number of acres of forest. To those persons of mere laborer qualifications it provided plots of five acres for a house site and vegetable garden.

By Kallio's law, landlords were to be paid in government bonds, and the purchasers were to pay 7 per cent per annum of the purchase price. In estates under 500 acres there were to be no forced sales in any case. If a man owning over 1,250 acres refused to sell, he could be forced to part with 50 per cent of his uncultivated area. The sales were almost entirely voluntary, for the landlord really got more for his acres than he might have got before the war. At the same time the price to purchasers was reasonable. By 1935 some 31,000 new farms had been created out of land that had never been worked, and some 2,000,000 additional acres had been added to Finland's cultivated area.

Everybody except the estate-owning Conservatives and the Communists were pleased with the land reforms. The extreme radicals recognized that the creation of a larger class of peasant proprietors was a powerful stroke against Communism. For by satisfying the land-hungry, the state had converted tens of thousands of smoldering revolutionaries into contented advocates of democratic government. The land reforms effected some moderate wealth distributing, improved the productivity of the soil, gave hundreds of thousands of unfortunates a new sense of responsibility and removed the likelihood of their ever becoming public charges.

And just as these peasants began to make material and spiritual progress on becoming independent small landholders, so every aspect of Finnish civilization flourished like the green bay tree.

WITHOUT PARALLEL

In 1919 the new republic was somewhat in the position of the tenant who suddenly found himself possessing the title deed to the farm he and his ancestors wrestled with for generations. And as a tenant who becomes his own master sets energetically to improve his buildings and his land and makes progress in four directions, the yeast of independence began working throughout Finland. The progress Finland made in two decades of independence is without parallel among modern nations.

Finland's phenomenal improvement is nowhere better exemplified than in wheat production. Before independence Finland had bought a great part of her wheat supply from Russia. Now she was faced with the urgency of raising her own under conditions that seemed peculiarly adverse—because of the very short season, the rigors of climate, and the unpredictable summer frosts. Her farmers, through experimentation in hardy, cold-resisting varieties of grain, proved the adage that the way will be found if the will is good. The mere printed figures of the increase in wheat production during the two decades of independence are dramatically eloquent of Finnish will and ways. In 1917, Finland's farmers raised only 6,178 tons of wheat; by 1927, they had increased the yield to 28,954 tons. Ten years later the yield swelled to 208,611 tons. In twenty years the agriculturist had increased the wheat yield more than thirty-three-fold. A mere doubling of the rye crop in twenty years was sufficient for the local demand. Larger barns and elevators and flour mills sprang up with the grain increase. The monetary value of the entire grain harvest increased fourfold in twenty years. And for the equivalent of each dollar a farmer received in cash at the end of 1917, he made four dollars in 1937.

Before independence, cattle farming was the most significant factor in Finnish agriculture, and it too has grown in bulk and quality. The revenue from animal husbandry constitutes three-fourths of the total in Finnish agriculture. Finnish farmers possessed half a million more cattle in 1937 than 1917. And even the number of horses increased 20 per cent despite great increases in motorized farm machinery, trucks, and private cars. Reindeer have doubled in number in the last two decades. Not only did the number of poultry increase more than three and a half times, but the breeds were so improved for better laying that the legion of hens laid almost six times as many eggs in 1937 as their ancestresses did in 1917. The output of dairy butter nearly tripled in tonnage, while almost five times as many tons of cheese were produced.

So much for progress on the farms.

An even more spectacular progress took place in industry, especially in the products of the forests, which account for over 80 per cent of the gross value of the country's exports. The output of Finland's sawmill industry rose from 245,000 standards in 1917 to 1,369,000 in 1937. In the first decade of independence the tonnage of cellulose rose over fivefold from 95,000 to 495,000—and to a twentyfold increase by 1937. Four times as many tons of paper were produced at the end of the second decade of independence as in 1918. The value of the output of the entire woodworking industries quadrupled between 1917 and 1927, fell off slightly in 1932 (when the depression hit Finland), but in 1937 more than doubled the 1932 figure. The total cash value of Finland's wood products rose from 1,398,000,000 marks to 9,095,000,000 marks in twenty years.

The progress was spectacular but not speculative; phenomenal but substantial; and more or less evenly distributed. And with the booming increase in agriculture, industry, and export trade came the new amenities and appurtenances of modern culture. But prosperity was accepted in Finland with as much self-contained calm as the first snowfall in November.

PRELUDE TO CO-OPERATIVES

Though when I talked with him at the ministry of finance Väinö Tanner did not refer to his own role in the advancement of co-operation, I knew it well from numerous first-hand sources.

The ex-premier had begun his career as the director of a small consumers' co-operative in Turku and had risen to be managing director of Elanto, the largest consumers' co-operative in the North. One of the reasons for the unprecedented success of the co-operative movement in Finland is that its leaders and managers are willing for the country's good to accept salaries at one-fifth and one-tenth of what they might receive managing any other concern of like magnitude. Tanner's ability as a business executive had been so signal that it pointed him to the leadership of the Social Democratic Party and placed him in the prime minister's seat in 1926. Because Elanto functioned so smoothly, owing to Tanner's genius for business organization, the govern-

JEAN SIBELIUS PLAYING AT HOME

AT ILOMANTSI THE FIELDS RUN DOWN TO THE CHURCHYARD

ment had been able to borrow him from time to time. From 1936 to the Russian crisis late in 1939, Tanner was minister of finance. And in December, when Premier Cajander resigned to placate Russia and Risto Ryti was asked to form a new government, the indispensable Mr. Tanner was made foreign minister.

"Co-operatives have never developed merely from the aid of a benevolent government," the minister of finance said across a desk piled high with documents and memoranda. "They have always come from the people themselves. Here they came out of a common need—a need of the people to stabilize prices which individual businesses had unjustly raised for private profits. All classes have thereby benefited, whether they buy at co-operatives or not.

"With co-operatives, tricks and meanness seem to go out of business. No special group is prospering, hence no necessity to make big profits. Everyone is getting the profits—why pay high prices to make dividends higher when they go right back into high prices? Of course, in regular business high prices mean high dividends, but the few who get the dividends accumulate them at the expense of the majority who pay the high prices, and the majority have enjoyed nothing except the struggle to pay the high prices for the favored few to enjoy dividends."

He picked up the telephone, answered in Finnish, made a notation, and then turned back to me.

"Finns have proved the value of propaganda," he said with emphasis. "Nothing has been done for the relief of Finland without propaganda. The greatest work in co-operation is really in the medium of education. The co-operatives have their own press—two weekly papers with combined circulations of almost three and a half million. We have lecture courses for adult education, so that men and women can study what to do with their leisure to make it productive and creative. . . . Our propaganda agency has engaged a staff of good architects to make factory buildings and shops an ornament to the landscape. We spend a great deal of time and money on window displays—because we feel if the people have attractive models continually before their eyes, they will inevitably improve their level of taste. And that is our aim—to raise our people culturally as well as materially.

"Formerly Finland was a backward country in living standards, because she was an agricultural country. Agriculturists as a rule do not demand particularly good living conditions. And because Finns are inherently patient and rather easily contented, their material progress was long held in leash. Now we are becoming an industrial country—and with the epoch of industry comes a demand for better material conditions.

"It is true that our wages are one-third lower than those of Sweden," Mr. Tanner replied to my question. "But real salary depends on living costs. And our living costs are at least a third lower than Sweden's."

I wanted to know how his government handled Finland's unemployment situation.

"In the last ten years there has been nothing you could really call unemployment," the finance minister said. "Any Finn who wants to work can find a job—if not immediately in his specialty, then in some other line of work. But we are prepared to meet an unemployment problem if it should arise. The moment a business crisis comes, we have only to press a button"—he made the gesture with his index finger—"to put into operation a five-year public-works program. We have been saving for this fund. And there is much to do in building roads, bridges, harbors."

"And to do all that you do by way of social services and amenities—how much do you tax your people?"

A faintly triumphant light shone for a moment in the shrewd and benevolent eyes.

"The highest state income tax a man pays in Finland is 20 per cent. On an income of $30,000 and over, a citizen pays 20 per cent and no more. There are so few rich men in Finland that it wouldn't add enough to the national income to bother to raise the higher bracket income tax."

My parting question before we spoke of the history of co-operatives was what the minister considered Finland's greatest need.

"Roads," he answered promptly. "If we are not involved in a war against our will, we shall build roads. Good roads are precursors of civilization."

CO-OPERATIVES

In one of the most just and lucid books that has yet been written about modern Finland, J. Hampden Jackson, the renowned English historian, says:

> What the Finnish people would have become without co-operation can never be known; perhaps there would have been no alternative between remaining a poverty-stricken, backward and exploited peasantry or becoming a regimented and collectivized community in the Russian model.

Certainly the most casual observer in 1939 could see and feel how profoundly the co-operative movement had stimulated the well-being of the Finnish people. Like a tonic that courses through the arteries to capillaries in every square inch of a man's body, this co-operative movement had given renewed vigor to the apathetic and hope to the despairing in the remotest regions. It was the isolated peasants' contact with the pulse of the new nation. In the farthest backwoods village the best-looking, neatest, most efficient, as well as the least expensive shop was invariably a co-operative. These shops of good design, with plate glass and stucco, were beacons of hope in formerly depressed and fruitless areas.

The co-operative spirit itself is not new to Finland. From early days, the Pellervo Society tells us, the Finnish people banded together for mutual help in various kinds of pure economy. They formed teams for hunting wolves, for fishing with dragnets on the gulf shores and in the lakes. They organized co-operative crews to look after the grazing of reindeer herds. They formed companies to clear new land for agriculture by burn-beating. Co-operation then, as now, was under strictly democratic management. These spontaneous beginnings of co-operation in individual communities prepared the population for the universal conformity "to a common principle and the distribution of profits in proportion to participation."

During the last two decades of the nineteenth century scattering dairies in Finland had formed companies that adopted the principles of modern co-operation in their management. Of course, farmers had had for a long time their bull societies, whereby some twenty men in a district would purchase a pedigreed bull for improving the quality of the community's livestock. And a few had seen the advantage in making wholesale purchases of fertilizers and imported cattlefeed.

As early as 1866 Professor Palmén made the first recorded effort to create a consumer co-operative society in Finland. He had studied the Rochdale experiment in England. He prepared and delivered an address urging the Finns to try it. Canvassing for members commenced, but the response was too meager and discouraging to push the cause further at the time. The idea, however, smoldered. Periodicals published occasional articles on the subject, and in Viipuri in 1878 a kind of co-operative society was actually established by the workers employed by an engineering company. Another organization—a kind of joint stock company—was formed in industrial Tampere, and in 1889 the first consumer's co-operative was established at Helsinki. Many farmers endeavored to stir up interest among their fellows in co-operative purchasing of supplies and the marketing of dairy products. But the farmers, instinctively hesitant as a class to try anything new, did not take to the schemes. The peasants were in such a depressed condition and so dominated by the shadow of their own landlords, who themselves lived in the menacing shadow of the Russian regime, that they had little initiative. Besides, there was no law that recognized co-operatives. And during the last decades of the century the Russian government actively disapproved of anything that savored of people's organizations.

When the Pan-Slavic Bobrikoff was appointed governor-general in 1898 and set about to deprive the Finns of their autonomy, the plight of the agriculturist became more desperate.

At this time there crystallized in the brain of one man a scheme whereby the farmer might be succored and imminent obliteration of the Finnish culture and economy checked. That man was a thirty-five-year-old lecturer in agriculture at the University of Helsinki. His name was Dr. Hannes Gebhard. He had gone abroad and made an intensive study of the working of co-operatives, particularly as they functioned in central Europe. He became convinced that only by mutual self-help could the masses of his people meet the new economic conditions that followed the industrial revolution with its cash and credit system. On his return he made a thorough examination of the small property holder, his needs and his capabilities.

Gebhard saw that if the doctrine of modern co-operation was to be spread effectively it had to be spread in a systematic manner. First, it needed a central organization to encourage and direct the movement. On October 2, 1899, he established such a society with a constitution that explained its purpose of "promoting the economic improvement of the people by means of co-operation and to establish a bond between the various different co-operative societies in the country." The organization was called the Pellervo Society, in honor of the God of Fertility, the farmers' favorite character in the national epic, *Kalevala.*

From the launching of Pellervo until his death in 1933, Doctor Gebhard, who was made a professor in 1909, gave his chief energies to the co-operative movement. Scarcely any man in any period of Finland's history can have beheld such abundant harvest from his own planting of a seed, followed by thirty-three years of devoted cultivation. What Professor Gebhard added to the sum of human happiness among his fellow beings and to the phenomenal advance that Finland made is incalculable.

With the founding of the central society, the propaganda campaign commenced. The next year an Act Relating to Co-operative Societies, which gave protection to every kind of co-operative combination, was passed. According to a stipulation of the act, the rights and obligations of the members were to be equal. Each member was to have one vote, regardless of how much or how little he contributed. But profits were to be divided according to the number of shares each member owned. Capital was to be gained by contributions paid by members, who might receive their money back on resigning. Any citizen might join a co-operative, but non-members might also benefit by its business. To increase membership and make it possible for the very poor to join, the contributions were to be as small as need be.

The legalization of the act stirred up fresh interest in the movement. By 1903 various co-operative societies to the number of 189 had been registered. Sixty-six of these were consumer co-operatives, 75 were creameries, and 24 were credit banks.

One of the most significant central institutions planned for the benefit of the rural population was the Central Bank for Co-operative Agricultural Credit Societies (O.K.O.). (It was established in 1902 before the existence of local rural banks.) For without reasonable loans the distressed farmers could not acquire land or implements or build houses or improve the breed of livestock. The purpose, of course, was to save the poor farmers from extortionists by providing credit on cheaper terms.

The rural banks were founded by Gebhard after a model created by Mayor Raiffeisen in a village of Anhausen, Germany, in 1862. Raiffeisen established his first rural credit bank on the principle that "the poor ought to help each other and themselves." Thorsten Odhe, in his admirable book *Finland, A Nation of Co-operatives,* quotes Luigi Luzzati's shrewd definition: "A bank is an institution where the money of the poor is lent out to the rich; a Co-operative Credit Bank is an institution where the money of the poor is lent out to the poor." Thus the peasants of Germany put their savings into a general pot that could be used for loans at low interest rates to their less fortunate but worthy brothers. But Gebhard was convinced that it would be too slow a process to begin in desultory fashion from the bottom and work up, so he immediately established his central bank for two reasons: for systematic propaganda and to provide material assistance to individual credit banks as they were formed.

To spread the new doctrine of co-operation, pamphlets were sent broadcast, preceding and following personal missionaries who were the school teachers, agricultural experts, humanitarians. Interested business men gave helpful advice. An agricultural journal called *Pellervo* was published. From its inception until today the magazine has never ceased its educational work of disseminating information in the rural districts. The circulation has reached over two hundred thousand, a high figure for a country of less than four million.

Credit having been provided, the next step was to rid the peasant of his dependence on the middlemen and dealers, who got the chief fruits of his hard labor. On the principle that the cream of the profits should go to the men who did the work, producer co-operatives were formed for selling their products to more advantage and attaining better facilities for distribution.

Most significant to the national economy of the producer co-operatives are the dairies. In foreign trade, dairy products followed forestry products as second in the list of exports. (Butter was one of Finland's earliest recorded exports, and even in 1260 the peasants were paying part of their taxes in butter.) But in the old-fashioned haphazard marketing there was a tremendous leakage. With the passing of the Co-operation Act, the first actual milk co-operatives began to function in 1901. And now those peasants with few cows have been enabled to increase their production of butter and cheese to the present high level only by the co-operative method.

By 1937 the number of co-operative dairies scattered over the land had reached 676. There were 77,155 members enrolled, who together owned 458,697 cows. The dairies were also supplied with milk by 20,395 non-members who milked 73,902 cows.

Not more than 5 per cent of the co-operative members own as large a herd as fifteen cows, and 37 per cent own less than four. Yet these small holders have all the advantage of modern units and expert management, of superior skill in butter and cheese making, and of marketing at home and abroad. Without co-operation such benefits would be impossible.

In 1905 at Pellervo's instigation the Valio Co-operative Butter Export Association was formed by a combine of seventeen co-operative dairies. Annual production of butter from this combine was 900 tons. Expansion was rapid. By 1928 Valio's production was listed at 15,350 tons. Not content with the export of butter, Valio in 1914 sent men to Europe to study cheese making and instituted cheese-making educational courses in Finland. In 1916 Valio established a bacteriological and chemical laboratory for promoting technical efficiency among the dairies. With great energy Valio set about to build up an export trade in cheese. In 1939 cheeses stamped with the trade-mark VALIO, which means "select," were exported not only to England and Germany but to North and South America and to Asia and Africa. The exports of cheese almost tripled in the past decade.

By 1938, Valio, by reason of quality, improved methods, and energy of salesmanship, had acquired such a dominant position in dairy-products exports that 93 per cent of the butter for foreign markets passed through its hands, and 66 per cent of the cheese. In 1938-1939 Valio became greatly interested in building up the home market to aid further the farmer's economy and to minister to the health of the citizens. It established great dairies in different consumer areas and put on a campaign to expand the retail trade in milk. In 1939 Finland was the greatest milk-drinking nation on earth. There was one cow for every three people in the land. Even the poorest Finns could afford to eat butter, and not margarine like the Danish peasants. In remote country districts margarine substitutes were as unknown as honeydew melons from Chile. Butter was the fat the people used to protect them against the rigors of winter. Pure Finnish butter gave the lumberjacks energy for the heavy work in the winter camps.

The great achievement of Valio's service to Finland's national economy could be reckoned in finnmarks or dollars. But what it did for the spirit of the small farmer is beyond computation. It raised him in his own estimation, lifted him from the bogs of the hopelessness of unrewarded labor to a place of self-confidence in the sun. He revalued himself, his abilities, his share in the commonweal. And he set about a course of cultural self-improvement as well as stock improvement and the betterment of his fields.

Besides the co-operative dairies formed after 1901, organizations for slaughtering and selling beef and pork came into existence and prospered. The Muna Egg Export Association was established in 1921. It has been so successful that Finland's annual export of fresh eggs rose from an estimated 100 tons in 1926 to a registered 8,900 tons in 1937.

The increased output and sale of dairy and animal produce due to co-operatives had a salubrious effect upon the peasant and his standard of living. Yet if he had had to purchsae his farm supplies and household and personal requisites entirely through the old-fashioned middleman, he might have had little enough to show for his increased cash. Here is where the consumers' co-operative safeguarded him from exorbitant middleman profits that could have raised the cost of living to unwholesome heights. The desire for mutual self-protection grew so strong that by 1938 the membership in various distributive co-operatives had reached 606,000. That figure means that at least 50 per cent of the retail shoppers of Finland were enrolled in one or more of the 6,355 shops scattered broadcast about the land in a chain of co-operation. At these shops the average man's family might purchase sugar, flour, coffee, fruit, canned goods; also boots and clothes, furniture and bedding, cooking utensils and drugs, thread and pins, bicycles, baby carriages, soap and cosmetics. The family needs were met at the lowest reasonable price. The aim of the co-operatives was never to make high profits for its members, but to keep prices down. The dividend rate averaged no more than 2 per cent for its members.

To supply these necessary articles of consumption for the numerous shops at low prices, a central organization was established back in 1904. It was called the Finnish Co-operative Wholesale Society (S.O.K.). Today this society supplies through its wholesale buying agencies or its own manufacture almost 60 per cent of what its affiliated shops need.

Among its own manufactories S.O.K. maintained a match factory, a hosiery mill, a machine shop, a dressmaking department, a coffee-roasting works, a plant for packing spice and fruit, and factories for making paper bags, brushes, candies, etc. S.O.K. owns two flour mills, one at Viipuri and one at Oulu, which were models in beauty of design and efficiency. The annual sales of S.O.K. amounted to more than a billion and a half marks in 1938, foodstuffs accounting for about 45 per cent, industrial articles for 30 per cent, and hardware for 25 per cent.

Energetic in its advisory and propaganda work, S.O.K. maintains a commercial school with a two-year curriculum for training co-operative staffs and publishes a weekly journal called *The Common Good,* which has the biggest periodical circulation in Finland. By diligent methods of improving service in co-operative shops throughout the country, S.O.K. has brought the whole retail business to a high level. Privately owned shops, particularly in the rural districts, have been forced to live up to the model of cleanliness, attractive display, and courtesy of clerks set by the co-operatives.

The country co-operative assisted the small property holder in the hinterland by buying his hay, potatoes, fresh vegetables, berries, eggs, fresh-slaughtered meat, and game killed in season. This was a significant service and meant better clothes for the children in winter, books, subscriptions to papers and magazines, tobacco, and oddments of civilized life that bolster a man's self-respect and add to Finland's general welfare.

The second central organization inspired by Pellervo, and one of inestimable value to the farmer, was known as Hankkija. Its function was to provide at wholesale prices almost everything necessary for supplying and running a farm—concentrated cattle-feed, fertilizers, seed, and agricultural machinery of every description.

Heretofore agriculturists had been at the mercy of the private manufacturer, as they are in most countries today. Nothing is so essential to a farm as the implements of cultivation, and because of this necessity, manufacturers of farm equipment often took "rugged" advantage. Because of the high prices, a farmer was forced to forgo buying many farm implements that were really imperative. He was retarded in improving his acres. If he did buy the requisite tools, he often had to mortgage his place to pay for them, and often he lost it by doing so. As this situation exists in non-co-operative countries today, it existed in Finland before Hankkija stepped in and forced prices down. The special function of Hankkija's agricultural-machinery section is to get machinery best suitable to conditions in Finland, to popularize it, and to sell it at the lowest possible cost. Its own great Agricultural Machinery Works has originated among other implements a high-efficiency threshing machine used all over Finland.

As the farmers became enabled to purchase the tools they needed, more fertilizers, and proper seed, agriculture in Finland began to come into its own. However, some of the prodigious increase in grain production during the past two decades was due to two other services of Hankkija: a large-scale sale of farm produce and a scientific botanical organization with an experimental farm of 150 acres at Tammisto, near Helsinki. Hankkija specialized in the selection of seed varieties best adaptable to Finland's soil and strove to achieve, by cross-breeding with foreign and local strains, grains that would combine cold-resistance features with high yield. Finland's foremost seed-culture expert was in charge, and a continual study was being made of all the more important grains and dozens of varieties of garden vegetables. During the summer of 1939, over 1,400 sample plots were under experimental cultivation. Hankkija maintained a "seed central" with special equipment for drying, sorting, packing. Forty varieties of Tammisto seed have been perfected and placed upon the market.

Some of Hankkija's supplementary offices were to construct central heating installations and water-supply systems. It sold refrigerators, electrical machinery, and fittings. During the past decade the factory specialized in developing dairy machinery especially adapted to Finnish conditions. It made its own design of steam engines, milk pumps, cheese pressers, churns, butter scales, and pasteurizers.

In 1939 Hankkija manufactured 15 per cent of the products it supplied, but no more, because it could get the rest at such advantageous prices that there was no need to set up rival plants. The society's mere existence, however, was a threat to the manufacturers to keep prices within bounds. By Hankkija's operation the nightmare of the middleman that kept the farmers tossing on their hard beds disappeared like hobgoblins at sunrise. For the Finnish small property holder became not only his own master but his own middleman.

By no means has co-operation been adopted only by the farmer. The movement arose among the industrial workers, not farmers. Co-operative distributive stores followed largely the model set by the Rochdale factory workers in England. After farmer groups and middle-class townspeople joined the movement, differences of opinion arose concerning the social and political functions of the co-operative stores. The attitude of co-operators toward the trade unions and the Social Democratic Party, to which the industrial workers belonged, became a critical issue. Each group tried to secure control of S.O.K., the wholesale society. Finally in 1916 there was a break, and the Socialists withdrew from S.O.K. and formed their own central organization, K.K., and a year later their own special Co-operative Wholesale Association, O.T.K. When the workers withdrew they called themselves the Progressive Co-operative Movement, while the farmers took the name of Neutral. Since 1918 the two factions have advanced and developed side by side—in all parts of Finland.

The rivalry between the Neutrals and Progressives has been on the whole stimulating and beneficial to the country. When there are two co-operative general stores in a small town they vie with each other in giving the best service in the most attractive manner. And the competitive propaganda of the two groups has brought many more members into the co-operative movement than would otherwise have joined. Membership between the groups is remarkably equal—approximately 300,000 in each, with the Progressives in the lead by a mere 6,000.

The most important of the consumer's co-operatives belonging to the Progressive group is the one called Elanto, which a Swedish economist has designated "the premier co-operative society of the North." For twenty-five years it has been under the management of Väinö Tanner, sometime prime minister, minister of finance, and foreign minister. Under the forceful Mr. Tanner's vigilance, drive, and imagination, Elanto became a model for all co-operation in Finland. Its reputation is that not merely of a mammoth business successfully managed, but of an institution with high purpose and a noble mission.

Elanto came to birth very humbly on October 15, 1905, when nineteen men at the Students' Hostel in Helsinki subscribed a capital amounting to some thirty-seven dollars. The generation that has lived in Helsinki from that date to the present has seen a phenomenal change in the city's economic and social picture. The consumer of 1905 was not aware of his own strength. The buyer was at the mercy of the private enterprises; he had to be satisfied with such goods, cleanliness, and service as they offered, and pay whatever they demanded. In 1905 and for some years afterward Helsinki was one of Europe's most expensive places for foodstuffs; today it is one of the cheapest.

A conflict among some workers connected with the bakery trade led to the conception and birth of Elanto. At the beginning of the century conditions of uncleanliness existed in the privately owned bakery shops. About a third of the bakeries were situated underground, and some served also as the family kitchen and sleeping room. The discontented workers decided to form a co-operative society and have their own hygienic bakery. But there were many difficulties to surmount in getting members, buying a factory site in the suburbs, and erecting a building. It was not until May 1, 1907, that the first cartload of co-operative bread passed through the gates into the town. The little organization persevered, continued to enlarge its operations and widen its scope until 1925, when a whole new bakery, the biggest in the Northern Countries, and one capable of supplying half of Helsinki's bread, was built.

But Elanto had been formed as a consumers' society, and as soon as possible it had opened little shops and then larger ones. In 1908 it opened its first restaurant. Before Elanto instituted its restaurants, eating places where factory workers congregated ranged from dingy to grimy to sordid, spiritually and physically. A large part of the food money was spent on liquor; workers adapted their manners to the surroundings. Elanto banned liquor and made its first café as bright and attractive as its moderate capital would permit. Instead of the predicted failure, within a short time the first café could not accommodate the crowds. By providing seventeen attractive restaurants in Helsinki and its suburbs for workers, Elanto has given the workman a new sense of self-respect and decent living. For as little as twelve cents he can get a full meal with meat in a pleasant place attractively furnished and decorated. Some of the better restaurants provide music and fresh table flowers, and all of them have efficiently trained and courteous waitresses.

In 1911 Elanto opened its milk business. In 1917 its sausage factory and meat business began operations. Today in its refrigerating cellars over a million pounds of meat at a time can be preserved. Among other productive establishments, Elanto runs a brewery, a flour mill, a canning factory, and a mineral-water bottling works. It has its own steam power station, machine shop, paint shop, upholstery shop, service workshop, and laundry.

In 1919 it opened a members' savings bank. In 1920 it started its retail drugstores and department stores. By August of 1939 Elanto had a total of 397 retail shops, including shops for drapery, shoes, household articles, and tobacco. A large number of the shops are situated in buildings owned by the society. Besides possessing buildings and building sites, Elanto owns and operates two farms with a total area of 3,500 acres. The business turnover for 1938 amounted to more than 460,000,000 marks (approximately $10,000,000), its surplus reserve being over 15,000,000 marks. In 1938 Elanto's members numbered 57,833, of whom 80 per cent were wage-earners, the rest being business men, independent craftsmen, farmers, and professional men.

To me one of the notable achievements of Elanto was the example it set all over Finland in hygienic and artistic shopkeeping and in the attractiveness and good taste of window display. There is nothing in the British Isles and little in the United States to compare with shop-window designs for fruit and groceries in Finland.

Some of the Elanto drugstores were designed by distinguished architects and are among the most pleasing shops in the capital. For the working women who wanted luxuries in perfumes and powders and notions, here was displayed a choice of the leading imported brands as well as the best local products. Everything was done in the Elanto shops to make the worker unconscious of class distinction. If he wanted to indulge his wife with a fox-fur scarf, he could get her one at an Elanto shop and save a neat sum. But anyone, Finn or foreigner, could buy at Elanto shops at a saving whether he was a member or not.

Elanto was one of the largest employers in Finland, and its operations extended beyond Helsinki into fifteen parishes. In the capital alone, where it employed 4,000 men and women, Elanto aimed to serve as a model for other employers. It paid slightly better wages than any other similar business, and provided excellent medical service free. It gave professional training of three-month courses in special fields. It provided pensions for superannuation and a loan fund from which employees could borrow money to build their own homes. And Elanto itself had built and was operating three huge model apartment houses for members.

Through its various periodicals and lecture courses, the society has carried on an informal but relentless process of adult education. It has taught domestic economy and dietetics to housewives. It has trained skilled labor. On all planes of activity it has made manifest the virtues of efficiency and good taste. It has enabled the Finnish populace to enjoy the benefits of modern technical processes and to profit from an intelligent use of leisure.

Across the harbor from Helsinki, Elanto maintained a green

island which was used as a recreation park, with sports fields and clubrooms. It provided a large motor launch for transporting members free, and during the summer it sent daily some hundred-odd children of employees to play. Elanto also encouraged amateur dramatics, band concerts, dancing, and gymnastic exhibitions. For the entertainment of its members it built, in 1931, a large community hall with stage and dressing rooms. The hall was opened with a workers' performance of a play by the profound and esoteric Strindberg!

So the social influence of the co-operative movement in Finland has been as important as the economic influence. And as Mr. Tanner reminded me significantly, co-operation in Finland profoundly strengthened the national solidarity.

In my talks with both Väinö Tanner and Risto Ryti the factor that stood out clear and bold was the pure democracy of the Finnish way of life. The purpose of the co-operatives and all the state's functions were related to principles of democracy. Whereas in the United States we tend to assume that a mere political democracy is a democracy, Finland's ideal was based on the assumption that people have economic rights as well as privileges.

PART FOUR

"Man is a spiritual being; the proper work of his mind is to interpret the world according to his highest nature, to conquer material aspects of the world so as to bring them into subjection to the spirit." ROBERT BRIDGES

Several Personages

SIBELIUS AT HOME

Practical as the Finns are with their co-operatives and other means of providing a more abundant material life for the commonwealth, no country of the size of Finland has spent more time and energy in the creation of or the provision for a more abundant life in the arts. At the capstone of Finland's artistic achievement stands the world's greatest living composer, Jean Sibelius.

Sibelius had invited us out to his place at Järvenpää for coffee. Arvi Paloheimo, the husband of his daughter Eva, came to take us. Therese decided not to go this time. Men can talk better when women are not about, she said. Mme. Sibelius unfortunately was ill and had not been seeing anyone all month. We started off in the new car that had stalled on the country road. Sibelius' grandson, the red-cheeked, sixteen-year-old Paloheimo son, just returned from volunteer labor on the border defenses, drove us. He would not talk, he said, because his English wasn't good enough. He offered to talk Latin—for he attended the Latin School—but that was too much for me. His father had been educated at the Latin School and had studied Latin eight to twelve hours a week for eight years.

"Latin is good for the heart," the glass manufacturer said, slapping his broad chest and pushing his Homburg back from his forehead. "Sibelius is a beautiful Latin scholar. When the Yale Glee Club sang here last month and went out to serenade my father-in-law, he amazed the undergraduates by making them a fine speech in Latin from his log balcony.

"After the serenade and speech-making was over, Sibelius invited the students in for refreshments. The director presented him with a silver cigarbox—and called him a Yale alumnus, because of the honorary doctor's degree conferred on him in 1914. Sibelius asked them to sing a favorite sailor chantey, *My Johnny Was a Shoemaker,* twice over, and enjoyed the afternoon thoroughly—all except the picture-making. The boys were shooting pictures, from every angle, every minute. He didn't like that much, for he hates being photographed."

"Stop!" Paloheimo said to his son.

We had passed an ugly Russian church with tarnished gilt cupolas and were driving through blocks of new modern apartment houses built on high ground.

"This was where we lived when we were children," said Paloheimo. "See how Helsinki has grown. That was a wood there not long ago." He described an arc with his hand. "Right here our father taught us how to ring foxes in the forest. On skis my brothers and I would go out from here, each carrying a big coil of rope on which we had tied pieces of rags. The fox wouldn't go by the rope; he was suspicious of a trap—he'd always turn the other way. We'd make a great circle and gradually pull the ring in closer and closer, knowing that if he was hiding somewhere in the circumference we'd get him. Only when we closed in on him and he saw us would he make a dash to get by the rope, and then we'd shoot him. If a fox was in the woods, we never failed to catch him. We felled many a one right there where those apartments now stand."

He signaled for his son to drive on.

"My father taught us about shooting and hunting when we

could hardly carry a gun. He's still a keen sportsman. At seventy-five he goes to his shooting box every week-end."

In the suburbs the car suddenly stopped, not far from the Arabia Porcelain and China factory, which had expanded into the biggest business of its kind in the Northern Countries. I thought we must be going to inspect the factory. But there was something wrong with the car, young Paloheimo said. His father was embarrassed. Alternately scowling and laughing, he shook his fist at the absent garage man. "I told him I would fix him, if he didn't fix this car right." The son went off to find a telephone to call a taxi—the taxi Sibelius always used, since he did not have a car of his own.

Sitting on a rock on the highway waiting, the glass manufacturer and I talked music. He knew a lot about it, for he was president of the Helsinki Orchestral Society.

"Finland is very much what you in America might call musically minded," Paloheimo said. "The concert season in Helsinki is gay and heartily attended. Sometimes we have two or three concerts scheduled for one evening. Even the most persistent concert-goer can't cover them all. But it isn't just city people who know good music. Most everything of Sibelius' has been recorded on gramophone records. In peasant cottages far out in the wilds you can hear his tone poems.

"Of course Sibelius overshadows other composers, but we have some excellent ones that will become better known after his death. Sixteen other Finns have composed symphonies—that's not bad for a little nation with the population of Missouri. Erkki Malartin, who died in 1937, wrote seven himself."

Paloheimo scratched the figure 16 on the ground with his heel.

"Sibelius is sometimes considered difficult and heavy, because he is bold and profound. And when he broke away from the conventional laws in the *Fourth Symphony* and called on his own inner greatness and touched on the mystical, people were at first bewildered. But wherever he is played in Finland now there is great enthusiasm and the people never get tired of hearing the same things over and over."

Paloheimo got up and peered down the road, saying, "What if the music is tinged with melancholy? So is our landscape. An old Finnish saying tells us, 'Music is born of sorrow.' "

But the taxi was not in sight, and I asked questions and began to see Sibelius through the eyes of his son-in-law. And I understood why he is Finland's idol. For Sibelius is the embodiment of the spirit of Finland, its classic simplicity, its intimacy with nature, its fearlessness, honesty and energy, and its *sisu,* that superhuman nerve force.

Though Sibelius has had peculiarly painful struggles on that unseen battlefield that lies within each man's heart, outwardly his life has been remarkably serene. And to compensate for threads of Finnish melancholy woven in the fabric of his being, the gods have blessed him with many of their most precious gifts.

At the start he was fortunate to begin life in an atmosphere of culture, in a family moderately comfortable but not rich enough to sap his ambition. On December 8, 1865 (the year Lee surrendered at Appomattox), Sibelius was born at the fortress town of Hämeenlinna in the lovely pastoral province of Häme. Sibelius' father was an army physician. At his christening, the baby was given the ponderous name of Johan Julius Christian. But from the first his playmates and relatives all called him Janne, the equivalent of Johnny. Johnny Sibelius—the first name was dignified by being changed to Jan or Jean after he was grown—was no infant prodigy, but lived the normal life of a regular boy interested in sports and the attractions of the woods and fields. Though he early became an orphan, he was lovingly reared by grandparents and a musical aunt who taught him to play on her white Swedish piano. His first regular instruction in piano came when he was nine, and during that year he composed a little piece for violin and cello, which he called *Water Drops.* At fifteen he began to take violin lessons under the town's military bandmaster. And at the same time he began definitely to look to nature for inspiration. He started listening to that "singing in the woods" which has profoundly influenced his creation. With his violin he would spend nights and days in the forest and wander about the edges of beautiful Lake Vanajavesi improvising, trying to reproduce a synthesis of his own emotion and nature's sounds and visible beauties.

When his elementary education in the Finnish schools was over, to please his bourgeois grandmother the stripling Johnny entered the law school of the University of Helsinki and dutifully took his degree. But he studied the violin more assiduously than the law, for he hoped to become a violin virtuoso. Impelled to follow the gleam of his genius, he left Finland when he was twenty-three to study music in Berlin under Albert Becker. With this first study under a master, Sibelius knew absolutely that music must be his life work.

For further study he moved on to Vienna, the glittering capital that "lived entirely in music." "At last I have found a place that was made for me!" he wrote home in an exuberant outburst. His boundless vitality gave him the power to study and compose while he reveled in the thrilling life about him. But in his compositions he drew inspiration from the native poetry of Finland, the *Kalevala* legends, and the soil of the Fatherland in which his roots remained.

When he returned to Helsinki in 1892, the gods again blessed him inordinately. He won the lovely Aino Järnefelt, a daughter of a noble family that boasted a string of eminent artists and soldiers in its lineage. Aino Järnefelt, besides being a paragon of virtues, was versed in the difficult ways of creative geniuses. Her three brothers all became renowned: one as a writer, another as a painter, and a third as the musical director of the opera in Stockholm.

Now twenty-six and married, Sibelius conducted a concert at which only his own compositions were played. To make a living for his family he taught theory at the Academy. And as his family increased—five daughters were born to him in time—he redoubled his teaching and had few hours left for composing. But after the production of the *Varsong* and the *Lemmikäinen* cycle, the citizens uprose and demanded that the state give the composer an annual grant. The newspapers joined in an impassioned campaign, insisting that Sibelius be allowed to devote his talents to creative work. The wise government heeded the popular clamor, acceded to the wishes of the taxpayers, and settled a modest annual sum on him. At thirty-one Sibelius was pensioned, and never has the subsidizing of a productive artist paid richer dividends to a nation. Through his music Sibelius became Finland's foremost ambassador.

In 1898, when the attempted Russification of Finland began under Czar Nicholas II, Sibelius' music became imbued with its deep nationalistic spirit, from which his tone poem *Finlandia* flowered. But the Russian authorities soon recognized the patriotic significance of the composer's music and tried in various ways to suppress it. When *Finlandia* was first played in Estonia, the title was not permitted on the program, and the piece was listed as *Impromptu.*

The music world at large first heard of Sibelius in 1900 at the Paris Exposition, when Robert Kajanus conducting his Finnish orchestra played Sibelius' *First Symphony.* Since then music lovers have listened to seven of his symphonies and a prodigious quantity of his other compositions. For Sibelius has been an indefatigable worker—already he has published one hundred fifty musical compositions, "from seven symphonies to little songs."

But now, having become almost abnormally critical of his later work, he continues to revise and polish. Admirers have been waiting eagerly for the *Eighth Symphony;* but the composer will say nothing about its release, or whether it is finished or not. He will talk of almost any subject on earth except himself and his work in progress. Some of his relatives believe he has not only the *Eighth Symphony* completed, but a ninth and possibly a tenth, but they wonder if they will be released before his death. "We do not really ask him, of course—we only gather from little things he lets fall." Ordinarily all Finland respects the sanctity of Sibelius' physical and spiritual retirement, and reporters do not question him any more than do his closest friends.

Only once in a quarter of a century had the outer serenity of his life and mode of living been interrupted—during the war between the Whites and Reds in 1918. Again and again the Red guards ransacked his house, and he and his wife never knew when they might meet death like so many of their friends. For weeks he was kept a prisoner in his own house.

But to still the fears of his littlest girls he would play the piano while the guards were tramping through the rooms. And during these tragic days of war and cold-blooded murder he continued to try to work on his *Fifth Symphony.*

Paloheimo's talk was interrupted when the taxi whizzed up alongside us and young Paloheimo hopped out.

"Do you play the piano, like your grandfather?" I asked the youth.

He shook his head and grinned. "No—not much."

"But he's a whirlwind on the accordion," his father said.

The boy laughed sheepishly. His teeth were good but not so

splendid as his "horse-bread-eating" father's—his mother had been slipping him soft white bread.

We drove off in the taxi, leaving the son to wait with the car for the garage man. "Of course, the piano is the instrument of instruments with Finns," Paloheimo said, "but the accordion has the greatest popular appeal. In early times Finns used different instruments for different moods. They sang laments to the *kantele* and used birch-bark horns and willow fifes for joyous occasions."

To the right, just before we reached Sibelius' place, was George Paloheimo's estate, with the three large houses he planned to turn into a psychiatric hospital for the poor when he returned to Finland. The broad acres along the road were richly laden with sugar beets.

The Sibelius home, which will some day be Finland's foremost shrine, sits on a rise of ground in a grove of pines. It is built of logs and stone and vertical white clapboards, and its roof is painted a deep, rich red. "Ah, the peace of this place," Paloheimo said, smiling luxuriously. And then as the chauffeur stopped, he looked suspiciously at a large car parked under a tree. "Who are those people?" he asked himself, puzzled, indicating the empty car.

The front door was wide open. Paloheimo rang the bell perfunctorily, and we went in without waiting for a servant to come. At the entrance to the drawing room, balls of silver light burst in our faces. We stopped in our tracks. Tripods like wigwam skeletons were set about the room. Three men and a woman stood by them like soldiers at machine guns. They were London photographers, all come to get pictures of Sibelius for British periodicals.

In his double-breasted white linen suit, with the coat casually unbuttoned and displaying a square-cut white waistcoat, the composer rose from a pose and crashed through the barricade to meet us, a smoking cigar in his trembling fingers.

Because I was the friend of his neighbor George—commissioner-general of the Finnish Exhibit at the World's Fair—and of Albert Spalding, I was thrice, thrice welcome. He had not expected to be photographed this afternoon, but here they all were and they seemed insatiable. Would we sit down? Would we have cigars? What could he offer us to drink?

The first impression I got of the great man was his intensely warm humanness. He had a magnificent head, bald as a birch-wood bowling ball, and his collar was as big as that of the heftiest Rex Beach hero.

"This reminds me of a war," Sibelius said, indicating the photographers. He returned to face the barrage.

Sibelius sat at the piano, but no notes came. The silver balls of light burst in the air. He sat at a table with a book, restlessly fingering the leaves. Four more flashes. He was asked to stand here, sir, if you please—stand there. Would you gaze out the window? Would you light your cigar? Docilely he complied, but his restless energy made it difficult for him to be still a moment.

"This isn't good for him," Paloheimo said *sotto voce*. "Strangers confuse him, and he hates publicity. He's doing it for Finland—for the coming Olympic games."

We walked softly about the rooms. The interior of the house was in no particular style and looked as if furnished with pieces inherited from various branches of the Sibelius and Järnefelt families, generations apart. It was a mixture of town and country, sophisticate and peasant, informal yet slightly stiff, but bright and spacious and thought-releasing. The newly added library was modern and paneled in cool butter-colored wood. The hangings and ornaments were in shades of copper, bronze, and parchment. Sprawling armchairs were upholstered in beige homespun. It was a relaxing room, made for masculine conversation. "Sometimes he will sit up until dawn talking to a congenial companion," Arvi Paloheimo said, "and his conversation is like an arc of flame."

But the photographers seemed not nearly ready to release their subject for conversation. Paloheimo said, "Let's take a walk in the garden." Sibelius called through the cordon of shooters, "Look at my peonies!"

The composer made a specialty of his peonies and was very proud of them. We strolled among the stiff-stemmed flowers that burst into pompons of crimson and white like fireworks. It was warm in the northern sun, and we took our coats off as we went down the slope to the edge of George Paloheimo's acres of sugar beets—fields he had not seen himself in six years. Where a group of alders stopped and before the vegetable garden began, Sibelius himself had built, a quarter of a century ago, a dollhouse for his five daughters—his "five best symphonies," he calls them. It looked like a miniature crofter's cottage, and was still sturdy. "He built it," Paloheimo said, laughing, "not merely for their pleasure, but to get them out of the house while he was composing." But he has never really done his major composing indoors. He still does it wandering about the woods—sitting on a remote garden bench, or staring from his upper balcony at the secretly smiling lake. Most of his work is done before he touches the piano.

We laid our coats on the stoop rail and sat on the steps for a cigarette.

"I am distressed that Mme. Sibelius is not well enough to see you today," Paloheimo said. "When you have met her, you have met a woman! She is superb—a beautiful woman, with the finest face you could ever see—and the brains of a man. Without her—who can say how far Sibelius might have realized his talents?

I have lived in Hungary, Spain, Germany, Russia, and Turkey, and I have known many women, but Mme. Sibelius is the lady I adore most of all the women I have ever known."

With that profound tribute to a mother-in-law, Paloheimo and I returned to see if the photographers had gone. As we reached the porch another car drove up. Out of it stepped Väinö Aaltonen, Finland's foremost sculptor, Mme. Toivola, wife of the foreign office's press chief, and a noted lady photographer from Paris, fully equipped with camera, tripod, and two suitcases of flash bulbs. Paloheimo and I swore softly.

In the drawing room one of the English photographers had not shut down his tripod. Just one more, sir, if you don't mind. Sibelius, very polite, very accommodating, was visibly tired and nervous. The fingers that held a glowing, fresh cigar trembled. Another silver bulb flashed like a bursting star as the French lady got out her lightmeter.

Sibelius groaned faintly, excused himself, and led me through the dining room to the wood-paneled study. On a low table Scotch and soda and a bowl of cracked ice had been placed. Sibelius mixed me a drink. He was distressed that he could not join me in one until the photographers were gone. He wanted to talk about America—of Olin Downes, the critic; of the Albert Spaldings.

He took my arm that held the whiskey glass and led me over to the long window. "Do you know who lived over there in the woods only a few miles away," he said. "Aleksis Kivi, our greatest writer. I fancy I can almost see his rooftop. You must make Arvi take you to see his house when you leave. Often, I sit here by the window and look toward Kivi's roof. Poor fellow, he went mad and died poverty-stricken at thirty-eight—and now his cottage is a shrine. If he had lived as long as Tolstoi and Turgeniev, how far might he not have gone! *Kivi* in Finnish, you know, means 'stone.' We have a pun and apply the biblical saying to him: 'The stone which the builders rejected has become the head of the corner.' The neglected man has now become our prime immortal."

I stood there looking at the famous living head that had been immortalized in marbles and bronzes and set up in museums and parks of alien countries. I regarded the great forehead, the kindly, brooding, pale-blue eyes, the well-shaped ears—big for better hearing the singing in the woods, I thought.

As I was half through a sentence asking the composer if as a child he remembered ever having seen the writer, Mme. Toivola came in with Aaltonen to say that the French photographer was awaiting Sibelius' pleasure. "We must be careful not to tire Sibelius!" Mme. Toivola warned me. "We must all leave as soon as the photographing is over." She was a romantic-looking woman, with black hair and eyes like a Portuguese and an air of quiet authority. I remembered my manners and did not say that I thought this was my afternoon. She and Sibelius left the room together.

Aaltonen sat in one of the big chairs, a thick, powerfully built, dark man with a jutting jaw and heavy-lidded eyes. The muscles of his shoulders bulged under his dark coat. I knew how he kept those muscles looking like a heavyweight boxer's. It was not just by chiseling and handling blocks of marble and making bronze casts. I had called at his house one evening with Mr. Toivola and had found hanging at the very entrance of the drawing room a pair of gymnastic rings.

I mixed the sculptor a whiskey and soda, and since we had no common language we sat in the big armchairs drinking in friendly silence.

Aaltonen had done the green bronze statue of Nurmi in the Athenaeum. He had done the massive head of Sibelius emerging from a huge block of marble. He had done the memorial to Aleksis Kivi in front of the Tampere Library and was doing another to be set in front of the National Theater in Helsinki. His sculpture had found pedestals in most of the European capitals.

Väinö Aaltonen's work affected people strongly one way or the other. He had many enemies in the Northern Countries who by periodically damning him had kept his name featured in the press. French art critics and the Italian and the Polish had praised him extravagantly. The intensive power and highly individualistic style of his sculpture one could feel in the man himself. He was born to carve heroes, real and imaginary.

As we finished our drinks and I was thinking how my afternoon had gone awry, Paloheimo came in to say that coffee was served in the drawing room. Aaltonen and I went in. Sibelius was again posing at the piano, looking like an amiable little boy eager to be left alone, but being very brave about an unjust punishment. With the silver bombs still bursting in air, we sat about the coffee table. Mme. Toivola continued the refrain, "We must all go as soon as this is over. We mustn't tire Sibelius." Paloheimo looked perplexed and helpless. I didn't demur. "We will come back another day," he said to me, with a defeated smile.

The composer passed cigars from the silver box the Yale Glee Club had given him, and he followed us out into the yard, shifting his own cigar from one hand to the other. He shook hands with everybody warmly. He and Aaltonen embraced affectionately, bull chest against bull chest.

As we got into the cars Sibelius stood white against a pine tree looking like a masterpiece of a statue of himself. He waved a white-sleeved arm as we drove off.

"I feel as if I had taken you on a lion hunt and we had been detoured by swarms of mosquitoes," Paloheimo said.

"He's extraordinarily charming," I said. "I've never seen more amiability under trying circumstances. And I have him as a human being: the perfect host, the genial erudite companion, the affable mystic with a passionate necessity for solitude."

"Ah, he is a very good man," the glass manufacturer said. "Good and simple and great."

KIVI NOT AT HOME

We went from the shrine of the breathing immortal to the shrine of a breathless one. Kivi's cottage was simple as a servant's house and no larger. But it was painted and well kept, protected and cared for by a historical society. Among Kivi's few possessions in the sparsely furnished hut was his father's sewing machine—his father had been a village tailor. The bed was a hard, shortish couch, where no man, sick or well, could ever have known real comfort. Yet there was something intimate and cozy about the little room, and the landscape outside had a delicate charm.

When Kivi died from want and that form of madness called melancholia, the national and personal mourners had been few. Now the place where he had produced his comic masterpiece was sacred ground, and he was accorded the place in Finnish literature that Spain gave to Cervantes and France to Molière.

Although the Finns had spurned Kivi's masterpiece when it first appeared, today it is a kind of Finnish testament. *Seven Brothers* is a red-blooded book, broad of shoulder and lusty of lung, as honest and earthy as a peasant's sweat, resoundingly humorous, and yet tinged with mystical speculations and nostalgic beauty. It is a patriotic book, too, full of adoration for the land and the people who inhabit it.

In Kivi's story seven orphan brothers, ranging in age from Juhani at twenty-five to Eero at eighteen, rather than farm the place they have inherited, rent it out and go to make their way unhampered in the wilderness. A fight with the parish clerk over the learning of their A B C's drives them to this reckless decision. For nine years they range the wilderness in a rip-roaring series of gusty and humorous adventures, then at the end return to civilization and the responsibilities of adult life. Juhani, the eldest and the leader of the brothers, the biggest and the most rebellious, the quickest to pick a quarrel or resent an insult, takes to learning the hardest. Juhani learning his A B C's after the return is a favorite passage of Finnish readers:

> Juhani sat in the cabin, stripped to his shirt and oozing sweat at the table's end, A B C book in hand. Greatly enraged and tearing his hair, he fingered his stout-leaved book. It often happened that, grinding his teeth with rage and almost shedding tears, he would bound up from his stool, snatch the chopping block from its corner, lift it on high, and dash it fiercely to the ground; and at such moments the cabin shook and the man's skimpy shirt fluttered. Thus he would pounce at intervals on the chopping block; for only with much toil did the alphabet take root in the man's head. But he would always sit down again at the table corner and go through a stiff paragraph anew. And at last, as spring came round, he too knew his book from cover to cover; and, with pride in his glance, could close it.

When anything as ordinarily quiet as learning letters calls for such heroic treatment, one can imagine how much might and thunder belong to passages calling for violent action. Fights better than anything Hollywood could ever conjure occur at frequent intervals. When Juhani's neck hairs begin to bristle and his eyes narrow, the reader knows he will witness a tumultuous riot in the next pages. And then when the shouting and slugging are over, the brothers will be sitting "battered, scabby, and one-eyed like tomcats in March," philosophizing on their wasted youth.

The brothers roam the wooded heights, bogs, and backwoods with a tremendous lust for life. With guns in hand they ski around the forest, and "their bullets fell white-furred rabbits under the snow-clad trees." At night they "sprawl like bull calves on the rustling straw." At some times they come near to starvation; at others they feed until their bellies almost split. And in their reformation they fight, struggle, strain, and wrestle "to escape the tangled backwoods of hard fortune to a free and open clearing."

Though they miss nothing, they have a sympathetic regard for almost everything. They can look understandingly on a bull "blowing out the mighty passion of its heart through its nostrils," and smile with affection on an infant that "tumbles and gambols" in its mother's lap one minute and then looks up at her "like a radiant morn."

Kivi possessed in rich measure that special quality of writing that is known as gusto—that quality which Rabelais had and which Shakespeare gives to Falstaff. Aleksis Kivi is the Henry Fielding of Finland, and *The Seven Brothers* is the Finnish *Tom Jones,* as in another sense it has been called Finland's *Huckleberry Finn*. But whereas Mark Twain was merely a superlative humorist, Kivi was also a poet, with compelling accents in his overtones.

He was also a dramatist—his *Heath Cobblers* is still Finland's favorite play—and Shakespeare had been his schoolmaster. The birth of the Finnish theater dates from May 10, 1868, when Kivi's *Lea* was produced—for that was the inspiration for the foundation of a regular Finnish Theater. The Swedish-speaking population fought it tooth and nail, but in the fall of 1872 the Suomalainen Teatteri was definitely established.

The scene of almost everything Kivi wrote is in the province of Häme, which he immortalized as Hardy did Wessex. Häme is called Finland's heart, and from the core of it emerged her two greatest sons, Kivi and Sibelius.

I had intended to ask Sibelius if he ever "once saw Kivi plain," but the photographers had kept me from asking him anything. He well might have, for there were only thirty-one years between their births, and Sibelius was seven when Kivi died. But though they came from the same province, their paths to fame had been markedly different. As if to make up for the neglect of one great genius, the gods seemed to have bestowed everything on Sibelius, not the least of the benefactions being that small state pension, conferred early in his career, that made it possible for him to compose instead of wasting creative powers in teaching.

Without complaint Kivi had endured his hard lot by courageously trying to live up to his own stated belief: "I would say that the world is toward us as we are toward the world, and that the one who always suffers wrongs had better look into his own breast." And probably it was because he found nothing but good will in his own heart that he was perplexed to account for misfortune and finally relapsed into melancholic madness. Kivi's own lines may have a reflection of his disappointment and foreboding:

> The scented field bloomed, the hopes of the men . . . were at their highest. But the wind suddenly veered round to the north and blew thence strongly a whole long summer day, making the air cool and chilly. . . . Like a grave, so cold and silent was the night, and on the bosom of the field a gray frost lay. . . . With horror they looked on the ruin worked by the frost . . . three days later they saw the flourishing crops white and withered.

As we left the place, the Kivi shrine was bright now in the glow of the low westering sun. Summer perfume rose like a mist from the meadows. It was hard to realize that there had been so much pain in this smiling landscape. But in Valhalla, or whatever other blessed afterplace Finland's heroes retire to on eternal pension, surely Kivi enjoys the place of honor at the feasting table and the best seat by the fire. And until Sibelius comes, there will be no concern about precedence.

"WE LOVE TO ACT"

That night Mme. Toivola took us to the National Theater to see a rehearsal of Kivi's *Heath Cobblers,* a classic that continued to hold the affections of the people. Another of Sibelius' sons-in-law, Snellman, the actor, received us in the green room. Pictures of himself as Romeo and Hamlet hung on the walls beside pictures of two past generations of Finnish stars and one of his wife, Ruth Sibelius, in a modern role. Snellman, a former matinée idol, was one of those Finns who at sixty look nearer forty, and he radiated a quality of personality which Isaiah calls "loving-kindness." "It is partly because he is a theosophist," said Mrs. Toivola. "He is innocent of the fashions of the world"—by which she meant he neither smoked, drank, ate animal flesh, nor ever spoke unkindly of anyone.

"The repertory of Finnish theaters is extremely varied and international," Snellman was saying while we waited for the director. "The plays of Molière, Ibsen, Strindberg, and Shaw are in high favor with Finns—and O'Neill, Maxwell Anderson, and Somerset Maugham are all popular. *Idiot's Delight* was a success last year. *Of Mice and Men* and *Our Town* are on the fall schedule. Traveling companies from Helsinki tour the provinces in busses and give *The Merry Widow* the week after a backwoods little theater has put on *Desire under the Elms.* We open our fall season with an adaptation of the Lunts' version of *The Taming of the Shrew*."

When the director came, we found him a reedy beanpole of a man with a long nose, a genial smile, and an extraordinary style of hand-kissing. He had had his professional training under the master of them all, Stanislavsky. His years of tutelage in Moscow had been paid for by the state, which offers traveling scholarships to actors and producers to study dramatic work abroad, besides subsidizing its opera and leading dramatic theaters.

In the darkened auditorium we watched a half hour of rehearsal on a stage crowded with players and set as meagerly as if for a performance of *Our Town* or *The Yellow Jacket*. It made one realize how superfluous scenery and costumes really were, for there we sat engrossed before actors speaking an alien tongue on a vast stage—furnished with some benches and a couple of pine tables. Kivi's vigor came out in all its force in the quarrel scene. The two leading male performers rehearsed with such gusto that they became drenched with sweat, the cords in their necks bulged, and their neck hairs bristled.

When the director wanted to stop the action and change a piece of business, he walked quietly down to the front and spoke so softly that the actors had to come to the edge of the orchestra pit and bend down to hear.

"If only you could understand the language and know how beautiful is Kivi's prose!" Mme. Toivola said in quiet ecstasy as we went into the director's study for coffee and liqueurs.

For her gift to the world's theater art, the director was willing to forgive Russia most of the sins the Finns laid to her door. "But though no nation has reached such perfection in dramatic presentation as the Russians," the director said, "we here in Finland are even more dramatically inclined than the Russians."

"Almost anyone you meet in Finland is an amateur actor," said Mme. Toivola.

"You know, of course, there are far more little theaters here than in any country of the world," Snellman said. "Every crossroads has its local acting group. Traveling producers are engaged to go from one rural community to another to train the backwoods players."

"It is good for our culture and social life," the director said. "The regular theaters of the towns have grown from amateur societies—so in a sense the Finnish theater has evolved from the heart of the people."

"The sum of all the state theaters, workers' theaters, Swedish-speaking theaters, out-of-door theaters, and all the little theaters dotting the land is between three and six thousand," the Romeo of yesteryear said.

"That means a lot of acting for a population about that of the State of Missouri." Mme. Toivola, who had spent April in the United States, drove the point home.

"Your taxpayers don't resent government tax money going to subsidize dramatic art?" I raised my eyebrows, implying what a row such an innovation would cause among our taxpayers in democratic America.

"They demand it," the director emphasized.

"And many who frown on gambling," said the theosophist, "help to swell the lottery fund just because part of our subsidy comes from that source."

TORCHES AWAITING FIRE

It was not only regrettable, as Mme. Toivola said, that I could not understand the Finnish of Kivi, but it is still more to be regretted that foreign translations of Finland's authors are so few. Although the best books of England and America, as well as those of France, Germany, and the Scandinavian countries, are to be procured in Finnish, there is hardly more than a one-foot shelf of Finnish books in English. Most all of these are done by one man, Alex Matson. Because Matson is such a painstaking artist in his translation, a stack of Finnish successes crying out for English translation are delayed—he has not had time to get to them. Conversely, while virtually every well-read Finn knows not only American classics but Hemingway, Faulkner, Steinbeck, and the late Thomas Wolfe, only a handful of Americans know Sillanpää and Seppänen, who have been translated, and fewer know Mika Waltari (invariably a best seller among the younger Finns) except for having read him in German or French.

Sigrid Undset had sent Mr. Waltari her love by me, and I went to have coffee with him at his apartment in Töölö, the shining new residential section of Helsinki that spreads a square mile between the parliament building and the sports stadium. We sat talking of the lack of translators. "It would be well-nigh impossible for one not born to and saturated with Finnish to make a translation that retained the initial power of our language," Waltari said. "Besides, to an alien, apart from the pungent infusion of dialect and homespun, Finnish is considered one of the most difficult of tongues."

The Finnish language belongs to the Finno-Ugric group, as do its cognate languages, Estonian and Hungarian. Finnish is peculiarly remarkable in that it has fifteen cases. To Englishmen and Frenchmen, Finnish seems a language of long words, because its compound words are written as one and some words become as elongated as rifle barrels. Virtually without prepositions, it is also innocent of the use of articles, definite or indefinite, and "a boy" and "the boy" are both simply *poika* in Finnish.

Nor is there any grammatical guide to the gender of pronouns —"he" and "she" are both *hän.*

I had learned one helpful rule my first day in Finland: the accent in all Finnish words is placed on the first syllable. And I had found Finnish simple to pronounce because a word is spoken as it is spelled—there is no English skipping of syllables to make "Maudlin" out of "Magdalene" or "Tolliver" out of "Talliaferro." Neither is there any concern over how to pronounce words ending in *ough* like "sough," "though," "trough." Whenever you hear a Finnish word correctly you know how to spell it correctly.

Whereas in English the vowel *a* has five or six pronunciations, in Finnish *a* is invariably broad like the *a* in "father." If the sound is long it is merely doubled in spelling, as *aa* instead of *a* (*matka,* "travel," and *maa,* "country"). Finnish orthography is so phonetic that phonetic transcription is unnecessary.

"Finnish sounds better sung than spoken," Waltari was saying. "Because of the frequency of *l*'s, *m*'s, *n*'s, and *r*'s you may have noticed it is peculiarly beautiful in song."

It was a rare pleasure to be with a young author who made enough on his writings to have as choice a modern apartment as Waltari's. Completely without pretentiousness, the place had just simple charm and simple comfort, but the pictures and vases and rugs had been selected with infallible taste and without stint on price. Except to the shrewd observer there was nothing obviously Finnish about the furnishings, unless it was in the little daughter's playroom. But Waltari himself was decidedly Finnish in type, strongly built, pale-complexioned, soft-voiced, and economic in his movement. Except for his eyes, he gave an impression of indolence. Yet he wrote steadily from nine to five, with an hour off for lunch, in summer. As prolific as Daniel Defoe or H. G. Wells, he was yet more versatile than either of those powerhouses. At seventeen he had published a volume of poetry, and at twenty his first novel, *The Great Illusion*. He wrote not only poetry and novels but novelettes, short stories, murder mysteries, plays, and cinema scripts. He was more or less a perennial prize-winner in one field or another. At the age of thirty-two he had twenty-odd volumes to his credit, eight of them novels. And up to 1937 he had held a salaried job as editor, so that his writing had been perforce an avocation.

I was considering the boundless fertility of the Finns when I recalled that Sillanpää, the greatest writer of them all, sometimes takes four or five years to do a shortish novel. While the young Mika Waltari produced one child and lots of books, the aging Sillanpää had lots of children but had produced only a few books.

"But Sillanpää," said Waltari, "has long periods when it seems impossible for him to write a line. And he revises as much as Hemingway is reported to do."

"Hemingway himself told me he wrote the last page of *A Farewell to Arms* seventy-six times," I said.

Waltari raised a blond eyebrow slightly and then shook his head almost wistfully. To him invention comes easy, and when he writes he rarely revises a line. "By the way," he said, "I think *A Farewell to Arms* is the most beautiful love story in the world —for the modern age."

But I had come to talk of Finnish literature rather than American, and while we drank coffee I turned the talk directly to the subject.

"The birth of modern Finnish literature," Waltari said, "dates from 1860, when Aleksis Kivi published his tragedy *Kullervo*. Because our literature was historically belated, Kivi's art fused traditions of several cultures in one. His *Seven Brothers* is the ancestor of our realistic school, for it handles the life of actuality; yet you see how full of romanticism it is—and of a robust sense of humor that stems back to the Renaissance."

"Isn't Kivi in the blood of all present-day Finnish literature?" I asked.

"Every good work to come out of Finland has drawn inspiration from him," Waltari answered, and then went on: "In the 1880's and '90's we were much under the spell of the great Norwegian dramatists and the Danish critic Georg Brandes. A group of realistic and thoughtful writers at this time became known as Young Finland—or the *Päivälehti* group—because they were loosely bound together by the liberal newspaper then called by that name. Now that paper has become the *Helsingin Sanomat,* and its editor today is Foreign Minister Erkko.

"The *Päivälehti* were social-minded young men who learned from Flaubert, De Maupassant, and Zola. Juhani Aho was the most important of them. Though inimitable in his way because his prose was intrinsically lyrical, Aho is accredited with having taught Finns to write like Europeans. Yet like Selma Lagerlöf, Aho had neo-romantic leanings, and his *Helkavirsiä,* a collection of old ballads, is one of our greatest treasures."

"Is it not true that Finland's greatest novels have all had rural settings?" I asked, fully aware that Waltari was about the only novelist who made good use of the city scene.

"Yes—Kivi's, Linnankoski's, Sillanpää's. Perhaps the second most popular novel among Finns after *Seven Brothers* is Johannes Linnankoski's *The Song of the Blood-red Flower.* Though it has a Don Juan theme, the setting is authentically rural."

"So," I said, "no matter how far Finns presume to wander into the dark and flowery paths of romanticism, they are drawn back to the problems of ordinary daily living?"

"Right," he answered. "Finland has had to struggle against too many alien forces as well as a rigorous nature to write much other than novels of the soil and the careers of simple folk. Though some Finnish writers have traveled in more sophisticated continental countries and felt the influence of French and Italian culture, on the return to the homeland the struggle for freedom and national integrity has seemed all-consuming. Sophisticated ideas have paled before the burning elemental necessity to exist as Finns and to fight for the dignity of the individual. A Finnish writer of lasting significance might make a beginning steeped in admiration for the neo-romantic school, but almost invariably he ends up in a portrayal of the simplicity of living in rural Finland."

After a pause he continued: "Neo-romanticism was finally left to find its expression in lyrical poetry—and lyric poetry reached its culmination in Eino Leino. Sillanpää, who is our prime exponent of the peasant-life theme, has some of that lyrical quality of Leino which combines vitality and delicacy so movingly."

"I confess Sillanpää moves me profoundly," I said, "but his genius is difficult to analyze. It's as if he saw with two minds—with one he notes an incident as it actually happened with all its realistic detail; with the other he beholds its mystical distillation and cosmic significance. The qualities that I get most definitely from his elusive art are his compassion and his poignant appreciation of beauty—he hears all the melodies that are to be heard, but he also hears the sweeter unheard ones—"

"Yes," said Waltari slowly, musing on what I had said, "he has a super-gift for making his readers see and feel things that they could never have seen or felt by themselves. His own inspired appreciation of nature, though too analytical and actual to be mystic, is yet so delicate that he must suggest it through the creation of a sensitive farm maid who dies at twenty-two."

We began running over the titles on his shelves of Finnish authors. The largest and most important group of the new generation of Finnish writers, those born since 1900, are known as *Tulenkantajat,* or "Bearers of Fire." Several of these who were lyric poets had dramatized their lives by dying of consumption in their twenties. Among the novelists of the group, the two outstanding Fire-bearers are Mika Waltari and Unto Seppänen. The prizes Waltari does not win seem to go to Seppänen. Twice, as the jackets revealed, he had won the Finnish Literary Society Prize, and four of his novels had won the State Literary Prize. But the only one of Seppänen's fire-bearing novels that had been translated into English was *Sun and Storm.* (Here Kenneth Kaufman had done a brilliant job of translation.)

Though the two leaders did not choose the same settings—the Helsinki-born Seppänen laying the scenes of his novels in the Karelian Isthmus where he then lived—strangely enough they had both succeeded best in the depiction of emotions of youth. According to the critics, each was eminent in revealing "the sensual stirrings at puberty" and the awakening to responsibilities of man's estate. I had read Unto Seppänen's *Sun and Storm,* and I thought his portrayal of the boy Matti in the second half of the book was as profound a revelation of male adolescence as I had read in any nation's literature. In fact, Matti had immediately become my favorite character among yearlings, because out of a complete normality and naturalness Seppänen had created a boy whose every move and thought were unfailingly interesting.

I ran my finger and eye over more titles and authors. "Many of the Finnish novelists who use the backwoods for settings," Waltari said, "are almost untranslatable because of the infusion of dialect." Ilamari Kianto writes of the primitive hinterland and Joel Lehtonen and Heikki Toppila are depicters of authentic rural life, but they will be tough problems to a translator. The same is true in a measure of Toivo Pekkanen, the leader of the proletarian group and a powerful portrayer of the lives and loves of working men.

As I talked with Mika Waltari, whom I had not read, I felt that all the more deplorable was the lack of English translations of Finnish literature. For those who cannot visit a foreign land and meet its people, an acquaintance with its literature is a boon. Music, dramatic acting, architecture, painting, sculpture, and athletics all speak a language that is universal like nature. Of all cultural arts only literature must be recast in another form to make it comprehensible to alien eyes and ears. And even to those foreigners who have traveled and resided in Finland, there is much that lies beneath the surface life that needs interpretation by its own men of letters. Without some literary guidance it is not easy to grasp the dual nature of the Finn with his mystic dreaming and his business acumen. It is hard to reconcile his even placidity with his occasional volcanic outbursts of passion. One needs a book like Seppänen's *Sun and Storm* to see harmonizing in one man the two tendencies of the race—as Kenneth Kaufman puts it, "the half-sad, half-affectionate looking backward into the homey folkways of the past on the one hand, and on the other a shrewd enlightened grasp of the possibilities of an agricultural-industrial economy."

There on Mika Waltari's special shelves in their Finnish sconces were ranged the fire-bearers' torches waiting to be lighted for the English-speaking public by the flame of translation. When I said good-by to Sigrid Undset's friend, my best wishes to him were for a worthy English translator.

SUCCESS IN THE TOMB OF THE CAPULETS

I was taken to call on Mme. Vuolijoki, Finland's most successful playwright, at her town apartment overlooking the bay and Suomenlinna Fortress. A blonde two-hundred-pounder, dressed in pink organdie, she sat on a gilded love-seat and talked of rehearsals of one of her comedies in London.

"The director didn't understand Finns at all. He was making the actors move about without reason—do this, do that. 'But Finns don't act that way,' I kept calling out. 'They only move when necessary. They are ten times more English than the English—unless they are drunk or fighting.'"

Shrewd, voluble, and big-hearted, with a genius for business, Mme. Vuolijoki had had a remarkable career. Born an Estonian, widow of a Finn who left her without funds, she was a self-made woman who had made good in three big ways. During the first World War she had realized a neat fortune as a food purchasing agent for Russia, buying coffee and sugar. When her Russian business connections were severed, she had turned to writing box-office attractions for the theater. According to formula, she wrote comedies people were eager to pay to see. Success followed success. Her opening nights became a vogue. The flowers and wreaths she received would have made any funeral spectacular. Even today her dining room—which I could see through the drawing-room arch—looked like a mortuary parlor. The walls were hung thickly with wreaths of laurel and acanthus leaves. The dried and brittle floral offerings were adorned with silver ribbons and a card bearing the name of one of her plays and the date of opening. "It is a custom to present playwrights with wreaths on the opening nights," Mme. Vuolijoki said. "It is bad luck to throw them away. So now I eat my meals in something like the tomb of the Capulets—that is, when I'm in town. But playwriting is only an avocation—I'm a practical farmer."

Her farm was famous. With some of her theater money she had bought an estate halfway between Helsinki and Viipuri and turned it into a model farm. She had managed it so successfully that every phase of it made money—dairy cattle, sheep, sugar

RUSSIAN ORTHODOX MONKS COMING FROM A SERVICE AT VALAMO

AT HEINOLA BATHERS EMERGE FROM AN OLD-FASHIONED SMOKE-SAUNA ON THEIR WAY TO PLUNGE IN THE LAKE

beets, wheat, flax, soya groats, and gooseberries. On the estate she entertained quantities of house guests with expansive and efficient hospitality, writing her witty comedies, as it were, with an energetic left hand, while receiving guests, rich or stranded, important or insignificant, with a plump and gracious right.

We talked wool-growing, slaughterhouses, and A.I.V. Cattle Nutriment. She used the system of preserving winter fodder that had been invented by Professor A. I. Virtanen, of Helsinki University, and was now being adopted throughout Europe. She explained how the last crop of hay is piled into a vast hole and all the tops of sugar beets and other root crops are thrown in too. Then a chemical liquid is poured over the mass. By the special process all but 5 per cent of the nutriment and vitamin value of the fodder is preserved. The cattle are kept healthier and the winter milk is made richer. "The A.I.V. method is in considerable use now in the United States, I understand," the playwright said. "A Mr. Chapman of Kansas City holds the patent rights."

Fiftyish and pretty without make-up, Mme. Vuolijoki bubbled on like a plump-breasted coffeepot at a boil, chattering common sense and cleverness, her feminine gestures almost skittish, her doll-like baby-blue eyes smug in their assurance that they couldn't be easily fooled and ready to endure unblinkingly all the limelight that might be turned on. Here was a woman of mettle and good fun, one who could deal with a hardboiled business man and not fear to be worsted. Astute and hearty, without any torturing complexities of genius, Mme. Vuolijoki knew precisely her worth, and she made the most of her talents by keeping as sharp a grip on the common pulse as do the editors of *The Saturday Evening Post.* Because she gave the public bounteously what it wanted, she was handsomely rewarded. Worldly-wise enough to realize the benefits of compromise, even though it made her suspect in certain circles, she continued to urge Finland to be friendly with Soviet Russia for the republic's own good.

In September I could see the opening of the new play she was just finishing, she said, but now I should see her farm in operation. I promised to bring my wife and spend some days at her farm when we returned from Karelia. With the charming gesture of a chatelaine, she offered to send her car to fetch us.

"OURS IS A REBELLIOUS NATURE"

Elli Tompuri's apartment happened to be in the same building with Mme. Vuolijoki's, two floors down. Paul Engle, the Iowa poet, had given us a letter to her, and she asked us to tea the day after her return from New York, where she had attended the opening festivities at the Finland Pavilion at the World's Fair. There she had given readings from the *Kalevala* and the Finnish poets and interpretations of Kivi's dramas. Mme. Tompuri is the best known of Finnish actresses outside of her own country. As a *diseuse* she had been a success in Berlin, Paris, London. For years she had her Helsinki experimental theater and had directed highbrow dramas and played roles she had not been able to play in the state theater. But because she was so individual in her art, she was said to be at her best in one-woman performances. She is the Cornelia Otis Skinner of Finland, with a difference, for she is a bit too much like caviar for the general taste, whereas Miss Skinner is a community attraction *par excellence.*

We sat in the little library amid original bric-a-brac and good paintings, including one of the hostess as Salome. The actress is a bronze-haired woman with violet eyes, and she wore a dress of burnt-orange color. A natural warmth and quick sympathy flowed from her, unconstrained by any conventional barriers. She had a certain tragic beauty like Duse, but there was little repose in her, and her personality could vibrate like a struck gong when she became excited. As we talked, Mme. Tompuri seemed to become reflections of parts she had played—of The Lady from the Sea, Medea, Hedda, Paula Tanqueray, and both Hamlet's and Oswald's mothers. When she spoke of world conditions, there was a flash of violence in her exasperation at man's stupidity, of the obtuseness of governments, of any brand of smugness. "Doubtless I shall become older and older, but I shall never become conservative," she declared.

While we were talking of the poet Eino Leino's death in 1927, she flew to answer a long-distance call about a funeral she was attending in Viipuri the next day. Because the connections were poor she screamed so loud—about a train schedule—that she might have been shouting to Suomenlinna Fortress out in the bay. When she came from the telephone, she paused in the doorway and recited a twelve-line poem of Leino with such consummate art and simplicity that the brief perfection of the moment went straightway into a special niche of my memory's museum.

"If anyone is as good for poetry as Sibelius is for music," she said, "it is Eino Leino, the lyric poet of the Nineties. And because he had to sell his art to live, he set such a standard for newspaper poems that no country can boast of anything like the high poetry of Finland's press when Leino was alive."

We turned the subject to Russia, as we so often did to get Finnish reactions.

"Finns do not hate Russians as individuals," Mme. Tompuri said. "They have been marvelous to Russian refugees. But they fear Russia. I was brought up in Viipuri. Finns liked Russians very well before the Russification began. After that all Russians became suspect. Soon we were not allowed to have anything to do with them even in school. It was sad, because I was devoted to two of my Russian schoolmates and couldn't believe they were incarnations of evil. I remember my mother commanding us, 'Be polite, children—Russians are coming to call.' And then when I was grown and went about on the Continent and met Russians in Paris, Florence, the Riviera, I was astounded to find them invariably the most charming people there. I came home and said, 'Look here, you've got these Russians all wrong—they are clever and gay and generous and some of them are profound.' But my praise was greeted with icy unbelief, and I had to admit they were undependable and even a little mad perhaps, and perhaps they didn't bathe so thoroughly as we did."

Tea was served in the drawing room by Hilma, a remarkable woman who had nursed the actress's two sons, now grown, and was her cook, housekeeper, typist, rental agent, personal maid, traveling companion, and chief critic. Any performance that did not get by with Hilma in the home, Mme. Tompuri did not risk on the public.

"Do Finns really love the theater as much as is claimed?" Therese asked.

"In one sense more than any other people since the Greeks," Mme. Tompuri answered. "Finns love to act—so much so that it really doesn't matter about the audience." She laughed. "Often there are more people on the stage than in the audience. This frequently happens in the little theaters, where they choose plays with enormous casts so that half the community can be in them." She paused, drank some tea, ate one of Hilma's delicious seed cakes, and said thoughtfully, "For all their boasted impassiveness Finns dramatize their own lives a bit. They take zest in bearing misfortunes nobly. Some like to behave over simple happenings as if they were holding in leash tearing passions. They make such a virtue of restraint that in many situations there is not more than meets the eye, but less—" she smiled and added "—as in some of Maeterlinck's poetic repetitions." Then she said more slowly, "Seriously, I think it is because Finns cannot bear to show their emotions in real life that they crowd the stages to let off steam."

She got up to receive a dramatic critic who arrived late for tea, in a top hat and morning coat. He had come straight from a fashionable funeral—and Finland followed the Swedish custom of dressing for a funeral as for a wedding. When the hostess was again called to the telephone, the critic bore out what we were both thinking—that if Mme. Tompuri had come along in the days of the Czars her art would have been more appreciated and she would have risen to greater heights. "Finns do not readily acknowledge superiority in a fellow countryman," he said. "They are likely to resent any marked publicity accorded to another. And Tompuri acts as she pleases. Perhaps she is a little too—shall we say 'original' or 'flamboyant'?—for Finnish taste. But she will not compromise to please the public. She gives them what she likes and how she likes—because she is an artist. So she makes enemies, and enemies make for frustration."

"This war, Elli, if it comes to Finland?" the critic asked lightly, as Mme. Tompuri came back into the room. "I'm a reserve captain of cavalry, but really I prefer to exercise on bridle paths—and I haven't the heart to shoot a rabbit."

With a grim smile and a fearless eye, the lady answered: "We can eat famine bread once more—and survive—start from the ground roots again if necessary. But oppression we can never again endure from any nation—for ours is a rebellious nature." She smiled deprecatingly at Therese and me. "We are so—inflexible. It is our weakness as well as our strength. But how can we change the way we are?"

DEFENSE PREPARATIONS WITH A DISCOUNT

It was less than four months before the Russian invasion that I was received by Minister of Defense Juho Niukkanen. We sat in front of the closed fireplace about a small round table on which was a banquet-sized chromium box with compartments divided for cigars and cigarettes. We smoked cigarettes and used the polished butt of a large gun shell for an ash tray. Mr. Niukkanen had a cold and kept a white silk handkerchief in his right hand, his cigarette in his left. The minister was a middle-sized, solid man with tow-colored hair and sun-ruddied complexion. He wore a scarcely perceptible stubby white mustache like Sumner Welles's. And like the governor of Lapland he looked stout as an oak stump in his suit of cream-colored wool. He had been brought up on a farm in Karelia, and working in the fields had developed his powerful physique. The minister of defense belonged to the agrarian party.

"How does the farmer's party get along with the social-democratic factory workers?" I asked.

"In a sense they have the same aim—to raise up the bottom stratum."

"But social democrats are generally interested only in improving conditions of laborers."

"Quite right. And all social democrats are more or less international. They have been helped by organizers from other countries. At first their international character made it impossible for us to collaborate. Then they had a change in attitude. One reason for the new collaboration between social democrats and farmers was the question of national defense. By 1937 they, too, saw the country should be defended and they also saw they had to change their program to get votes. They did and in that year they came into top power. The elections this summer showed their decision was right, because they gained many more votes."

"But what about farm workers' wages in comparison with those of unionized factory labor?"

"Farm laborers' pay here corresponds very well to factory wages."

"You've achieved something remarkable, then," I said, and we turned back to the question of defense. I asked for a comparison of Finland's defense with that of the other three Northern Countries.

"The will to defend the country is more developed in Finland than in other countries," he replied. "In parliament the vote for defense measures for three years now has been virtually unanimous. Besides the regular army we have the civic guard, a strong voluntary defense organization with 100,000 men enrolled—something like a territorial army. They drill on Sundays and holidays. The girls of the defense organization, called Lotta Svärd, are being trained as nurses, telegraphists, and telephone centrals, and for kitchen duty and antiaircraft defense. All the country is divided into small districts. Women are trained in what to do if the place is bombed. All clothing will be manufactured by them during a war. They will take charge of reloading of cartridges. Now at the frontier thousands of men volunteers are working on antitank defenses. The Lottas prepare the food for them."

"What about supplies in wartime?"

"We will be almost self-sufficeint so far as food is concerned. We are storing up our own grain and some foreign grain. We are in close co-operation with the methods of Norway and Sweden. We are developing our own plant for producing hydrogen from the air. At Jyväskylä, in the central part of the country, we have a state gun factory for making artillery. Since 1927 we have made rifles and machine guns there. Since 1937 we have made cannons. There are several other factories, state and private, for making guns. We have a factory for explosives, a factory for making gas masks. During this past year we have spent about $32,000,000 on defense. That's a lot of money for a small country."

The minister got up and led me over to a big map that covered half a wall. The significant thing was that the map was merely an enlarged sector of that part of Finland that joined Russia on the southeast. With a stout forefinger he began tracing the black lines of fortifications that came to be called the Mannerheim Line and the lines of tank traps and barriers that curved like sickles across the chart.

I said I did not see what could prevent the Russians from landing along the gulf shore. But the minister said ice made it impossible for boats in winter, and in summer the waters were difficult and shallow—and the Finns had a special method of defense that could keep Russians from landing.

I asked him what that method was. The minister sneezed into his handkerchief. His inclination to sneeze seemed to come on him whenever I asked a question he preferred not to answer. It was convenient and diplomatic. He did not refuse to answer my questions—he just sneezed.

"Of course," Mr. Niukkanen said, "after the ice melts the Russians could bombard the coast from their ships in the bay, but it wouldn't do them much good."

He used his forefinger as if it were a piece of chalk, making short marks to the right and east. "See," he said, "no railways go into Russia, except these lines to Leningrad through the narrow Karelian Isthmus. All dirt roads stop within fifteen or twenty kilometers of the eastern border. The terrain is so difficult that

I do not think they would attempt to come in where there are no roads."

I asked about the antiaircraft defenses of Helsinki and Viipuri. The minister sneezed into his handkerchief. "But," he said, recovering from the sneezing, "defense in our country is so well organized and so strong that if there should be a European war I do not think any nation would be willing to attack us. By every means possible we shall certainly try to avoid being drawn into war. And our army officers and all those serving in defense work are of the same opinion as the whole population—not to mix up in the struggle."

A secretary came in and said quietly that General Mannerheim had been waiting some time. We turned from the map.

"But Finland will not give up like Czechoslovakia," the minister said with emphasis. "Quite independently of any English-Russian pact that may be made or any other pact, Finland will fight the minute any foreign troops cross our border. The mentality of the Finns is such."

In the anteroom a tall, distinguished man in a smartly tailored dark-gray suit rose from a small sofa. Baron Mannerheim was the perfect product of his aristocratic breeding and his military training. But his athletic figure and his hair and eyes belied his seventy-one years. After the formation of the republic Mannerheim had retired to private life, but was recalled in 1931 to help organize the nation's defenses. "The George Washington of Finland" was the phrase with which some Finns explained him to Americans—"the Father of the Independent Republic." "The White Butcher" the Reds called him in the Soviet press. Whatever he was called in history books, he was already one of Finland's immortals. The door closed on his soldierly back, as he went in to give professional advice about those fortifications I had seen outlined on the map—and which were soon to be publicized in the world's headlines as the Mannerheim Line.

When I came out of the ministry I ran into the dramatic critic whom we had met at Mme. Tompuri's. "Ah, yes," he said, "defense! But Russia can put fifty men where there was one. When Finns are killed, there are no more to take their place. It is sometimes hard for us to face the truth. Finns like to discount Russians as nothing, because they want to think they are nothing."

PART FIVE

"And one more thing, set plainly before the eyes of your soul what will be our final victory: we shall be men."

ALEKSIS KIVI

The Fateful Southeast

VIIPURI AND THE FRONTIER

The minister of defense arranged for the colonel in charge of constructing the anti-tank barricades on the Karelian Isthmus to meet us at Viipuri early Sunday morning and take us to the frontier. The foreign minister, Eljas Erkko, had offered us an interpreter for a trip into the wilds of eastern Finland where only Finnish was spoken and where there were no railroads. I asked for one of his own men, Heikki Brotherus, a young Finn who looked like the portraits of Napoleon in his late twenties and who was the son of the chancellor of Helsinki University. Accompanied by Brotherus, we left by train for Finland's second largest city.

The history of Viipuri goes back to pagan times, when it was a trading post. And as long ago as 1293 a Swedish lord, Torkel Knutsen, built a great fortified castle there as an outpost against the medieval Muscovites. Throughout the subsequent years Viipuri has been periodically engaged in prolonged and bloody sieges. One of the most famous of these occurred in 1495, when Russian hordes attempting to storm the city were routed by Knut Posse, commander of the castle. Posse, who had studied chemistry and physics at the University of Paris, tried tricks on the besiegers, who took them for magic. Filling a copper kettle with lime, lye, and mercury, seasoned with a mess of reptiles and turtles, he caused the mixture to explode in a cave with a noise ten times greater than anyone had ever heard before. At the same time he drenched the invaders with barrels of flaming pitch and tar. The enemy retreated pell-mell in terror back to Russia. Viipuri was not seriously endangered again until the reign of Peter the Great.

Then in the spring of 1710, following Czar Peter's victory over the rash young Charles XII at Poltava, the Russians came over the frozen bay from Kronstadt and began a siege that lasted three months. The Finns held out with superhuman courage, slowly starving or dying from untended wounds. Only when the last bit of food had been scraped from the bins and the last spoonful of gunpowder was spent did the defenders give up the castle. Like the head of John the Baptist, the keys were presented to Peter on a silver salver. What had been Finnish for over four centuries became Russian. Viipuri remained Russian until it was returned to Finland in 1812, and even then, like all Finland, it became a part of the Grand Duchy that was dominated by Imperial Russia. In 1918 it was the last stronghold of the Reds, and when the town fell before the White forces on April 29, Finland's independence was assured.

But Viipuri was to remain free and Finnish for less than twenty-two years. In March 1940, Russians again came over the ice, surrounded the city with their overwhelming forces, their mechanized units and heavy artillery, and began blowing the town to bits. On March 13, when the fall of Viipuri was hourly imminent, the Finnish government mercifully signed a peace treaty. Viipuri again became Russian.

Of all places in Finland Viipuri has suffered most from gunfire. Its blooming gardens and shadowed parks have been more rankly fertilized with human blood than those of almost any other town in Europe. Yet Viipuri was noted for being the gayest of Finland's cities, and the Karelian Finns who inhabit the surrounding districts were said to be the lightest of heart and the quickest to laugh and forget of any of the Finnish people.

Like Finland's capital, the second city of importance was set flatteringly in the midst of water. Parts of it were broken off into islands and peninsulas, with bridges grappling the green chunks together. Even more than Helsinki, Viipuri was a city of contrasts. Memorials of a medieval city wall and narrow, secretive streets merged into boulevards with modern shops and modern architecture. Cobbled streets wound purposefully down to numerous separate quays where the harbors were jammed with ships of a hundred different models. For Viipuri did a big export business and was the outlet of wood products for eastern Finland. The city had the look of a seaport to which sailors had brought home ideas of architecture and decoration from other lands. Here Russians, Swedes, and Germans as well as Finns had erected structures, and yet iron balconies that belonged to the tradition of none of those nationalities adorned second stories of blocks of houses. Although redolent of many centuries of age and change, Viipuri was happily in repair, and the past and present amiably linked arms together in the shade of flowering chestnuts.

Within a seven-minute walk of each other were the warlike thirteenth-century castle, its masonry sides nine feet thick, and Alvar Aalto's new municipal library with walls of glass. A gem of modernity, this most lovely and original library in all Europe was like a palace of crystal held together with chromium and pure white stone. And within was every device for convenience and comfort to encourage the diligent pursuit of knowledge. Its luminous walls had been reared to bring in the light and keep out the weather, to allow the student pausing in his reading to remark the summer glory on the watered garden, or to receive the full benefit of reflected light from opulent winter snow. The building belonged to an advanced age of perpetual peace, for no thought of direct shellfire or shattering detonations had gone into the clarity of its conception. Those outer sheets of glass, those inner walls paneled in pale-yellow birch, with hangings of cream- and silver-colored stuffs, were designed to lift man's mind and lighten his heart as he read or studied or listened to lectures. The library was a gift to the municipality from one of Viipuri's merchants, who having made a fortune in trade returned it when he died in the form of art and learning. Yet not ten blocks to the west, on its compact rocky island, stood Torkel's ancient castle with towers and bastions and cannon, all charged with romantic memories of past wars. It stood with its once impregnable walls—now ivy-clad and faintly pink in the evening light—as a reminder to peace-lovers that they still lived in an earthly world and that at the end of the bottle-necked isthmus fifty miles to the southeast lay Russia with all its mighty menace.

In the park between the ancient fort and the new library townspeople and tourists dined *alfresco* and the military band played Viennese waltzes in its pavilion under the silvery birches. Citizens sat on benches along the sidewalks or stood in groups by the flowering shrubs, swaying slightly to the rhythm. When the band played Grieg's *Morning,* they stopped walking or sat very still, as if the piece held some special significance for them. The Norwegian Grieg, who loved the woods like Sibelius, could speak to them in a musical language they immediately understood.

For coffee and liqueurs the townspeople of Viipuri went back to medieval times. In the southwest corner of the market square stood the famous Round Tower, built in 1550 beside the former cattle gate in the city wall. The Tower, later nicknamed Fat Catherine after the full-bodied Russian empress, had been converted into a restaurant in 1923. The walls were decorated with

AT OULUJOKI THE WORK OF SEPARATING THE MILLIONS OF LOGS ACCORDING TO THEIR OWNERS MUST GO ON AT NIGHT UNDER THE BIG LIGHTS, AS WELL AS BY DAY

REFLECTION OF CELLULOSE MILL IN RIVER AT KAUKOPÄÄ

amusing chalky murals depicting momentous hours in the city's history. The waitresses wore ruffed costumes of the sixteenth century. But though uniformed officers danced with their girls and the orchestra played with spirit, there was little evidence of the Karelian merriment everyone hears of, no hint of the insouciance and glitter and debauchery of days of Russian soldiery. Since the Nazis had high-handedly marched in and possessed Czechoslovakia in April, the people of Viipuri had paused to think that sooner or later they too might be faced with dark threat.

The amplitude of Fat Catherine in the old town stood in contrast to the slender grace of the seven-towered flour mill in the new. On one side of this masterpiece of industrial architecture seven round towers rose from the ground to great height and shone resplendent as alabaster in the white night. Utilitarian in function, co-operatively turning out the stuff that sustained life at the lowest possible price for Finland's wage-earners, the flour mill of Viipuri was audacious with originality and classical economy. Against the bright Finnish night sky, with the electrical illumination of the town twinkling like the Milky Way behind it, the seven-towered flour mill was as startling and impressive as some fantastic monument reared on the plains of India in memory of a maharaja's dead love.

This co-operative flour mill and that municipal library were symbols of the new Finland, where the people provided themselves with the gift of good bread and the rich patriot-merchant bequeathed to them proverbial hyacinths to feed their souls.

Though only fifty miles from Russia, though for one hundred eight years under Russian domination and just before that an actual part of the Russian Empire for more than a century, Viipuri was Finnish to the core. Except for a handful of faltering shops where refugee Russians sold to tourists the remnants of heirlooms, embroideries, ikons, and samovars, there was no soupçon of Russian flavor in Viipuri. The Finns here, as elsewhere, drank coffee like the Swedes, not tea like the Russians. In fact, they rather prided themselves on their ignorance of tea-making. And it would have been easier to get borsch, that ubiquitous Russian soup of beets and cabbage and sour cream, in Peoria, Illinois, than in Viipuri. Such was the tenacity of the Finn for the mores of Western civilization.

I. "WE SHALL BE MEN"

The Colonel called for us early the next morning. He was a tall, slender, slightly stooped man in the middle forties, with sandy hair and a sensitive, English type of face. He was as natural as the outdoors in which he worked, one of those cultivated Finns who find no reward in a sophisticated world to match the satisfaction and thrill of being in the woods—and the wilder and remoter the woods, the greater the zest for him. His smile radiated good will, but his pale gray eyes were sad now at the follies of mankind—the hatred, ambition, and greed of men that made the building of defensive fortifications expedient.

Like the rest of Finland, which is 75 per cent forest and water, Karelia was compounded largely of woods and lakes. The way the Colonel chose to the anti-tank barricades did not go straight, but wound through endless forests. But there were goodly farms too, and wheat grew abundantly in the well-watered isthmus. And now the wheat was at its richest maturity. As the late August breeze passed troublingly over the ripened grain, the fields turned from gold to burnt orange and then burnished copper with rich purplish lights. Never have I seen alien corn so beautiful. Never have I seen a painting with such opulence and harmony of autumnal harvest colors. And around the edges of the fields, the tall silver birches were beginning to herald the fall's approach—slim golden sprays drooping among the fresh green boughs.

Since it was Sunday, no workers were abroad in the fields. The cream-colored cows lay at their mid-morning rest. The good-natured, company-loving Karelians had already set off afoot or on their bikes to the nearest church village or to the seaside. Into our dust on her bicycle rode a buxom golden girl in a pink silk shirtwaist with a sailor straw hat set at the angle fashionable in 1905. She looked like a Gibson girl model returned to life in a Finnish byway.

As we drove along, the Colonel and Brotherus explained the work of the civic guard. It was a volunteer organization, a patriotic citizen militia. It evolved out of the White Guard of 1918 that defeated the Communists. Defense in Finland meant one thing, as I had learned at the ministry: defense against Russia. Because the government had little enough money for materials, to say nothing of wages for labor, the men of the civic guard offered their services in the construction of fortifications. For two years now men belonging to the organization had spent their vacations at hard labor digging, blasting, carrying rock for their country's protection.

Sons of rich men, clerks, landlords, small farmers, railway conductors, musicians, lumbermen, actors, students, city men, and country boys worked side by side for the defense of *Suomi*. The volunteers came for a week or a fortnight. And although the majority of them came from the ranks of the politically conservative or agrarian groups, many factory workers belonging to the dominant social-democratic party, which was dedicated to peace, came to help in the work. In the eleven weeks since the first of June, the Colonel said, 35,000 of these civilians had worked under his direction in setting up anti-tank barricades. In his pocket was a letter from the company physician of a factory who wrote that never had the workers returned from a holiday in such excellent condition. The government allowed eighteen cents for each man's food and this small amount was so skillfully spent that it was sufficient to send them back well-nourished and hearty. The men slept in tents or in barns and sometimes in temporary barracks. Whatever their quarters, they were always close by a river or a lake where they could swim before breakfast or in the evening after the day's work was done. Meals were cooked and served by members of the Lotta Svärd. Shopgirls, schoolteachers, milkmaids, daughters of titled families spent their vacation serving their country, feeding the men that built the defenses.

In the midst of a spruce forest the car came to a sudden halt. We had arrived at our first line of anti-tank defenses. On either side of the narrow road stood rows of jagged pink boulders chest-high, four abreast. As far as the eye could see among the trees to the right and the left were these thick slabs of granite, stiff as soldiers at attention and looking like pink monuments in a cemetery.

At first glance the arrangement of rocks appeared to be something boys had devised at play. But the jagged blocks were set in holes two meters deep in nests of concrete and pebbles. And the chest-high stones, solid in the ground, could not be moved except by blasting. Blasting, the Colonel explained, would leave such holes that the enemy tanks could not pass until the holes had been filled. During the delay the Finns would be at work sniping and blowing up the tanks.

The Colonel was proud of the work. Finland could not afford the concrete blocks for tank barricades that the Germans had built. So he had thought up the idea of blasting the native granite from its bed in the earth and turning it to its country's defense.

We walked half a mile in one direction, half a mile in the other. To the left where the terrain became marshy, and the granite could have no suitable base, the water hazards were reinforced by stout ten-foot walls of logs and mud.

"At any rate, if they ever come, this will hold them off awhile," Brotherus said. And the soundness of the ingenuity was to be shortly proved when tanks by the hundreds were stopped at the barricades and blown to smithereens.

A half hour away was one of the Lotta Svärd camps in an old barn in a sloping hayfield overlooking a river. When we arrived about half-past ten, six pretty girls were washing out great boilers where the breakfast porridge had been cooked. Dressed in gray-blue cotton dresses with big white aprons, they looked like Red Cross workers without the flowing veils. An older woman chaperoned the half-dozen girls.

The men were standing around idle because it was Sunday. Some had just arrived, some had finished their fortnight's work. They were a varied lot, ranging in age from fifteen to sixty-four. Many just arrived were not yet in uniform. But Finnish summer uniforms of blue-gray denim were so sloppy that they looked no smarter than the farm clothes. The Finns were too sensible to waste money dressing their soldiers for parades and admiration. Despite the friendliness of officers with men, very strict discipline was maintained. It almost made us smile to see an officer stiffly salute our Colonel in his wrinkled denim uniform, clicking his dusty boots with all the manner of a German captain on parade.

The soldiers crowded around us with amused curiosity, as we examined this and that. Lottas bustled about, clattering dishes, setting tables for luncheon on boards set up on dirt floors of the barn where cows lodged in winter. Rungs nailed on a log wall led to a loft where the girls slept on quilts spread out on the hay. I wanted to see their quarters. So did the Colonel. The boys looked at each other and grinned involuntarily when I started climbing the ladder. They burst into laughter when the Colonel followed me up. The Colonel did not mind, but smiled good-naturedly. On the sweet-smelling hay lay seven quilts: six for the girls, one for the chaperon. A suitcase lay beside each quilt and a blanket at the foot for cover. When these girls went others would come, and they too would learn to make adjustments to primitive living.

The hundred-odd men who fed here at the camp lived on other properties—except for six who slept as armed guards in a low tent near the shed kitchen. The atmosphere was like that of a summer camp. Uniforms seemed merely masquerades for a vacation—like slacks and shorts. There was no feeling of imminent war. The outing seemed devised for the purpose of keeping youth in touch with simplicity—and here the meeting of all classes on an equal footing was as humanizing and fraternal as in a real war.

While the Lottas boiled fresh coffee for us, the boys gathered in the barn and sang. One great lusty youth with a broad handsome face and straw-colored hair stood in the front line leading the singing in a resounding baritone. He spoke a little English and smiled much. He came from above Oulu in the west. He was going to be a Lutheran priest, and in six more months he would finish his theology course. I noted the gold band on his third finger. Yes, he was married already—in June. He had left his bride to come to help with the defenses. But his fortnight work was over—it had been great fun—and he was returning to his wife tomorrow. He asked if we'd like to hear them sing the Finnish national anthem, written by Runeberg in 1848.

The volunteers gathered close together, and never was there such fervor of patriotic singing under the beams of a cowbarn. Men outside who couldn't get in crowded to the door until they almost shut out the sunlight. They joined in the singing, opening their mouths wide, making masculine music like the leader. It was a stirring anthem. Therese and the Colonel and Brotherus and I stood in the corner by the ladder to the loft and listened with everything we had as they sang *Our Land.*

Three of the verses, into which they put a particular intensity of emotion, run like this in the Stork translation:

> Oh, who could tell the fearful tale
>   Of what that folk withstood,
> Their hunger in the wintry gale
> When war ran red from dale to dale?
>   Who counts the drops of heroes' blood,
>   Their feats of hardihood?
>
> 'Twas here they shed that crimson tide,
>   Yea, here for us it flowed,
> 'Twas here they thrilled with victor pride,
> 'Twas here in bitter grief they sighed.
>   The folk that bore our heavy load
>   And broke for us—a road.
>
> To us there is no fairer spot—
>   We lack not, feel not dearth;
> However fate may cast our lot,
> A land, a native land we've got.
>   What better could men ask on earth
>   To love and hold of worth?

When they came to the lines asking what could men better ask on earth than to have a native land to love, the eyes of the men took on an expression of such moving intensity that it was like a glimpse of the very essence of patriotism at its purest and noblest.

This was the thing itself unmixed with a trace of alloy, and I had never seen or felt patriotism like this among any people in any land before. It was not inspired by martial excitement, for the Finns were at peace and they did not believe a robber nation would ever really come to crash their boundaries and barricades. But as I watched these men sing and reveal their hearts on that peaceful Sunday in a Karelian barn, I knew how terrifically they would fight for their land if beset. I did not need to see the Finns at war to behold the composite face of the courage and sacrificial devotion which was soon to amaze the world.

Again, as many incidents in our travels about Finland recalled lines from that most Finnish of Finns, Aleksis Kivi, I thought of another passage that bore out what the Finns had already achieved and what future historians must truthfully report of them:

> And one more thing, set plainly before the eyes of your soul what will be our final victory: we shall be men.—And our graves on the misty coming shore of life will not seem a home of terror for us, but a place of delightful rest, a shadowy porch to the halls of the blest.

The coffee was ready in the great room under the loft. I wanted to talk with the theological student who had led the singing, and I asked the Colonel if I might ask him to have coffee with us. The Colonel hesitated for only an instant and said, "Why not?" We paid a small tribute to military proprieties by having three of us sit between the Colonel and the volunteer. But the young man was quite at ease, and though the Colonel did not talk with him he smiled at him reassuringly. "In war-time, Finnish officers and men are served precisely the same food," Brotherus said, "though for discipline's sake they eat separately. Such is our real democracy."

The captain in charge of the camp was addressing the new men when we left. They were standing at attention in their civilian clothes, their hands straight and held tight against their thighs. The captain was telling them to remember their honor as soldiers. They were new here in this particular countryside and they might never come again. But they must remember that the people in whose midst they had come were innocent folk, unschooled in the fashions of the world; soldiers must not take advantage of their innocence, but must ever deal with them in gentleness and with honor, as they always did with their own neighbors back home.

II. RUSSIAN GHOSTS

On the way to Terijoki the Colonel had the chauffeur turn off on a side road, and we went some thirty kilometers out of our way to visit a wood that contained the tallest trees in Europe. It had been planted by a Russian empress a century and a half ago. It was an enchanting wood of a special rare breed of larch trees. The great tall trunks, straight as columns in a Grecian temple, seemed to support a green fretted roof, for the delicate needled branches shut out the sky except for faint traceries like blue enamel in a cathedral ceiling. The ground was a thick carpet of damp moss and blueberry bushes. And the light along the paths was like that sifted through old stained glass. It was just such a wood as might have been planted by an empress as a trysting place for future empresses and all the ladies-in-waiting of an imperial court.

The trees should be cut, the Colonel said, as we stood looking up at their incredible height. But we protested it would be a desecration to destroy such beauty. The wood might as well be used, he retorted, for the trees were more than one hundred fifty years old—past maturity. If not cut, before long they would begin to fall of their own rottenness—as the empire had.

Besides, he added as we wound down to a little river where fresh-water pearls were gathered, if there was trouble with Russia, the Reds would quickly take this forest, because the first significant line of fortification was behind us now. The trees were worth money—Finland would lose a valuable equity if all these square kilometers of forest passed into the Reds' possession.

When we had returned to the white glare of noon on the dusty road and headed again for Terijoki and luncheon, a mirage-like vision appeared on the horizon beyond a hill to the right. A jade green tower topped by gleaming gold stood out spectacularly above the pine trees.

"What's that?" Therese asked with some excitement.

"The Grave of Love," Brotherus said, "a chapel built by a Russian count in memory of his wife. She's buried there. Andreev, the playwright, is buried there, too. The gold on that tower is pure."

"But let's go—by all means," I urged.

We were all hungry, but Therese and I wanted to see the gold-topped chapel and Andreev's grave. The accommodating Colonel ordered the chauffeur to turn back and find a connecting road. It had not occurred to our Finnish companions that we might be interested in anything so bizarre. It was Russian, and therefore to Finnish eyes it held little interest.

On a bare ugly hilltop, surrounded beneath by skinny pine trees, the domed church rose, with its crown of gold flashing in the sun like a powerful lighthouse lamp. Around the chapel and the private cemetery were stone walls twice a man's height, so that the only view within the grounds was through locked iron gates. Andreev's grave was marked with only a simple black cross, Brotherus said. The poet had died there while on a prolonged visit under the patronage of the countess. We could not tell which was his grave—or how many of the crosses marked the resting places of other poor pensioners befriended by the lady.

The countess had been a famous beauty, Brotherus explained, an intellectual woman and a patron of artists. Her husband had loved her devotedly, but he had had an affair with an actress in St. Petersburg. There was trouble, a separation, and finally a reunion. As expiation for his infidelity he had built this chapel for his wife. Brotherus did not recall the story precisely—some romantic tale of Russians—hardly worth remembering.

We walked around the barren hillside past the front of the chapel. A little below it in an open space protected by a spiked iron fence the lady herself was sitting lifelike in bronze on a rock. Her hair was slightly pompadoured in the fashion of 1910, and her Edwardian dress spread in soft natural folds. She was a beautiful woman with the chiseled features of Greek sculptures but a contemporary expression. She sat there in the glaring sun, looking as if she were alive, staring out over the treetops to the sea and the Russian shore. At her feet sat a frolicsome bear cub, also in bronze. The countess had had such a pet about her always, and now the cub kept her company in her long vigil.

Nothing but a Russian nobleman of that dead, extravagant era could have conceived of anything so fantastic as a statue of a lady, in the costume of 1910, sitting on a barren hillside with a playful cub at her feet, against a background of Byzantine towers and a pure gold dome erected in expiation of marital infidelity. To the Finn it was typical of the foolishness of Russians. The waste and disproportion irritated his common sense more than the romantic tale stirred his imagination.

"A funny, mad lot, those Russians," Brotherus said. "They tell a story of a nobleman, Duke Demidoff, who managed to escape with twenty of his servants into Finland when the Reds were slaughtering the aristocrats. Accustomed as he was to a prodigal regime, his money was soon gone, his jewels sold, the twenty servants dispersed, and he and his family reduced to threadbare want. Some sympathetic Finns gave him a purse of five thousand marks for food and clothes. When they called to see to what good uses he had put the money, he showed them with great pride and joy two Pekingese pups. In ragged grandeur he and his duchess used to parade with the brace of snooty little dogs, which kindly neighbors had to feed. Finally Demidoff got a job as a coachman, and then became a farmer's helper. One day, driving a cart of manure into the fields, he absent-mindedly toppled from his seat and broke his noble neck."

"But I must say," the Colonel added, "Russian aristocrats were remarkable at greeting misfortune. If Finns should lose all like those Russians, no happy day could one have."

We were hot and dusty and very hungry as we covered the last ten kilometers to Terijoki. In the imperial days before the revolution, Terijoki had been a favorite summer resort for Russian society. The miles of bathing beaches and the gardens of estates had been thronged with gay holiday-makers. After the strain of a glamorous winter season in St. Petersburg, they loved to lie "lazing" in the sun on the lawns or on the beach. Like all aristocrats they strove for complete simplicity in the country as a relief from the artificiality of the city and the court. The young women wore flounced white organdies with bright sashes and floppy straw hats. Entertaining was informal, and consisted mostly of small supper parties in the gardens by candlelight.

But the privileged Russians, who never had a money sense and could not be simple about spending, threw their money about in cavalier prodigality. And though the peasants on their estates in Russia might be too poor to buy salt for their cabbage stew, Russian gentlemen rarely bothered to take change for a five-rouble note when they bought a bunch of wild flowers in Finland. The irrational extravagance filled the thrifty, hard-working Finns with as much contempt as amazement, though many a Finn got rich off summer visitors.

The revolution of 1917 had come in October just after the Russians had closed their summer houses in Karelia and returned to St. Petersburg for the winter season. Now the villas were still standing on either side the road, many of them with their windows boarded up just as the Russians had left them twenty-three years ago. The owners had never returned to rehabilitate them, because those owners had been destroyed by the violence their ways had fomented. Here the houses remained, rotting away under the great shades trees, but the people who had inhabited them had gone with the wind. Hardly ten out of the ten thousand owners of villas in the district had lived to return to their property. Prosperous Finns had bought some of the houses, repaired them, and used them for summer residences. Many of the finer ones had been bought and removed to other parts of Finland. When the villas were sold, the Finnish government scrupulously put the money in the state bank for the owners or the heirs, who by all counts must have been murdered long ago.

"By now," said the Colonel, "all trace of the poor devils seems to have disappeared. But the money is still here in the banks, waiting for them—and drawing interest."

An air of decadence and dismay now pervaded the ghost-thronged properties. Fences drooped and weeds intruded on the gravelly walks. Grass choked the struggling flowers that still volunteered gallantly in the gardens. And though casinos and bathing establishments and pensions had been set up to revive Terijoki to a semblance of its former self, the town, for all its lovely situation, was a saddening relic. The loudspeakers of radios blared horridly under the trees of the park to excite the visitors to gaiety. But the few Finns sitting along the edges of the restaurant's glassed veranda were not a joyous-looking lot.

We ate luncheon quickly and drove to Rajajoki on the Russian border, where the Helsinki-Leningrad railroad crossed the boundary. The approach to Rajajoki was forbidden territory. Even our Colonel had had to get permission from the war department to take us in, and he had to show his pass to three different guards along the way.

A narrow river separated Finland and Russia and made their common frontier. On the Russian side vicious tangles of barbed wire stretched along the river bank. In the center of the railway bridge white Finnish paint met red Russian paint. On the Russian side the train had to pass under an arch decorated with a great red star. Beyond lay the station of Beloostrov—and a little farther on the outskirts of Leningrad began.

A youthful Finnish guard with a bayoneted gun stood in the doorway of a sentry house by the tracks leading over the bridge. On the opposite end of the bridge a form moved in front of the Russian sentry house.

The Colonel borrowed a pair of field glasses from the guard. The powerful lens brought the form across the river within seeming touching distance. The Russian guard, too, had a pair of field glasses to his eyes. He stared back at me as if hating my curiosity. He put down his glasses and hid behind a screen of bushes. He was only a youth, slim and pale, with reddish hair.

He would peep over the bushes and then duck back out of sight.

While we were standing there, two busses drove up in a cloud of dust and disgorged Finns: some of them were backwoods country folk, the older women with headkerchiefs tied under their chins. It was Sunday, and they had come out of curiosity to try to catch a holiday glimpse of Bolsheviks. They must have gone to no end of trouble to get permission. It had seemed all right for the four of us to have curiosity, but two busloads of pleasure-seekers on the same mission made our curiosity seem vulgar. The Colonel and Brotherus felt it, too, and we prepared to leave.

A long train appeared on the Finnish side, coming slowly down the track to the bridge. We stood aside, watching it. It approached cautiously, as if feeling its way across the border. It was a Russian freight train with empty cars. The Russian engineer stared out of his window, arm propped on the ledge. His pale, immobile face with theatric dark eyes and brows looked like a countenance from another planet. He regarded us with sullen disdain as the long, empty train crept over the bridge into Russia.

The black-eyed man in the box looked as if he would kill with no more compunction than a robot. The red-headed Russian youth looked as if death around the corner would not surprise him. The ill-will and the fear all seemed so tragically wasteful. By a mere changing of mental concepts the Russians on the red side of the bridge and the Finns on the white might have commingled freely and wished each other well.

From Rajajoki we drove to another border place. On the way we passed a monument before a farmhouse at a crossroads called Joutselkä. The memorial was a pyramid of granite erected in 1931. On this battlefield, the inscription said, 560 Finnish soldiers and embattled peasants had routed a Russian army of 5,000 —in the year 1550.

Throughout the ages the Finns had repelled Tartar invasions against tremendous odds. This particular parcel of ground had been lost and regained, lost and regained, time after time. But despite long periods of Russian domination the Finns had never ceased to cling tenaciously to their Finnish individuality and independence of spirit. "Not two centuries of attempted Russification here," Brotherus said, "have made the Finns one whit Russian."

In a pleasant, red-stained farmhouse with a pretty garden some hundred yards from the border lived a jolly group of Finnish sentinels. Accompanied by an armed guard, we walked down a country road banked by shade trees, with grass growing in the roadbed smooth as a lawn. In former days this was the main highway to Leningrad. It had been untraveled now for two decades. We stopped before barbed wire stretched across the remains of a concrete bridge, which had been dynamited in 1918. There was no sign of life except for a tinkling of a cowbell. On the Russian side we could see only a watchtower like a water tank above the treetops. A short barbed-wire fence edged the willow-shadowed creek on our side.

"That little fence wouldn't do much good," I said, pointing.

"It's good enough for cattle," the guard said. "It's to keep our cows from swimming the stream and wandering on Russian soil to be milked or eaten by the Reds."

Except for the blasted bridge, it was a peaceful rural scene of idyllic peace, such as Corot put on canvas. Then a figure moved in the top of the watchtower in Russia, and the sylvan setting took on an air of secrecy and menace.

All during the rest of the afternoon we continued to pass four-rowed lines of pink granite boulders cutting across farmers' fields, traversing cow pastures, winding through forests and linking the natural defenses of lake to lake.

At a village of two thousand Russians we paused to see the church. The original inhabitants had fled from Russian oppression to Finland during a past century. The houses were in shocking disrepair, the only evidences of abject poverty we had yet seen in Finland. Some of the men made pottery for a living. A few cultivated patches of flax. It was backward poverty of the past, unrelieved by that hope for a future which we had felt in the poverty of Lapland.

At the Greek Catholic church we saw a Madonna incrusted with real pearls hanging on a gold filigree wall. Pearls under glass in a village where men and women were in want seemed as irrational as Duke Demidoff's purchase of the brace of Pekingese he could not feed.

Evening had come, and we still had a long journey before us, but the Colonel directed the chauffeur to drive home by a roundabout back road among the lakes. He seemed to relax as he got away from Russia into the security of his own simple land with its clean-smelling woods and its "secretly smiling lakes." We felt a great admiration for this military man, so understanding, so without ostentation and superior attitudes, as genuine as the country of which he was a part.

The gray-blue lakes among the trees grew black under the evening shadows. As we passed farms, milkmaids moved silently in the dusk like figures on a screen. The atmosphere was full of contentment and blessed with the peace of a Finnish evening on the threshold of autumn.

Within four months every acre of meadow and wood that we

had traversed this Sunday, every town and industry we had remarked, had passed into the possession of Russia. Hardly a house or barn in all the district was left standing intact. The people who had had their homes here for generations had moved into cramped temporary quarters west of Viipuri or had begun to fell logs to start a new life in a wilderness.

POWER OF WATER

After supper the Colonel's super-sinewed little chauffeur drove us on to Imatra, where we were to spend the night. From the dim past Imatra had been famous for the most mighty rapids in Europe. In the mauve decade Russians had made it a favorite vacation spot, and to accommodate them Finland in 1903 had built an ornate hotel in the grand Russian manner. Here reservations had to be made long in advance, for the upper-class Russians flocked to Imatra before 1917 to make use of its dramatic scenery as a background for their merrymaking, and sometimes for their spectacular suicides.

Beneath the very window balconies of the State Hotel the deep granite gorge ran tortuously among the trees. The rushing water had formed gigantic waves that broke into high-flung foam like a prodigal scattering of diamond dust. The clamor of the rapids was so insistent that men could make love only by sighs and touch, and would-be suicides could not hear restraining inner voices, but only catch the compelling call that said never could one die more cleanly in a setting more sublime. Here every year Russian men and women had leaped romantically to their death.

But the Russians were gone now, and with them the personal drama. The pink plaster palace of Prince Obolensky a few miles away was falling into disrepair, and today it housed some of the office force of the pulp factory at Kaukopää. The tumultuous water had been turned from the gorge to pragmatic rather than romantic uses. A power station with its dam had diminished the sensational force of water. Imatra had become the center of the greatest industrial area of Finland. Spreading out over an area of a few kilometers were paper mills, sawmills, cellulose mills, sulphite spirit plants, bobbin factories, and plywood factories, and brand-new plants for making rayon. At the Imatra Electric Smelter, Outokumpu's purple ore yield was made into iron. The Imatra Iron works manufactured rails and forgings and billets. The works were being extended, and shortly the output of steel was to be increased to eighty thousand tons a year. At the Kaukopää sulphate-cellulose mill on Lake Saimaa a million dollars' worth of cordwood lay stacked in the yards.

At the new Imatra power station, owned by the state and built by the state, six powerful Francis turbines had been installed, developing in all 174,000 horsepower and coupled directly with generators. Not only were the large copper, iron, and chlorate works in the neighborhood and all the agricultural consumers round about supplied with cheap electric power, but the whole of southern Finland, as far as Kuopio to the north and Helsinki and Turku in the west, drew vitalizing power from Imatra.

The most striking factor in the mechanized setup was that the surrounding countryside still looked like a countryside and not like the edges of an industrial center. Forests and well-pruned orchards and meadows joined industry with industry. The workmen's cottages were not jammed together but were set pleasantly in the midst of little gardens. Sometimes they were strung through the woods like shooting boxes in the Adirondacks. All the new plants had been designed and furnished in the smart Finnish functionalist style, and they made the pretentious bedizened hotel and Obolensky's pearl-pink palace seem as obsolete as serfdom.

When we arrived at the hotel, the antithesis of a fashionable Russian society thronged the corridors. The crowd looked more like a sheriff's posse returned from a successful search. It was completely masculine—hundreds of hatted men in khaki breeches and puttees were moving about, many of them bearing rifles. A great shooting match in progress for several days had been concluded that evening. Men from all stations in life and all parts of Finland had competed for honors in marksmanship. In Finland to be able to shoot straight is regarded as a part of a man's equipment for life—just as an intensive study of plant life and animal life is a requirement for all Finnish school children. Some of the popular appeal of Pehr Svinhufvud, former president, is due to his having once been champion marksman of Finland.

In the midst of the confusion of marksmen's celebrating we said good night to our chauffeur. He had had a grueling day of driving—he had been up since six, and now it was nearing midnight, and tomorrow he had to be ready to drive the Colonel at seven again. Brotherus and I pressed on him money that came to more than his weekly salary. "No, it is too much," he kept insisting. Because he was so tired, tears almost came into his eyes when we forcibly stuffed the money into his pocket and shook his hand fervently in gratitude and friendship.

In the morning Brotherus and I did a round of mills and factories, talked with managers and foremen, examined statistics on the astounding industrial progress of the last two decades. We had driven home to us what we already knew, that the forests were the be-all and the end-all of Finnish economy. Finland's lifeblood was arboreal sap. For Finland to survive, the nation's forests had to be preserved. Legislation for tree conservation was not merely prudent and rational; it was an absolute necessity. And a threat of any foreign power at war to set fire to Finland's forests was like holding a loaded revolver at Finland's heart. In the early months of 1940 Russia threatened to burn the Finnish woods when the snows melted and the spring sun dried the trees.

From one of the directors of the famous Enso-Gutzeit combine we learned many things about the wood industry. In spite of contraction of business since 1929, Finland has nevertheless been the largest exporter of sawed timber in the world for several years past—Finland is followed by Canada, Soviet Russia, Sweden, and then the United States. Great Britain is Finland's foremost customer, and South Africa occupies first place among her overseas customers. The powerful growth of the sawed-timber trade in Finland is seen in the export figures: in 1860, about 85,000 standards were exported; in 1900, about 500,000. The average yearly export since 1920 has been approximately 1,000,000. The joint interests both at home and abroad are supervised by the Finnish Sawmill Owners' Association, to which all the most important concerns of this kind belong. In good times nearly 700 sawmills operated in the little country, and 500 of these sawed for export.

Pine is the most important wood in the sawed-timber trade. The climatic conditions of Finland are particularly happy for the growth of pine. The trunks grow straight and tall and are generally free from branches right up to the crown. Because growth is so slow, the timber is strong and hard, easy to dress and polish, and signally resistant to atmospheric conditions. In the southern and central parts of Finland it takes a pine tree 80 to 160 years to grow large enough for milling; in the north, 200 to 300 years. Whereas in the southern United States a tree requires only seven years to become large enough to cut for pulping, corresponding trees in the warmest latitudes of Finland require at least fifty years.

Finland does a big business in wood pulp, boards, cardboard, and fiberboard. But the most spectacular example of her progress attained since independence is that shown in the chemical pulp industry. The industry has increased tenfold in twenty years, and Finland has risen to second place—following Sweden—among the countries of the world exporting sulphate and sulphite pulp. In this industry, as with almost all others in Finland, co-operation has proved most successful. The Finnish Cellulose Union manages the sale of 90 per cent of the nation's exports of chemical pulp.

The manufacture of paper has increased only threefold in two decades, but in the export of newsprint Finland ranks second only to Canada, which leads the world by a tremendous margin in tonnage.

The Enso Company owns considerably over one million acres of forest. It employs 16,000 workmen, not counting the corps of workers in the woods. Although 80 to 90 per cent of the employees vote the Social Democratic ticket, only 20 to 40 per cent belong to labor unions. They do not join the labor unions, because they know it could be of no benefit in getting better wages. The company pays as much as it can afford, and in 1937 it raised the wages of the workmen three times without their once asking for a raise.

The average worker gets what amounts to about $40 a month in American money, although sometimes for overtime he can make two and a half times that amount. But he and his family can live comfortably in Finland on a $40 wage, since the cost of living is low. All education is free, and amusements cost nothing. The company maintains six sports places for the workers. There are halls for dramatics and dancing, swimming pools and cinemas. The company maintains professional orchestra leaders to train the musically inclined; there are three amateur orchestras and two bands. If men want to build their own homes, the company gives them the land and lends them the money at low interest rates. It furnishes free plans for houses and sells all materials and tools at 10 per cent above cost.

We drove about, visiting workers' houses at Kaukopää. At one where we called, a bailer and wrapper named Malmikoski had been living in his own home for three years now. It had cost him only $1,000 complete, with an outside *sauna*. He had built it himself in his spare time. Within ten years it would all be paid for. He had a vegetable garden where tomatoes were growing against a wall, and a flower garden with dahlias, asters, and gigantic cosmos. His electricity even in the long dark winter cost him only fifty cents a month—"And," he said, "we boil coffee by electricity, many times a day."

Malmikoski, the factory worker, was as contented with his lot in life as the bear-killing farmer in Lapland had been. Perhaps he would never own an automobile—but he had a cupboard in the basement stocked with skis, and there were bicycles for all the family. He did not need a car or train or bus to get him to work. In summer it was only a pleasant walk along a berry-bordered footpath under spruce trees. And in winter, when the snow made a white floor in the forest, what Finn would choose to sit inert in a motor car when he could go on skis?

Finland is struggling to increase the productivity of her forests. The state has begun to dike some of the woods and survey the land to ascertain where new forests can be established. But even Finland has faults in her wood conservation, for it is not economical to burn as much birch for fuel as she does. A large percentage of the Finnish railway engines are fired entirely with birchwood. This practice has been going on for three quarters of a century and will be ended only when Finland can afford to electrify her railways. "Until we electrify our trains we should import coal," one of the men showing us about some plants said. "The next generation of Finns will think it as foolish to burn birch as it was for Mexicans to make their railway crossties of mahogany."

When the crisis at the end of the 1920's hit Finland like every other country, she realized that her weakest economic factor was her one-sided dependence on the export of timber, which accounted for 60 per cent of the value of her total exports. So her leaders set out to find new industries and new ways of utilizing wood, with the result that in 1937 the total output of all industries was 49 per cent higher than in the climactic year of 1929. The sawmilling industry had lost so much of its relative importance that in 1938 its share of value amounted to only 40 per cent of the total exports, while paper exports had doubled, plywood had more than doubled, and pulp had trebled. If this development can continue unhampered, Finland will leave the group of countries producing raw materials and semi-manufactures and take her place among the modern industrial countries, by reason of both her economic structure and her economic standard.

"But remember," said Jaako Kahma, head of the Finnish Export Association, "Finland's industrial development must be based in large measure on the international division of labor. Finland's foreign trade has of necessity proceeded parallel with her industrial expansion. Finland is dependent on foreign trade more than most other countries. In relation to national income, she sells more to other countries than any other country in the world except Belgium and New Zealand—her exports amounting to 35 per cent of her national income. In 1939 Finland's total foreign trade amounted to about $115 per inhabitant, while in the United States it amounted to only $50.

"Finland's policy in trade treaties like that of Cordell Hull has preferred 'the most-favored nation' principle and avoided bilateralism. A policy of autarchy would be impossible for Finland. It would retard exploitation of our resources and curb our people's enterprising spirit. Besides, compulsory restrictions go against the grain of Finnish national character. Finland will always favor freedom of trade, and she will do all she can to lower or remove the present barriers to foreign trade."

Three miles below Imatra lie the magnificent rapids of Vallinkoski, where the colors shift magically from green to luminous white and silver like the flickers in a kaleidoscope. The swirling waters plunge and leap over the gigantic boulders as uncurbed as wild horses. Now their chief value lies in their wondrous free beauty. But soon a new power station will be built to harness the horsepower and bring more light and prosperity to inhabitants of Finland.

One cannot drive to the edge of Vallinkoski—he must approach it humbly, by footpath, through a tended forest. We sat on a boulder at the rapids' edge with the spume dashing high before us and making a pierced and patterned screen. And although a café pavilion was somewhere on the hill behind us, we were as removed from industry and modernity as the first Finnish trappers who stumbled upon this savage beauty. Nature's music that we heard here was as primordial as creation, as pure as Mozart's, as mighty as that of Sibelius.

"Well," said Brotherus, "men may come and go, but Finland will ever be rich in wood and water—those primitive elements so essential to mankind."

As we returned to the place where we had left the car a

quarter of a mile back, I stopped to take a picture from between two great pine trees. In one shot I got the main economy of Finland—the edges of a forest; a field with stacked wheat; beyond that, a meadow with grazing milch cows, and in the far background the smokestacks and spreading roofs of a plant that turned the wood to cellulose. The scene lay in levels of harmony and beauty under a benign blue sky where fleecy clouds trailed each other like slow-moving barges in a pageant.

As we approached our car, we saw a girl carrying two buckets of water across a field to a farmhouse beneath the road. "With all this electric power," Therese said, "in this modern place of industry, couldn't they have plumbing on farms?"

Brotherus regarded the girl with the buckets, and then said, "Too much plumbing is not good for peasants. If life is made too easy it will degenerate the Finns."

I laughed. But Therese, indignant at man's smug attitude toward the hardships of country women, retorted, "Good plumbing never degenerated anybody."

THE BIG SHOW

Sortavala on the shore of Lake Laatokka linked the last vivid evidence of old imperial Russia to the modern world. To reach the world-famous monastery of Valamo one embarked at Sortavala. Geographically farther east than Leningrad, Sortavala was as Finnish as Rovaniemi in Lapland, and it looked as new and vitally progressive, although in 1939, after three hundred seven years of history, it had only five thousand inhabitants. Four-story modernistic buildings were replacing the one-story wooden structures, and a newly opened hotel stretching along the tree-lined river was more attractive than any hostelry in Helsinki. Though from its quarries Sortavala had supplied the granite for most of the public buildings of old St. Petersburg, the town of 1939 was using modern concrete and chromium and glass blocks for its own construction. Sortavala was the economic and cultural center of Laatokka-Karelia. It was the market town of a fertile farming district and an educational center. It was the seat of the Finnish archbishopric of the Greek Catholic Church and the nucleus of sawmills and plywood factories. But the industries were under discreet control—the town council had bought up sufficient surrounding land to prevent industry from crowding in and despoiling the town's natural beauty.

Lake steamers for Valamo sailed daily from the Sortavala docks—a slow journey of some two and a half hours that took one within fifteen miles of the Soviet half of the lake and centuries backward in time. The steamers were owned by the monastery, and though their skippers were trained Finnish seamen all of them had monks for pilots and ticket collectors. The monks had gone into the tourist business on a big scale. Their dramatic way of life and their magnificent surroundings had a show value richer than any other attraction in the Northern Countries.

In the pilot box a gray-robed brother with flowing gray beard and hair rippling down over his shoulders held the wheel and steered us through a wooded archipelago toward the open water of the largest lake in Europe. On our masthead was a silver cross atop a silver ball. The pilot was as intent on his job as a saint about to go into a trance. It was like the beginning of a storybook voyage into a mythical land.

But the sober-hearted Finnish captain in his cabin kept up a running commentary on reality. "It's all theatrics," he said to me quietly. "They put on a good performance, and they put money in the bank. They are rich, very rich. They carry money by the bagful to deposit in Finnish banks. There used to be 1,400 monks back in 1914, but the Russian government took 700 of them to fight. Not one single one ever came back or was heard from again. Now there are only 164 monks and a few novices left. They can't get any more monks from Russia. Reds don't make good monks—so they have a school for Finnish orphans on the island and try to turn them into monks. Often when a poor man dies, his widow brings the boys here to be educated as novices. It's all right until the boys get to be eighteen and have to do their yearly military service on the mainland. Then they get a different feel for life—they get a taste of girls and liquor, and they don't come back to be monks."

Out in the open water the lake seemed limitless as the ocean. In the intense sunlight the surface of the water sparkled like a scarf of azure sequins. A lone woman rowing a great boatload of marsh reeds was all that we passed in the vast expanse. "Taking them home for mat-tres-ses," the captain said, and picked up a book from his desk. "All the time I am improving my English—see?" He handed me the book. "This is an up-to-date English study."

I flipped the pages to Lesson 3, a dialogue between Billy and Tommy. I read:

Does your brother work now, Tommy?
Yes, he is in a new talkie.
What part does he take?
He is a mute fellow.

I turned to Lesson 6.

Do you know what a film star is?
Yes, she is a girl all hair, smile, and teeth. All young girls have clear skins, but if their teeth is not good, their mouths are not pretty.

"Look, they are in sight," said the captain.

I turned from the simple language lessons to gaze upon the

fantastic outlines of Byzantine cupolas and minarets shimmering with the brilliance of the ancient East. As the vessel approached the islands, the colors became more intense—the deep electric blue and the contrasting powder blue of the domes of the cathedral topped with a gold cross gleamed against the paler blue sky and made a memorable symphony in blue. From the fjordlike bay the monastery and the hotel came into view, set on a rise above green banks redolent with wild flowers.

Two horse-drawn droshkies and a scattering of black-robed monks waited on the dock to greet the boatload of tourists and pilgrims. At high speed we were driven up the hill to the hotel. Droshkies are exciting vehicles, with nothing but a shallow tray for a seat and no back or sides to cling to. They rock and sway, and the spirited horses were as nervous as the monks, who met us at the steps of the monastery-hotel with eyes trembling in their sockets as if on springs.

The "office" on the second floor was merely an oilcloth-covered table with a series of great keys strung on brass rings set in the corridor. Behind it stood the specterlike manager with piercing black eyes, a dead-white skin, and false hair switches hanging from his high, brimless hat. Here, assisted by student interpreters, the guests were assigned to their accommodations. Poorer pilgrims remained on the ground floor and stayed for nominal fees, cooking their own food in a common kitchen and making their ablutions at basins set up in the corridors.

We were shown down a long corridor, where footsteps reverberated as if during a parade in a prison. Our simple corner room was clean and neat, and looked out on banks of lilac bushes. The walls were faintly washed in blue. Over my bed hung a chromo of the murdered Czarina, and over Therese's a chromo of the little Czarevitch. The iron beds were hard, but the sheets were of pure linen.

A young Russian handsomely dressed like a well-tailored monk in the movies was appointed to show us about. He had glistening red hair that curled, and he spoke English in a soft, rhythmical voice. A senior at the University of Helsinki, he served at Valamo as guide in the summers to pay his board in the winter. He was a White Russian—his refugee father and mother, the Baron and Baroness von Knorring, worked in a chocolate factory in Helsinki. They had no money except their factory wages, the young man told us later, but they were quite happy in their new way of life.

Because Brotherus of the foreign office was with us, we were invited to have tea with the Igumen, the head of the order. The Vice-Igumen himself came to conduct us to the audience. His little coal-black eyes looked us shrewdly through and through, while his red sensual lips smiled welcomingly. He was a big fellow with a curly chestnut beard covering his chest like a dickey, and iron-gray hair flowing over the shoulders of his belted black robe. The three of us had become keenly conscious of back hair and beards, lengths and shades, and various color combinations. Long hair is one of the dominant impressions one receives at Valamo.

When we knocked at the Igumen's house an emaciated servant-monk, with a silky beard and cascading hair white as tuberoses, cracked the door suspiciously, with all the caution of a speakeasy attendant. Then, recognizing the Vice-Igumen, in a tremulous whisper he bade us enter. Nervous as a girl, he bolted the door behind us and then fluttered to usher us into the Igumen's presence, his long locks floating behind and making me think of the Sutherland sisters.

The Igumen awaited us on a stiff rosewood chair in a stuffy little sitting room with a large center table covered with flowered velvet. He stood up and shook hands with us in simple dignity and motioned us to sit. His beard was quite gray, but his thinning gray-blond hair, though bald at the top, still retained some strands of its younger gold. His gray-blue eyes were pale, their expression serene, intuitive, and kindly. He looked like a level-headed, clear-seeing business man, firm but never overbearing, shrewd but trustworthy. We all three liked him at once.

As we sat around the velvet-covered table waiting for tea, we looked about the flowered walls, studded with holy ikons and oil portraits of the late Imperial Family, and brought up to realistic date by an enlarged photograph of President Kallio of Finland. Therese commented on a large cross of emeralds and diamonds that hung from a heavy gold chain about the Igumen's neck. Ah, yes, he explained, it was an imperial gift from Czar Alexander I to the incumbent Igumen in 1819. But this was only a poor replica. Would we like to see the original?

He disappeared into a little side room and brought forth a magnificent cross made entirely of large, square-cut diamonds and glittering emeralds, with barely enough gold to hold the stones together. We passed the jewel about the table, made much of it, and delighted both high priests with our admiration. As if a feeling of former Russian elegance had been revived in the stuffy little parlor, the Igumen took from his neck the chain with the false-jeweled cross and put on the genuine one to honor us during tea.

The servant-monk brought in a great tray set with five glasses and one cup and saucer. He moved about, jumpy as a jack rabbit, nervously clutching at his long white beard to keep it from flowing into the tea things. The cup and saucer were for Therese. In old Russia men drank hot tea from glasses; only ladies used cups—their hands were supposed to be too delicate to manage a hot tumbler. With fresh home-made bread we had delicious strawberry jam—the fruit grown by the monks and preserved by them. We had never tasted any strawberry jam comparable to it except at Pont Aven in Brittany. Therese asked for the recipe. The servant was called in and, as stage-frightened as if making a maiden speech in the Duma, he related the process to the guide, who translated it to English.

We must see some of the beauties of the place that evening as his guest, the Igumen said. Would we prefer a droshky or a motorboat? A motorboat, Therese said at once, remembering her brief, frightening ride from the dock. The boat would await us at seven-thirty, after dinner—the Vice-Igumen himself would accompany us. And now we must see the church.

Bells were booming—great, deep, tumultuous bells, then little jingling chimes like children mocking their elders. "The largest of the belfry bells weighs over thirty thousand pounds," the Vice-Igumen said, as the Igumen put on a high, brimless hat with a long, flowing black veil like a widow's and took a patriarchal staff in his hand. Leading us down the steps and across to the great red brick Church of the Transfiguration, he looked neither to the left nor to the right to acknowledge respectful greetings from lesser brothers. Black-gowned monks, all with flowing veils, appeared from every path, rushing as if in terror of being late.

The great church with its five cupolas is really two churches, one built on top of the other. In the lower ancient church reposed the sarcophagi of Sergei and Herman, two hermits who founded the order, Sergei having arrived at Valamo in 992.

The service was in mid-career when we entered the upper church. Bearded monks were sweeping about in black robes with trains. The smell of incense was mixed strongly with that of turpentine, for the church was being redecorated. Scaffolds reaching to the ceiling took up one corner space. Young boys with girlish bobs—orphan-school novices—were painting at different levels while priests and monks murmured the service in Church

CO-OPERATIVE FLOUR MILL

WORKER'S COTTAGE

Slavonic. One lad jumped down from the scaffolding and ran up to greet the Vice-Igumen. He curtsied and cupped his right hand within his left. The Vice-Igumen laid a big soft hand on the boy's cupped palms. The boy kissed it reverently, and then curtsied again, in gratitude for the privilege. The Vice-Igumen smiled and patted him affectionately, like a favorite sheep, as the lad scampered away back up the scaffolding and seized his paintbrush.

The church was magnificent with gleaming gilt. Every conceivable space—walls, ceilings, columns—was covered with ikons, religious paintings, and filigrees of pure gold. The Igumen had taken his seat in a high throne chair facing the altar. The Vice-Igumen stayed beside us. Pilgrims were standing about crossing themselves, tourists gaping wide-eyed. Some of the monks were so old and feeble that they clung to the railings of stalls. Some who stood by themselves shook with palsy; others with sniffly colds blew weakly into squares of cloth. A younger monk robed in garnet velvet embroidered with gold braid went about the crowd swinging a brazen incense pot. As he paused before pilgrims he would give the pot an extra swish under their noses and they would make genuflections in humble adulation.

A black-browed monk with sweeping train passed among the spectators, motioning them up if they attempted to sit in the few benches along the walls. Everyone must stand during a Greek Catholic service. Before the high altar door a priest paraded back and forth carrying an enormous holy book held open, his long widow's veil rippling behind him. The service was being chanted in a profound rich bass, and the acoustics were so remarkable that it sounded as if fifty were speaking instead of one. A young laborer-pilgrim lit a candle before an ikon affixed to one of the great columns. The Virgin in the ikon was outlined in real pearls, and from the hem of her enameled garments a pure gold foot protruded. The laborer knelt before the image, reverently kissed the golden foot, made his petition, and went away, his eyes shining with seraphic fire.

With so much moving and confusion we wondered how any-one could feel devout. It was like a dress rehearsal for some religious drama like *The Miracle*. Yet the lives of the monks were built around this spectacular worship—three services a day, beginning at three in the morning, three hundred sixty-five days a year. It seemed a far cry from the teachings of the simple Nazarene.

Twice the Vice-Igumen nudged us and raised his eyebrows questioningly. Had we not had enough of the service?—there was much he wanted to show us. At length we followed him out. We saw the library stacked with musty, rare volumes in ten tongues. We saw the old cemetery, serene under great shade trees, the mounds reduced by time to the size of babies' graves. Gardens with heavy-scented flowers, petunias, heliotrope, phlox, and spice pinks, wound in and out among the scattered buildings, with seats for meditation concealed in nooks behind lilac bushes. The colors of some of the buildings formed a rich background for the color of the flowers. Besides the electric blue and powder blue of the cupolas, there were the red brick of walls and the pink granite of great columns. Window frames were of bright yellow or black. Signposts were lettered in white on royal blue. On a lower level bordering the lake front, apple orchards with reddening fruit and well-tended vegetable gardens stretched as far as we could see. And behind the buildings hayfields and acres of potatoes were cultivated to the edges of the dark green woods. In the barnyard, laborer-monks in dirty gray work smocks and crushed leather boots were at their evening tasks—among them a strapping yellow-headed monk with a leg missing who hobbled agilely about on a single crutch under his right arm.

A coal-black tomcat left the crippled chap's company to join us. "His name is Gypsy," the Vice-Igumen said, smiling, leaning down to stroke the unascetic beast. "See his black coat; he is a monk, too."

As we returned to the guest house to get ready for dinner, the Vice-Igumen led us to an apartment in the monastery where Alexander I and Alexander II had stayed when they had paid visits to the order in the last century. Then he took us to his own apartments in another part of the same building, where he had a little organ with which he entertained himself in the evening. We urged him to play for us. Hesitantly he seated himself at the keyboard, pushed his long hair from his shoulders with both hands, pulled up the skirts of his cassock, and set his big feet against the pedals. First he tried a Russian hymn, but without much interest. Before it was finished, he stopped, shook his head distastefully, and said, "This is too sad." He took a book of Finnish temperance songs and selected one. It was a rollicking jiglike tune, and he put gusto into it, nodding approval. "This is more like it," he said, leaning forward and pedaling up and down as if he were bicycling on holiday.

When it was over the guide suggested a Ukrainian love song. "Ah, yes—" He had come from the Ukraine. He played with feeling, raising and lowering his head, moving his lips silently, singing the song in pantomime. Then he wheeled round on the piano stool, shrugged, and smiled as if to say, "I know I'm no musician, but I enjoy it—and the nights are long."

"He's got to do something besides pray," Brotherus said.

After dinner the boatman, a monk named Serge, was waiting for us at the dock. The air was cool now and fragrant with perennial phlox that grew profusely everywhere. When we stepped down into the big motorboat, the Vice-Igumen gathered his flowing hair into a tight stream at the nape of his neck and tucked it securely between his robe and the collar of his greatcoat. We turned off the fjord into a narrow isthmus. The boat just cleared the arch of a low masonry bridge, and we steered into secluded water, black and glossy as onyx, with the slim white reflections of silver birches stretching like shredded moonlight across the dark surface.

The guide touched my coat sleeve. A white temple with cupolas of pale jade appeared romantically on a small promontory backed by shadowy spruce. The boat was steered expertly to the wharf, as if guided by magic. In the intense stillness we disembarked and climbed a winding, fern-strewn path to the chapel Prince Nicolai Nicolaivitch had built in memory of the Russian monks killed in the Great War. The cupolas were constructed like inverted tulip-shaped bowls, and in the prince's conception the inverted bowls were full of heroes' blood that spilt forever over the separate roof parts of the church. But now the chapel stood immaculate white and pale green, like a white tulip. The hermit who kept the key had already gone to sleep in his hut at the water's edge because he rose for prayers at three in the morning. So we did not disturb his rest, but quietly slipped away from the wharf to another bay and another island.

Between a double colonnade of larch trees, we followed a path of resilient larch needles until we came to a wooden bridge traversing water edged with yellow water lilies. Above the spears of motionless pines a setting moon shaped like an orange section lingered in the sky. Its reflection lay tranquilly on the black water like a topaz on an Ethiopian's breast. We stood in silence for some time. Then the young Russian said, "It is the essence of peace, is it not?"

He spoke in a low musical voice that might have belonged to the youthful Saint John. The shrewd old Vice-Igumen said nothing, but he watched us. We merely said, "Quite," and the young Russian took bread from his pocket and broke it and cast it into the lake. For a moment, nothing; and then little ripples, as carp mouths began to pierce the dark surface and to nibble soundlessly, as though sneaking a meal in secret. Suddenly there was a leaping and a scurrying and a great troubling of the waters. A huge fish had arrived unwanted at the feast, and the smaller guests had fled in terror. Then, when the last crumb had been consumed, the water was again smooth as onyx.

"I always like to bring something for the fish," the youth said, as we went on over the bridge to a wooden chapel so small that hardly a dozen pilgrims could stand in it at one time. We had to stoop to enter the low door. The dark room smelled of old wood and generations of stale incense. The Vice-Igumen lit a holy candle, and the flame picked out some gold leaf and the variegated colors of the screen. "It is a favorite shrine for the troubled in heart, because it is small and so simple," the guide said.

As we came out again, an earth-colored figure approached like a moving shadow down a winding path that led to a shack on the hillock. It was the aged hermit who tended the chapel. He was a little bearded man with great soft eyes and no teeth. He looked simple as a child who knew naught but good of the world. Yet he was one of the few brothers who had ever been married. He came from beyond the Ural Mountains in Siberia, where he had married a girl of Turkestan. When she died he was so disconsolate he had become a monk to regain equanimity. Now he had lived as a happy hermit for forty years, tending the chapel and his five apple trees and his potato patch, and meditating himself into the life beyond. He looked already nine-tenths in the spirit. He bowed before the Vice-Igumen and cupped his right hand within his left palm. The Vice-Igumen blessed him with the sign of the cross and dropped his large soft paw into the gnarled, unwashed hands of the hermit, who bent to kiss the padded knuckles. Then the great man and the lowly kissed each other on the bearded cheeks, and the hermit was told that we came from America. He mumbled softly and looked as if he wished us well, but that for him America and Finland and the moon might be all the same.

"Do the monks keep up at all with world affairs?" I asked the student, as we walked back over the path of pine needles.

"They do not have radios, but some of them get old newspapers. And this summer I have heard them murmuring to each other, 'There is a big trouble going on in the world.' "

We all laughed, but softly, so as not to disturb the peace in the woods.

"Each week I discover new places," the young Russian said in his poetic voice, while the boat was chugging back over the dark water, "each one more charming than the last." He was obviously fascinated by the idea of the contemplative life amidst plenty and beauty. The authorities were trying to persuade him to become a monk. They needed capable young men to carry on the order. As he was telling us about his problem, the intuitive Vice-Igumen gathered the drift of the conversation.

"You would make a fine Igumen," the Vice-Igumen said to him beguilingly.

But the young man merely smiled and said, "If I should come, it would only be as a simple monk."

"What is the good of all this praying?" Brotherus wanted to know. Like the Russian student he was moved by the poetry of the place, but its abnormal aspect was disturbing to his Finnish reason. "What is the good of a monastery?"

The guide was thoughtful—then he said quietly: "They do good. Pilgrims come here because of sorrow or guilty consciences or some maladjustments in their personal lives. They stay for a day or all summer. It's like psychiatry or a rest cure. They live in peace for a while and then go away to face difficulties purged or refreshed. And then it is very beautiful here even if one does not pray."

Despite the spell of the place and the great natural beauty, I kept wondering if the monks were happy. Out in the woods there was peace, but in the routine of the monastery a nervous unrest was obvious. The head men seemed happy enough in their functions, for they were directors of a successful enterprise. But the workers' eyes were those of zombis—as if their bodies were directed not by minds but by puppet wires. And there was an unnatural nervousness as well as apathy. The monkish lives seemed spent in constant tension, as if listening for bells, terrified lest they be late for constant services.

"Tell me—are the monks happy here?" I asked the Russian waitress at breakfast next morning. She was a White refugee, the daughter of a former wealthy tile manufacturer of Kiev.

She stood still for a moment, looking out the window.

"Happy? No," she said slowly, "not happy, if you speak of happiness for this world. The monks take no thought for pleasure in the ordinary pursuits of this world—only in thought of the world to come. When walking quite alone in the woods, lost in their own thoughts of a coming spiritual life, then I think they are happy. But in daily living as we know it, they are human. This abnormal life breeds irritation. They bicker, they have their petty quarrels and jealousies. But it is like a thing apart from their real selves. In their human dealings—no, they are not altogether happy; but in themselves, yes, I should say, they are. They look at things quite other than we—at death, for instance. It is a thing accepted, quite as natural as eating their porridge for breakfast. They feel no sorrow, no shock.

Their lives are spent in contemplation of death. Yesterday—it is a pity you could not have been here—one of the old monks died. He had been a hermit. The other monks did not grieve. *I* cried—because to me it seemed so pitiful—they are old, and going fast now, one by one. But for them it was a simple order of the day. They buried him as naturally as they would have fed him. It was neither relief nor sorrow they felt—just acceptance."

I thought of the little old hermit emerging in the mist by the still pool the evening before—how outwardly he was holding to mundane life by a sack of frail bones and with a mind that had been dead a long time. He was seventy-four, they had said. I thought of Sven Hedin, the famous Swedish explorer—he, too, was seventy-four. But he sat up working all night, writing from eleven to eight in the morning. He had shown me planned work that would take an ordinary man a lifetime to accomplish. His was a life spent in the activity of ceaseless interest. And here was this hermit, a pathetic relic of a body and a mind, spent in a lifetime of escape.

After breakfast, as we prepared to leave, the hotel manager with the piercing black eyes and false switches presented Therese with a bouquet of white phlox as a last mark of our being honored guests. We said good-by to the young Russian aristocrat in the tumultuous confusion of monstrous bells ringing. The echoing little bells mocked derisively as we walked down the hill to the steamboat, where a gray-bearded monk stood at the wheel. With almost a sense of relief I watched the blue gilded domes fade into the sky like clouds that disintegrate and vanish. Not for much would I have missed the conscious or unconscious theatrics of Valamo or the extraordinary natural beauty of the place. All in all, it was the best show in northern Europe. But it was pleasant to be getting back to Finnish normality.

How long would Valamo last? we wondered. "Not more than ten or twenty years," Brotherus guessed.

Within four months Russian troops had already taken possession of the islands. The brotherhood had to flee for their lives across the ice. By the treaty of March 1940, Valamo and the whole of Lake Laatokka became a part of the Soviet Republic. "The big trouble going on in the world" had become a reality even in the monks' own little world.

SPIRIT OF PEACE

From Sortavala the railway headed northeast toward the shore of Lake Saimaa. When we stopped at the junction of Elisenvaara, where we had to change trains for Punkaharju, Brotherus bought a local paper. His eyes grew wide with un-Finnish excitement.

"Look at this!—Germany and Russian are signing a pact!"

We peered at the Finnish letters. No, we said—all three of us—it can't be true. It doesn't make sense. The report was not absolutely confirmed, but the correspondents were commenting eloquently on dire possibilities of such a step. Though we consciously denied it to ourselves and to each other, a cold foreboding ran through us. If it was true, just what would it mean to Finland? To Poland? To the world? Did it mean war or peace?

Brotherus was troubled. "Russia!" he said ominously.

"You're more concerned about what the Russians might do to you than Germans?"

"But Germans are so far away that they are not a reality for us. Sunday we looked across the fence at Russians. For seven hundred miles our territory marches with theirs."

We were still repeating inwardly, "What will it mean?" when we reached Punkaharju. The name of the place in Finnish signifies Beautiful Ridge. To us it came to mean Perfect Peace. Punkaharju is a high narrow ridge that runs like a green stake fence for seven kilometers between two still blue lakes. In places it is no more than fifteen feet in breadth—just barely wide enough to make of itself a natural railroad embankment. The pine-covered slopes of the ridge are steep, rising at the highest point to ninety-five feet above the lakes. A motor road follows the crest of the ridge, and one reaches the mainland by ferry, but the railway crosses two channels on bridges.

By its wise Nature Protection Act of 1923, Finland made Punkaharju a national park and saved it in perpetuity from industrialists and real-estate promoters. In the conserved area the forests are supervised by the Forest Research Foundation, which maintains testing tracts where millions of seedlings are grown in its nurseries. The pines of Punkaharju have adapted their style to the strange narrowness of the topography. On either side of the road atop the ridge the slimmest, tallest pine trees in the world rise like an army of magnified javelins aimed at the sky. The top roots are buried in blueberry bushes and lilies of the valley. At the base their rugged bark is gray-green and bronze-colored, but on the upper part of the tree the bark becomes flame-colored and scarlet. The upper bark flakes off in paper-thin pendants and drops to the ground like transparent tongues of fire.

The state-owned hotel was called "Finlandia," and the girl who managed it was more like the spirit of Finland than a flesh-and-blood woman. We had heard of this remarkable Miss Kouhi. But we had not expected to find the shadow of an angel running a tourist hotel. When she spoke to us, her voice was so soft and gentle that we had to lean forward to hear. When she gave her low-voiced directions, the porters looked at her as they might have looked at the Virgin Mary. As she talked, she occasionally brushed the thin-spun gold of her hair back from a pallid brow. Her glance was shy, and she held her head just a little to one side.

As she saw us to our rooms, I realized where I had met her before—in Aleksis Kivi's book. She was the girl who had become Eero's wife: "Seunala's slender daughter, the flaxen-haired, shy-eyed Anna, she who had seen wondrous visions and in delirium prophesied many miracles." But we were to learn that this shy creature, unlike Eero's wife, not only carried the pantry keys but had a will as resilient and tough-fibered as a seasoned vine.

Brotherus telephoned the foreign office, but they could not give him any certain confirmation about the Berlin-Moscow pact yet. There were rumors, and things looked dark. They might know in a few hours. In the interim Brotherus and I had a *sauna.* The brisk, red-headed laundress, who was also bath attendant, beat us and scrubbed us with mighty energy. Then in the cooling room she wrapped us in sheets as tenderly as if we had been newborn babes and gave us cold home-brewed beer to drink while we cooled.

After dinner Therese and I walked across a white wooden bridge and climbed the ridge to watch the sunset. The pines, reflecting scarlet from the flaming sky, stood rigid and slim like shipmasts—all the same extraordinary height, properly spaced, and scrupulously groomed.

On the crest of the ridge we sat around a granite obelisk erected to the memory of Runeberg, because he had written his poem "The Fifth Day of July" here a century ago. As the sun turned from apricot to burnt orange, the western lake became lacquered copper and the pine trunks silhouetted against the sunset glow turned into columns of ebony. On the other side of the ridge, the moon, as if taking its cue from the declining sun, appeared before the sky's blue curtain and cast its image like a pearl into the darkened lake. The world was intensely still—not even one egotistical sound from a bullfrog or a crane. In the perfection of quietude a strip of tissue bark detached itself from a near-by pine and wafted down to drape a vagrant flame on the Runeberg obelisk. Runeberg had found this ridge the loveliest spot in the world. He compared it with the most perfect woman he had ever met or could create in his imagination. Her name was Hilda Holm. "See Hilda Holm on Punkaharju," he wrote, "and in one glance you glean the most beautiful things that life and nature can offer."

The foreign office in Helsinki was calling Brotherus when we got back to the hotel. The Moscow-Berlin treaty was a fact. A man at the office read a brief report over the phone. Would it mean war or peace? No one in Helsinki knew. All visas for Russia had been canceled. We were sorry to hear that, for we had expected to go to Leningrad in a fortnight for a brief visit.

An American woman of German descent who had just now arrived at the Finlandia after a week in Leningrad had an answer to "peace or war?" She brought Russia so close in a half-hour conversation that we felt there was no need to go.

She was a funny, natural, awkward woman, with a bottle nose, a big heart, and frumpy clothes. She was suffering from a kind of rheumatism which made her shift her legs suddenly and pull at her nose.

"Those poor Russians—" she said—"so ignorant that some of them don't look quite bright. And what a time I had at the customs! It took us hours to get through, going and coming. They found a ratty piece of skunk fur in my bags. 'Ah,' they said, holding it up for everybody to see, 'sable!' I was never more embarrassed. Anybody could see it was moth-eaten skunk. But they kept saying, 'Sable!' and nodding their heads at each other. I said, 'You can have it.' But they had to send for an expert.

Then they found a stack of receipted hotel bills, odds and ends of papers I should have had the sense to throw away. They examined every one!—And worst of all, I carry a little portable gramophone around with me for company, because I am traveling alone. I had thirty records. And what do you think those silly fellows did? They held the train up two hours and made me play every record. I guess they were looking for spy messages. Of course, I was a fool to take it with me, but I never dreamed they'd make such a fuss. And did I get dirty looks from the fellow passengers? Some of them even said they didn't like my taste in music either." The woman laughed, gave her nose a vigorous pull, and jerked her leg.

It had cost her ten dollars a day at the best hotel in Leningrad, she said, but the hotel was so shabby it was downright depressing. It was grand in the old style, but so run down, dilapidated—the proletarian contempt for elegance, she guessed. Torn sheets, torn towels, filthy rug, abused furniture. So strange—an elaborate suite with marble bath and furniture such as an empress might have, and ragged towels and veneer half off the tables. The room she had had first, for eight dollars a day, had bedbugs. She'd bought her tickets in New York before she left, and they'd assured her everything would be first class. But she couldn't sleep a second night in that bed. They said they had nothing better for eight dollars, but if she would pay ten, they could give her a suite with a better bed. So she had taken the suite.

The Russians looked so poor, she said, that it made her heart ache. The women didn't wear dresses like Americans, but just sacks without a belt. She heard they tried to keep women from wearing headkerchiefs, but they couldn't stop them, she reckoned, for they nearly all had them on. They looked just awful—like immigrants. The men wore blouses—all dirty, too—and awful-looking. But they must have some money, for they came to the hotel to eat, and it certainly wasn't cheap. Came in the dirty white blouses—and the sloppy way they sat at the table—with arms all over it—contemptuous, she supposed, for nice appearances. Occasionally you'd see a girl on the streets dressed like us—but not often.

Everybody was kind, though, and helpful. The guides were nice as could be, and they only showed her what she wished to see. She was left free to go about where she liked. She went shopping alone. In the shops the people were kind, but she didn't buy anything—she'd never seen such prices! An ash tray she wanted cost twenty-seven dollars! She went on a trolley car—they were all full, too—to see a cathedral—past flat ugly land and awful working houses built before the revolution—they hadn't had time to tear them down and rebuild. But they had some fine hospitals and schools. And you certainly felt they were doing all they could to help the people. But it looked like they had so much to do—it was pitiful. But they *were* trying. You could see that everywhere.

We asked her about the people's food.

"Food? I don't know in general. I ate nothing but chicken and caviar. Yes, plenty of caviar. Good, too. So fresh. But it made the hotel smell fishy. I couldn't read anything on the menus, and the waiters—so dirty and greasy their clothes were, too—though they wanted to help and were kind, they didn't know any English word but chicken—and at every meal they'd suggest chicken—so, as I didn't know the name of anything else, 'Yes, I'll take chicken,' I'd say—and I ate chicken till I felt I'd turn to one."

Her legs twitched and she yanked at the end of her nose with her thumb and two fingers.

"What's the latest war news there?" I asked.

"I don't know a thing. But I have a notion something may be

happening in Russia. When I left Leningrad the girl who was the guide said something curious was going on—the radios for the past few days hadn't had anything nasty to say against Hitler. The week before they were all blaring hot propaganda against Germany like they always did—but the past few days they hadn't said anything dirty."

"Why, don't you know," Brotherus said, "that Germany and Russia have signed a non-aggression pact?"

"You don't mean it!" she said in amazement. "You don't mean it!" she repeated in high delight. "Then that settles it." She shifted her legs and pulled her nose in gratified relief. "Germany will take western Poland, and Russia will take eastern Poland. That's all there is to it. That settles that. There won't be any war."

The next morning the foreign office said Brotherus was to continue his trip with me but to keep in touch with Helsinki by telephone each day. While he took Therese out in a rowboat on the lake, Miss Kouhi and I went for a walk. I wanted to know more about her, for Brotherus and I were going to start tomorrow for the backwoods and Therese was going to remain here during my absence. Now with the war imminent I wanted to be assured she would be as happy as possible with her hostess and as little troubled.

Miss Kouhi led me past the Finlandia's ski-jump down a hill through birch-shadowed paths where the sun was filtered coolly. We passed a white-painted folk school deep in a birch wood, the silver trunks of the trees ankle-deep in lilies of the valley and blueberry bushes. Behind walls of clipped fir hedges ten feet high were myriads of green seedlings with which the government would replenish the Finnish forests. Over another hill was the first state-owned tuberculosis sanitarium. There in an atmosphere purified by fresh pine needles and the breath of millions of wild flowers, the ill were restored to health at a cost of a dollar a day. We went on past a sun-drenched field, fragrant with the white bloom of meadowsweet, until we came to a deep dell of pines carpeted with delicate, fan-shaped ferns. Low, moss-covered boulders were spread about casually like seats in a summerhouse. No other foliage marred the pattern of fern and pine. It was a beauty ordered by nature in her own way, not by man.

We stood still, intense quietness all about us.

"When I come here alone," said Eero's wife, and her voice was so soft it was like the stillness speaking, "it seems—all this—made just for me."

Her red lips were parted in wonder at the quiet beauty, and she pushed the spun-gold hair back from her pale brow.

"When the spring comes—it is so unbelievably love-ly at Punkaharju." She hesitated as if doutbful of my sympathetic interest.

"Tell me how spring comes, here," I urged her.

"First, the ice breaks with an eerie kind of music, and then—it moves—" Her voice would pause, and she would say "then" with a little lift at the end. "Then—the trees, they become green. Not green all at once, but slowly, a little, a little—then—more green, and then—the birds, they begin to sing: the cuckoo, the nightingale, the oriole. And, then—the lilies of the valley, they bloom. The scent becomes so strong that we must close the windows at night to sleep."

"It must be lovely," I said, as we walked on.

"It is just love-ly."

"But what do you do in the winter to amuse yourself here?"

"Always we have skiing," she said. "And last March we had a love-ly horse race around the island that you can see from the

MODERN RAILWAY STATION AT TAMPERE, THE GREAT INDUSTRIAL CENTER

FINNISH ENGINES BURN BIRCHWOOD AND THE SLEEPING-CAR PORTERS ARE WOMEN

ISLANDS LIKE THE SHADOWS OF CLOUDS AT KOLI

hotel out on the lake. The ice is always two meters deep, and the snow was thick and hard."

"But how did they race?"

"In sleds. Little gray wooden sleds that you see in the farmers' yards now. I knew a farmer from whom I bought meat. He had love-ly horses, and I suggested we have a horse race. It was dull—we were bored—and the hotel needed to make money. All the farmers who had horses raced. The sleds slid on the hard snow. It was—just love-ly. People from everywhere came. Hundreds and hundreds. They stood along the shore and watched. And all had dinner and coffee at the hotel. All day they ate, and into the night. It made a gay break in the winter."

We had come to a fir wood. On either side of a shadowy road low-branched firs stretched unending, the thick carpet of moss pale in a shade so deep that the morning seemed suddenly late afternoon. The trees were marked with numbers in white paint.

"The government owns it," the girl said. "That is why it is so cleanly tended."

A sudden whir of wings, and a covey of brown grouse flew up before us, their bodies too heavy to disappear quickly among the firs.

"Wood grouse," she said. "See, they are brown. But in winter they will be white, like the snow. They are protected by the government here, but nature protects them everywhere."

The moss looked deep and soft as velvet in the thick shade. "Let's sit," I said.

It was like sinking into a bed of down. I got out a pack of cigarettes. Eero's wife did not smoke. I lit a cigarette and put the burnt match in my pocket.

We sat silent for some time, I waiting for her to talk.

"It is strange," the girl said finally, "how at times like this one remembers things—little things. I remember when I was a little child—"

"Yes," I said. "What was your childhood like?"

"Well—my father died when I was four. And then—my mother had to bring us up. We were three—two sisters and myself. I was the middle one. And, then—it was very hard for my mother. My father had been a teacher in a school. He left money—but it was in war times and the money was not worth much when the finnmark was devalued."

"And what did your mother do?"

"At first she sewed. And then, she bought a shop for hats and dresses. And a cottage for us. She still lives there and keeps her shop too. My mother was determined we should be educated. I thought first to be a teacher—but, then, I saw my friends who taught often had such narrow lives, their minds became narrow too, and they gossiped and bickered. I decided I would not teach. But I wanted to know languages. I borrowed money and went to London. I got a job as housemaid. They paid me ten shillings a week."

"No," I said. "Good Lord, we pay a Negro in the South a pound at least."

"They finally gave me a pound—and one pound ten before I left."

"And were they kind to you?"

Her eyes darkened slightly. "The English are not unkind, but they look upon servants as mechanisms run by money. It hardly occurs to them a servant is a human being. I had eleven rooms to clean every day besides the dishes to do and other things. I worked very hard—for I so wanted a smile. But not one little smile or word of praise did I ever get.

"And then—I went to Paris—to learn French. And I got a job as maid with a French family. The French are worse than the English to servants; they have no mercy. I ran all day instead of walking. At night when I lay down I would be so tired I would think, 'Surely, I can never see another day.' But—" she laughed— "I did. And, then—I came to Finland and I went to Ivalo in Lapland as a waitress."

And now this fragile-looking creature was running one of the most popular hotels in Finland, with a staff of forty persons, including the gardeners who took care of the great hothouses, where they raised fresh vegetables in winter for all the state hotels, even those in Lapland. She bought beef on foot and saw that farmers did not cheat her. For four weeks now she had been encouraging the wife of one of Sweden's cabinet ministers out of a nervous breakdown. The bellboys came to her with their love affairs. She read books aloud with the maids in the evening, and because the waitresses were university students, she had to see to it that there was no class feeling between them and the maids, who were farm girls from the neighborhood.

"Has it been difficult?" I asked.

"No—not difficult. Sometimes a little trying—when drunken men demand liquor after eleven-thirty, when it is against the law to sell it. They call me names, but I say, 'No. It is a rule.' And I just stand there. They even curse me. I say, 'No, it is a rule.' And I think, how can a man drunk with liquor and cursing me affect me? Finally they quiet down and go away. Drunkenness is very strange to me. Some rare and beautiful souls get drunk. Our greatest writer, Sillanpää, gets drunk. I have met him only twice, and one time he was very drunk. But what an artist and what a heart! Unless you know Finnish you cannot dream how marvelously Sillanpää writes. Like Shakespeare he takes this simple word and puts it next to that one and makes something quite wonderful." She looked up at a spray of gold-turned leaves on a birch tree. "Take a phrase like 'September-colored leaves.' In Finnish that is so beautiful it almost hurts. Yet Sillanpää can get unpleasant with drink. I suppose it is because he sees life as a tragedy and he must sometimes forget."

We did not talk much more. We sat listening to the silence of the morning, a silence made more intense by the even heartbeats of the woods. Our wordless thoughts coalesced into a profound sense of peace. I smoked another cigarette.

"Tell me," I said, "do you find it hard living in this workaday reality?"

"The days go," she answered. "I am busy with many things. But what is called reality is like dreams to me. At night when I go to my room, and am alone, and can lose all sense of even myself—there is peace, and in peace is happiness."

" 'Commune with your own heart and be still,' " I said, quoting.

"Yes," she said quietly.

Her strength, I thought, lies in this very quality of spirit and removal—she is too remote to be deeply touched by a world of things.

I thought of the monks at Valamo and the Russian girl, saying, "In themselves, yes, they are happy—when they are alone." But this Finnish girl was not escaping life like the monks. Fearlessly she was facing it—running a tourist hotel.

"If Russia comes to take Finland, what will you do?" I asked.

"We will fight."

"But with all their man power and resources, what can you do?"

"We will fight."

"Russia would be bound to win. She outnumbers you fifty to one."

"Still we will fight!"

When Brotherus and I started on our journey next morning,

to be gone five days, I felt quite safe about Therese, not only because she loved the place already above all others in Finland. I had left her in the protection of a guardian angel—armed with a spirit that served better than a flaming sword.

"REMOVED FROM THE SOIL OF THE EARTH"

The old town of Savonlinna lies picturesquely on islands and a cape clasped together by bridges between two great lakes. The city's jewel is Olavinlinna Castle, built on a rocky island in the midst of a swift-running channel. Tourists who come to Savonlinna because of the castle's fame are hardly aware that it is also an industrial town, with a large plywood mill, machine shops, and various factories, because innumerable parks do all in their power to camouflage the fact. It is also the most important lake center of Finland, and at the docks of the flagstoned harbor square steamers of various routes and schedules are continually arriving or setting forth.

Brotherus and I took our luggage straight from the bus station to the quay. Two boats were leaving for Kuopio, the capital of Savo, at precisely the same hour and arriving next morning eighteen hours later, but traversing two different routes—one going by the Leppävirta route to the west of the large island of Soisala; the other, by the Heinävesi, to the east. The Leppävirta route was a century old, having been channeled in 1839. But the Heinävesi route had not been opened to shipping until 1906. We chose the newer eastern way because it ran through a more rugged territory, where for long stretches there was nothing but primordial wilderness. We selected our staterooms and left our luggage with a bulky, red-faced skipper, who chuckled to think of his older brother in California who had boldly changed his name from Harju to "a great name like Harrison, after a President of the United States."

"These lake captains," Brotherus said, as we started on foot to see Olavinlinna, "are said to be so skillful that they can pilot their ships through anything as deep as morning dew."

One reaches the island of Olaf's Castle from the prettiest little park in Finland—a park tended by old women who groom it as tenderly as they would an only daughter for her wedding. An old boatman rows visitors across a swift current and deposits them on a stone terrace before the great portcullis. Here university-student guides greet the guests and conduct them through the halls and towers.

The castle was built in 1475 by that famous Swedish constable of Viipuri, Erik Axelsson Tott, as a defense against the Muscovites. In its history it has often changed hands. Passing from Swedish to Russian control, its architecture has been augmented by extra towers and bastions. The forty-foot-thick walls are constructed to the very edges of the rocks, where turbulent waters of the lake form a glorified moat. In past eras the massive pile of masonry contained all things needful for maintaining a governor's seat and a military headquarters, with barracks for a garrison and workshops, armory, smithy, flour mills, and brewery as well as banqueting halls, chapels, and dungeons. Today Olavinlinna is a many-leveled labyrinth of halls and stairways and vaults and inner galleries. The vast, cold rooms are shadowy in midday and cheerless as a prison. The unmitigated grimness of the interiors is relieved only slightly by the courtyard, where in one corner, on a raised earthen terrace, mountain ash trees droop their pendent berry clusters over an *alfresco* restaurant. Ruin-haunting pigeons flutter in the sunlight and tread the flagstones lightly on golden feet. By moonlight the courtyard is said to be strangely evocative, and here in summer grand opera is sometimes given, just as *Hamlet* is often played in the courtyard of Kronborg Castle in Denmark. But visitors cannot help but shudder when the guide reminds them what winters must have been in the medieval ménage. Fireplaces are as rare as those quaint W.C.'s which jut as tag-ends of alcoves out of the masonry and hang perilously over the mirroring water four stories below.

The *Heinävesi II* sailed at one-thirty, and we made ourselves comfortable in wicker armchairs in the stern, I with Alex Matson's translation of Sillanpää's *The Maid Silja* and Brotherus with the Finnish translation of *Gone with the Wind,* which he had bought at a local bookstore next to the restaurant where he had lunch.

Almost from the moment the steamer pushed out into the lake, a sense of delicious content stole over me. Eighteen hours of perfect relaxation were in store, where quietly as if through parted curtains in a pleasant dream I could see through the green wooded screens and behold the mighty core of Finland's simple heart and the strong roots that bound her to the earth.

"At such times"—I marked the passage in Sillanpää's moving story—"the loveliest mode of travel is by water. The shores blossom, and the transparency of the green lends to the air around a special appearance. The road, too, along which one floats, is new and virginal for every traveler, innocent of the tracks of any preceding voyager. No dust is raised by others, no annoying intruders from the roadsides; and those who chance to be making the journey together in the same boat are in some manner humbler to each other when resting on the mysterious element. For a moment they are removed from the soil of the earth."

The part of Finland we saw this day was innocent of railroads and bus service. The waterway was the only convenient way from May to November. When the lakes were sheeted in winter ice for six months of the year, travel and transportation were by ski and horse sledge.

Conversation among the passengers was not necessary to make one feel the friendliness and harmony in the air. The Finns do not talk much or idly, but in their silences you can often sense what they are feeling. Their nostrils took in the scent of the woods like hounds let loose in the field after being kenneled in a city backyard. When strangers' glances met theirs, they smiled quietly as if sharing a special benison.

The trees came down to the lake's edge in massed battalions, erect as king's guards at attention, their green-plumed crests setting off their bronzed uniforms. For miles on miles there was nothing to see but the polished lake, the scrubbed blue sky with white clouds piled like opalescent soapsuds, and the green-bronze trees lining the shore and exuding tonic odors. Sometimes the banks were so near that you felt as if you were riding in a high tallyho through the forest. And sometimes the devious channel was marked for long stretches by black and white poles to the right and red poles to the left, as if the course of a royal water pageant had recently been charted. Then out in a wide expanse of water we would pass commercial launches chugging south, trailing great piles of logs chained together like coupled boxcars and as long as a coast-to-coast freight train. Like monstrous sea serpents the trains of logs would glide sinuously over the greenish level, while the log floaters walked professionally up and down their corduroy surfaces.

The lake borders were not all unmitigated forest. The phalanxes of green trees were broken by occasional farms. More and more the farmer's husbandry was nibbling at woodlands and lake marshes. We passed an island with three separate farms—

and only sixty years ago that island had been sold in fee for the exchange of a single cow.

There were no Rhineland castles, no resort hotels, no bustling towns. But the boat had many regular stops on its route and would halt along the way to pick up a lone passenger waving a beseeching handkerchief. There were occasional co-operative dairies, a peckerwood sawmill or two, and landing stages where as many as thirty persons were sometimes gathered. We passed summer villas built on rocky spurs set far out of sound or sight of neighbors. Finland's foremost operatic star and director, Aino Ackte, had built herself a charming lodge far from the madding crowd and had painted it the rich country red of Finnish farms. At one landing stage where there was no sign of habitation we stopped for a sad-faced little girl in a pink gingham dress. She brought on board a china soup tureen full of fresh raspberries, handed it to the cook, and departed with some paper parcels and a smile.

There was much the same feel on the lake steamer that one got on the Lapland post bus. We delivered and accepted freight of any and every kind—live pigs, milk cans, bicycles, coils of trace chains, machinery parts, bales of hay, kegs of nails, tubs of butter. Old women with headkerchiefs, some fat, some thin, teetered up and down the single-plank gangway. Sometimes they traveled in pairs and would sit on the lower second-class deck impassive as nuns. A girl delivered a bundle of laundry wrapped neatly in brown paper. At a mill we handed over a bag of money —the laborers' weekly wages. Once in a place where we couldn't get quite close to the shore we took on a baby carriage with a baby in it. The feat required considerable manipulation, with five or six men helping and passengers from the upper deck calling down advice. Everyone was calm except a dog that barked frantic disapproval at such a hazardous procedure.

Some stops were hardly long enough for a man to swing himself over the rail of the lower deck. But once we stopped for half an hour to take on wood. The boat's firebox consumed prodigious quantities of cut birch. At the landing the piled wood was brought aboard in little wooden sledges, dumped down manholes into the maw of the ship, and stacked in every spare space on the lower deck. To facilitate operations passengers took off their coats and toted armfuls of wood onto the boat, where nimble ship boys dispensed it. Brotherus and I got out and helped. Even the captain lent a hand.

"On each trip," the skipper said, "we burn enough birch to build a church." Then, to prove his sixty-year-old agility, instead of boarding his ship in the regular way he sprang from the ground onto the lower deck rail and climbed like an energetic bear to the upper deck about as quickly as a fireman could slide down a pole.

"Why didn't you tell me you were going to do that?" I called up. "I would have taken your picture."

"I'll do it again for you at another stop," he called back. He disappeared into his bridge house and tooted his whistle, and we were off by the time I had leaped aboard. "You see," he said, grinning, after I had joined him on the upper deck, "in Finland a boy is a man at fourteen and at sixty he's still young." I was to remember his words later when men of all ages were fighting for *Suomi.*

The lake trip was a lesson not only in co-operation but in economy and efficiency as well. The lower deck was loaded to the beams with cargo, and the waitresses had to pass over manholes and loose piles of wood to get to the refrigerator. The kitchen could not have been more than six feet by four. Yet the dinner that was served to Brotherus and me in the little dining saloon was as varied and well-cooked as we could have wished in the capital's best hotel. I saved the menu of the ship's *table d'hôte* for August 25, 1939. Here is what was set before us: first, a smörgåsbord with six kinds of cold meat, three kinds of herring in tins, a bowl of whole tomatoes, a dish of stewed mushrooms, fish salad, cucumber salad, pickled beets, sardines, and boiled new potatoes with dill. Then came cream soup, and then the main course of roast pork with a delicious cauliflower soufflé, wax beans, and carrots. For dessert there was French toast with raspberry confiture, followed by coffee and Finnish liqueurs. To achieve such a dinner in such tiny space was one more telling piece of evidence of the Finns' resourcefulness and natural gifts. And the girl cook weighed 220 pounds. "She's only twenty now," the captain said. "When she gets her full growth, I doubt if she'll be able to get into the kitchen."

Dining with us were two small-town shopkeepers, who were off on a fortnight's holiday. They showed us their folder of tickets, covering all four corners of Finland south of Lapland by train, bus, and steamer for 455 finnmarks, a sum slightly less than ten dollars. Such cheap travel was possible because the state owned and operated virtually all the transportation facilities of the country.

One of the men wondered if anyone cared to pass the time playing cards, but cards were for winter nights, his friend said.

"Queen Wilhelmina's husband used to sit up all night playing cards in this very room in summer," Brotherus said. "This was his favorite boat, and when he traveled on it he stayed down here gambling and drinking and eating, and never came out on deck.

"What was *he* doing *here?"* I underscored the words in my question.

"Going to see his lady love. He came every summer. He had a Finnish mistress, whose husband owned an estate on one of these lakes farther up. The husband threw big parties for him."

"The husband!—and he was a Finn?"

"He was a Finn, all right," Brotherus said, "but he wasn't much of a man. Maybe he was proud that a prince consort preferred his wife to a queen."

"Like the doddering French nobleman," I suggested, "who used to present his beautiful new spouse proudly as 'My wife—former mistress of the late Lord Byron!'"

"Yes, yes," he said, chuckling. "And then of course maybe the Dutch prince's friend was one of those cuckolds who never catch on to what's happening under their nose. But he came year after year, and there were royal goings-on."

"You astound me," I said, really surprised. "Finnish women involved in high intrigue?—and in the heart of the backwoods? I didn't know they ever let themselves in for scandal."

"Um-m, it's very rare, but even Finns have their little vanities."

The sun was setting when we came up from dinner. In the evening atmosphere the brief jaunt we had just taken back into "the soil of the earth" dissolved like a mist. The gray-blue surface of the lake had now become vivid as an artist's palette. The western sky was ablaze with crimson and rose like a forest fire, and not only was the spectacle mirrored in the water, but the trunks of the white birches became luminous as pink waxen tapers that caught the sunlight through the stained glass of a saint's red garments. When the passion of the sunset was spent, a cooling lavender twilight began to fill the air.

At a quarter past eight we passed through the first locks. With consummate skill the pilot guided the boat into the narrow concrete groove, with hardly a foot on each side to spare. A little fuzzy black dog with a white ruff barked and leaped and walked on his hind legs about the platform. The captain, grinning, slipped some sugar lumps into my hand. "He's always here and he always expects it." The upper deck was level with the concrete platform. I leaned over the rail and dropped a lump in the dog's open mouth.

"Finns are very fond of animals," Brotherus said. "They treat them like folks. Some are uncanny with them. We had a cow once that was always running off. We heard of a peasant who had a way with cows. We asked him to cure her of the bad habit. My little brother spied. The man took the cow off into a lonely part of the woods and whispered something in her ear three times. Then he brought her back and she never ran away again. He wouldn't tell what he had said to her, because it would break the charm."

As we proceeded, the lake turned to pale copper and the farther islands became jet-black. Lanterns were lighted at the stops now, and the evening quiet was broken only by the steamboat's demure tooting. At a hillside farm, men and women were finishing their labor in the wheat fields. They paused in the twilight beside their garnered sheaves and waved at the lighted boat. The moon rose behind them. As I stood at the ship's railing, the lines of an eighteenth-century poet came to me.

> Ye harvests, wave to him,
> Breathe your still song into the reaper's heart
> As home he goes beneath the joyous moon.

We tied up for the few remaining hours before daylight at the village of Heinävesi. Here the passengers were always offered the hospitality of a steambath in the *sauna* by the landing. But Brotherus and I turned in to read in our bunks. I soon fell into a deep sleep and did not know until I had waked at eight that a heavy fog had risen in the night and delayed us three hours.

We did not reach Kuopio, the capital of Savo, until ten o'clock. Our travel by water was ended. As we stepped from the boat,

I regretted returning to what Sillanpää called "the soil of the earth." In a droshky we drove straight from the dock to the governor's mansion so that Brotherus could telegraph the foreign office. The governor, Gustaf Ignatius, was his father-in-law. When we were ushered into his office, he was seated at his desk examining a new gas mask. It had just been sent to him by the government.

The international situation was tense, things looked ominous, but Brotherus was to proceed with me into the wilds of Karelia for two days and then call Helsinki. After telephoning, he tried on his father-in-law's gas mask. His Napoleonic features were metamorphosed into nightmarish idiocy. The governor and I could not help but smile, however grimly.

"Very un-Finnish," the governor said apologetically. "But we are forced to be realistic."

Brotherus hired a Ford, and we headed northeast to spend a night at Koli, the Finns' favorite beauty spot, before going into the eastern backwoods.

"ALMIGHTY BEINGS"

"In Kuopio," Agnes Rothery had said rightly, "no one is rich as we know riches in America and no one is poor as we know poverty." But as we passed from the province of Savo eastward into western Karelia, the landscape became barren ground and specters of penury lurked about many thresholds. Some of the weather-stained cottages were empty and abandoned. Others were new and roughly thrown together. The clearings were rich only in stones and boulders. The soil was shallow and anemic. Scraggly beds of potatoes grew in uneven rows, and oats stacked in wispy sheaves looked apologetic, as if trying to hide their meagerness behind the stalwart rocks. These were the places of the new pioneers, who out of stony wilderness had the hardihood to carve a homestead for themselves. Most of them had been hired men or lumberjacks, and now they had become property owners. They were struggling with Finnish might and main to make a go of their new way of life.

In the neighborhood of Kuusjärvi I looked closely at the men and women we passed. (We had to drive slowly, because the side road we had taken was in sad repair.) On the lined faces of some of the men were expressions which almost made you wish you had not seen them and yet filled you with such admiration for dogged courage that it hurt. In their grim countenances a consummate pride and defiance mingled with haunting fear of failure. In this stark region I beheld the spectacle of man's naked will pitted against malevolent nature. I looked at the rocky clearings where only a pauperish vegetation could ever result from Herculean labor, and I wondered at man's o'erweening faith in himself. Here men with responsibilities to wife and an increasing brood of children battled with fate, determined to stick out the contest even though the cards ran steadily against them. "But the Finns," said Brotherus, "have become the people they are because of faith in their ability to surmount obstacles."

At one flinty farm where a well sweep marked the unfenced entrance, we stopped for a drink of water. A flock of ragged children crowded shyly about us. One extremely thin little boy, with the face of an angel framed in golden curls, looked more like a hothouse son of a king than a peasant lad. He had delicately chiseled features and enormous violet eyes that smiled back friendly-wise at us. He offered to show us his dog, which could dance on its hind legs. I got a box of chocolates from the car and gave them to him to pass among his brothers and sisters and friends. We went up to the house to see the dog. The mother came to the door with a baby in her arms. We asked permission to get the drink of water we had already taken. She smiled amiably and declined a piece of candy. In her manner was the dignity of a mistress of a home, even if half her children might sleep on the floor.

As we came back down to the car, the husband returned leading a horse with dangling trace chains. Although he muttered *"päivää"* under his breath, he did not look at us, but went to water his horse. He was a powerfully framed man, but battered and stooped, with a hard and tragic look in his eyes.

"We have seen his naked poverty, and it hurts his pride," Brotherus said.

The children followed us hesitantly to the car, but the father did not call them back. I opened up the angel-faced kid's pocket and slipped some loose coins into it. He backed off smiling in wonder, with one hand feeling the wealth in his pocket and the other holding a piece of chocolate up to make the dog walk on his hind legs.

"It's like one of Juhani Aho's stories come alive," Brotherus said.

I knew the story called *The Pioneers*. I had read Nesbitt Bain's translation. Aho recounted movingly how the hearts of a stable-boy and a housemaid turned toward the wilderness and a place of their own. They made a clearing in the raw forest, planted grain, and worked themselves like galley slaves. Finally frosts, debts, fast-coming children, and overwork broke them down. The wife died first. The husband made a rude coffin and fastened it across a pair of shafts hitched to a starving nag.

Now he had to carry her to the grave, but the roads were so very bad. He only hoped that the coffin might hold out till he had reached the church. He tweaked the reins, for the horse had overstepped the path and was searching for a little grass among the withered leaves. The beast was in just as wretched a state as the man; it looked like a skeleton.

Ville took leave of me and went on his way without lifting his eyes from his load. The shaft poles cut two parallel furrows in the sandy path.

The story-teller goes on his way until he comes to the deserted house of rough logs with the forest looming up beyond darkly, "thick as a wall."

The first pioneer had fulfilled his task; the man can do no more good there now. His strength, his energy are gone, the fire of his eye is extinguished and the self-confidence of his marriage morn has forsaken him.

Another will certainly come after him and take over the cottage plot. He perhaps will have better luck. But he will have a lighter task to begin with, for before him no longer stands the savage forest quite untouched by man. He can settle down into a ready-made hut, and sow in the plot of land which another had ploughed up before him. That cottage plot will, no doubt, become a large and wealthy farm, and in course of time a village will have grown up around it.

Nobody thinks of those who first dug up the earth with all their capital, the only capital they possessed—their youthful energies. They were merely a simple lad and lass, and both of them came there with empty hands.

But it is with just such people's capital that Finland's wilderness has been rooted up and converted into broad acres. Had these two only remained at the parsonage, he as a coachman and she as a housemaid, then perhaps the course of their own lives would have been free enough of care. But the wilderness would not have been cultivated, and the foreposts of civilization would not have been planted in the middle of the forest.

When the rye blooms and the ears of corn ripen in our fields, let us call to mind these martyrs of colonization. We cannot raise monuments upon their graves, for the tale of them is by thousands, and their names we know not.

"These pioneers are your great heroes of Finland," I said to Brotherus, as the smokestacks of Outokumpu Copper Company came into sight. "But, great God! The courage it must take to start from scratch, as these fellows do in some of these places. It's like trying to make bricks without clay and without straw."

A little later on I said, "Do you remember in *Seven Brothers* what Juhani said to Aapo's question, 'What can we build out of nothing?' Juhani replied, 'The whole of the world was created out of nothing, so why could not even a little chaff bread be made out of it?' And Aapo rejoined, 'Ay, if we were almighty beings.'—That's what these fellows unconsciously put themselves up to be—almighty beings."

"Well, the race deserves a rest now," Brotherus said as we turned into another branch road, which headed north toward Koli. "We've been pioneering a long time. Today you've seen about the last of the pioneers."

But before the lake ice had begun to break up the next spring, Finland had lost a tenth of her territory, one Finn out of every eight was homeless, and there were new pioneers by the thousands.

MAPS TELL LITTLE

"If you follow a good map of Finland you may find a quantity of names along the capriciously meandering line of the border," Ralph Enckel had written me, knowing I was planning a motor trip. "But do not imagine they are the names of towns or boroughs. Those names so difficult to spell belong perhaps to a small farm or a wayside church with pointing roof or a clock tower glistening with tar. In the churchyard the tombstones lean more and more to the ground, the wooden crosses wither slowly, and the wild grass threatens to cover it all. But the next place name may be that of a factory built close to some rapids on land uninhabited a decade ago. Now thousands of workers, miles from the nearest town, toil before the most modern machinery and live in unending rows of trim cottages and enjoy strawberries grown in their own gardens."

And on the drive to Koli we found it to be precisely as he said. We would find an important-sounding name on the map, aim for it, and discover it was the place name of a lone, tumbledown farm. Then a simple-looking name would turn out to be a sizable milltown.

Koli on its white-gray rocks sits so high above beautiful Lake Pielinen that motor cars must be parked on a plateau and guests must climb tiers of winding stone steps to reach the inn. Koli is a favorite resort of the Finns in winter as well as summer. When the ridges are covered with snow, skiers spot and streak the landscape, and slalom instructors are kept busy teaching the new technique.

In the purple evening we sat enjoying the view from the terrace, where coffee was served. Islands lay scattered on the damask sheen of the lake like rich crumbs on a banquet table. The clouds above were opal-colored, and they hovered above the islands much in the same contours, as if the sky were a mirror reflecting earth and water. Lambs bleated from somewhere down the rocks. The tinkling of cowbells and the musical calls of herd boys came pleasantly through the cooling air to the top of Finland. But for me, despite the beauty and the pastoral sounds, there was little restfulness at Koli. The terrace was crowded with German tourists, and that evening they packed themselves about the white soapstone fireplace of the lobby and listened tensely to the radio. When I went to bed, Brotherus was arguing with a German woman professor. There would absolutely be no war, she maintained. Hitler had promised them peace. It was only England that wanted war. Of course, Hitler must have Danzig and the Polish Corridor. But Hitler would keep the world out of war.

I was not loath to leave Koli and the radio and the German tourists. Early next morning, after an hour's walk along the ridge in the most spectacular scenery in Finland, we departed. The time was too much out of joint for me to enjoy the place or even be fair to it in my memory.

We drove south along the Sunday road full of church-goers—even the young girls in this part of Finland wore white headkerchiefs instead of hats. Haystacks bronzing by blue rivers were never more lovely than on the road from Koli to Joensuu, nor was a landscape more sweet-scented with summer. And although the month was not May but August, I thought of Sunday hours in spring that Sillanpää had made to sound so delightful. "The young foliage of hedges and trees is so irresistible, so alive with the might of nature, that admiration of it throughout a Sunday is no shame even to a manly man."

At Joensuu, the trading center of north Karelia, with a population of barely six thousand, we found a delightful hotel which was another last word in modernity. It was designed by a young architect named Ypi and erected by Joensuu's leading hardware company. The building inside and out made Saarinen's masterly town hall, built in 1914, look a century remote instead of only two and a half decades.

From Joensuu we headed again toward Russia. East of Joensuu there was no railway, and for strategic reasons all roads petered out into trackless nothingness fifteen miles from the frontier. We were going to visit an old peasant whom Brotherus knew and whom he called the Patriarch. "Typical of his kind," Brotherus said, "but his kind is no longer typical." We trusted he would give us lodging for the night, for there were no inns in the district.

LAST OF THE PATRIARCHS

The road from Toupavaara to Konnuniemi ran scantily between grassy ditches and undulated up and down like a measuring worm. But the August sun was by no means unpleasantly hot, and except for the exciting hazards in the rock-strewn road, the afternoon was peaceful with the houseless backwoods quiet of three o'clock of a Sunday. The only sound beyond the ditches and the diagonal split-sapling fences was that of occasional cows tinkling their bells in surprise at the clatter and grinding of our car. At each curve the road held camouflaged ambushes, concealed traps and hurdles, to confound the unwary. Once or twice we came to places that looked like the top of practice ski-jumps. The car would drop down suddenly, giving us all the feelings of an elevator's sudden plunge, and then we would shoot up the other side like an ascending roller coaster. Not a vehicle did we meet in our staccato pace, not a person. To right, to left, stood the walls of forest, and before us as well, for the labyrinthine road never ran straight enough thirty yards ahead for us to see the sky in front of us.

"If the old man takes a liking to you," Brotherus said, "he will slip off with us somewhere and bring out a bottle of schnapps."

Finally the zigzags of the road became fewer, and the forest halted. To the right at the top of a short incline fields extended in sweeping yellow curves. "Those are the Patriarch's," Brotherus said. "I know where I am now."

Haystacks under the full floodlight of the sun looked like a series of gigantic golden beehives. Curving row after row, hill beyond hill, they were silhouetted in ordered richness against a white-blue sky. Then came another brief stretch of shadowy woodland, and the road turned sharply to the right and down. We headed for a dozen shingled rooftops, stained a brick-dust red, scattered on a grassy plateau between hilltop and meandering river.

Eight of the structures were ranged about an open rectangular court of untended grass. The barns and stables and lofts and woodsheds were built of huge squared logs, painted the conventional rich country red. Only the house of the owner and the washhouse far down by the river broke the rule. The washhouse was weathered gray. The dwelling house was painted the neutral cream of uncolored winter butter; the doors, cornices, and window frame were trimmed with beige. It was a long house with a superimposed half-story. Two glassed-in outdoor vestibules some fifty feet apart jutted out near the opposite ends of the façade. The typical vestibule is a conventional Finnish architectural device to keep men from bringing snow and winter winds into the house with them. Here the two vestibules distinguished between the master's entrance and the servants', but they looked almost identical. We came to the servants' entrance first. Brotherus stopped the car with noisy éclat to announce our arrival.

A silence like that of a household gone to church greeted us. We got out, stood shaking out the kinks in our backs and legs. We looked at each other with concealed apprehension. I slammed the car door with a resounding bang. From the panes of the glassed-in master's vestibule a bearded face peered. I smiled toward it hopefully. It disappeared. There was a sudden alert movement. The outer door opened, and the profile of a vast belly emerged, followed by a black crushed-leather boot. The Patriarch himself was coming to greet us.

It was Falstaff in Finnish; Falstaff sobered and grown prosperous, an ornament to society, the first citizen of his district. We *päivääed* and shook hands. Brotherus and he talked in their language. I was being explained. The old man shot appraising oblong glances from shrewd blue eyes. I regarded him in detail. His silver beard was like Edward the Seventh's with a flourish of natural curl—a well-groomed, prideful beard that would have been as distinctive on the boulevards as in the local councils. His short-cropped white hair ran forward, country-style, like Gertrude Stein's, to make a cap for his handsome, worldly face. His tanned cheeks were rouged with health, and his full lips red as any mouth in a Rubens canvas. He wore his tan-striped shirt open at the huge neck. His chest was broad like a bull's, and below it swelled the most affluent belly in Finland. Where shirt and khaki riding breeches met, the girth was marvelous to behold. It was no sloppy, sagging, loose-made appurtenance, this patriarchal belly, but sound and solid and evenly rounded. If one thumped it, it would have resounded like a ripe watermelon. But there was no overripeness—only a mighty maturity.

"You are welcome," the Patriarch, turning to me, said in Finnish. "Be so good as to come into my house." He stepped forward to lead us. The aggressive belly kept the front, preceding its master like a prancing drum-major leading the band. Into the vestibule we followed, through a hall, and into the living room. Several males, adult and adolescent, and a few females of various ages were gathered listening to a low-tuned radio announcing sports events in Helsinki.

Brotherus went about holding out his hand and saying, *"Päivää.* Brotherus," to each of those who did not disappear. I was not introduced to anyone. So I said, *"Päivää.* Strode," and captured somewhat awkwardly the hands nearest me. The people who escaped and those who stayed were all members of the family—

sons, daughters-in-law, grandchildren. Cats are especially adept at catching Finnish tongues, for the Finns are the least voluble of people; but when a stranger who speaks no more than twenty words of Finnish enters, country cats have a field day catching tongues. A great hush fell. The radio stopped.

In a few moments there was no one left in the room except Brotherus and me and the Patriarch. The master's presence had swept the room of relatives like a strong wind. We sat in high-backed, brown leather chairs about a coffee table, while the Patriarch spread himself on a stiff, high-backed leather settee, thronelike, with arms too far away for one to reach both at a time. On either side of the settee, slender-fronded palms in tubs reached to the ceiling, and in a corner between the radio and a couch a straggling oleander blossomed feebly. Cacti drooped from baskets slung from the ceiling. (The Finns have such a fancy for tropical plants that hardly a house is without its indoor window box of cacti.) In a corner, behind a palm, a stuffed crane stood quite naturally. Glass-eyed owls perching on pedestals stared at me with the same cold, inquisitive look that one of the married sons had given me as he vanished. Though the Finn is so in harmony with the outdoors that he must bring some of it indoors with him, yet winter has taught him to keep his double windows tightly shut, and on this sunny August afternoon there was no crack to admit air into the living room. It seemed as if the green-tile floor-to-ceiling stove had not cooled since the spring fire went out.

The Patriarch opened eight different boxes of cigarettes and spread them out on the table for us to choose from. Then he began to chat with Brotherus, his eyes twinkling and canny, self-conscious and proud, by turns. With only three of us there, he seemed just barely to have elbowroom, though he did not smoke or make flamboyant gestures. Brotherus would translate bits of the conversation into English for me.

No, the host had not killed any bears lately, though last winter four were killed in the next parish. Wolves no longer came so far south. But when he was a youngster the Patriarch saw his grandfather kill a huge fellow right on the living room hearth. In those days the house and the stable were one building together, and one evening his grandfather arrived to hear a terrible kicking and commotion in the horse stall, and when he went to see, a creature ran over into the living room. He held the lantern up and saw a huge wolf snarling on the fireplace. Just as the beast sprang, he grabbed an ax and split its skull.

As he talked the old man stroked his belly abstrusely and affectionately, as if a favorite tomcat were purring on what might have been his lap.

"But a neighbor of ours had a really fine experience with a wolf," the Patriarch went on expansively. "He was driving home with a load of timber on his sled when a wolf tore up behind him. He dumped the timber from the sled so that his horse could run. But that frightened the wolf. Instead of springing at him or the horse, the glutton jumped the timber and ran on ahead. The horse pricked up his ears and pawed, and the man on the empty sled, seeing that the wolf had already been running a long way, decided to give chase. He let out a yell, whipped up the horse, and away they flew on the hard snow. The doors of the cottages flew open and people stared. There was a wolf running for dear life, a horse behind him, snorting like a demon, and a man whooping like a war trumpet. They had never before seen a wolf chased by a man. They grabbed guns and axes and ran cheering after the flying sled. The road was fenced all along the way with high split saplings and the wolf couldn't turn off. But he was tired and getting more tired, and the horse was gaining on him. After about two kilometers the wolf made a break for the fence. He had to leap a ditch to clear it. He fell short and caught in the sharp sapling points. The man jumped from the sled, hopped the ditch, and grabbed the wolf by the tail. The man was an extra stout fellow, used to lifting heavy logs. He held the snapping beast by a hind leg, thwacked him dead with a stick. That night there was the biggest celebration the neighborhood had ever seen. The drinking and the singing and the fighting went on for days."

The old man gave his belly a resounding, pleasurable pat.

"Fighting?" I said.

"Yes. When Finns celebrated, they always ended in a big fight. It took that to make them know they'd had a good time. That was in the old days. Now, of course, we are more civilized." He rose with dignity and said, "Let's drink some coffee."

The little room between the entrance hall and the huge baronial kitchen contained a money safe tall as a highboy, and a sideboard and a table set against the window. The table was laden with breads and cakes and three after-dinner coffee cups. A pleasant red-cheeked, black-haired woman, and a fair-haired, athletic girl stood in attendance and poured coffee from a large brass teakettle. One was the daughter-in-law and one the daughter. I waited for the women to sit.

"It's a custom," Brotherus said in English, "for country women to stand and serve. They never drink coffee with the men—only afterward."

The daughter-in-law was the wife of the youngest of the three sons, the only one who lived on his father's place. Before she made her great match she had been a village chemist's assistant. Now her high position as daughter-in-law to the richest man in the district brought with it the privilege of cooking on a wood stove two major meals a day for the seven current members of the family and the five male farmhands and the six dairymaids and the two little girls of the widowed washerwoman who helped with the sheep. Besides, she prepared coffee and bread and butter three times a day, according to the Finnish custom, and she cooked for and served the Patriarch and whatever guests he entertained at meal hours differing from the farm routine.

"She must be worth more than her weight in gold to you," I said to the host. He looked a bit taken aback. Then he laughed politely at my American pleasantry. The daughter-in-law blushed and passed me the blueberry jellycake. It was delicious. I complimented her skill. She blushed again and filled my coffee cup to the brim.

After coffee we made a brief tour of the farm, the proud belly leading the way. The old man held his left hand jauntily on his flank, drum-major style. In his right, he carried a stafflike unpolished stick which from time to time he used for emphasis, as he pointed out special aspects of the feudal abundance.

Outhouses are more abundant in Finland than in any other land. Even the humblest Finnish cottage has three or more: for bathing, for wood, for a cow, for tools, for hay, or for any expectation of plenty. Here in the center of an estate of two hundred acres of cultivated land and eight thousand acres of forest, the supplementary houses flourished in the grand manner. From outhouse to outhouse we went, following the belly and the staff with increasing wonder. My amazement and praise became eloquent—all the more so because the Patriarch could understand only my expression, not my words. He opened doors with increasing dramatic effect, punctuated his explanations with pauses for applause.

Acres of purple-blossomed potatoes cascaded down the hill to woodsheds big as village churches. In the icehouse, where tons of ice cut from the river were stored annually, great trays and baskets of fish were spread about and quarters of sheep were hanging. "The fish were caught fresh this morning before breakfast," the Patriarch said, "thirty-two pounds of them." In the cooling house tubs of golden butter and earthenware jars of cream stood in rich abundance on the dirt floor. On the shelves mounting to the roofbeams crowded glass jars of preserves and jams and lucent jellies, glittering in the pale electric light like garnets and amethysts and topazes. In the vegetable gardens that extended to the river every good thing that could be grown in eastern Finland was growing, and the food house built half into the side of a hill was ready to receive the beets and carrots and other varieties of root vegetables that were to feed the household bountifully in the long winter.

As we walked through waist-high wheat I said, "Everything seems to flourish here. Is the land extraordinarily fertile or do you use an especially potent fertilizer?"

The old man paused, winked at Brotherus, and said to me, "We have a proverb: The master's steps fertilize his fields."

He marched on to show us personal inventions—his scheme of concrete curbs and drains in the great cow stable for washing the manure into a concrete reservoir large as a Long Island swimming pool. Here was conserved the dung of the eight months during which the cows were immured. He had devised an economical motor that furnished power for threshing wheat in one house and for sawing lumber and making shingles in another. We examined the little electric unit, which furnished electricity for the whole place at something less than a cent and a half an hour.

As Brotherus and I paid mounting tribute to the ingenuity and the plenitude of the place, the old man became visibly younger. He was a boy showing the marbles he had won from the gang, the miraculous slingshot that could bring down birds you could hardly see, the persimmon tree in the woods that nobody else knew about. And the belly strutted, and even seemed to swell as its master acknowledged our appreciation.

We came to a newly built garage. The double doors were rolled back. There, as resplendent as if on display in Madison Square Garden, stood a 1939 special-model blue Buick. Only five times in the four months had the old man driven it. It was for important occasions. But there it stood, like a king's carriage, a symbol of the Patriarch's high position—to be used and exhibited on any market day the owner chose. The Patriarch stood a bit in awe of the elegant car, for at heart he was a simple man. He felt more at home in the three-year-old Ford that stood under an open shed and that better suited the dirt roads of Karelia.

The Patriarch drew forth a thick silver watch and glanced at the time. It was almost five—the hour for dinner.

We dined at the private table, in the room with the money safe. Again the daughter-in-law served, assisted by the daughter. The daughter-in-law had cooked the dinner. They kept no kitchen or house servants. She was apologetic for the jumped-up meal—on Sunday they had their regular dinner at two. We had to content ourselves with two kinds of broiled fish, cold chicken and lamb, cauliflower au gratin, string beans, tomato salad, a platter of delicious fresh blueberry gelatine served with thick golden cream, three kinds of cakes, and coffee.

"Fifty years ago farming was hard," the Patriarch was saying. "When a lad I worked in summer eighteen hours a day. I was so tired at night sometimes I couldn't eat supper. Fifty years ago many people starved. But not now. Today farming is simple if you have brains."

"If you have good soil and some money to begin on," I

amended politely. I commented on the rocky scarcity we had passed through yesterday and the hungry-looking children we had noted.

The old man was unimpressed. "Some people aren't fit to farm," he contended. "It's their own fault. The trouble is, the forest workers think they must have farms too. A lumberman marries and then he must have a house for his wife and the likely children. Soon he begins to think it wouldn't be respectable not to clear some land and plant some potatoes or something. Then they may get a cow and raise hay and a little wheat. The woman and children keep the garden and tend the cow. Of course, it's a poor-looking place. But the husband makes his money on woods. Farming is a side job. A lumberman is not the type to make a farmer. It's a question of prestige. He wants to be a landowner to look well in his neighbor's eye."

He dismissed the claims of the land-hungry and turned to his overloaded plate. He held his fork poised in the air and said with assured conviction, "It is better to have a few great farmers and the rest laborers and woodworkers."

"Yes, wonderful for those who happen to be the great farmers," I said. Brotherus did not translate.

I did not pursue the issue. There was no use in antagonizing the old man—in emphasizing that Finland's salvation had been in making tenants proprietors and creating tens of thousands of new small landholders.

When I was full I wanted to stop, but the Patriarch urged me on, eyed my middle and my mouth critically. I recalled to my chagrin that I had not been offered a glass of schnapps—infallible sign of approval—nor had Brotherus. It put me on my mettle. I began matching the Patriarch, mouthful for mouthful. He was obviously pleased with my appetite. The platter of blueberry gelatine melted into oblivion. The Patriarch pushed his chair back and let his hands fall into an embrace about his midriff. I felt ballasted to my chair forever. Perhaps my reward would be the schnapps.

But instead, when we went into the living room the old man showed me his tickets to the Olympic Games for 1940. He had bought them the first day reservations were received. He was going to take the family, seven of them, in the new Buick. We sat about the living room discussing Mäki's style of running. As we talked Nurmi and American football, the Patriarch's son sat with us in silence, his little three-year-old boy asleep in his lap.

The sun was going down behind the hills beyond the river. We had not yet been asked to spend the night. "How far away is the nearest hotel?" I asked Brotherus.

"Sixty miles, back where we came from."

Finally the Patriarch rose and said perhaps I'd like to see the river view from upstairs. Brotherus looked at me hopefully.

By narrow stairs behind a door in the hall we reached the upper floor. At the top was a heavy trapdoor that could be bolted down. It was like a hangover from medieval days when the owners barricaded themselves in the upper stories. The hall was unfinished, unpainted, stored with odds and ends. From the naked rafters hung dozens and dozens of pairs of boots and skis, as if troops of soldiers were billeted in the house.

We entered a severe but femininelike room with a couch bed, a sewing machine, and pictures of male movie stars pinned to the wall. The Patriarch carefully closed the door tight behind him, waved us to a view out the window. While our backs were turned he produced a key from his pocket, opened a large home-made desk, brought forth three liqueur glasses, and set them on the sewing machine. Then he cleared his throat and un-wrapped a bottle of aqua vitae and pulled the cork. He filled the glasses precisely to the brim.

"I beg you to join me in a drink," he said. We skåled. I downed mine with relief. I had been accepted. Brotherus congratulated me with his glance.

"He wouldn't think it proper to drink with his sons," Brotherus said in English. "He makes believe his family doesn't know about his little drinks." It was like prohibition days, tapping at speakeasy grills or slipping up into a hotel bedroom to take an illicit dram. But I had never heard of a father using his daughter's room as a hideout for secret drinking.

The Patriarch pointed out of the window toward the southeast. "You see the hills in blue there at the horizon. There is my wilderness, my thousands of acres of trees."

"He owns not only what is in sight, but beyond the horizon," Brotherus said.

The Patriarch poured out another drink. We skåled, and tossed it off. The old man took up the glasses, put them back unwashed into the desk, and carefully locked the door.

"You like my farm," he said. "But wood is the only consistent factor in Finnish economy. Long ago, before the present prosperity in wood, I foresaw it coming. I joined three different forest-surveying expeditions sent out by the government. I learned all I could about trees and timber. I began buying forests to add to what my father had left me. This summer I bought a thousand more acres of forest as soon as I got inside information that the railroad was coming within four kilometers of my woods next year. And now I am fixed. I sell a million marks' worth of wood a year."

"Something over $25,000 worth," Brotherus translated. "A fortune in Finland. A bigger annual income here than the combined salaries of the president and the prime minister and a couple of other ministers."

"It's clear profit. I sell the marked trees standing. The companies do the cutting and hauling." He rose. "Would you want to see some of the forest close by?"

He grasped his stick and led the way through a green pasture extensive enough to graze a whole cavalry regiment's mounts. A colt and two caramel-colored mares with taffy manes had it for their private domain. The colt and its mother cantered up to us as if we had been playfellows. The mare nuzzled against the Patriarch, tickled him in the ribs. He laughed and caressingly pushed the mare's head away. The colt caught Brotherus playfully by the seat of his trousers. "They expect sugar," the old man said indulgently. "They are spoiled."

We cut diagonally through the pasture and out on the road. In half an hour we turned off on a path that led through a wood. The light was fading like a glowworm at dawn. The forest was peculiarly evocative in the strange, leaf-sifted twilight. The Patriarch's eyes were sharp as an owl's or a youngster's bent on mischief. He would pat this pine, that spruce, and say, "Here, see this mark. This tree is for sale next season. The government's agent must mark the trees before they can be sold."

We walked into the denser forest among the centuries-old trees that make the beauty and the economy of Finland. As he explained this and that, the old man would stop to pay tribute to a tree of special girth or straightness or quality of bark with the same affectionate pride with which he stroked his symbol of prosperity. It was almost dark in the forest now. Once the Patriarch stopped and made a complete circle, looking about him with possessive passion. "It's the wood that counts," he said fervently. "Farming gives a living, but the forest gives the surplus."

When we got back to the house it was ten o'clock and dark. Our luggage still remained in the car.

"Now we must have some coffee," the host said.

"Did you say the nearest hotel was sixty miles?" I asked Brotherus.

The daughter-in-law had laid out the evening coffee in the living room, and plates of cake and more blueberry rolls. It was surprising how the long tramp had made it possible to swallow again already. She poured from the copper teakettle and then went to put her little boy to bed.

Our anxiety about our own bed became acute. Brotherus tried strategy. He asked permission to bring in one of the bags to get out his pipe. I helped him, and we brought in all the wrong bags first and my raincoat and Leica for good measure. I yawned ostentatiously, and Brotherus explained that we'd been doing a lot of heavy traveling.

"Perhaps you'd like to take your bags to your room," the Patriarch suggested.

We thought it might be a happy idea. Behind the master we trooped up the stairs through the trapdoor. The daughter's room had been prepared for two. Of course, they'd been expecting us to spend the night all the time. The couch was spread as a bed and another pair of box springs and a mattress had been laid on birch logs. Scarlet silk quilts and lace-bordered pillowcases made them look like twin cardinals lying in rude state. In one corner had been placed a white enameled pitcher and wash basin supported within a frame of storklike legs. Beside it was a galvanized tin bucket into which I learned we were to make our arrangements for the night.

I thought of the resplendent blue car idling in the garage, and I wondered if the next generation would compromise enough with modernity to install a modern bathroom and give the country women a dividend on their generations of hard labor. When the living was scanty and hard-wrung from poor soil, it could not be helped if sometimes women had worked themselves into early graves. But on an estate overflowing with cash, as well as plenty, it seemed a bit too patriarchal not to save the mistress unnecessary drudgery.

Long after I had gone to bed, I heard what sounded like stirring about of women. I lay there thinking of Kivi's conception of a Finnish housewife as he puts it into the mouth of Aapo:

> A home without a mistress on its storeroom path is like a cloudy day, and dullness sits at its family table like a mournful autumn eve. But a good mistress is the bright sun of a house, that lights up and warms.—Lo! she is first to leave her bed in the morning, mixes her dough, lays the breakfast for the men, puts up their food for the day, and then hurries with milkpail in hand to the rear, to milk her mottled cattle. Now she kneads bread, hustles and bustles; now she stands at the table, now trips with a loaf on her palm to the back bench, and now like a tempest she stirs the fire, which spews out flame and smoke from its glowing bowels. Then, while the bread is rising, she finds time at last, with a baby at her breast, to break her own fast, a hunk of bread and a broiled sprat, with sour milk from the bowl. Nor does she forget the dog, or the cat that peers sleepily down from the oven-top.—And now again she hustles and bustles, trips and turns, mixes another dough to rise in her trough, kneads it into loaves and bakes it, and the sweat flows in streams from her brow. And see: when evening falls she has hung the loaves under the ceiling, pole over pole, full-loaded, from which new life breathes down. And when the men return from the forest a steaming supper awaits them on the newly-scrubbed table. But where is the mistress herself? There in the yard she milks her crooked-horned cattle again, and the hissing, foaming crest of the milk rises high in the pail.—So she hustles and bustles, trips and turns, and only when the others already rumble in deepest sleep, does she sink down in prayer beside her own bed. But even then her labors are not over. Uncomplaining she rises from her couch during the night for a moment, for an hour at a time, to hush the child which cries in its cradle.—Such, brothers, is a good mistress.

Our brief morning with the Patriarch was another round of feasting, beginning with coffee in the living room at six-thirty, followed by a whopping big breakfast at seven-thirty in the private room. For breakfast we had porridge and cream, two platters of fried fresh fish, a platter of eggs, cold meats, breads and preserves in profusion, and always the coffee. At half-past nine we had luncheon: smörgåsbord, with herrings, sardines, eggs, mayonnaise, pickled dishes and salads, followed by hot meats and vegetables and a huge dish of fruit pudding with cream and more coffee. The Patriarch ate with us in the private room and set us a Flastaffian example. The daughter-in-law who had cooked the meal served, and stood behind my chair with teakettle poised to pour more coffee. Her cheeks were red as winesaps from the stove's heat, but she smiled with sweet-tempered hospitality.

I had hoped to eat with the family and the field hands in the kitchen. But the Patriarch said their hours did not accord with our habits. They had continental breakfast at five, luncheon at eight-thirty, coffee at noon, dinner at two and final evening coffee at six. But he invited me into the kitchen to watch his household eat and to take snapshots of the scenes. In the castle-sized kitchen, big as half the house, there were two tables, one in one corner, one in another. The seven current members of the family and a more intimate guest, a vacationing mathematics teacher who helped with the threshing, ate at one table. The five male laborers, three dairymaids, three female haymakers, and two orphan girls who tended the sheep ate at the other.

I regarded the two groups critically. Informal harmony seemed to exist between them. They all served in the patriarchal scheme, and none of them was in the least afraid of the old man, for he was no slave-driver, even if his authority was absolute. There was one outstanding difference. The people in the family group all bordered on plumpness. The workers were as spare as factory hands on strike. Their main dish was potatoes boiled in milk.

A round of brownbread passed among them and they cut off hunks as desired. They had butter for their bread and milk to drink as well as coffee. Four of the male laborers were youths under twenty. They were bronzed and healthy-looking and not afraid of smiling or being photographed. Only the fifth seemed to mind having his picture taken. He was middle-aged, stoop-shouldered, myopic. He wore thick glasses and hung his head.

"The boys are new this year," the Patriarch said. "The older man has been with me twenty years. It's hard to keep boys these days. They are restless and full of notions. They haven't got the stuff in 'em they had in my day. Factories have ruined them. Big pay, few hours."

"How much do your laborers get?" I asked.

The figure amounted to about forty cents a day. "Besides, they get all their food and their room."

As we were about to leave the kitchen, a woman in a housecap rose feebly from the family table. It was the Patriarch's wife. I had somehow taken it for granted she was dead. So had Brotherus. "This is our hostess," he said, astonished.

A faint smile flickered in her deep-set black eyes. She was not old. Her hair was still black, but her face was blanched. I stepped forward to shake hands and to receive her kindly welcome.

"She has been sick for a year," the Patriarch said casually. "She has to lie down a lot."

We went to inspect the men's living quarters—in a combined blacksmith and machine shop and toolshed. They slept around the edges of the room. Lathes and tools stood against one wall. A huge open fireplace jutted from another with iron racks for drying boots and work mitts. Along the other two walls were rows of what looked like wooden chests, six feet long. The Patriarch stooped down and pulled open a long drawer in one of the chests. It contained a mattress and a red blanket. When night came, each man hauled out his mattress and made his bed on the wooden top of the chest. It was an ingenious space-saver. I looked for a washstand and a mirror, but I didn't see any and I didn't inquire further, for I didn't want to appear to have "notions."

As we left the men's living quarters I said casually to Brotherus, who voted the conservative ticket, "Ask the Patriarch if he is a conservative."

No, but the Patriarch used to be. But now he belonged to the Patriotic People's Movement Party—the name was the euphemism for Finnish fascism. "I believe in order," the Patriarch said, "order above all things. We must keep order. There are a lot of worthless fellows in this very district who might turn Communistic and want to take over things that didn't belong to them. We need more armed control to handle them."

The Patriarch led us to the climax of his possessions. He had saved the best for the last. It was a storage house for grains. We climbed a ladder. Great bins two stories high lined three walls. They were filled to the brims with tons of wheat, rye, oats—enough to last a prolonged famine or a war. They had been arranged so that grain poured into the second-story level could be drawn out on the ground floor. The Patriarch opened compartment after compartment. At one, he said, running a handful of grain lovingly through his fingers, "This wheat is ten years old. It's the finest grade—taste it—see how sweet it is." I tasted. It was sweet after ten years.

"It will be fine for all your poor neighbors to have you near—if the war comes and food is scarce," I said. Brotherus translated.

The Patriarch's eyes widened and then narrowed. "Yes," he said, somewhat uncertainly, "I should get a good price."

To complete the emotions of the morning before we started

our journey farther into the hinterland, the Patriarch directed us to a commodious white garden swing, the kind with slat-backed seats facing each other, which you put in motion by pushing the floorboards with your feet. It was the very kind of swing that everybody had in his yard or on his veranda in Alabama when I was a child. The Patriarch's bulk filled completely one side that was made for two, and Brotherus and I sat opposite him. As his belly settled itself in his lap, he pushed on the floor and we were in motion. The Patriarch liked to swing—and the movement loosened his tongue the more. I decided the psychological moment had arrived to speak of the national epic, for here I was in the very home of the *Kalevala.* And Eljas Erkko, the foreign minister, had assured me that this particular region was full of venerable men who could chant the verses for hours on end.

I began by asking the Patriarch some zealous questions about the *Kalevala.* But the old rascal pursed his lips, frowned slightly, and said, Polonius-like, that he found the *Kalevala* too long. Twenty-five thousand lines were a big doseful for one poem, he said with a dignified snort.

"Kun hän kulki kuusikossa!" Hopefully I quoted the one line in Finnish I had memorized. Because it described the hero walking among spruce trees I thought it might awaken response in the timber lover. But the Patriarch merely pushed the swing into faster speed and dismissed the matter with the observation that he found the constant alliteration and repetitions monotonous. "If I hear much of it at a time," he said with half-closed eyes, "it always puts me to sleep."

Brotherus glanced at his watch and said it was time to go, but we weren't permitted to leave before we had had a farewell cup of coffee in the private room. The son lurked in the kitchen near the door. I rose and nodded toward him. "Of course, you must join us," I said, as if my feelings would be hurt if he didn't. I made a gesture of making room. "And you, too, of course," I said most innocently to his wife, the daughter-in-law, just as if she were accustomed to having coffee with the Patriarch's guests. Without looking toward the head of the house the son and his wife sat uncertainly, and took coffee. I addressed my conversation to them, Brotherus interpreting.

The crisis passed. At the beginning I thought I heard the old man snort, but by his second cup he seemed to find nothing offensively subversive in the situation. He even beckoned the grandson to the table to have a cup of milk flavored with coffee. He became almost charming, as his hands passed contentedly over and over his great mound of belly. "Coffee is good in the morning—and all day long," he said with a half wink.

He had good reason to be content. He had not wasted his father's heritage. He had followed the Biblical injunction and increased his talents. "I hoed in my youth," he said. "Now I don't have to hoe in my old age." He was a success through his own efforts, and he was the complete center of his little world.

As we said good-by, I regarded the proud old peasant as I might the last of a species of game.

"The reason the patriarchal system is finished," I said to Brotherus as we drove off, "is that under it the only one who is really happy is the patriarch himself."

COLLECTORS OF THE PAST

Although Ilomantsi is the nearest town to Mekrijärvi, the lake district where Lönnrot collected the most prized verses for his

Kalevala, the town is not even mentioned in the guidebooks and few are the Finns who have ever visited the district. Far from the beaten path, without benefit of railroad and river boat service, the lovely, unspoiled country offers unrivaled possibilities to hikers. In the entire district, of which Ilomantsi is the administrative center, only thirteen thousand people inhabit the five thousand square kilometers—less than three people to one square kilometer.

It was at Ilomantsi, the last town in eastern Karelia before one reaches the Russian border, that the sheriff showed me the knife which belonged to the young man who had more *sisu* than anyone he had ever known. We were having coffee in the drawing room next to his office, in another one of those Finnish rooms that brought the outdoors within. Tables, lampstands, taborets were made of knotted and twisted tree stumps, polished until they glistened like the white tiles of the stove. The brown and green leather of the upholstery gave the room a masculine as well as woodsy appearance. Only in the vases of Danneborg dahlias—red and white like the Danish flag—was there the feminine touch of the sheriff's wife.

As we drank coffee and ate almond cakes we listened to the radio report of Hitler's army, poised and ready to descend on Danzig. Then, as if to shut out the menace of the future, the sheriff switched off the tense contemporary voice and from a safe brought forth some boxes and bags full of the past. He was a collector not only of knives but of ikons, coins, and rosaries. He spread out on the table a collection of holy medallions in silver, bronze, and brass—specimens from the fifteenth, sixteenth, and seventeenth centuries. One, in azure enamel on a silvered bronze, was a virtual replica of that picture of God I had coveted in the Lapp woman's hut—in a spiderweb halo that surrounded the figure from head to foot, Christ was healing the sick. Fingering it reminiscently, I told my story of the Lapp's rebuke and asked if there were any ikons to be bought in the village.

"I have scoured the countryside, and there are no more to be procured," the sheriff said. "The last Catholic priest got them. He blessed little colored pictures and swapped them for silver ikons. He told the people the pictures would be more efficacious with the saints. The ikons he sold to antique dealers abroad."

The sheriff took up a loaded, parchmentlike sack and balanced it in the palm of his hand. He handed it to me. It was a dried ram's bag, heavy as if weighted with gold. He undid the parchment tie, opened the bag, and poured from it a stream of golden profiles. Russian emperors and empresses piled up in a scramble or played leapfrog across the green table cover. Some of the coins were very old and valuable. The sheriff took up two at random, looked at their noble features, nodded toward the radio, and said, "Wouldn't they be dumbfounded?"

From a cardboard shoebox he spilled ancient rosaries that belonged in museums. They were made of all kinds of materials and wrought in varied strange designs. The rarest one and the oldest was fashioned of little balls of polished leather. It had been sold to him by the bastard son of a monk. One rosary that might have been designed for a princess's confirmation was made of triangles of silver-colored silk embroidered in delicate flowers and partitioned by minute disks of copper. It was an exquisite thing, and the sheriff handled it respectfully.

"Some day," he said, "my collection will go into a museum. But Lönnrot was the real collector in this hinterland. A hundred years ago he got the cream of the *Kalevala* a few kilometers from here. I collect only coins and symbols. He collected the breath of poetry, and just in time—before it was forgotten."

He rose and reached for his hat. "Let's drive out to Mekrijärvi, where Lönnrot got his best songs."

We went into a region where men and women lived as primitively today as when the scholar-doctor accepted their rude hospitality and coaxed from them unwritten literary treasures to be added to his collection and Finland's glory. "Odd, isn't it," Brotherus observed, "that two impecunious village tailors—and one of those a drunkard—begat the sons who were to give Finland her greatest literature."

From a hill above the shadowy lake, the sheriff pointed to lonely cabins, dim and weather-grayed. "There and there lived Runo singers who twanged the *Kantele* and sang their magic songs for Lönnrot. All the good singers in this district are dead now. Their descendants still have the high foreheads, but they are empty." The sheriff touched his foreskull. "They have degenerated—and can recall almost nothing of the songs their ancestors created."

We passed a two-century-old house that was dwelling and stable and outhouses all in one. "Such houses are very rare in Finland today, and the people who inhabit them are like something from the dim past. But it was from just such humble households that Lönnrot got his most precious materials."

By sled and ski and afoot, the country physician traveled winter and summer doctoring the sick and cajoling cantos out of aging peasants. At deathbeds he collected verses in lieu of fees and delivered bawling babies for unwritten songs.

The one thing most Americans know about the *Kalevala* is that Longfellow borrowed its four-stressed trochaic meter for his *Hiawatha*. It was a shrewd borrowing, for the meter lends itself particularly well to any story of a brave and primitive people, attuned to the spirit of woods. Here, surrounded by the pines and birches, I thought of the Finnish hero's complimentary address to the tree from which he desired material to build a boat:

> O thou pine tree, shall I take thee,
> For the boat for Väinämöinen,
> And as boat wood for the minstrel?

and Hiawatha's similar plea:

> Give me of your bark, O Birch-tree,
> Of your yellow bark, O Birch-tree . . .
> I a light canoe will build me.

And when at the end of the story Väinämöinen departs because of the immaculate birth of a child who is baptized "King of all Karelia" and "the Lord of all the mighty," the old hero

> . . . prepared himself to journey
> From the lake's extended margin,

and he

> Sailed away to loftier regions,
> To the land beneath the heavens.

So Hiawatha, when the white men came,

> Launched his birch-canoe for sailing,
> From the pebbles of the margin,

and the people watched him as he

> Sailed into the purple vapours,
> Sailed into the dusk of evening.

It has often been remarked that the mythology of the *Kalevala* has as little connection with the Norse as with the Greek. Although some of its creators certainly had an acquaintance with Scripture, its feeling is animistic. It is tinged with the sort of black magic known as "shamanism," a faith in shamans or wizards, who knew "words of origin" that could bring about events. The chief hero of the *Kalevala* is a minstrel, knowledgeable in words of origin. He comes to Finland when it is a barren, treeless country and by magic incantation makes it fruitful.

The most interesting thing about the *Kalevala* epic is that though it deals with heroic and miraculous deeds, yet the characters are really simple people living a simple life in a rough land where nature is hard. There are no palaces, no luxurious display, no great kings, no military conquerors, which one finds in the other epics. Even in their imaginings the Finns did not concern themselves with material grandeur or military glory. Heroes with supernatural powers are really only peasants. And all through the epic the characters go about their daily tasks of felling trees, plowing, planting, marrying, housekeeping, just as they do today. The accomplished housewife is lauded above all fair women in the *Kalevala.* The bride is instructed in minute details of housekeeping:

> Then the tables must be scoured
> At the week-end at the latest,
> Wash them, and the sides remember,
> Let the legs be not forgotten . . .
> If there's dust upon the windows
> Dust them carefully with feathers.
> Wipe them with a wetted duster,
> That the dust should not be scattered
> Nor should settle on the ceiling.

"Finns have ever made more of poets than soldiers," the sheriff said. "The minstrel Väinämöinen, who could conquer his enemies with a song instead of a sword, is still their favorite hero." And despite the Patriarch's professed lack of interest in the *Kalevala,* Finns do read the epic for pleasure and many love to recite the songs of Väinämöinen—songs so responsive that

All the leaves called gaily to him,
And the heath was all rejoicing;
Flowers breathed their fragrance round him,
And the young shoots bowed before him—

On our way back to Ilomantsi Brotherus recited snatches of the poem, first in Finnish, and then in translation.

You at least were never present
When the ocean first was furrowed,
And the ocean depths were hollowed . . .
When the hills were heaped together,
And the rocky mountains fashioned. . . .

He skipped to another part:

Filled with wrath and indignation,
And himself commenced his singing . . .
Sang the aged Väinämöinen;
Lakes swelled up and earth was shaken,
And the coppery mountains trembled.

"There, you see," said the sheriff, as a man on a bicycle passed us with a birchbark bag like a knapsack strapped to his back. "Men wear bags made of birchbark today just as in the *Kalevala* days. And many of the people hidden in the depths of the forest have never yet seen a railway train—they live in a past age of folksong and superstition. But state schools are reaching them now."

When we got to Ilomantsi the foreign office was calling Brotherus. He was ordered back to Helsinki at once. The situation was explosive. Germany might strike at Poland any minute, and such a spark could set all Europe on fire.

As we said good-by, the sheriff slipped something cool and metallic into my hand. It was the ikon I had fancied. There was no refusing it, this souvenir from the land of the *Kalevala*. It made me a collector, too—of more than memories.

Our trip was cut short, but I had seen far more than most Finns have seen of their eastern border country. Now I was to make my way back to Punkaharju by bus tomorrow from Joensuu. Brotherus was to take the car to Kuopio and there catch the train to Helsinki.

He drove toward Joensuu as wildly as John Gilpin involuntarily went on horseback. We tore down a twisting hill and at the bottom skidded into a granite boulder, and for one jarring moment we each expected death. But we were miraculously unhurt. Only our car's rear was knocked cockeyed in the crash. We were able to proceed at sober pace to Joensuu's repair shop.

"I'm glad I didn't kill you—I would have had to resign," Brotherus said, practically, recalling that a chauffeuring guide recommended by the foreign office to Burton Holmes and his wife had had a collision near Koli which broke the legs of both passengers.

That evening from the hotel at Joensuu I telephoned Therese. The toll for speaking from a distance that took a bus five hours to cover was twelve cents. So much for the virtue of government-owned long-distance telephone lines. Therese had heard no war rumors at Punkaharju. Idyllic peace still reigned there.

THE PEACE IS BROKEN

At Punkaharju these last days Therese had reveled in the quintessence of peace, for the frail guardian angel, "Anna of the shy glance," had thrown her flaming spirit against the intrusion of war talk. Newspapers had mysteriously disappeared; something had strangely gone wrong with the radio. Guests of six nationalities, restive at first, had quietly come to accept the peace under the pines. The weather had been ideal, each day like a last lovely day of summer.

At dinner that evening Therese had asked an Englishwoman named Miss Bent to join us. "She is a teacher in a factory town of Cornwall," Therese explained, "and has a quality of mind as beautiful as her speaking voice." Yesterday Miss Bent had had a wire from a friend telling her to come home at once. But she was so happy in this secluded spot that she could not bear to go. She had telephoned the English legation in Helsinki, and they had said things were tight but that there was no immediate necessity for returning.

"I know I should go," she said. "I am staying on here in blind faith, without belief. I know that this peace here in this heavenly spot is only a dream—and when I leave I shall wake up to a terrible reality."

"But England must not fight," Therese insisted. "She would be torn to pieces whether she won or lost. She should never have said she'd fight if Germany took Danzig. Why not let Germany go east—and sooner or later meet Russia?"

"Ah, yes, I wish we would keep out of it," said Miss Bent. "Why should we continue to rule the world? We've had our go at it for a long time—and what has it brought us? Perhaps it is time we gave another nation a chance. We could get on. We would have enough for ourselves alone. These people here in Finland—they stay in their own country, and they, the whole of them, have more than we. We say we shall be fighting for freedom. But fighting can never bring freedom of spirit. Only peace and consideration for our fellow man can bring spiritual freedom."

"Are you a pacifist?" I asked.

"Yes—and a Quaker. I cannot believe in war for any reason.

THE GAY AND GLITTERING HOTEL AT THE ARCTIC CIRCLE FLIES THE FLAGS OF ALL NATIONALITIES REPRESENTED AMONG CURRENT GUESTS

LAPP SETTLEMENT AT KOLTTAKÖNGAS

UNMARRIED KOLTTA LAPP GIRL WHO WOULD NOT SELL THE PICTURE OF GOD

And yet—" she ran her fingers into the hair above her temples. "When I think of some of our towns like Manchester with belching smoke and dirt and the people herded together in hovels—a bomb dropped there, destroying it all, might be a kind of blessing."

We looked at her in astonishment as Miss Kuohi joined us for coffee.

"What's the news?" I asked.

"There is nothing—quite nothing."

"Then you really think there will not be war?" Therese said.

"No," said Miss Kuohi, smiling quietly, as if reassuring a child. "No. There will be no war."

"But the porters say Germany is on the march."

"But that is nothing. Germany is always marching about."

We looked over at the three tables of Germans who were guests at the Finlandia. They seemed in no hurry to finish their meal and get home. There was some cheer in that.

Therese and I made the most of what turned out to be the last evening of peace, sitting out the ecstasy of twilight's metamorphosis on the wooden wharf at the lake's edge. Like so much that is Finnish, the beauty of the evening held a hint of melancholy and foreboding. The moist mirror reflected the pale spears of trembling marsh grasses and the proud columns of the pines, the color of gunmetal and straight as rifle barrels. A powder-blue mist crept across the lake, shrouding it in mysterious beauty. And then a waning moon rose, and the lake became as somber as black marble.

The lights in the hotel behind us went out one by one. A pair of wild swans streaked southerly, directly over our heads; but the whiteness of their wings was unreflected in the dark water. Along the grassy banks, field crickets fiddled minor melodies.

And from the direction of the gardeners' cottages came the sound of masculine singing. We listened intently—and recognized a Finnish folksong we had heard before. A baritone voice was singing a song of love—"If I should die, my sweet, would the night still be lovely?"

The next morning dawned—Friday, the first of September—and Hitler seized Danzig. But we did not know it until noon, for we stayed in our rooms, busy at writing until lunch time. When we came downstairs and saw Miss Kuohi's face, we knew her peace was at last disturbed.

"Hitler has made a speech," she said, distraught. "The Germans have all gone. We had to let the radio be fixed."

"And what does England say?"

"England still says nothing. But Hitler spoke—hard—as he does. The Germans listening at the radio turned pale—Hitler told them to come home. Fifteen minutes ago they all left—the big happy boys were sick at heart—they had tears in their eyes as they told me good-by. I had pity for them."

At two o'clock we listened over the radio to an English translation of Hitler's speech that came from Berlin. The Führer left no doubt that if his action in Poland provoked war—which he obviously expected—it was a struggle to the death with England for power.

That night at dinner the large dining room was empty except for Therese and me and a young bearded Hollander and his mother, who was a replica of Queen Wilhelmina. Everyone, including Miss Bent, had left Punkaharju. Out of the emotion of the crisis the old Dutch lady came over and asked if she might talk with us. She and her son were motoring, she explained, and she wondered how they could get home. She foresaw the invasion of Holland. "Only God can help us now," she said like a prayer.

When we took the train for Helsinki, Miss Kuohi walked with us to the station. She was pale, and violet shadows lay under her eyes. Her white-gold hair was in disorder and her hands were cold. Though she tried gallantly to keep discord from her spirit, her peace was broken.

It had turned chilly, and a fresh wind made us put on our topcoats. The shadows of late afternoon lay across the wheat fields. Sheet lightning played about the horizon. The underbrush along the road had become tinged with autumnal red. Winter overcoats and furs hung on doorstoops airing. A hay wagon passed us, piled full of a last load of summer. But the feel in the air was that of fall.

Therese put her arms very tenderly about Eero's wife as she kissed her good-by. As I kissed her hand I could feel her spirit still struggling to hold to its belief in peace. But the evening with its weight seemed heavy like a burden on the girl's shoulder, and I thought of Seppänen's line about the woman who sometimes felt "a lonely blade of grass over against a mountain."

As the headlight of the engine appeared down the track, I repeated the question I had put to her once before: "If Russia tries to take you some day, what will you do?"

"We will fight, of course," she said, lifting her head resolutely.

"But it will do you no good," I reiterated.

"We will fight." She spoke with stubborn insistence.

"But you couldn't win—"

"Still we will fight."

PART SIX

"In the moral world we are ourselves the light-bearers, and the cosmic process is in us made flesh. For a brief space it is granted us, if we will, to enlighten the darkness that surrounds our path. As in the ancient torch-race, which seemed to Lucretius to be the symbol of all life, we press forward torch in hand along the course. Soon from behind comes the runner that will outpace us. All our skill lies in giving into his hand the living torch, bright and unflickering, as we ourselves disappear in the darkness."

HAVELOCK ELLIS

Farewell to Finland

NEWS OF WAR COMES SOFTLY

Saturday in Helsinki passed with showers and a suspension of activity while all waited for the blow that was to fall or be withheld. We ran into Urho Toivola, chief of the foreign office's press department. He was calm and cheering. England had issued an ultimatum to Germany to withdraw troops from Poland—but had set no definite time limit. War might yet be avoided.

"War is probable, but not inevitable. In any case it is quite safe to stay in Finland—the little countries will not be drawn in for three or four months."

Sunday we lunched at the Royal Café on the Esplanade. The terraces were not crowded as usual, because almost all the tourists had left and the Finns had gone to the beaches for their last Sunday swim of summer. Though the sun shone splendidly, Helsinki stood at the threshold of autumn. Because of the tang in the air Therese wore the Spitzbergen blue fox scarf we had bought in Hammarfest and I had put on a winter-weight suit. Occasional leaves from the horse-chestnuts detached themselves one by one from the branches, like guests departing from an *alfresco* feast. They drifted leisurely to rest among the blue and white pigeons on the grass. Some fell upon the glistening pebbles of the walks and were crushed by passing feet. One or two adventurous ones made detours to the white napery of the luncheon tables, while some hid themselves among the hydrangeas. The songbirds had gone now and abandoned their summer homes to the winter's ruin.

A great stillness hung in the air. There was no sound of excavation and drilling, for the builders were taking their Sunday rest. On its dais the string quartet played muted music, while the diners at the tables talked tensely and abstractedly, as people do in a courtroom when a jury is expected any moment to bring in a verdict.

We had finished dessert and were waiting for coffee when Miss Bent, the Englishwoman, passed. We asked her to join us. Yesterday, she told us, she had put her luggage on the boat that was to take her to England, and had gone to do a couple of hours' shopping, and when she had returned at noon ready to sail she was told that the boat would not be going, and that there would be no more passenger boats from Finland to England. She had been routed by train through Sweden and Norway, and the agents hoped she could get a boat from Bergen, though they could not guarantee it.

"But that is probably just precaution," we said.

"No, it means war," she said calmly, resigned, but without fear.

While she was speaking I noticed a boy passing in and out among the tables, handing out single, half sheets like circus handbills. People were paying for them with copper coins. I got up and went after the boy. I read the Swedish headline, EUROPA I BRAND, and knew what had happened. I bought one of the extras and came back to the table. A brief paragraph below the headline that announced "Europe on Fire" said that England had declared war on Germany at eleven o'clock—one o'clock by Finnish time. Now it was half-past one. Therese turned a little pale. The English woman said quietly, in anguish of heart, "Oh, I wish they had not done it. Why didn't they wait a little longer and try to compromise?"

At the tables, people read the extras in silence, handed them to their companions, made low comments and went on with their luncheon. The newsboy walked away, never once having raised his voice. On our return to the hotel, we passed other newsboys, but they did not shout their wares. They merely held the papers so that men might see them and buy if they liked. No loudspeakers blared the exciting news. There was no outward interruption in the Finnish Sunday peace.

"I knew I should have been gone," Miss Bent said. "I let myself be beguiled by the spirit of peace at Punkaharju. I didn't want to face reality. Now I have waited just one day too late. In times like these one should be in his own country."

"I think we too must go home," Therese said, sadly. "These people can't be feeding alien mouths, too."

The next morning at the Swedish-American Line office I got the last stateroom on the *Gripsholm,* sailing from Gothenburg on the nineteenth. Because there was much to be done in Sweden, and because the Swedes began to make it difficult about visas, we decided we had better get back into Sweden at once. Besides, I had accepted an invitation for a dinner to Thomas Mann and H. G. Wells for the next Saturday in Stockholm, and had already intended to fly there for the week-end. So we broke a fortnight of engagements and got boat reservations for Stockholm again by way of Turku.

On Thursday I received a telephone message from Heikki Reenpää, head of the publishing firm of Otava. He had read a Swedish translation of my book on South America, *South by Thunderbird,* and he wanted to publish it in Finnish. I went to call on him at his office—a great room more like an ambassador's than a publisher's, with his desk near a corner between a floor-to-ceiling window and oil portraits of Sillanpää and Selma Lagerlöf. As he offered me a contract, he said with a wry smile, "I have put in a clause which I hope will prove superfluous—it reads here—so—'provided Finland is not drawn into war before the end of the year.'"

DEVOTION

When I got back from Otava's and was doing my last packing, Ralph Enckell telephoned that he had arranged to have me meet Nurmi that afternoon at three, and that Nurmi might show me his collection of modern paintings. I said we were leaving on the boat train at five, that I was packing, and couldn't possibly make it, but could he possibly persuade Nurmi to come here to the hotel at four? Enckell said he would try, but that Nurmi was difficult and extremely shy. I knew this was so because several important officials had tried to arrange a meeting for me and had failed.

At three he telephoned that Nurmi had said he would come. And at five minutes to four Enckell arrived at the Torni with the athlete that had caught my imagination beyond all others. In my twenties I had been thrilled by the Phantom Finn's fleetness. And I had always liked the way the very name, Paavo Nurmi, looked in print—the five-five letters, the liquidity of the vowels. It had a strong and beautiful sound, like something noble and heroic. This meeting was one I had looked forward to for many years—and now it came in the midst of telephone calls, bill-paying, luggage being brought down, and all the annoying interruptions of departure.

In features Nurmi was as obviously a Finn as any other man in Finland. Medium in height and weight—about five feet nine and weighing some one hundred sixty pounds—he was a blond with a broad face, high cheekbones, pale gray eyes, and hair without luster. He was dressed in a gray suit and wore a gray hat that looked too small for him. Outwardly, the noted runner looked superlatively average. But his famous poker-face stolidity was no more than a mask, for visible through it was another face, excruciatingly sensitive. His manner was shy, his greeting gave next to nothing of himself. When he attempted a smile, his discontent was the more revealed. The strain of high-minded obstinacy lurking in the corners of his face was almost absorbed in a cold impassivity of disillusion. I wondered what poison he was peculiarly susceptible to. For some unaccountable reason, Nijinsky came to my mind. But Nijinsky's consuming unhappiness had driven him mad. Whatever had made Nurmi critical of life had merely intensified the coolness of his logic.

I had learned these last weeks something about the private life of the Finnish idol, who by 1930 had held thirty-seven different world records for distance running. The son of a working man, the Phantom Finn began his career as an errand boy at twelve and later became a filer's apprentice. After his success in Antwerp, some people interested in his future paid for his studies at an industrial school, where he finished second in his class. He then became a skilled mechanic. When he gave up running, he went into business for himself. I had bought things at the haberdashery shop that he owned, and I knew he was also making considerable money in a contracting concern. He had the reputation of being a shrewd business man and driving a good bargain. The energy he had once put into running he was now putting into business. His wife had divorced him some years ago and had gone off with his son, who was now eleven. Like an ascetic, Nurmi lived in one room and invested his money in modern art, for which he had astute appreciation. The walls of his room were covered with paintings, and crated pictures leaned against the walls, while many more were stored in a warehouse.

These things ran through my mind as we sat in a parlor of

the Torni, my eye periodically on the clock, just as Nurmi used to consult the watch he always carried in his fist when he ran a race.

"It is somewhat idiotic, a man chasing after a record," Nurmi said, and Enckell interpreted. I looked at him in some amazement as the words sunk in. "God did not intend man to train himself into a perfect machine," he said grimly.

I thought of Housman's poem to *An Athlete Dying Young:*

> The time you won your town the race
> We chaired you through the market place.

Not only fellow countrymen, but the world, had borne Nurmi shoulder-high with honors time after time.

> Smart lad to slip betimes away
> From fields where glory does not stay
> And early though the laurel grows
> It withers quicker than the rose.

But Nurmi's laurels were kept fresh in the hearts of Finns, who saw in every new champion the spirit of Nurmi. In the Athenaeum Museum the place of honor was given to his own contemporary nude figure, racing in green bronze, a statue done by Finland's foremost sculptor. And on the posters printed in twenty tongues, Nurmi ran bearing tidings of the XIIth Olympiad to far-flung nations of the seven seas.

Here was no case of a forgotten champion, sour because his medals were tarnished. In his retirement from active sport a halo still hung about his early-laureled head. But perhaps it was because his career had begun at its "highest, purest level"—because he had seen himself proclaimed an immortal twenty years ago—that the salt of fame had lost its savor for Nurmi.

Nurmi's discontent, though, seemed to lie too deep for any consideration of egotism. It was a thing of the spirit—something ageless and racial. Melancholy is a kind of frost blight that lies quite naturally on Finnish natures. Sillanpää is said to be a suffering victim. Sibelius' most memorable passages of music have flowered from it. The humorist Kivi went mad with it. In every Finn over thirty I had met, I had found this tinge of melancholy in greater or lesser degree. Taisto Mäki, alone of the really noted men of Finland, seemed to have no trace of it. But Mäki had not quite reached his thirtieth birthday—and he was continuing to break his own world records.

"Success in sport as in almost anything," Nurmi was saying, "comes from devotion. The athlete must make a devotion of his specialty. Devotion is the real thing. Without it one will hardly be successful. Devotion cannot be forced on anybody—neither can it be got forcefully. It is given to you. You simply have it or you don't. I had it. I was born with it, and so I do not boast about it. I never wanted to be taken for an exceptional being. I made a champion's career, but still I have no memories. Perhaps it is regrettable, but that's the way it is."

He spoke in a low, monotonous tone, as impassive as his mask. Then he raised his voice slightly, as if he wanted to drive home a point. "The fault with sport all over the world nowadays is that it overreaches itself. It has been driven to a far higher level than it should be. If anyone desires success in the Olympics, he must sacrifice all possible time to training. And that is why we are going toward a false amateurism." He looked away from both of us. "A man must sacrifice too much for it. There are many other professions far more profitable than sport." He turned back and looked at me with quiet challenge. "At the present time sports do not interest me. It is impossible today to combine pleasure with a sportsman's career."

"But you encourage youth in sports—you help train them," I said.

"Ah, but because I have acquired experience, it is my duty to give the younger generation the profit of it—if they want it. That is the reason."

For a moment we sat in silence. Enckell gave me a glance that seemed to say, "I told you he was something quite different from other men."

I made no comment on Nurmi's last remark. I asked what he did for exercise now, and drew an amused smile. "I walk," he said. "Now that the government has stopped the sale of gasoline for private cars, I walk all over the place to look after my construction. But soon there won't be any more building—because we can't get materials." That had him worried, because he was under contract to finish work at a certain time.

As I looked at the clock again, our load of luggage was brought down. What with typewriter, manuscript, boxes of books and clothes for winter and summer, it made ten pieces. Therese came down, and the taxi was waiting. Enckell and Nurmi said they would go to the station with us to see us off.

I sat in the front with the chauffeur, and the other three got in the back. Another taxi followed with our luggage. At the station we could find only one unengaged porter, and Enckell and Nurmi began to pick up some of the stuff from the sidewalk. As Nurmi walked off carrying her overnight bag, Therese in horror said, "But you can't let Mr. Nurmi carry luggage." Nurmi, understanding, half-grinned, and we all went on through the gates.

After the bags were stowed and we stood outside on the platform by another line of cars away from the confusion of other travelers' good-by's, I asked Nurmi his definition of *sisu,* the Finn's favorite word.

"Every Finn has his own pet definition," he said. "To me, *sisu* means patience without passion." Then he added thoughtfully, "But there are many varieties of *sisu—sisu* can be a sudden outburst or it can be the kind that lasts. A man can have both kinds. It is outside reason. It is something in the soul. It comes from oneself—for instance, it makes a soldier do things because he himself must, not because he has been told."

A young man, smartly dressed in double-breasted gray flannel, came down the platform with a bunch of red roses in his hand. He was Lorenz von Numers, a young Swedo-Finnish poet and scion of a noble family that had fallen on meager days. He was a friend of Ralph Enckell. One evening we three had sat in his one-room apartment in Töölö in high-backed painted leather chairs that belonged in palaces, and had talked Finland and poetry, Enckell playing with a riding crop and looking like a portrait of a regenerated and intellectual Hapsburg, with his long body and long face and long lower jaw. Von Numers, now living with his three ancestral chairs in necessitated simplicity, had laughingly confessed to being perhaps the only Finn who longed for a monarchy. Yet he loved the root and soul of Finland with a poet's and a sportsman's passion, as he revealed when he recited impromptu translations of his poems.

Von Numers had brought the roses to Therese, and he bent to kiss her hand. Tomorrow he was going to join his regiment, he said, with the air of one invited to a wedding feast. He stood with his hat off, the sun gleaming on his gold hair. Therese looked tenderly at the smiling, handsome face. "But Finland must keep out," she said sadly, meaning that it would be too horrible to contemplate this beautiful young man and the other young Finns with bullets through their heads.

"We shall try with all our might," Enckell said. "But if any nation comes to upset our independence, we shall have to fight. Finns are an inflexible people—we can't make compromise."

As I looked at the disillusion that shone through Nurmi's

mask, I realized that it was so. Herein lay Finland's weakness and strength. Inflexibility was a key to the champion's fate and to Finland's.

Nurmi smiled gently at Therese when she said good-by, and we went to our seats in the train. Against the other parallel line of cars the sun shone in full afternoon splendor and illuminated the three Finns: the athlete, the diplomat, and the soldier-poet. Beside them like a stretched banner the embossed white letters SUOMI stood out boldly on the red railway carriage.

The conductor called out the Finnish "All aboard." We said the meaningless, quickly forgotten things one says in farewells. From the vestibule I raised a hand in my good-by. The three waved back—their hands above the line of SUOMI, their heads in line with it. As our train moved off, the symbolic letters seemed to draw together and unite in one vertical white line. The Phantom Finn and his two companions turned and started toward the station.

I came into the crowded compartment and sat down by Therese. Her face still reflected something she had seen in Nurmi —something she wished she could have comforted. "He was so nice, poor fellow," she said, and wondered what she should do with the red roses in her lap. I laid them on top of the piled luggage in the racks, and soon they perfumed the whole compartment.

"The papers used to say that Nurmi always finished a race taller than when he began," I said, settling down and relaxing from the emotions of packing and departure. "I imagine that's the way I feel, leaving Finland—a little taller than when I came."

But I was heavy-hearted at leaving, heavy-hearted with apprehension for Finland, yet more grateful for having seen the land, I think, than for any I had ever visited. Not only had I come to look upon the strange strong people as most remarkable for

FISHERMEN'S HUTS ON THE ARCTIC OCEAN

IN LAPLAND ONE BECOMES QUITE ACCUSTOMED TO REINDEER GRAZING ON THE ROADSIDES

what they had done with what they had, but my admiration had grown into a kind of depersonalized love for the race. I had seen the traces of victorious activity from one end of the land to the other. And I had seen in many manifestations democracy at its noblest.

As the train ran through the countryside, the stubble fields luxuriated idly in the late afternoon sunshine. Boys were practicing pole-vaulting in a farmyard, their cheeks bright as the ripened apples in the orchards behind them. Two little girls in dresses the color of mountain-ash berries waved gravely at the passing cars, and a gray goose flapped her wings. As the sun touched the horizon and shot its level rays across the meadows to the woods, the trunks of the birch trees rippled like white silk, and autumnal sprays glittered like a shower of gold. When dusk came, the infinite forest turned black, and the sky became a pierced lantern with its pattern of stars. A nostalgia surged through us—not yet for that southern homeland to which we were soon returning, but for this alien northern land to which we were not ready to bid farewell.

PART SEVEN

"But all your fine poetry is about wars you have lost."

FIELD MARSHAL GÖRING
IN CONVERSATION WITH A FINN

"And when the multitudes saw it they marvelled, and glorified God which had given such power unto men."

MATTHEW IX, 8

War with Russia

FROM GREEN ROCKETS TO SCORCHED EARTH

As the first month of the New World War advanced, Finland was never more beautiful with the gold and copper and crimson of its September-colored woods. While Hitler's blitzkrieg made a shambles of Poland and Russian troops massed on the Polish frontier to gobble up the eastern half, life in Finland went on in its accustomed orderly rhythms despite the disturbing echoes from the continent. Preparations for the Olympic Games never abated. Doggedly optimistic, the Finns had no serious misgivings until the U.S.S.R., taking advantage of the critical world situation, suddenly forced the Baltic republics of Estonia, Latvia, and Lithuania to provide Russia with air and naval bases to such an extent that the concession amounted to the relinquishment of their independence. On October fifth, the first fateful note from Foreign Commissar Molotov arrived at Helsinki inviting a delegate to come to Moscow to discuss "concrete political questions."

This note marked the beginning of seven weeks of proposals and counter-proposals, demands and compromises, exchanged in the forms of notes or at conferences. Finnish commissioners shuttled back and forth from Helsinki to Moscow three times for prolonged conversations. But though the Finns did not believe a war between the two countries would actually come, it was virtually inevitable from the first.

Russia had demanded territory in the Karelian Isthmus so that the frontier, which was within thirty-two kilometers of Leningrad, would be moved back some fifty kilometers farther. She also required all of Rybachi Peninsula on the Arctic Ocean, and four islands in the Gulf of Finland. For creating a naval base with coastal artillery, she demanded the leasing for a period of thirty years of the port and peninsula of Hanko, which controlled the entrance to the Gulf. And she required that the fortifications on the frontier be eradicated.

In return for 2,761 square kilometers of strategic and valuable territory, the U.S.S.R. would cede to Finland 5,529 square miles of Russian territory in the districts of Repola and Porajärvi. The latter was infertile, sparsely settled, and of no strategic importance. To avoid a fight, the Finnish government conceded more and more, but continued to refuse to turn Hanko over to the Russians or "to grant to any foreign power military bases on her own territory."

Moscow was ominously silent for a breathing spell, and then *Pravda* in the best Nazi manner began to work up home zeal for protecting the Finnish proletariat. Gripping stories of the hardships of working classes under the iron heel of warmongering rulers appeared with recurring frequency in the Soviet press.

On the last Sunday afternoon in November, imitating an old Nazi dodge, the Soviet government declared that Russian troops had been wantonly fired upon seven times by Finnish artillery near Mainil on the Karelian Isthmus. It was claimed that a noncommissioned officer and three privates had been killed and nine men wounded.

Premier Molotov, calling the faked incident "provocational shelling," summoned the Finnish minister, Baron Yrjö-Koskinen, to the Kremlin and handed him a note demanding that the government of Finland withdraw its troops without delay twenty to twenty-five kilometers farther from the border of the Karelian Isthmus.

The Finns categorically denied that Finnish guns had fired on Russians and offered to withdraw the same number of miles from the frontier that the Russians would.

At this show of independence, Soviet threats in the newspapers and on the radio began to come thick and fast and dire. In staged demonstrations students and factory workers shouted for vengeance. The "people" of Russia clamored for action against the Finnish "militarists" and urged the masses in Finland to overthrow their evil government.

On November twenty-seventh the Soviet press reached a violent climax of vituperation against Finland, and the next day the U.S.S.R. proclaimed the cancellation of its non-aggression pact with Finland.

In answer to this drastic move Premier Cajander telegraphed to the Finnish legation in Moscow, offering to withdraw troops the requested distance from the frontier, whether or not the Soviets did likewise. But the Moscow telegraph office held up delivery of the note until Vice-Foreign Commissar Potemkin had announced to Finland's representative that Russia had severed diplomatic relations and had handed the minister his passport.

As one last effort at appeasement, Premier Cajander called a secret meeting of the parliament the next evening and resigned. A new coalition government was formed with Finland's two foremost men in public affairs in the key positions: Risto Ryti was made prime minister, and Väinö Tanner foreign minister.

It was too late. The Kremlin did not want to be placated. Already orders had been given to launch the invasion the next morning at dawn. The Red soldiers were even now getting their last winks of peaceful sleep, and the green rocket signals were set, ready to be fired. At eight o'clock in the before-dawn darkness, heralded by the green shooting stars of the rockets, the advance commenced. Cannonading began at five different places on the border. At half-past nine three Soviet airplanes dropped through the low clouds hanging above Helsinki and loosed five bombs on the airport. As one hangar burst into flames, citizens in the capital knew that the undeclared war was on.

At lunch time a second air alarm sounded in Helsinki. Steel-helmeted wardens took their posts in the street, and within an hour the evacuation of women and children to the country began. As the railway station became jammed with outgoing hordes, ten Soviet pilots made it a target and began dropping 550-pound bombs from their roaring planes. The bombs missed all the buildings in the vicinity, but tore great holes out of the station square and killed forty persons. In another part of the town a bomb wrecked the Technical Institute, killing two professors and several students. Some apartment houses were demolished, and flames leaped up here and there as stray incendiary bombs started conflagrations. The coastal export centers of Viipuri and Turku also received aërial attacks. The sea fortress at Hanko was bombed. The power plant at Imatra and even the gas-mask factory at Lahti, far in the interior, were bombed. The awful news of Russia's invasion of Finland reached American homes on Thanksgiving Day.

After two days of bombing, during the night of December second snow began to fall softly, like a blessing. When Sunday morning dawned, a downy white blanket covered the capital in protective camouflage, and reports from the fighting area told of a blinding blizzard raging through the forests. The hearts of the Finns lifted with gratitude. Their old friend and enemy, the elements, had entered the fray as their only ally.

In the Karelian Isthmus the Russian infantry advance was

preceded by an artillery barrage and a tank attack. The Finns gave ground slowly and sold each square yard of territory dearly as they moved back to the Mannerheim Line. At the end of the first five days they had wrecked irreparably or blown to bits over fifty of the supposedly invincible Russian tanks.

At Suojärvi, on the northeastern end of the defense lines some sixty miles above Lake Laatokka, the Russians launched a fierce attack. There the Finns experimented with original tactics. Armed with "machine pistols" that fired 250 shots a minute, in squads of six they deployed themselves behind granite boulders and tree trunks, and annihilated two companies of Russians as they picked their way through the forest.

Wherever parachute jumpers baled out and began floating to earth, Finnish sharpshooters with their super-skill in marksmanship had such a field day of wing shooting that the Reds in the south soon gave up such strategy. In the Petsamo district in the north the Finns allowed the parachute jumpers to reach the ground and gather in bands, then surrounded them and shot them down *en masse*.

In this farthermost northern district, where there were only some eight hundred Finnish soldiers, the Finns had to think fast and work fast. They sent the women and children by bus, by reindeer sled, and on skis across the ice-coated boulder-strewn border into Norway. Busses camouflaged with white bed linen made poor targets for the machine gunners in Soviet planes that pursued the busses wherever they could pick up the trail. All the livestock that could not be driven over the snowy wastes into Norway was slaughtered. The thriving little port of Liinahamari on the Arctic turned from white to red, as flames from the Finn-lit fires greeted the invading Russians. Every village building and farmhouse and barn that might give the Russians shelter from the icy blasts were set on fire. Perhaps a lucky

Russian picked out a tasty bit of roast pig in some embers, like the Chinaman whose house was burned in Lamb's tale; but scarcely anything else in all the land was found to do them service. For the Finns had imitated the famous "scorched-earth" tactics of the Chinese.

The invaders captured Liinahamari and then began to freeze to death—ill-shod and ill-clothed as they were for such winter temperatures. The Finns swooped down on skis, recaptured the ruined town and took a horde of miserable prisoners. When reinforcements began to disembark from Russian warships and the harbor was thick with small boats taking the troops to shore, the defending Finns dynamited the cliffs of the fjord. The great rocks, hurtling into the bay as from a volcanic eruption, capsized the boats and drowned the Reds in the icy water. When thousands more, better-equipped Russian reinforcements poured into Liinahamari, the Finns fell back to Salmijärvi, leaving the enemy to enjoy the bitter fruits of victory in the snowbound "scorched earth," where dusky daylight came for only two hours a day in December.

HYDRA-HEADED ATTACKS

Attempting a stupidly blatant trick to stir the proletariat to revolution, Moscow announced the formation of a new Finnish People's Government, with Terijoki as its capital. Otto Kuusinen, a Finnish Communist who had fled to Russia in 1918, was set up as premier. His fake government proclaimed a policy of mild sovietism, by which all banks and industries were to be nationalized and the larger estates broken up and divided. The declaration called on the Finns to overthrow their criminal government of "hangmen and war provocateurs."

"Arise, long-suffering, toiling people of Finland!" Kremlin-inspired Kuusinen shouted over the radio and in pamphlets. "Arise to the courageous fight against the tyranny of your oppressors and hangmen! Arise, all citizens to whom the future of our country is dear! Let us throw down the black pack of reaction from the shoulders of our people! Let us clear the road for the progress, welfare and culture of the people. . . ."

Not a Finn stirred in response to the exhortation, except to give it a laugh that was echoed and re-echoed all around the globe.

With the intention of sovietizing Finland now made patent, Premier Ryti, speaking for the valiant will of Finland, declared, "We shall not consent to bargain away our independence. . . . We will fight alone and we expect to win." Knowing that she had not a single ally who would officially come to her aid, and beset by a foe fifty times as strong as she, Finland braced herself for a battle to the death.

The world cheered such resolution. Finland, a country of small resources and a population about equal to that of Missouri, now faced a major war with a nation possessing one-eighth of the world's land surface. As Russia continued to proclaim that Finland had provoked the war and thrice invaded her, the entire world began to mock Russia's travesty of justification. "The U.S.S.R.'s grotesque impersonation of a bear being bitten by a rabbit," *Time* in America quipped maliciously, "did the U.S.S.R.'s waning prestige and corroding ideal no world of good." Most silly of all was the fantastic apology of the American Red organ, *The Daily Worker,* which shrieked that the Soviet army had merely taken up arms in self-defense to hurl back "invading Finnish troops."

As the world press splayed indignant headlines across front pages, Italy all but outdid the United States in demonstrations of resentment. Yelling themselves hoarse as if news of another Abyssinian conquest had ended in triumph, lusty Blackshirts were not satisfied until they had borne the embarrassed Finnish Minister Eero Järnefelt through the streets on their shoulders. In London, dignified M.P.'s rose to cry "Shame!" at any mention of Russia in Parliamentary sessions. The *Daily Herald,* mouthpiece of the British Labor Party, shouted in red-inked headlines, "The Union of Soviet Socialist Republics is dead. Stalin's new imperialist Russia takes its place. Now finally Stalin's Russia sacrifices all claims to the respect of the working class movement."

Editorial writers in the United States pounded more sincere eloquence out of their typewriters than they had in years. But despite the clamor of righteous indignation and admiration there was no material succor in sight for Finland. The three tall old kings of Scandinavia were silent as their future sarcophagi. Their three premiers, with heavy caution, urged calmness. None of the three sister Northern Countries dared stir to go to the aid of the fourth. But scores of Swedes and Danes and Norwegians began to volunteer. Funds to aid Finland were started immediately. Within two days Sweden alone had raised a quarter of a million dollars. In the United States, President Roosevelt, strongly condemning the Soviet Union and protesting against the bombing of cities, set up a moral embargo against the shipping of war materials to Russia.

Making one last effort for peace, Finland appealed to the faltering League of Nations for help and asked for Russia's expulsion from the League. Russia pretended hurt astonishment. She was not at war with Finland, Molotov protested, and did not threaten the Finnish people with war. Russia's relations with Kuusinen's government were entirely friendly. Brushing aside the mockery of such moronic hypocrisy, Argentina's delegate made the speech demanding Soviet Russia's expulsion. For the first time in its wavering history the League expelled a member.

Bolshevism's prestige was in the mire, but on the battlefront little David still faced Goliath alone. The Finns had to rely in large measure on nature and their own wits. Destroying everything they left behind that might be of use to the enemy, they also filled the village wells with earth and in the abandoned seaside village of Terijoki they planted mines which blew up hundreds of entering troops.

In the Isthmus a farmer's family was routed out in the middle of the night by Finnish soldiers and told to save what they could carry, because the farm had to be fired to keep it from succoring the Reds. The next noon, in the midst of the shooting, to the amazement of the soldiers the old peasant turned up. Looking at the charred ruins fallen about the stone foundations, he said the farm had been burned twice before to keep it from helping the Russians—once in his father's time and once in his great-great-grandfather's—and he just wanted to make sure the soldiers had made a clean job of it this time, too.

The elements continued to help the Finns, completely concealing the tank traps under innocent-looking snow. As the Russians charged with their mechanized units against the thin Finnish defense, they were rudely shocked with a breaking loose of hell. Out of snow mounds Bofors anti-tank guns punctured the tanks with such precision that within the first fortnight of warfare one hundred tanks were made impotent. The Finns themselves swooped out of snowstorms and let go with their machine guns and "machine pistols." When their cartridges ran out, they unsheathed their knives and fought like cool-headed demons. They did not pause to take many prisoners.

Day after day, with their mechanized outfit stalled, Russia poured companies of infantry into the Isthmus forests. At a terrific human cost to the enemy, the Finns gave up their land acre by acre and fell back to the concrete trenches. As Russians dropped, in a few hours there were more to take their place—like cattle lined up for slaughter in the mammoth abattoirs of Bueños Aires.

The Finns lost incredibly few men. And the tales of audacity and prowess in hand-to-hand fighting that came back to Helsinki sounded like the boasts in the sagas. But they were true and authenticated. One Finn, a local marksman, shot down in one day forty-eight Russians with fifty-one shots.

The Finns were, however, caught napping in one respect. They had believed the 700-mile frontier between Finland and Russian Karelia safe because the uncharted terrain was too tough to negotiate. "All roads peter out with malice aforethought within fifteen miles of the border," Finnish Foreign Minister Erkko had said to me. And it was believed to be impossible for the Soviets to maintain supply lines, for Russia had only one railway, which paralleled the frontier from Leningrad to Murmansk. But Russia sent into Finland from the east four columns, separated by approximately a hundred miles, the intention being to cut through Finland's supply lines and eventually destroy rail communications with Sweden at the junction of Tornio, the western point of Finland's waistline. One detachment reached Nurmes and damaged the railway that ran from southeastern Karelia northwest to the Swedish border. Other Red troops reached Suomussalmi and prepared to turn south to despoil the rail junction in Finland's center. A third column approached not a railhead but the end of a road system at Kuusamo. A fourth entered Lapland over the mountains and reached Kemijärvi, where the northernmost railway branch ends. This fourth column aimed at Rovaniemi, the capital of Lapland on the Arctic Circle, for here the line that turned southwest to Tornio was the only rail connection with Sweden.

These moves of Russia were as daring as they were strategically clever. But the Soviet forces were now in danger of being cut off from their own supply lines, and the Finns went forth speedily on their skis to maroon them if they could.

In the third week of war Finland was attacked in seven distinct sectors, along a frontier of eight hundred miles with less than a hundred miles of it fortified and with an army of only two hundred thousand to defend the entire country. The President of Finland called upon the civilized nations of the world to help Finland to stem the Red tide. Premier Risto Ryti in a radio broadcast rallied his country by declaring, "The Finnish people at this moment are fully united, firm as steel and ready for the greatest sacrifices in behalf of their independence and their existence. . . . If compelled to do so, we shall fight to the end—even after the end."

The Finns took fresh heart and began to more than hold their own on all fields except the snow-covered tundra in the far north. Here, because of their very small force, the embattled Finns had to give way again. As they retreated to a new position southward, all the civilian population possible was sent across the ice into Norway. The rest went down the one road, the Arctic highway, toward Ivalo and Inari, driving their cattle and reindeer before them and carrying what household goods they could on reindeer sleds. The just completed hydro-electric plant at Jäniskoski the soldiers blew up, and the handsome new bridge likewise was destroyed. They burned the wooden houses erected for the two thousand workmen. The bright new town of Salmijärvi went up in flames. The advancing Reds, numbed with cold, had only a few hours of warm relief around the burning buildings that might have given them shelter during the whole campaign.

The Russians, having made no progress with their intended blitzkrieg anywhere but in the desolate north, now began taking more desperate chances at scoring some gains and victories. In an effort to outflank the unyielding Mannerheim Line, the Russians organized a big attack in the sector near Lake Laatokka, where the Finnish lines lay behind the two-hundred-yard-wide Taipale River. The river was not yet frozen, and under cover of an artillery barrage they attempted to send infantry across in boats. Both their aim and their shells were bad—many of the latter failed to explode. The Finns held their fire until the boats, sardine-thick with soldiers, were in midstream. Then they opened up with artillery. The boats were blown to bits. The current became choked with dead and dying men. A few who attempted to swim to shore in heavy overcoats were drowned or were picked off with rifles. Hardly a man of the five hundred in the vanguard escaped.

In the southmost sector, above the yielded Terijoki, the Russians continued to put their faith in tanks and sent waves of them charging across the landscape. But the advance gummed, because the soldiers were afraid to leave the tanks, and the tanks caught in the granite slab defenses were ruined by skillfully aimed hand grenades thrown under the treads. Finally the Russians turned tail, abandoning scores of tanks to the enemy. After less than three weeks of fighting the Finns announced the capture or destruction of two hundred of those tanks that the Russians had believed invincible.

Because of their small man power the Finns prudently refrained from any sort of massed attack themselves. They conserved men and munitions and stayed in watchful waiting behind their defenses. But nightly harassing parties of three, armed with machine guns and hand grenades, would slip silently in rowboats across the intervening waters and, like avenging angels, swoop out of the forest gloom, spread terror and death among the bivouacking Reds, and disappear.

At Salla and Suomussalmi, at the end of four days of maneuvers, the Finns had cut the Russian divisions from their bases. With the roads cut behind them, with no chance of getting to each other's aid, the Russians had been trapped. Most of those who were not mowed down by the Finns perished from starvation or freezing.

On December eighteenth, before dawn, a Russian cavalcade led by tanks and followed by Ford trucks of supplies, horse-drawn sleds, and a troop of cavalry, crossed a northern section of the Kemi River after having gone through a Finnish forest. Believing their approach unnoticed in the funereal darkness, they were astounded when Finns made a rushing attack and sent them back across the river doubling up on themselves. Another Finnish company dashed out of the woods and cut the infantry off from its supplies.

The Finns picked off the drivers of the trucks neatly, so that the machines clogged the roads. Those drivers who did not flee to the woods left blood-stained seats as they toppled dead into the snow. The fight went on for forty-eight hours of darkness and twilight in a temperature of twenty-two below zero. When it was over, some twenty-five hundred Russians lay dead. A Finnish soldier, observing the slain, said, "The wolves will eat well this year."

From the abandoned supply trains the Finns salvaged not only machine guns, shells, rifles, and gas masks, but stores of canned tuna fish, soup powders, rice and bologna, and great truckloads of black bread. "The best equipment and ammunition we have got from any power so far is from Russia," said a Finnish officer. And they gave some of it back generously—with a difference.

But for all the chalked-up Finnish successes and the generous gifts from Sweden, the little nation was still sorely in need of material and men. She was more than ready to declare the war off if any kind of honorable peace could be made. Over the radio Väinö Tanner, the Finnish foreign minister, once more asked the Soviet Union for some peaceful settlement, and promised "even greater concessions." There was no reply.

While the Finns were destroying the two regiments at Tolvajärvi, chasing Russians back into Russia, and striking toward the Murmansk-Leningrad Railway Line, the Finnish minister to the United States, Hjalmar Procopé, handed the Secretary of the Treasury a check to pay the annual installment due on the famous debt.

With the fourth week in December, the year came to its shortest day just before Christmas. Even in the south there were scarcely four hours of daylight. The matchless beauty of white landscape cloaked in snow was enhanced by the silvery twilight effect of Finnish midwinter. In most regions of the country the serenity of the peace-on-earth season seemed to lie like a blessing on whatever the eye beheld. But deep under the folds of the white mantles lay the stark bodies of the dead.

In Russia, four days before Christmas, Josef Stalin celebrated his sixtieth birthday. Such adulation from a nation's press had never been heaped on any living man. Among Comrade Stalin's shower of gifts was a portrait of himself made entirely from precious stones on which the Leningrad jewelers had been working a year and a half. But in the tumultuous fanfare of jubilee there was one discordant note that spoiled the swelling harmony. Zhdanoff, the "political boss of Leningrad" and as strong a Finnophobe as Czarist Bobrikoff, had promised Stalin the annihilation of the Finnish troops for a birthday present. And had that promise been fulfilled? The reports from Finland were indeed enough to turn any Russian birthday stomach sour. Instead of news of subjugation, long trains with drawn blinds crept into Leningrad bearing wounded by the thousands. Theaters and schools had to be quickly converted into hospitals. In Moscow, Russian casualties were already reckoned at thirty thousand, while the Finnish were still under four thousand.

Even from the far north, where the Russians were having their only success, came bad news to Moscow. In the Petsamo corridor the few Finns had fallen back to Nantsi, seventy miles from the Arctic Ocean. Ten thousand Russians pursued them with all the pride and assurance of their mechanized units. These new Soviet troops were efficiently trained and well-equipped for the rigors of winter campaigning. As the armored cars, aëro-sleds, and fleet of protecting bombing planes proceeded southward, it looked as if they might march straight down the Arctic highway to the Gulf of Bothnia. But the Finns, changing their tactics, slipped through the forests around behind the Russians and smashed asunder their communicating lines. Once again Finland's only ally, the elements, played a major part in stopping the Russians in their tracks. The temperature dropped to twenty-five below zero. A blizzard tore out of the skies with the fury of vengeance, cracking up or grounding the planes, freezing the radiators and the oil in the tanks, obliterating objects beyond a horse's length and stinging men into insensibility. Harried by the ski-swift Finns, whose white capes made them one with the snowdrifts, the Red advance about-faced to retreat to the Arctic seacoast, where the temperature was moderated by the Gulf Stream. Salvaging what they could, the Reds abandoned a vast deal of their motorized gear on the road beside the lines of their rigid dead.

Again the Finns sorted out those things of the Russian equipment useful to themselves and dug in while the weather fought for them. In a triumphant message they announced that there was no live Russian south of Salmijärvi, and then settled down to enjoy Christmas.

Below the narrowest part of the Karelian Isthmus Russia's massed forces were estimated at three-quarters of a million—more than twice as many in that one spot as Finland could ever hope to muster from all its man power. But now more material help from abroad seemed imminent. The U. S. Navy released forty Brewster pursuit planes, France sent some weapons, the enthusiastic Italians sent some bombers, Sweden contributed thirty-seven airplanes and ten thousand volunteers were released from military service to fight for Finland. Even if most of these gifts were not to arrive until long after the Christmas holidays, still they were heartening gestures and Finland was duly grateful.

When the sun came out for the first time in two weeks, Soviet bombers in groups of tens dashed from Estonian bases to shatter buildings and morale in the factory town of Tampere, in the ports of Viipuri and Turku. But here the batteries of anti-aircraft Bofors guns brought down many planes or frightened them to a height where aim was difficult. When they failed of their urban objectives, the Russian bombers took to pursuing trains in open country, machine-gunning the carriages and forcing the passengers to flee to snowclad forests. Alexander Matson, Finland's foremost translator, narrowly escaped death on one of the raids on moving trains.

On Christmas Eve a Finnish patrol a hundred and twenty-five miles north of Lake Laatokka skied across the Russian frontier. It was no invasion, but it did carry the war briefly into Russian territory.

Farther north near Lake Kianta the Russians hurled their entire 163rd Division, with some eighteen thousand men, into action in a violent attempt to cut Finland through the waistline.

The Finns let them come on, then surrounded them and began cutting them to bits. By using a streamlined version of American Indian tactics, in two days after terrific fighting the Finns more or less annihilated the Red troops, only small detachments and stragglers escaping into the woods and across the Russian frontier.

On December twenty-third, Russian planes had scattered threatening leaflets in the capital: "If Finland has not given up the fight by 1 P.M. today, we will destroy Helsinki by bombs on Christmas morning. The town will be leveled to the ground."

Christmas passed apprehensively and soberly in Helsinki. But the capital suffered no significant damage. The burden of snow that lay protectively on roofs made them look from above like patches of open fields.

ENTOMBED IN WINTER

As the New Year dawned, neutral experts, once more taking stock, changed their reckoning of Soviet casualties from thirty to one hundred thousand. The lengthening trains of the wounded no longer stopped at Leningrad, but proceeded to accommodations in Moscow. Finnish fliers began to make bombing raids on the Murmansk-Leningrad Railway in an effort to cut off the Russian supplies for the northern Red contingents.

At the beginning of 1940 the Russians had made virtually no progress, though they had been lavishly extravagant with cannon fodder and expensive motorized equipment. Stalin in irritable exasperation recalled the Soviet commander, General K. A. Meretskoff, and appointed General G. M. Stern chief of the armies attacking Finland. This thirty-eight-year-old son of a Jewish physician in the Crimea had fought in the little war against the Japanese in Siberia in 1938.

In the second week of the New Year the Finns repeated their phenomenal success with the 163rd Division by surrounding and destroying wholesale and piecemeal the Red army's Forty-fourth Division near Suomussalmi. After a three-day torturing blizzard that served the Finns better than any artillery barrage, the discomfited Russians went into the battle half-exhausted. With their resistance lessened and their faculties weakened, they could not distinguish the white-parka-enveloped Finns from the snow-covered hillocks. They did not recognize the Finns until they saw the flash of fire that killed them.

On the central front the Russians were being harried by the Finns everywhere. Salla was recaptured. Helsinki reported Finnish skiers had dynamited a small segment of the Murmansk Railway. In the northeast General Kurt Wallenius drove the Reds back thirty miles behind the point to which they had advanced a fortnight earlier. Though Russians possessed the "scorched earth" of the Petsamo Corridor, the Finnish troops that had settled themselves in winter quarters at Ivalo now reported, "The winter war in the North is ours." And it seemed that Russia had given up hope of cutting the waistline, for now the coldest weather Finland had experienced in fifty-one years enveloped the land in sheets of ice. Not since 1878 had the thermometer dropped to 58 degrees below zero. All the rivers and lakes froze solid, and on the Karelian Isthmus, General Stern ordered the Red troops to dig in temporarily, while fresh detachments brought up vast stores of ammunition and new outfits of artillery.

Finns now fought not only on skis but on skates. One of the skating patrols flashing across Lake Laatokka to the relief of Finnish troops encamped on an island was led by Birger Vasenius, the twenty-eight-year-old world champion speed skater. He was shot by a Russian sharpshooter and died on the ice with his skates on.

The wooded countryside of Finland became transfigured into the quintessence of sublimity. The patterned tree branches shimmered like a jeweler's designs created of moonstones as the light shifted within four hours between twilight dawn to twilight dusk. And on clear days when the blood-red disk of sun made its brief spectacular appearance the white *mise en scène* became diffused with ruby light. The commonest man among the invaders, as well as the patriots, could not but feel the spell of breathtaking beauty. But for tens of thousands of the Red soldiers this whitened wonderland was journey's end. As they had dropped to their knees and sprawled face downward to make fantastic frozen statues, they turned the scene of alien enchantment into a hideous mockery. And as soldiers' blood began to make pink pools in the snow and the agonized cries of wounded men answered the chorus of the crackling guns, many an observer from a hilltop was moved by the contrast of nature's prodigal gift of beauty to mankind and man's tragic treachery to himself.

After visiting the battlefield of Tolvajärvi, Correspondent Leland Stowe of the Chicago *Daily News* sent back a moving dispatch which seems destined to become a classic in war-reporting.

In this sad solitude lie the dead: uncounted thousands of Russian dead. They lie as they fell—twisted, gesticulating and tortured. But they lie beneath a kindly mask of two inches of new-fallen snow. Now they are one with the cold, white shapes of the illimitable pine and spruce trees. . . .

When we rode out upon the narrow finger of Lake Tolva's peninsula, we were not prepared for this. . . . All along the roadway we saw strange shapes bulging beneath the snow among the trees and shapes sometimes which might have been logs. Sometimes they looked like crooked limbs cast into the discard by the woodsman's ax. Sometimes heavy felt boots, bared of snow by the stumbling contact of some passing Finnish soldier, protruded suddenly and revealed the naked truth. Sometimes, too, we saw soldiers dragging frozen shapes, like pieces of cord wood, from the forest—and here and there bodies lay in crude contorted piles waiting for a final nameless common grave. . . .

Suddenly we found ourselves among whole groups of white-covered figures. Some lay straight on the ground, but mostly the arms were drawn convulsively upward to project stiffly above the shoulder. Mostly their legs were bent or doubled. . . . These were the Russian dead and soon we saw that most of their boots were good and that all had carried gas masks. They belonged to a picked shock-troop division of the Red Army. Now they were strewn on both sides of the road for more than a mile along the extended peninsula and then further on, and yet further—among the spruces and beside the road that leads to Aglajärvi. . . . We could not look for long.

In the second half of January news reached Sweden that three of the Swedish volunteer aviators had been killed fighting for Finland. The campaign for aid went on with renewed vigor. Over $2,000,000 was raised by private subscription. And the industrialists, who knew the jig was up with their way of life if the Communists took over Finland and proceeded to devour the Scandinavian peninsula, subscribed $4,000,000. Trainloads of supplies began pouring into Finland over the railway at Tornio at the head of the Gulf of Bothnia. In four of Stockholm's principal newspapers appeared challenging full-page advertisements. Large-type letters called out, "Now that the world knows what it is to be a Finn, it is your duty to show what it means to be a Swede. Join the Swedish volunteers! With Finland for Sweden—"

And in the Swedish Riksdag rose Rickard Sandler, recently foreign minister, who had resigned because of German enmity toward him and because he could not persuade the government to fight shoulder to shoulder with the Finns. Eloquently and caustically he created a hubbub among the dignified Swedes by condemning the government's attitude. "This neutrality is pure idiocy," he proclaimed, and the Riksdag walls resounded with wild cheering. Then as the unprecedented noise subsided, Premier Per Albin Hansson, rejecting all of Sandler's proposals, quietly announced that Sweden would maintain her neutrality. The parliaments of Norway and Denmark simultaneously declared for absolute neutrality.

In the face of ardent pro-Finnish sentiment in the United States, our Congress did a lot of pussyfooting and hedging about a loan to Finland. Many a good Democrat threw suspicious glances on the President's formal request for Congressional action to aid Finland. Carter Glass was among the few who spoke out loud and strong for "any kind of aid to them." Representative Hook of Michigan desired the passage of a bill to lend $60,000,000 with no strings attached. The public at large began to howl for more aid to Finland, and telegrams poured into Congressional offices. Funds for Finnish relief (headed by Herbert Hoover) mounted, as benefit performances and charity bazaars were given all over the forty-eight states. Shiploads of clothes and foods and medical supplies went to supplement checks. But Finland was still in as dire need of armaments as of man power.

"We are deeply grateful," said President Kyösti Kallio, "for the help America has extended us with humanitarian materials, but such help must be altered if the Finnish population is not to be massacred. . . . If our civilians are to be killed in their houses, as is happening every day in our cities, towns and villages, they will have no need for food and clothing."

President Kallio pleaded for antiaircraft guns and desperately needed pursuit planes. For although there was a lull in the fighting at the front, the air raids became worse than any since the war had begun. In a fortnight the Russians bombed forty-two localities.

The world continued to pay passionate tribute to Finland's superhuman defense. At least a hundred newspapermen and magazine writers about the globe almost simultaneously began to compare the Finnish stand against the Red onslaught to that of the scanty band of Greeks that held the pass at Thermopylae. At the beginning of February the redoubtable Commander-in-Chief Mannerheim did not try to conceal his pessimism about the future: the Allies must render significant help quickly. There was some talk that they would come in force in the spring. By spring, however, it might be too late, Mannerheim warned them. But he declared that if the necessary help did not come the Finns would fight on alone. "We shall fight," he proclaimed, "to the last old man and child. We shall burn our forests and houses, destroy our cities and industries, and what we yield will be cursed by the scourge of God."

With this bitter Old Testament pronouncement sounding out of Finland and across the continent, the Finnish attitude reached its climax of cold fury and resolution.

"SAVE FINLAND!"

Instead of lying quiet for the winter to subside, as many had thought the Russians would do, the new commander-in-charge, Grigory Stern, now commenced fiercer attacks to take Sortavala, the strategic railway junction on the northern point of Lake Laatokka. For two months now the Reds had been trying to take the sawmill town. On the east they could get no nearer than Kitelä—twenty-four miles away. Here the Finns repeated the tactics that had annihilated the Red troops at Suomussalmi:

they retreated strategically while bands of fighters encircled the enemy and slashed their supply lines. "Hit them in the belly," General Mannerheim had commanded, well aware that soldiers could not fight on empty stomachs and knowing that Russia was ever notoriously weak on supply. Trapped by the Finns who drew the circle close about them, the hungry Reds were in a desperate condition for a week. Their only food was what provisions their comrades could drop to them by parachutes. There was no escape to Russia by the road, because shells from Fort Mantsi covered it with a rain of fire. The surrounding woods bristled with Finns. Scattered groups of Russians attempting escape were either cut down by Finnish machine-gun fire or hopelessly lost to freeze or starve. Russian rescuers from the south were sacrificed in a withering crossfire. Finally, as the Russians grew weaker, the mobile Finns closed in aggressively, captured armored cars, tanks, and ammunition, and made a holocaust of the demoralized Red forces.

But for all the Finnish talk of this being the greatest victory of the war, the Finns found their own ranks thinned when the week was over. And Finland had few reserves to take the places of the dead. In the air she was still outnumbered by some twenty-six planes to one. It was the first week in February before the first eleven of the forty-four Brewster pursuit planes from the United States were unloaded in Bergen, Norway.

With the clearing weather that came in late January, the Russians began concentrated bombing raids on Finland's west coast ports and the smaller towns in an effort to demoralize the people and undermine the industrial structure. Rovaniemi, on the Arctic Circle, now became the target of a series of raids that killed many civilians and demolished dozens of the new buildings.

The general destruction from the air was accompanied by the demoniacal attack on the western end of the Mannerheim Line near Summa. For seven hours at night an artillery bombardment poured a steady rain of shells on the Finnish defenses. Then at daybreak a mass of planes thick as pests of locusts flew high over the Finnish lines and dropped their loads. Waves of Russian tanks crept forward, pushing before them armored sleds, filled with crouching soldiers. At the granite-boulder defense which they could not crash through, the tanks stopped and moved around into protective positions for the infantry-filled sledges. When the soldiers charged the Finnish lines, they were hurled back by machine-gun fire and well-aimed grenades. All day the bloody fight continued, and the Russian dead piled up on one another. That night the Reds continued their blasting artillery barrage. The shells could not actually reach the Finns in their little blockhouses, but they gave them a terrible shaking, and the din and reverberations made sleep impossible. For five days the unceasing bombardment continued, and gradually the unanchored blockhouses began to tilt so that it was impossible for the Finns to keep their guns in line.

With artillery now hub to hub, the Reds poured continuous fire on the Finnish positions. Day and night the bombardment went on, until the fields behind the Finnish lines were plowed for miles back. The shelling was so intense and incessant that the stout-fibered young Finns could not bear it for more than a week at a stretch. Six times in one day legions of Russians surged forward to attack, and each time they were sent back with staggering losses. But Stalin had millions of men in reserve, and now a hundred thousand fresh troops stood ready to aid in the attack on Viipuri, which was only twenty-five miles away. The world wondered how long Finland could endure.

Once again President Kallio offered to make any kind of "honorable" peace. The Soviet reply came by way of a Moscow broadcast: "The Finnish bandits will be destroyed and exterminated." The broadcast bore out what many Finns believed—that the purpose of the invasion was a scheme to liquidate the Finns as a unified people by removing those who were not killed into the Russian interior and settling Soviets in their places.

What the Finns needed was fighters by scores of thousands. And the promised planes from England and the United States had still not arrived. In many sectors there was such shortage of antiaircraft guns that rifle fire against low-flying planes was the only protection. In some places the citizens' defense was reduced to an impotent but defiant shaking of fists at the murderous aircraft.

As the Russian menace loomed still darker, more and more Swedish volunteers left for Finland—God-sped on the way by crowds singing that great old Lutheran hymn, "A Mighty Fortress Is Our God." But the world wondered why the Allies did not send troops to help the Finns stem the Red tide—particularly since the British War Office announced at this time that in the first five months of the second World War only five British soldiers had been killed in action and one more had died from battle wounds. There were hundreds of thousands of British and French soldiers frankly bored and, in the phrase of Bernard Shaw, "eating their heads off."

Despite tremendous losses in men and material, the hydra-headed Red army kept advancing over the bodies of their slain comrades. And in the far north where the Finns believed they had beaten the Russians back for the rest of the winter, the Reds now massed some fifty thousand ready to resume the southward drive on Ivalo and thence to Rovaniemi. In the Salla section the Russians were still held twenty-five miles from Kemijärvi, the northern terminal of the Finnish railway, but they were massing new strength and preparing to launch an offensive.

When St. Valentine's Day came, the Russians started attacks

on all fronts. They bombed communications, both railways and telegraph lines. They dropped showers of incendiary bombs on industrial towns. The entire town of Sortavala went up in flames. Civilians in villages were made to feel the sting of war as they had not yet felt it. Their homes were blown to bits or burned down by incendiary bombs. During the daylight hours, villagers were forced to seek refuge in the woods and to camp all day in the snow.

Fearing imminent Allied intervention, which was widely rumored, Russia poured all the hell possible into Finland to make her give up before an English or French force could enter the fray. The fighting became so savage at Summa on the road to Viipuri that the Finns used up the last scraps of their ammunition and held back the Russians with bayonets and sheath knives.

In the last fortnight of February the Finns were called on to make a display of *sisu* that was superhuman. "*Sisu* makes men do the impossible," Paavo Nurmi had said, "and it comes miraculously in times of stress." Bone-tired, nerve-shattered, after twelve days of ceaseless bombardment and attack, the Finns valiantly fought on to save their land. Like the doughty warrior in the old English ballad, men merely paused to sit and bleed awhile and then return to the fight. The same hundred thousand Finns had to do all the fighting in the south—and as their blockhouses tilted more and more, they began making strategic retreats, carrying their wounded with them. The roads they left to the Russians were so choked with fresh Soviet troops and abundant supplies that the Reds could not bother with their own wounded, but left them to freeze to quick death among the stiffened carcasses of their brothers.

As the weakened hundred thousand Finns who defended the way to Viipuri now faced the most formidable onslaught that Russia could muster, the Finnish government called up the men of forty-two and forty-three and within two days all men of forty-four and boys of nineteen. But already many volunteers past sixty and boys as young as fourteen were in active service.

The Russians now forced a wedge into the defense lines at Summa, twenty miles from Viipuri, and pushed on to the next town of Kämärä. Weary young Finns covering the well-ordered retreat fought hand to hand, using their hunting knives with cool and deadly ferocity, until at last they fell gloriously—heroes who were not aware they had been heroes. The world bemoaned that such men should pass in their flowery prime. But still no foreign army came to their rescue.

On the sixteenth day of the offensive, the thundering Russian advance finally broke through the Finnish defenses between the Vuoksi River and Lake Muolaa. The Russians poured through the gap and plunged into flat land to the east of Viipuri. This was the beginning of the final crack-up, though the Finnish people were unaware of the danger. Mannerheim urged his soldiers to stand unfaltering and announced that new fortified positions were being raised.

Foreign Minister Tanner was now in Stockholm emphasizing Finland's desperate situation and asking for two divisions of Swedish troops. The Swedish prime minister pointed out that Sweden by now had sent $70,000,000 worth of material to Finland and over $8,000,000 in voluntary contributions from Swedish citizens. But they could not officially send soldiers. Even the intimation that Finland would be forced to sue for a peace that might be hazardous to Sweden could not budge the Swedish premier, nor was he influenced by the fact that a great proportion of the Swedes felt that it was their battle as much as Finland's.

Then Mr. Tanner appealed to England and France for help. But the Swedish government, trembling at German threats, said, "Sorry, no passage through Sweden for Allied troops." The

Swedish attitude, right or wrong, seemed to presage the end of independent Finland. One of Sweden's most highly respected newspapers, Göteborg's *Handels-och-Sjofartstidning,* took the government to task in a condemning editorial: "It is Finland that is Europe's advanced guard against Asia, right up to Sweden's border. We have refused her aid. . . . Sweden has failed democracy's case." Yet it is possible that Sweden's official neutrality saved not only Sweden but Finland from destruction.

But whether Per Albin Hansson's stand was prudent or not history will have to decide. Without question, if Allied troops had entered Sweden on their way to Finland, Germany would have invaded southern Sweden, and that lovely ordered land would have become a major theater of the war.

Without hope of armed assistance, the valiant Finns fought doggedly on. The world held its breath for them and sent up prayers.

But hordes of Russians advanced, spurred on by the battle cry of "Comrades, destroy the White Finnish snake." By the last week in February the Reds were within six miles of Viipuri, which had often before been "the Death Gate of the Muscovites."

When it seemed humanly impossible for the Finns to prolong their defense many more weeks, the three Scandinavian foreign ministers met at Christiensborg Palace in Copenhagen. They agreed they must continue their stand for neutrality and decided to urge renewed mediation of the Finnish-Russian war. Meanwhile in Sweden the manufacture of armaments and gas masks was feverishly speeded up.

On the twenty-first day of the battle for Viipuri a detachment of Red soldiers came across the ice and isolated fortified Koivisto with its heavy guns. The Reds were within five miles of Viipuri now, and shells as well as bombs unloaded from airplanes played havoc in the historic town. The last civilians had departed with

A LAPP WOMAN OF PETSAMO. HER HEADDRESS SHOWS SHE IS MARRIED

THE WEAVING OF RUGS IS STILL PRACTICED AS AN ART AMONG THE PEOPLE

what they could cram into suitcases. Country women and boys bravely helped the men dig trenches and throw up breastworks to protect the soldiers who were to relinquish the last concrete defenses east of Viipuri.

In an effort to replace the Finns who had been killed or removed to hospitals, the government now issued uniforms to men with physical defects and to convicts released from prisons. Though the situation was desperate, the Finnish populace was still confident of victory. Even if Viipuri fell, they said, the Reds would still be only fifty miles from the Russian border. They were still a long way from Helsinki, they argued, and in April the ice would break and the spring thaws would incapacitate the motorized units.

While Viipuri defenders were making their super-heroic stand at the end of February, the helpless people in the towns of Lapland, with virtually no antiaircraft defense, had to endure bombings every day that the clouds lifted. But instead of weakening Finnish morale by the air raids on civilians, the Russians merely succeeded in making the people more determined to resist.

In the United States, as Finland's plight became more patently tragic, every community in the nation joined the heartfelt chorus of "Save Finland." Even many rigid isolationists made chameleon changes and virtually said, "To hell with isolation—Finland must be saved. Send her bullets and buckshot, not butter." Already through cash donations, concerts, lectures, bazaars, and gifts of jewels, Herbert Hoover's committee had gleaned $2,500,000 for the relief of evacuated Finns. And now, with the fall of Viipuri daily expected, the word-wasting Congressmen, after two months of hesitation, had finally juggled bills about so that Finland was to get a loan of $20,000,000.

The coming of spring presaged both good and bad for the

Finns. Good, because highways over the deep ice of rivers and lakes would vanish, and the Russian tanks would bog down in the mire of the thaw. Bad, because the spring would bring blue skies, dissolve the roof-snow camouflage, and render towns and factories clear targets for destructive bombs.

Already in the first week of March the Russians had bombed all the seacoast towns except Helsinki with devastating effect. North of Lake Laatokka the Finns, far from being defeated, routed the Reds' Thirty-fourth Tank Brigade. But now Viipuri was surrounded on three sides by the ceaselessly pounding artillery. In the city's center the beleaguered Finns, tortured with fatigue, held on. Ever resourceful, they made strategic use of the ruined buildings for fortifications, as Russia now poured her best troops across the isthmus to attack the unyielding city.

When the first seven days of March had passed, Finland entered the grimmest week in her history. Rumors flew about from capital to capital over the radio-telegraph and transatlantic cables as fast as snowflakes in a March storm—and as quick to melt. The Allies were declared to have an expeditionary force of fifty thousand men equipped and ready to go to Finland's aid. Sweden still said, "No passage for those troops," because Germany said, "No Allied troops in Scandinavia." Sweden was officially and unofficially making ardent moves for peace mediation. Eljas Erkko, now Finland's minister to Sweden, conferred with Madame Alexandra Kollantay, the Soviet minister to Sweden. (Mme. Kollantay was known to have opposed the war and to have sympathy for Finland.) Ex-President Svinhufvud journeyed to Berlin to see what his once potent diplomacy could do. Sven Hedin, the famous seventy-six-year-old explorer and the best friend Hitler had in Sweden, flew to Berlin for a two-hour conference with Von Ribbentrop. Axel Wenner-Gren, the richest of Sweden's industrialists, conferred with Göring. Germany wanted peace almost as much as frightened Sweden, for Allied intervention would not only prolong the war and stop Russia from sending promised supplies, but cut off indispensable shipments of iron ore from the Swedish mines at Kiruna.

On Friday, the eighth of March, Paris announced that the Allies had offered Finland official military intervention—provided the Finnish government made a direct plea for it. The only absolute fact among the rumors was the statement issued by Foreign Minister Tanner. Said he tersely, "The Finnish Government acknowledges that the Soviet Government had forwarded demands." But though he declared he was unable to state his government's attitude at the moment, the world believed there was a likelihood of peace.

The news threw the British cabinet into what the English sometimes call "a state of mind." It was to Allied interest for the war to continue, but the cabinet knew it would be a laborious process to transport a force sufficiently large to do the Finns any good. And the Finns wanted an adequate army or nothing.

A German broadcast now revealed the surprising news that a plane setting out for Stockholm and then doubling back and proceeding across Latvia to Moscow had borne four prominent Finns. Premier Risto Ryti headed the delegation.

The Soviet radio invectives against Finland ceased for two nights, but on Monday they began again with malicious attacks on Premier Ryti, who was in Moscow. Though Stockholm reported late Monday night that the Russian demands had been modified, bombing in Finland was resumed with increased intensity. The hearts of citizens of every country in the world except Russia were full of wishes for Finland's good.

On the night of Tuesday, the twelfth of March, a peace treaty was signed in Moscow. Hostilities were to cease at eleven o'clock next morning. All Finnish planes were grounded by ten o'clock, but the Reds dropped bombs up to the last five minutes. In Viipuri the Reds renewed the siege with violence, but at the very last hour of the war the Finns still held the city.

VOICES

For one hour there was a strange stillness in the land, and at noon Foreign Minister Tanner made the fateful announcement over the radio. The cessation of fighting had come as a surprise, and the acknowledgment of Finland's defeat came as a distinct shock. That very morning, when word went about that Russia had made peace, the Finnish people believed that the Reds were admitting they were licked. A workman putting up protective boards before the plate glass of a shop front replied to the New York *Times* correspondent who asked him about the peace that he had not heard about it, but that doubtless the Finns had at last thrown the Russians out of the country. When soldiers on the staunchly held part of the fortifications north of Laatokka heard the news, they took it for granted that the Reds had had enough.

But in the towns where there were flagpoles left standing, people saw the flags at half-mast and knew from the symbol that there was some cause for national mourning. Then over the radio came the measured words of the man the majority of Finns trusted above all others. Väinö Tanner, controlling his emotion with incomparable Finnish self-mastery, announced their fate.

In a speech stripped of high-sounding phrases, with a firm emphasis on common sense, Tanner spoke to his people. Profoundly aware of that superlative ability to take it that lies in the heart's core of every real Finn, his sad announcement was charged with faith that his people would build something victorious out of defeat.

"Our army did well and fought with all its might," he said. "They have behaved—I will not say as heroes, for that would be too everyday a word—but as men. . . . We had many great victories and only on the main frontier were we forced to withdraw somewhat. . . . But we are a small nation. . . . The same men have had to remain under fire the whole time. And even the pluckiest troops gradually become tired. . . . We could not win this war alone. The inevitable end would have been the destruction of our country. . . .

"Peace has returned to this country. But what a peace! . . . Yet we must forget the past and look toward the future. . . . Our country has been devastated before in the course of its history. Its population has once been reduced by nearly half. We have land in abundance. Our opportunities for fruitful work are boundless. And our army is still whole. It can watch that our peace will not be disturbed in the future. . . ."

The Finnish-Russian War had ended abruptly on the one hundred fifth day of hostilities. By the peace terms Finland gave up more than was demanded of her in October. She relinquished the entire Karelian Isthmus, including Viipuri, her third largest city and one of the world's largest timber-exporting ports. She gave up all claim to Lake Laatokka and the land bordering its shores, including the railheads of Sortavala and Suojärvi. She lost between 8 and 9 per cent of her industries . . . half the riches of the beautiful Vuoksi Valley with its wood products and cellulose and paper mills. She lost important water-power plants. But—most significant to military men—she lost her ingenious southeastern defense system, which still remained intact, except for the break of a few miles between Summa and Viipuri.

Instead of getting the slice of Russian Karelia which the U.S.S.R. had offered in trade in November, Finland now gave up an extensive chunk (7,000 square miles) east of Kemijärvi in the north central region, so that her waistline was further narrowed. Finland furthermore promised to extend the railway from Kemijärvi to connect with a Russian railway built from the head of the White Sea. Russia was to have free transit in perpetuity over this joint line, which could bring her in quick communication with the Swedish iron mines and the Swedish military fort at Boden. In the Petsamo district Russia left Finland the corridor, but got the Rybacchi Peninsula (200 square miles), which dominated the harbor and Liinahamari. Finland was forbidden henceforth to maintain an Arctic navy or any armed aircraft in the vicinity. She was to make no alliances aimed against Russia. Besides relinquishing four strategic Finnish islands in the Gulf of Finland to be incorporated into Soviet territory, moreover, Finland was forced to lease to the Soviet for a naval base the peninsula at Hanko, commanding the entrance to the Gulf of Finland and Helsinki itself.

From the human rather than national point of view the hardest result of the war and the peace was that almost half a million people were homeless. In the areas passing to the Soviets there were still a hundred thousand who had remained during the terrors of war. Now, with the bitter treaty ratified, a grief-stricken but unbowed people took leave of their homes, some of which had been in their families' possession for generations. Ninety-five out of every hundred chose to give up their homes rather than become sovietized. Gathering together what movables they could manage to transport, they began a painful trek along the ice-encrusted roads amid a heavy snowfall. Empty trucks sent east returned west piled with furniture, bedding, handicraft work, pigs, and poultry. Men, women, and children followed in their wake. Here was a mass migration greater than any Finland had ever known. The people did not know where they were to settle.

They had perforce become involuntary pioneers, and many now were to face the vicissitudes of clearing a wilderness.

The peace that had come was a thoroughly unpopular peace. It was a government-made peace—not a peace of the citizens or the soldiers. The people at large and the private soldiers refused to believe they were beaten. Exhausted troops were more than willing to continue to face grueling fire. Civilians who had made courageous sacrifices would gladly have repeated them many fold. Mothers were prepared not to make it hard for their fifteen-year-old sons to join the fighting ranks. Mannerheim's subordinate generals were said to have believed they could have carried on the war much longer, that the Allies would eventually have come to their assistance, and that in the end a decisive victory would have been theirs. Minister of Defense Juho Niukkanen resigned—he could not stomach peace at such a price. But the Finnish Parliament ratified the peace treaty by a majority of 143 to 3.

Premier Ryti could only remind his people that sometimes it takes more courage to make peace than to wage war. He and Mannerheim knew that the struggle might have been carried on to the last pound of effective resistance—with the painful deaths of many more hundreds of thousands—and yet there might have been nothing favorably conclusive in the result. And it was easily conceivable that prolonged fighting might have resulted in the obliteration of the Finnish people or the complete absorption among the Siberians of those remaining alive. However strong Russia's intentions to swallow Finland may have been, they were perforce altered by the war's course. The Finns suffered defeat, but out of the tragic sacrifices of war they saved their independence as a nation.

Despite the severity of the peace terms, the Finns did not give way to despair. They accepted their fate with Finnish philosophy. They had defended and held what was dearer than life—

their freedom. Finland, though maimed and a tenth smaller, was still Finland, with its own individual sovereignty.

To mitigate the troubling of heart among the Finns, an aura of glory lay upon the land—a glory to which the contemporary world paid the highest possible tribute. The Finns themselves and men of every nation knew they had lost the war only because of lack of man power and inadequacy in the implements of defense. Field Marshal Mannerheim exaggerated only slightly when he claimed his men had outfought by thirteen to one an enemy that outnumbered them fifty to one. He first reckoned the Finnish dead at fifteen thousand. But even when foreign observes put the figure above twenty and as high as twenty-five thousand dead, the superior fighting qualities of the under-equipped Finns remained prodigious; for the Russian dead were numbered at two hundred thousand and the wounded at a quarter of a million. And the U.S.S.R. had lost as heavily in prestige as in material.

When the seventy-two-year-old Mannerheim addressed his men on the peace and bade them, as it were, farewell, it was for him the most moving hour in his half century of great soldiering.

"Soldiers of the glorious Finnish Army," he began in a profound voice, as if he were proclaiming a victory. And then he paused until the atmosphere was charged with stupendous stillness.

"Peace has been concluded between our country and the Soviet Union, an exacting peace which has ceded to Russia nearly every battle field on which you have shed your blood on behalf of everything we hold dear and sacred.

"You did not want war. You loved peace, work and progress; but you were forced into a struggle in which you have done great deeds, deeds that will shine for centuries in the pages of history.

"More than fifteen thousand of you who took to the field will never again see your homes and many have lost forever their ability to work. But you have also dealt hard blows, and if two hundred thousand of our enemies now lie on the snowdrifts, gazing with broken eyes at our sky, the fault is not yours. You did not hate them or wish them evil; you merely followed the stern rule of war: kill or be killed."

He paused again, and then came resounding words.

"Soldiers! I have fought on many battlefields, but never have I seen your like as warriors."

Then after a moment he went on:

"I am proud of you as though you were my own children. . . . After sixteen weeks of bloody battle, with no rest by day or night, our Army still stands unconquered before an enemy which, despite terrible losses, has grown in number.

"Nor has our home front, where countless air raids have spread death and terror among women and children, ever wavered. Burned cities and ruined villages far behind the front, as far even as our western border, are the visible proof of the nation's sufferings during the past months.

"Our fate is hard, now that we are compelled to give up to an alien race, a race with a philosophy and moral values different from ours, land which for centuries we have cultivated in sweat and labor. Yet we must put our shoulders to the wheel, in order that we may prepare on the soil left to us a haven for those rendered homeless, and an improved livelihood for all, and, as before, we must be ready to defend our diminished Fatherland with the same resolution and the same fire with which we defended our original Fatherland.

"We are proudly conscious of the historic duty which we shall continue to fulfill: the defense of that western civilization which has been our heritage for centuries. We also know that whatever debt we may have owed to the West we have paid to the last penny."

Now out of that West came a ringing tribute that might have been the voice of the world speaking. The English poet Alfred Noyes, more or less silent these latter years, was inspired to write eight stirring lines that uttered what millions of less articulate men were groping to express:

> Far off between the mountains and the sea
> In ancient days this word was sped:
> "Tell them at home we held Thermopylae
> According to their word and lie here dead."
>
> Now from the North there comes a mightier cry—
> "We fought and failed against titanic powers.
> But ask mankind—whose is the victory
> When every unchained heart on earth is ours?"

PART EIGHT

"The territories left to Finland constitute now the symbol of all that is finest in what we of the democracies call civilization. In both a spiritual and a physical scene Finland is the thin front line to be held, cherished, supported, and allowed to shine in example to all of us."

JOHN TEMPLE GRAVES, II

Finland Rebuilds

While the world wondered what the future would bring Finland, the Finns doing the needful business of the day girded themselves for rehabilitation with the same energy and spirit with which they had girded themselves for defense. Though Finland was dismembered and her economy broken up, her morale was still intact. The people did not pause to salve their wounds or waste time exulting in the editorial orchids tossed them by admiring nations. They went straight to work to repair the damage and to prepare places for the shelterless. The mothers of Finland hardly waited for the embers to die from hostile flames before they began to re-establish their homes. Childless families assumed the care of orphans. Those with available unoccupied bedrooms put up the evacuees.

Within seven days after the cessation of war the government was laying plans for the reconstruction of Finland's cities and public institutions and for the creation of homes to house the half-million homeless. Alvar Aalto, Finland's leading architect among the younger generation, headed a commission whose charge was a speedy rebuilding. The program included the construction of four entirely new towns, which were to be models of efficiency and comeliness.

With their ready resourcefulness to turn defeat into victory, the Finns now purposed to make their scarred and battered country serve as a laboratory for civic planning and building. Instead of being staggered by the enormity of the undertaking, the indefatigable architects and artisans welcomed the task of reconstruction. And the Finns are a nation of builders—they are born carpenters and stone workers and have an inherent sense of design. Aalto and his associates expressed the hope that they might organize the rebuilding as "a good example of new kinds of towns, new kinds of cities, which architects and engineers and sociologists of all nations might come to study with profit."

Despite their resolution to rehabilitate quickly, the Finns faced a Herculean task. There was not only an urgency to find homes for an eighth of their population, but it was necessary to create a new means of livelihood for them. One tenth of the cultivated fields was lost and about one ninth of their industries. The towns, particularly the provincial interior towns, became seriously overcrowded. In Kuopio, for instance, there were two and a half occupants to every room.

In late March the well-to-do in the best club in Kuopio sat about talking over the new situation. The large landholders said, "We must make a new deal for these people and share our land with them. The boys of the poor were fighting for nothing material, but our sons fought to preserve the land they will inherit. The poor must be rewarded." But they could find no institutions which could make such a deal. It is difficult to make such regulations quickly in a democratic country. "But the law means nothing, if these fellows aren't provided with farms now," the landlords of Kuopio said. And they began to divide the land according to their own self-made temporary laws. From the example in Kuopio, landlords all over Finland began making voluntary new deals on the big estates. And then the government passed laws to make the transfers legal. A "Colonization Act" was rushed through to allot homes and farms to the former farmers of

Karelia. A compensation bill was also passed to make up at least partially to those who had lost their property and holdings.

The crowding was dangerous for epidemics, but the psychological effect was still more dangerous. During the summer many of the evacuees preferred living in the forests to staying in the overcrowded dwellings or old diaries hastily fitted out as barracks. But people could not exist in the forests in winter—and so all over the land, building was begun with an energy that surpassed even that of the building for the Olympic Games. But owing to war restrictions and blockades it was well-nigh impossible to get all the necessary materials. Fortunately Finland had plenty of wood and granite. And in the chill rains of autumn sounds of drilling and hammering were strong in the air as building, governmentally supervised or privately done with neighborly co-operation, raced against winter.

Sweden, which had contributed magnificently to Finnish relief (to the amount of $12,000,000 when collections were finally closed in September), performed a super-service by a gift of 2,600 prefabricated houses. Sweden even contributed the skilled labor to boss the job of setting-up. All the Finns had to do was to supply the unskilled labor, the foundations, and the steambaths. The cottages were of three or four rooms, and altogether they provided space to accommodate comfortably 12,000 persons. Following Sweden's example, Finland began to establish factories to manufacture prefabricated houses on her own, and with a Finnish forward-looking eye even planned to expand the new factories to furnish similar houses for foreign export.

The government had to grapple not only with the problem of shelter for families, but it had the problem of providing for invalided and permanently disabled soldiers and widows and orphans. A club house was established in Helsinki to function as an information and advisory center for war invalids. The

Helsinki Municipal Building Commission approved a project for a new "own home" settlement for war invalids in the outskirts of Helsinki, and planned for the erection of nine apartment buildings with accommodations for 263 large families. A program of vocational training for war orphans as well as disabled soldiers was devised. Work was started on a new children's hospital in Helsinki and several new tuberculosis sanitoria in various parts of the country. And to curtail the increase in infant mortality special itinerant instruction courses were instituted over the land. Labor-service camps were established for the evacuee youth of Karelia, where in groups of twenty to sixty they worked four to six hours a day in the forests and devoted the rest of the day to educational activities and recreational sports.

The whole nation joined in the rehabilitation, even the school children volunteered for work without pay. The boys and girls of the Four-H Agricultural Clubs—an adaptation from the United States—offered their services on farms where husbands or sons or laborers had been killed. They helped in the weeding, threshing, hay-making, and dairy work. Finland expected every child to do his duty; and, recognizing the seriousness of the national situation, the children worked with a willing energy.

On the whole the rehabilitation, difficult as it was, proceeded with remarkable efficiency and good will. Of course there were some who became disgruntled and complained and made demands. In August the discontent of a small group became acute and the extreme radical element of the Social Democrats broke away from the party. A near riot occurred in Turku when a parade of malcontents bearing banners demanding "true friendship with the Soviet Union" got out of hand. The leaders were said to be jobless men, who had served jail sentences and who were now in the pay of the Communists.

Except for these few agitators, Finland publicly and privately

KITCHEN-LIVING ROOM OF TYPICAL FINNISH PEASANT HOUSE. NOTICE THE DISKS OF BREAD ON THE POLE

NEW PIONEERS BEGIN TO ERECT NEW HOMES IN THE WILDERNESS

responded to the task of reconstruction with the devotion of those volunteers who had set up barricades of boulders in the Karelian Isthmus. As Fanny Luukkonen, Chief of the Lotta Svärd, said, "Voluntariness is our strength in this country. In Finland everyone goes dutifully and quietly to his or her post, whether it be a front line trench or a windswept potato field in the Arctic."

But despite the good will, the spirit of sacrifice, and the brotherly help and sharing, on November first, 200,000 of the evacuees were still "on relief." Because of the difficulty of importing both consumers and capital goods, the Finns, for all their foresight and energy, faced a trying winter. For the general welfare, the government had to impose restrictions to counter the critical shortages. All clothing and footwear, fabrics and yarns were confiscated on October 22, preparatory to the rationing that went into effect in November. All stocks of soap were confiscated. The government regulated the price of hay, oats, and cereal straw, and imposed severe penalties on profiteering. And because of a new trade agreement with the Soviet Union, by which Leningrad was to be supplied with Finnish dairy products, butter and milk were rationed in this land where there was a cow to every three persons.

With the war holding Europe in its restricting grip, Russia, her next-door neighbor, perforce became one of Finland's best customers. In 1938 Russia's part in Finland's foreign trade had amounted to no more than to nine tenths of 1 per cent. But during the summer and fall Finnish manufacturers and business men made repeated trips to Moscow to improve trade relations. And a year after the outbreak of the Russian-Finnish war, Finland was promulgating a cultural exchange with Russia, whereby dramatic actors and opera singers would perform on each other's stages, and museum exhibits and motion pictures would be exchanged. The innovations did not mean any lessening of ties with Sweden, where there has always been an exchange in business, art, music, science and sport; and now Sweden and Finland, for the first time in their joint histories, were like brother and sister. Finland's trade with Germany as well as with Russia began to expand; a delegation of Finnish business men attended the Industrial Fair in Leipzig. In exchange for wood products Germany sent Finland some coal and steel and machinery necessary for rebuilding her industries.

Despite the discomfort from crowding and notwithstanding the scarcity of soap, shoes, cattle fodder, gasoline, and coal, Finns in general met the rigors of early winter as courageously as did their ancestors. And unlike Czechoslovakia, Poland, Belgium, Holland, Norway, Denmark, and the Baltic States of Estonia, Latvia, Lithuania, when 1941 approached, Finland was blessed by being still an independent state. Though the future holds no guarantees of security, Finland is still free and she intends to maintain her liberty by all the means in her power. While she prays for peace, she strengthens her defenses. The vulnerability of her geographical position is greater than it was in 1939. But at the end of 1940 Finland's army of 250,000 was stronger than at the signing of the peace treaty in March. The men of thirty-five have now had their training. The war planes from the United States which arrived too late for use last spring have bolstered the air force. Artillery and antiaircraft guns which were ordered from several European countries and arrived after the peace are now ready for emergency. The very day after the peace Finland began taking up contributions for a new defense line; jewels and gold and silver ornaments went into the collections to buy more pursuit planes, more antiaircraft protection. All during the summer Finnish volunteers were digging new trenches, and, according to a private letter from a high official, "pouring concrete everywhere."

In the midst of uncertainty, the Finns go on quietly setting an example to the democratic world in their happy balance of individualism and social-mindedness. Without any guarantees of security, they are rebuilding with as much thoroughness of creative planning, as if their inviolability were assured. No one inside Finland or outside can know whether or not the Finns can remain at peace or if on her soil the interests of Germany and Russia may yet clash. But somehow the Finns hold to a simple faith in their destiny. As an expression of that faith they are given to quoting two lines from the *Kalevala:*

> Might of earth will never fail us,
> Never while the world existeth.

And as an example of the national never-say-die spirit, they love to tell a brief anecdote of a simple peasant: "The game is not finished yet," doggedly declared the old man of Huljava, though he had only two cards left, both deuces and neither of them a trump.

AFTERWORD

"A new day can still change everything."

FINNISH MOTTO

Afterword

"THERE WAS NO MANNERHEIM LINE"

All during the course of the war I was receiving letters from Finland and since the bitter peace more have come. Many were moving and inspiring, some were witty, all were calm. One that came late in October from my friend Ralph Enckell of the Finnish foreign office seems peculiarly worthy of quoting. Of his seven closest friends not a single one was left alive—they had been officers and every single one was killed. Because of his gift of languages, Enckell was drafted by the High Command as an interpreter and chief cicerone to the war correspondents. As he writes it: "I was called to High Quarters and traveled with the foreign correspondents to the front lines, back and forth, back and forth, being a commercial traveler in death and blood and horror, trying to get hold of corpses not yet stiff, of wounds still bleeding, of battlefields not yet covered by the all-forgiving snow—in order that all over the civilized world men could have every morning with their toast and coffee, their fresh ration of shuddering war horrors."

Then he writes a confession that may mightily surprise those who followed in the newspapers the daily accounts of the Finnish defense. I quote verbatim:

"Now that it is over, it can be said: *There was no Mannerheim Line*. I created the phrase, giving it away as a secret—the best way to get it spread—to your U.P. man. I did it mainly in order to intimidate the Russians, and partly because some 'sensible' explanation was to be given for the fact that our defense did not collapse under the immense Soviet push. Well, the Russians, in their communiqué from the H.Q. of the Leningrad Military District, issued on December 23, declared the Mannerheim Line could stand every comparison with the Maginot and Siegfried Lines. It really consisted mainly of trenches and some scattered concrete bunkers—it was not commenced until the summer of 1939, and the main part of it remained unfinished."

The truth is that the Creator casually constructed most of what was called the Mannerheim Line eons ago. The terrain, with its lakes and forests, its narrow necks of land lying between lakes, its granite outcroppings, were all utilized in the broad belt of defense measures. Occasional concrete pillboxes and little blockhouses had been embedded at strategic points in the open; and in the defended sectors of the forests, trees had been felled and their branches sharpened into murderous looking pikes. The correspondents made much of the term "Mannerheim Line," but for descriptions they drew on their own imaginations and the subtle implications of Finnish interpreters.

On the anniversary of the beginning of the outbreak of hostilities between Finland and Russia, the Finns' defense seems all the more remarkable in retrospect. The real power of that defense lay not in any Mannerheim Line, but in the *sisu* of Finland's soldiers and the deadly precision of their marksmanship.

DO YOU REMEMBER?

As the writing of this book was drawing to a close in November, I received a letter from Lorenz von Numers, the young poet who (with Paavo Nurmi) had said good-by to us at the railway station. I had pictured him as dead on the battlefield. But he had come through the war without injury and was recently married to a girl "whom you yourself would adore." His letter brought back a surge of nostalgia for *Suomi*.

"I wonder if you remember?" he wrote. "The mountain stream making its way northwards from the rolling heights of rust-red heather purred softly like an enormous cat in the twilight. There were some small trees, dwarf birch, otherwise nothing big enough to make a fire to boil the coffee. The flames licked round the sooty copper-kettle hanging from its stick. The mosquitoes sang in their multitudes, swarmed in clouds over the gray slope of the fell, danced in the hollows, climbed in spirals. You had put a switch through the trouts' gills, slung the glittering catch over your shoulder, and came jumping from boulder to boulder through the spray of the swirling stream. Your rod was a pest in the birch thicket and I heard you swear like a stoker who has found the dock gates locked. Your friend in Chile, on your South American trip, had tipped you a capital way of cooking fish. Cover in clay and bury in the embers—and wait. And while we waited and daubed ourselves with gritty mud and swiped at the mosquitoes, a flock of wild geese, with wings splayed out stiff, swept over us in blunt formation. They settled on the fen higher up to the north, where the night sun just brushed the water.

"Finland was mostly forest—you will remember that well enough—with now and then a meadow and a barn. But on the plains which you woke up to from your creaking bunk you saw an infinity of these little barns, silver-gray and lopsided, and rivers curving lazily round lonely villages. The people you saw were hardly beautiful: they wore dark clothes, the women as well as the men, and drove over the plain in high carts behind their tow-colored nags. You said, 'It is odd about you Finns, you all have individual faces and individual eyes.' Do you remember the sullen-looking yokels in the post-bus who sat and eyed your fine tackle with the envy and approval of an expert, and the men we met on the tundra bent under their heavy packs and tramping with long strides over the carpet of reindeer moss? . . . They were my people."

Yes, I remember them and all the rest and much more. I can close my eyes and see the forests that never seemed to come to an end, but bounded the road like gigantic green fences, mile after mile of stockades of virgin pine. And then like an oasis in the forest would come a brief cleared tract with a houseyard as bare of vegetation as Sahara sand. I remember the flash of heavy-antlered reindeer through the trees, as if to remind me that it was not the piney-woods of Alabama.

I remember the stark reality of August noons and the lovely face of August evenings mirrored in the lakes. I remember the singing of the sawmills in the wilderness—that paradox of sleek white chimneys rising like shipmasts above a sea of soughing pines. There was something fantastic in throbbing factories of glazed tiles and glass bricks with their thudding pistons and whirling belts in the midst of a forest where birds continued their tranquil song. The workmen, coming home from the factory in the cooling evening to potter about their kitchen gardens, spoke politely to the foreigner who tried to fish in the wrong river.

I remember the waving wheat fields in the fertile south, and through the alders the long yellow façades of the manor houses. The peasant farmers worked among the waving rye or harnessed broad-buttocked cart-horses, sturdy under the heaviest load. And I remember by an inland lake-side neat stacks of butter-colored timber, and pit-props for mines in Wales, and boatloads of bobbins for Manchester.

Afterword

I remember the pavement café under the limes and the stars, with the plash of a fountain and Sibelius' youngest son-in-law conducting the orchestra, while pigeons murmured above the city traffic where no motor horns were permitted to sound. I think on Finland's brave new architecture, independent, full of light and harmony, and peering into tomorrow. And I recall the taciturn, high-booted farmers at village fairs giving the whole landscape "a solid sense of everyday."

I remember the gold of a declining sun glowing on the bare athletic backs of farmers' sons, bending with pick and shovel, widening a drainage ditch between fields. And I recall how the social fabric of the state is impregnated with co-operation. I think of a certain student waitress at an Arctic inn, with her smile brimful of summer, and of such a fresh and desirable beauty that three Oxford youths all fell in love with her at sight. And I remember the unearthly beauty of mid-summer Arctic nights.

And as I think of the contours of Finland's geography, I recall that the soil lies lightly on an underbedding of granite and that in the backbone of every Finn runs a vein of that granite. In perspective I see the labyrinthine waterways, with the sixty thousand lakes and the rapids and the rivers, like pieces of blue and silver in a jigsaw puzzle predominantly green. And the map of Finland suggests a figure in hooded Arctic cape, with arms outstretched—one into Norway and one into Russia—like a crucifixion between the East and West.

When Europe has spent her passion in the present conflict, and if Finland is allowed to pursue her creative ways in peace, I hope to accept my friend's invitation to visit Finland again and once more light a good campfire somewhere north of the nickel mountains, and send flies dancing over an Arctic river.

In the meantime, when in memory I am in that land of champion athletes and bookworms, builders and music-lovers, dirt farmers and warriors and mystic dreamers, I involuntarily recall the words of Runeberg, "I saw a people able to do everything except betray their honor."

Bibliography

Abregé de Histoire de Finlande. Helsinki, V. K. (1936)
Aho, Juhani: *Squire Hellman and Other Stories.* Trans. from the Finnish. London, Fisher Unwin (1893)
Atchley, T. W.: *Finland,* With a Chapter on the Birds of Finland, F. J. Campbell. London, Sidgwick & Jackson (1931)
Bakken, Henry H.: *Cooperation to the Finnish.* Madison, Wisconsin, Mimir (1939)
Brotherus, K. R.: *Staat und Kirche in Finland.* Königsberg, Graf und Unzer (1931)
Chydenius, Anders: *The National Gain.* London, Ernest Benn Limited (1931)
Coles, K. A.: *In Finnish Waters, from Estonia to Sweden.* London, Edward Arnold and Co. (1932)
Danielson-Kalmari, J. R.: *Finland's Union with the Russian Empire.* (1891)
Ekman, Karl: *Jean Sibelius, His Life and Personality.* London, Alan Wilmer (1936)
Fox, F.: *Finland To-day.* London, A. & C. Black (1926)
Finland, a Practical Guide Book. Helsinki, Finnish Tourist Association (1931)
Finland Blue Book. (1940)
Finland, the Country, Its People and Institutions. Helsinki, Otava (1926)
Finnish Trade Review. Helsinki
Finland Year Book—1939-1940. Helsinki
Fisher, J. R.: *Finland and the Tsars.* London (1899)
Gilmour, K.: *Finland.* London, Methuen & Co. (1931)
Gray, Cecil: *Sibelius.* London, Humphrey Milford (1934)

Hallsten, Ilmi: *The Position of Women in Finland.* Helsinki, V. K. (1924)

Harmaja, L.: *Effects of the War on Economic and Social Life in Finland.* Yale University Press, New Haven (1933)

Hemmer, Jarl: *A Fool of Faith.* Trans. from the Swedish by F. H. Lyon. New York, Liveright (1935)

Hilden, Kaarlo: *The Racial Composition of the Finnish Nation.* Helsinki, V. K. (1932)

Jackson, J. Hampden: *Finland.* New York, The Macmillan Company (1940)

Jukola, Martti: *Athletics in Finland.* Helsinki, Werner Söderström (1931)

The Kalevala—The Epic Poem of Finland. Into English by John Martin Crawford. 1-2, London, J. M. Dent & Co.; New York, E. P. Dutton & Co.

Kallas, Aino: *Eros the Slayer.* Two Estonian Tales. Trans. from the Finnish by Alex Matson. New York, Macmillan Co. (1927)

Kallas, Aino: *The White Ship, Estonian Tales.* Trans. from the Finnish by Alex Matson. New York, Alfred Knopf (1924)

Kivi, Aleksis: *Seven Brothers.* Trans. from the Finnish by Alex Matson. New York, Coward-McCann (1929)

Land Reform in Finland (Official Statement). Helsinki, V. K. (1922)

Maury, Pierre: *La Question de Iles d'Åland.* Paris, Presses Universitaires de France (1930)

Medill, R.: *Finland: Its People.* New York, Robert M. McBride & Co. (1925)

Murray, Levick G.: *Young Pioneers in Northern Finland.* London, Walter Judd (1933)

North, F. J.: *Finland in Summer.* Cambridge, W. Heffer and Sons (1937)

Ohde, Thorsten: *Finland: A Nation of Cooperators.* London, Williams and Norgate (1931)

Pavolini, Alessandro: *L'independenza finlandesa.* Roma, Anonima Romana (1928)

A Quarter of a Century of Cooperation in Finland. Published for the twenty-fifth anniversary of the Pellervo Society 2. X. Helsinki, V. K. (1924)

Rahola, I.: *Agricultural Cooperation in Finland.* 2nd ed. Helsinki, Pellervo Society (1936)

Rosvall, Toivo: *Finland: Land of Heroes.* New York, E. P. Dutton & Co. (1940)

Rothery, Agnes: *Finland, the New Nation.* New York, The Viking Press (1936)

Runeberg, J. L.: *The Songs of Ensign Stål.* National Military Song Cycle of Finland. First complete English translation of Clement Burbank Shaw. New York, G. E. Stechert & Co. (1925)

Runeberg, J. L.: *Sainte Miseré.* Trans. from the Finnish by Jean-Louis Perret. Paris, Rieder (1928)

Scott, A. M.: *Suomi: The Land of the Finns.* London, Thornton Butterworth (1926)

Seppänen, Unto: *Sun and Storm.* New York, Bobbs-Merrill Company (1939)

Silberg, K. P.: *The Athletic Finn.* Hancock, Mich. Suomi Publishing Company (1927)

Sillanpää, F. E.: *The Maid Silja.* Trans. from the Finnish by Alexander Matson. New York, Macmillan (1933)

Sillanpää, F. E.: *Meek Heritage.* New York, Macmillan Company (1938)

Söderhjelm, Henning: *The Red Insurrection in Finland.* (1919)

Sutherland, Halliday: *Lapland Journey.* New York, Dodd, Mead Company (1938)

Suviranta, B. R.: *Finland and the World Depression.* Helsinki, V. K. (1931); London, Harrison and Sons (1931)

Topelius, Zacharias: *Canute Whistlewinke and Other Stories.* Translated from the Swedish by S. W. Foss. New York, Longmans, Green and Co. (1927)

Van Cleef, Eugen: *Finland, the Republic Farthest North.* Columbus, the Ohio State University Press (1929)

Wuorinen, John: *Nationalism in Modern Finland.* New York, Columbia University Press (1931)

Wuorinen, John: *The Prohibition Experiment in Finland.* New York, The Columbia University Press (1931)

This book was set in 12 point Linotype Granjon and printed on paper supplied by W. F. Etherington & Co. The composition, printing and binding were done by Quinn & Boden Company, Inc. The illustrations, which were reproduced by the Photogravure & Color Company, were supplied by Suomen Matkat and Hudson Strode. Warren Chappell designed the labels, Richard Edes Harrison the endpapers, and Charles Lofgren the jacket.

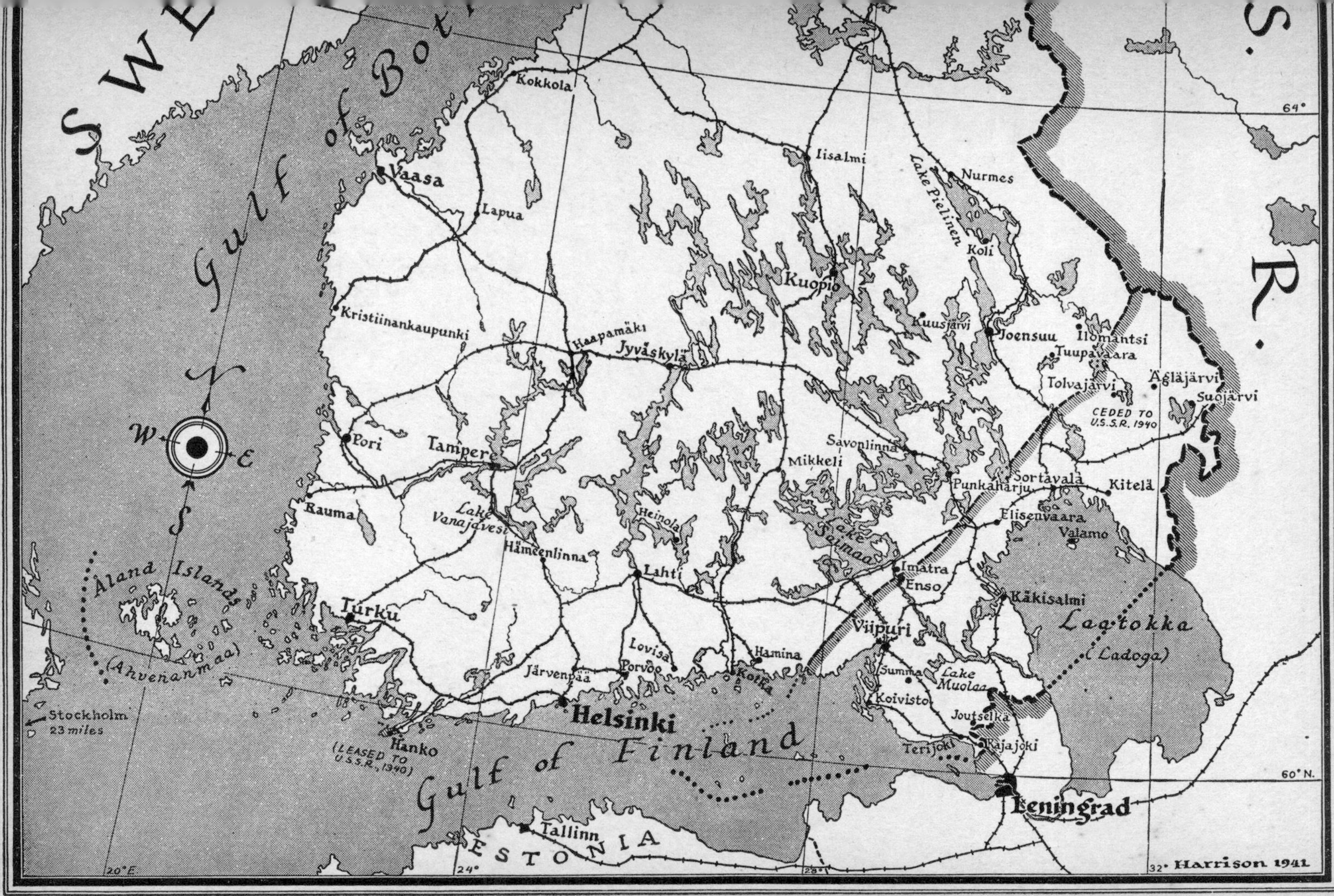

SWE
Gulf of Bot
S.
R.
Kokkola
Vaasa
Lapua
Iisalmi
Nurmes
Lake Pielinen
Koli
Kuopio
Kristiinankaupunki
Haapamäki
Jyväskylä
Kuusjärvi
Joensuu
Ilomantsi
Tuupavaara
Tolvajärvi
Äglajärvi
Suojärvi
CEDED TO U.S.S.R. 1940
Gulf
N
W
E
S
Pori
Tampere
Savonlinna
Mikkeli
Punkaharju
Sortavala
Kitelä
Rauma
Lake Vanajavesi
Heinola
Lake Saimaa
Elisenvaara
Valamo
Hämeenlinna
Åland Islands
(Ahvenanmaa)
Lahti
Imatra
Enso
Käkisalmi
Turku
Laatokka
(Ladoga)
Viipuri
Lovisa
Hamina
Järvenpää
Porvoo
Kotka
Summa
Lake Muolaa
Koivisto
Stockholm 23 miles
Helsinki
Joutselkä
Hanko
(LEASED TO U.S.S.R., 1940)
Gulf of Finland
Terijoki
Rajajoki
60° N.
Leningrad
Tallinn
ESTONIA
20° E
24°
28°
32°
64°
Harrison 1941